Chaplains Investigate Their Practice

TRANSFORMING CHAPLAINCY SERIES EDITORS

George Fitchett, Cheryl Holmes, Steve Nolan, Anne Vandenhoeck

Contemporary spiritual care, as practiced in healthcare contexts, is very different from the way many healthcare professionals and patients perceive it. Two factors are responsible for effecting this change.

First, spiritual care is plural. The days are gone when spiritual care was the sole domain of religious clergy. Representation of a variety of faith traditions is now the norm in chaplaincy teams, and an increasing number of professional chaplains identify as religiously unaffiliated. In addition, the concept of generalist/specialist lends the idea that every healthcarer has a responsibility to care for the spiritual needs of their patients.

Second, healthcare itself has changed. Since the turn of the century, the culture of evidence-based practice has become part of the fabric of contemporary healthcare. In part, improvements in medicine and healthcare practice have driven that cultural change. But allied to improved medicine, health economics are such that interventions have not only to be effective, they have to be cost-effective. Spiritual care is no exception.

These dynamic factors are transforming chaplaincy. Chaplaincy is now a plural profession and empirical research into chaplaincy and spiritual care is growing year on year. However, considered reflection on the issues raised by chaplaincy's altered context has not kept pace with the changes affecting the profession.

The Transforming Chaplaincy series aims to thoughtfully address strategic gaps in the literature, in ways that are relevant to both chaplains and other spiritual care practitioners. Edited by an international team that has wide expertise in research, practice, and policy development, the Transforming Chaplaincy series is planned to include, among other topics:

- Spiritual Needs Assessment
- Spiritual Care Interventions
- Humanistic Chaplaincy
- Theories of Spiritual Care Practice
- Chaplaincy Management
- Chaplain Competencies

Titles are planned to include book-length treatments of a topic by single authors, as well as specially commissioned edited collections of research-informed papers, written by academics and spiritual care practitioners. All the topics covered will be directly relevant to chaplaincy and spiritual care practice.

Chaplains Investigate Their Practice

The Dutch Case Studies Project

Edited by
MARTIN WALTON, JACQUES KÖRVER,
and NIELS DEN TOOM

Foreword by George Fitchett

☙PICKWICK *Publications* · Eugene, Oregon

CHAPLAINS INVESTIGATE THEIR PRACTICE
The Dutch Case Studies Project

Transforming Chaplaincy Series

Copyright © 2025 Wipf and Stock Publishers. All rights reserved. Except for brief quotations in critical publications or reviews, no part of this book may be reproduced in any manner without prior written permission from the publisher. Write: Permissions, Wipf and Stock Publishers, 199 W. 8th Ave., Suite 3, Eugene, OR 97401.

Pickwick Publications
An Imprint of Wipf and Stock Publishers
199 W. 8th Ave., Suite 3
Eugene, OR 97401

www.wipfandstock.com

PAPERBACK ISBN: 978-1-6667-7027-8
HARDCOVER ISBN: 978-1-6667-7028-5
EBOOK ISBN: 978-1-6667-7029-2

Cataloguing-in-Publication data:

Names: Martin Walton, editor; Jacques Körver, editor; Niels den Toom, editor.

Title: Chaplains investigate their practice : the Dutch case studies project / edited by Martin Walton, Jacques Körver, and Niels den Toom.

Description: Eugene, OR: Pickwick Publications, 2025. | Transforming Chaplaincy. | Includes bibliographical references.

Identifiers: ISBN: 978-1-6667-7027-8 (PAPERBACK). | ISBN: 978-1-6667-7028-5 (HARDCOVER). | ISBN: 978-1-6667-7029-2 (EBOOK).

Subjects: LCSH: Chaplaincy Service, Hospital. | Military chaplaincy. | Pastoral care.

Classification: BV4335 C28 2025 (print). | BV4345 (epub).

The publishing rights for the five photographs are held by the photographer, Jacques Körver, from Eindhoven, The Netherlands. The photographs are selected from the series "Om en nabij Igny, 2014–2018" [Around and Near Igny], all taken in northern France in the period from 2014 till 2018. The photographs' titles are

- Fort de la Pompelle, Reims, 2016, p. xii
- Railroad station, Fismes, 2016, p. 9
- Road from the abbey of Igny to Cohan, 2014, p. 65
- Bridge at railroad station, Fismes, 2018, p. 161
- Road from Cohan in the direction of the abbey of Igny, 2018, p. 249

Contents

Contributors | vii
Foreword | ix

Introduction. *Martin Walton, Jacques Körver, Niels den Toom* | 1

PART ONE: THE DUTCH CASE STUDIES PROJECT: BACKGROUND AND METHODOLOGY
1. Context and Objectives of the Case Studies Project. *Jacques Körver* | 11
2. Observing, Interpreting, and Participating. *Jacques Körver* | 26
3. What Makes a Good Case? *Martin Walton* | 43

PART TWO: EXEMPLARY CASE STUDIES
4. Energy *and* Inspiration: Case Study from Oncological Rehab. *Jowien van der Zaag, Jacques Körver, Martin Walton* | 67
5. The Enigma of a Day: Case Study from an Oncological and a Palliative Ward of a General Hospital. *Rob Vos, Martin Walton, Jacques Körver* | 76
6. Exposure? Case Study from Mental Health Care. *Marie-José van Bolhuis, Hanneke Muthert, Jacques Körver, Martin Walton* | 87
7. I Do It My Way: Case Study from Mental Health Care. *Irene Plaatsman, Hanneke Muthert, Martin Walton, Jacques Körver* | 95
8. Reiteration of Ritual: Case Study from Eldercare for Dementia. *Joke Zuidema, Martin Walton, Jacques* Körver | 106
9. A Church for Charly: Case Study from Care for Persons with Intellectual and Developmental Disabilities. *Marieke Termeer, Martin Walton, Jacques Körver* | 117
10. Wounded Warrior: Case Study from Mental Health Care. *Guus van Loenen, Jacques Körver, Martin Walton, Reijer de Vries* | 126

11. To Honor and Confirm: Case Study from a Military Ritual. *Helga Knegt, Carmen Schuhmann, Theo Pleizier, Martin Walton, Jacques Körver* | 138
12. From Slumped to Upright: Case Study from a Psychiatric Penitentiary Center. *Bart van den Bosse, Reijer de Vries, Jacques Körver, Martin Walton* | 149

PART THREE: EMERGING THEMES
13. Chaplaincy in Context. *Jacques Körver* | 163
14. Apprehending Goals. *Jacques Körver* | 183
15. Aesthetic Counseling. *Martin Walton* | 197
16. Rituals in Chaplaincy. *Jacques Körver* | 209
17. Roles in Chaplaincy. *Niels den Toom* | 222
18. Serving the Care Community. *Martin Walton* | 236

PART FOUR: APPRAISAL
19. Consensus in the Research Communities. *Niels den Toom* | 251
20. Chaplain Researchers. *Niels den Toom* | 264
21. On Method and Evidence. *Jacques Körver* | 282
22. Answering the Research Question. *Martin Walton* | 298
23. Looking Back and Forward. *Martin Walton, Jacques Körver, Niels den Toom* | 323

Appendices
A. Organogram Dutch Case Studies Project | 330
B. Format Case Study Dutch Case Studies Project | 332
C. Consent Information and Forms Dutch Case Studies Project | 340
D. Case Studies in Chaplaincy: Inventory of English Language Publications | 345
E. International Publications Dutch Case Studies Project | 354
F. Ritual Interventions by Chaplains in Research Community Hospital | 358

Contributors

Marie-José van Bolhuis works as a chaplain at GGZ-Noord Holland Noord, Netherlands (mental health care). m.vanbolhuis@ggz-nhn.nl

Bart van den Bosse is a Buddhist prison chaplain in several prisons in Netherlands. b.vd.bosse@dji.minjus.nl

Helga Knegt-de Boer is military chaplain with an Airmobile unit in Assen, Netherlands. hc.knegt@mindef.nl

Jacques Körver is (retired) Associate Professor of Practical Theology and Chaplaincy Studies, Tilburg School of Catholic Theology and former director of the University Center for Chaplaincy Studies (UCGV), Netherlands. j.w.g.korver@tilburguniversity.edu

Guus van Loenen worked thirty-five years as a spiritual counselor for the patients of a mental health hospital in Venray, Netherlands. vanloenenguus@gmail.com

Hanneke Muthert is Professor of Psychology of Religion with special attention to Spiritual Care and Wellbeing, Head of the Department of Comparative Study of Religion at the Faculty of Theology and Religious Studies, University of Groningen, Netherlands. j.k.muthert@rug.nl

Irene Plaatsman is a chaplain in mental health care in Groningen (Lentis), Netherlands. irene.plaatsman@gmail.com

Theo Pleizier is Associate Professor Practical Theology, Protestant Theological University, Groningen, Netherlands. t.t.j.pleizier@pthu.nl

Carmen Schuhmann is Assistant Professor in Practical Humanistic Studies at the University of Humanistic Studies, Utrecht, Netherlands. C.Schuhmann@UvH.nl

Marieke Termeer works as a chaplain at Lunet, a foundation for support of persons with intellectual disabilities in Eindhoven, Netherlands. m.termeer@lunet.nl

Niels den Toom is Assistant Professor in Spiritual Care and Chaplaincy Studies at Tilburg University, Tilburg, Netherlands, and chaplain in a nursing facility in Breda, Netherlands. j.n.dentoom@tilburguniversity.edu

Reijer de Vries is Associate Professor emeritus of Practical Theology and Prison Chaplaincy Studies at the Protestant Theological University, Amsterdam, Netherlands. ds.rjdevries@planet.nl

Rob Vos works as a hospital chaplain, Hilversum, Netherlands. rovos@tergooi.nl

Martin Walton is Professor emeritus of chaplaincy studies, Protestant Theological University, Utrecht, Netherlands. walton@kpnplanet.nl

Jowien van der Zaag has worked as a chaplain in a specialized oncology hospital, Amsterdam, Netherlands. dewilde_vanderzaag@quicknet.nl

Joke Zuidema presently works as a minister in Velserbroek, Netherlands. She served previously as a chaplain in nursing homes in the area of Maastricht, Netherlands. jokezuidema@home.nl

Foreword

THE DUTCH CASE STUDIES PROJECT (CSP), described in this book, addresses the vital "need to make the qualities of chaplaincy visible" (p. 21, Chapter 1). In the U.S., and probably in most other national contexts, the work of healthcare chaplains is poorly understood and poorly integrated into the care of patients and their families. Two studies from palliative care, the clinical context with possibly the best integration of spiritual care, illustrate the problem. The first was a retrospective review of the medical records of 402 deceased patients who had been hospitalized with serious illness (Ernecoff et al., 2020). Investigators examined each record for documentation of key elements of palliative care. In 81% of the records, they found documentation of pain control and in 76%, documentation of discussion of goals of care. Screening for spiritual needs was documented in only 55% of the cases. The second was a study of audio recordings of 249 meetings between the clinical team and families whose loved ones were hospitalized in one of 13 intensive care units across the country (Ernecoff et al., 2015). Chaplains were present in only 2 of the meetings. Chaplains' involvement in helping patients and families with difficult medical decisions was also the focus of a survey of 463 U.S. healthcare chaplains (Wirpsa et al., 2018). Among these chaplains, only 38% reported being frequently or often integrated into health care team discussions regarding medical decisions.

Several factors may contribute to this poor utilization of healthcare chaplains. Physicians, nurses, and other healthcare professionals receive little education about religion and spirituality (R/S) or spiritual care (McGee et al., 2023). Many may think that chaplains only provide religious services. They frequently don't know how to determine if a patient should be referred to the chaplain (Winter-Pfändler et al., 2011).

Chaplains contribute to this problem by emphasizing the process that informs their work, "a ministry of presence," in settings where attention is focused on outcomes (Lyndes et al., 2012). Chaplains' documentation of their care in patient medical records could help educate healthcare colleagues about their contribution to patient care, but in many cases their notes are vague and filled with jargon (Lee et al., 2017). An international survey of 1,657 healthcare chaplains during the COVID-19 pandemic (May/June 2020) found that many were unclear about their role not only during the pandemic but prior to it. The investigators comment, "It follows that it would be unreasonable to expect managers and colleagues to be clear about how best to deploy chaplains when they [the chaplains] are not clear themselves" (Snowden et al., 2021, p. 13).

What can be done to help chaplains be more articulate and effective in communicating what they do, to help them be more visible? In 2009 I brought together three oncology chaplains to write and share case studies with one another (Fitchett, 2011). Participation in the project had an impact on them. One wrote, "In writing the case and being in dialogue with colleagues also engaged in spiritual care of oncology patients, I found myself being more aware of the needs-interventions-outcome relationship so that I am more intentional in my approach." Another wrote, "I find myself much more attentive to the construct and implementation of spiritual care assessments, and more disciplined about considering and characterizing spiritual care interventions before applying them and evaluating them afterwards" (Fitchett, 2011, p. 11). This little project hinted at the impact that writing and discussing case studies could have on chaplains' ability to articulate what they do and why they do it.

As you will read in the pages that follow, in 2016, colleagues in the Netherlands launched the Dutch Case Studies Project. Over the next four years 62 chaplains from diverse settings, including healthcare, aged care, corrections, and the military, worked together in six research communities (small groups). They produced 101 case studies, over 20 of which have been published. The main study question for the project was to describe what chaplains do, why they do it and the effects of their care.

Importantly, like the chaplains who discussed their case studies with me, participation in the CSP had significant effects on these Dutch chaplains. They became more reflective about their practice including its effects on their clients. They reported that it also strengthened their expertise. They reported being better able to articulate, to professional colleagues and managers, what they were doing with clients and why.

This included changes in their charting with increased emphasis on the effects of their care. In short, they experienced "increased confidence in their professional actions" (p. 275, Chapter 20).

Helping chaplains be more reflective, articulate, and confident about their work holds the possibility of increasing the integration of spiritual care in healthcare and other care settings. Reading this book will show how colleagues in the Netherlands realized these changes. Hopefully this will stimulate broad replication of the Dutch CSP. When chaplains are more reflective, confident, and better integrated, more clients, patients, and their families will experience the benefits of quality spiritual care.

George Fitchett
Rush University Medical Center
Chicago, Illinois, USA

REFERENCES

Ernecoff, Natalie C, et al. "Health Care Professionals' Responses to Religious or Spiritual Statements by Surrogate Decision Makers During Goals-of-Care Discussions." *JAMA Internal Medicine* 175 no 10 (2015) 1662–69, doi:10.1001/jamainternmed.2015.4124.

Ernecoff, Natalie C, et al. "Elements of Palliative Care in the Last 6 Months of Life: Frequency, Predictors, and Timing. *Journal of General Internal Medicine* 35.3 (2020) 753–61, doi:10.1007/s11606-019-05349-0.

Fitchett, George. "Making Our Case(s)." *Journal of Health Care Chaplaincy* 17.1 (2011) 3–18, doi: 10.1080/08854726.2011.559829.

Lee, Brittany M, et al. "Documenting Presence: A Descriptive Study of Chaplain Notes in the Intensive Care Unit." *Palliative and Supportive Care* 15.2 (2017) 190–96, doi: 10.1017/S1478951516000407.

Lyndes, Kathryn A, et al. "A Survey of Chaplains' Roles in Pediatric Palliative Care: Integral Members of the Team." *Journal of Health Care Chaplaincy* 18.1 (2012) 74–93, doi: 10.1080/08854726.2012.667332.

McGee, Julia, et al. "Assessing the Impact of Provider Training and Perceived Barriers on the Provision of Spiritual Care: A Mixed Methods Study." *Journal of Cancer Education* 38.1 (2023) 301–8, doi: 10.1007/s13187-021-02115-x.

Snowden, Austyn. "What Did Chaplains Do During the Covid Pandemic? An International Survey." *Journal of Pastoral Care and Counseling* 75 (1 supplement) (2021) 6–16, doi:10.1177/1542305021992039.

Winter-Pfändler, Urs, et al. "Referrals to Health Care Chaplaincy by Head Nurses: Situations And Influencing Factors." *Holistic Nursing Practice* 25.1 (2011) 26–32, doi: 10.1097/HNP.0b013e3181fe266c.

Wirpsa, M Jeanne, et al. "Interprofessional Models for Shared Decision Making: The Role of the Health Care Chaplain." *Journal of Health Care Chaplaincy* 25.1 (2019) 20–44, doi:10.1080/08854726.2018.1501131.

Introduction
—Martin Walton, Jacques Körver, Niels den Toom

Case Study

In each case
some detail
is decisive.

A bird sings.
They stop, listen.
He begins to speak.

There is the other
who weighs each word
and listens between the lines

until the lyrics rhyme
with his melody.[1]

AN EYE FOR DETAIL

OUR INVESTIGATION OF CHAPLAINCY care is guided by the conviction that in chaplaincy, as in life, attention to detail is crucial. Consequently, understanding how chaplaincy care is efficaciously provided requires paying attention to the details of care provision. That initial conviction became even stronger in the process of developing the Dutch Case Studies Project (CSP) with its format for description of case studies and for analysis in research communities of chaplains. The conviction was fed by the case studies

---

1. The moment pictured here (by Martin Walton) is based on a turning point in a case study in Van der Meer, "Is MacDonald's Freedom."

themselves, as chaplains developed their own capacities for observation, description and reflection and provided rich and detailed reports on instances and trajectories of care. It is telling that in response to the material and feedback provided by the participating chaplains, the format was amended about ten times during the first two years of the four-year project. We kept learning how to look for, observe, uncover and appreciate the details of care.

In this volume we want to share many of those details with you, drawn from 101 case study documents. In analyzing and interpreting the details, we looked for patterns in chaplaincy care provision and for indications of what makes chaplaincy care meaningful and efficacious. In other words we have sought to understand and explicate chaplaincy care as a coherent and intentional practice that includes observations, interactions, interventions, reflections, emotions, and effects, all at the service of providing good care.[2] That was the primary focus of the CSP in seeking to answer the questions: What do chaplains do, for what reasons and with what effect? That is also the primary focus of this book. At the same time, we appeal to the reader's peripheral vision to address a number of other issues with respect to method, logistics and outcomes: What is a case study in chaplaincy care? Why and how can a case studies project be developed? And what effect does such a project have?

CHAPLAINCY CARE AS AN ARTISANSHIP

When investigating the practice and performance of chaplaincy care we do well to understand the work of chaplaincy, as Trace Haythorn and Jason Callahan have done,

> as both a science and an art. As a science, it is increasingly centered on evidence-based understandings of effective spiritual care and informed by an emerging body of research. As an art, it is always and already being refined, reimagined and challenged, even as its history is recognized for its important grounding and shaping of the field.[3]

There are any number of publications on chaplaincy, spiritual care, pastoral care and counseling with art in the title.[4] Some of the publications are more

---

2. With MacIntyre we understand a practice as being related to some good, some striving for excellence (MacIntyre, *After Virtue*). See Walton and Körver, "Dutch Case Studies Project," 260.

3. Haythorn and Callahan, "A Commissioning," 259–60.

4. Boelsbjerg and Leget, "Art of Spiritual Care"; Friedman, *The Art of Jewish Pastoral Counseling*; Gladding, *Counseling as an Art*; Hansen, *The Art of Pastoring*; Pembroke,

conceptual in their approach; some of them more specific in detailing the practice, the step by step handwork of care provision. We would like to emphasize the latter and, in doing so, understand the interplay of science, art and actual practice as an artisanship.

The word artisanship, while including the dimensions of art and science, also turns our attention to what chaplains actually do when they provide care. When the chaplains in the CSP took a closer and more investigative look at their practice, they discovered that they do a lot more than they realized that they were doing, certainly more than they often expressed in very general terms like "just being there" or "simply listening." And often they had become unaware of the theoretical fundaments of their care. But like contemporary artisans whose work is increasingly based on scientific knowledge of the materials and tested methods, their care is based on a professional body of knowledge they have gathered in education and training.[5] Their attentive and skilled interactions as reflective practitioners[6] are an embodiment of practical training, worldview wisdom,[7] empirical evidence and attested theory.

One must never take a metaphor too far. For the artisanship of chaplaincy does not lead to the creation of an artifact.[8] Chaplains work with living, unpredictable and vulnerable human beings. The personal and existential issues that chaplains address in their care are constantly in flux. They also stand in a relationship of reciprocity, of shared humanity with patients, residents, clients, prisoners, soldiers, family members, other professionals and colleagues. However, the chaplains do shape the encounters in which they become involved in specific ways. And the effects of what they do are often tangible, observable and verifiable. What they do leads to describable outcomes. It would help if they could learn to express those outcomes like the artisan who can be very concrete and detailed, not just talking about being a potter and making pottery, for example, but clarifying how the artisanship of pottery led in a specific instance to a particular design, shape, pattern, function, glaze and luster.

The Art of Listening; Peterson, *The Contemplative Pastor*; Snodgrass, *The Art of Spiritual Care*; Stratford, *Art of Interfaith Spiritual Care*; Willows, "Editorial."

5. Muthert, "Daar aansluiten." See Chapter 22.

6. Schön speaks of a reflective practitioner and offers the metaphor of how all the architect's knowledge, experience and awareness of the context come together in the point of a pencil. See Schön, *Educating the Reflective Practitioner*.

7. Den Toom, *The Chaplain-Researcher*.

8. Ostrom, "Artisanship and Artifact."

DEVELOPING OUR CASE

We have arranged the material in four sections. Part I sets the stage. In Chapter 1 we explain why the project was initiated and how it took shape in the context of Dutch chaplaincy practices. In Chapter 2 the research design is introduced and issues of methodology are discussed. Then in Chapter 3 we discuss what makes a case a "good case" that is reviewed not for supervision purposes, but for the development of the profession. At the end of Chapter 3, the case studies in Part II are briefly introduced.

In Part II, Chapters 4 to 12, we provide nine case studies that were produced in the framework of the project. The case studies exemplify the primary aim of the research: structured and detailed descriptions of care provision by chaplains, that have been submitted for analysis and review by colleagues.

Part III is more analytical in nature as it reviews, in Chapters 13 to 18, the work of the research communities in their discussions on multiple cases. Where an individual case study describes provision of care in a specific situation, the analysis of multiple cases seeks to offer a case for chaplaincy care on the basis of patterns, perspectives and themes that emerge from the material as a whole. The chapters deal with discerning the contexts in which care is offered, recognizing the goals, aesthetic forms of counseling, the use of rituals, roles of chaplains and the horizon of community in care.

In Part IV, Chapters 19 to 23, we seek to appraise the process and harvest the results of the project. How was consensus developed in the research communities and what were the effects of the appreciative approach? What were the effects of participation in the project for chaplaincy practice, as researched in a secondary study? What did we learn during the project about method and doing research? Then it is time for a summary answer to the research question: "What do chaplains do, for what reasons and with what effects?" and return to the question in Chapter 3: "What makes a good case study?" The last chapter offers concluding remarks both in retrospect and looking forward.

The epigraph of this introduction is a poetic rendering of a turning point in one of the case studies from the CSP. It describes one of the aesthetic moments that often played a role in care descriptions.[9] One of the convictions that grew during the project is that research on chaplaincy needs to bridge the waters that sometimes seem to separate scholarly analysis from narrative, wisdom and the arts.[10] A symbol of that is the inclusion

---

9. See Chapter 15.
10. Walton, "Test All Things Spiritual."

of epigraphs for all of the chapters, with the exception of the case studies in Part II. Also, each of the four parts of this volume is illustrated associatively by a photograph in black and white.[11]

A COLLABORATIVE PROJECT

Who are we? That question can be answered in a couple of ways. We, the primary authors and editors of this book, are researchers in chaplaincy care, who work or have worked on Protestant and Catholic theological faculties in the Netherlands. Jacques Körver and Martin Walton were initiators and coordinators of the CSP that ran from October 2016 to March 2021. Niels den Toom was a PhD researcher who studied the effects of participation in the project on chaplaincy practice.

At the same time the Dutch Case Studies Project was a collaborative endeavor involving sixty-two chaplains from various fields of chaplaincy and thirteen academic researchers from five universities, organized in six research communities and an academic advisory board. The participants were Catholic, Protestant, Humanist, Muslim, Buddhist, Hindu, Jewish, and without an explicit religious or worldview affiliation. At this point we emphasize that the "we" of the CSP is the "we" of all those seventy-five participants, collaborating for an extended period in description, analysis and publication. Almost all publications of the CSP have multiple authors reflecting the collaborative effort. That is particularly visible in this volume in the authorship of the individual case studies and in the list of contributors. As the primary authors of this book, we are deeply indebted to all who collaborated in the project and express here our appreciation. Supporting the research participants were employers, chaplaincy departments in care institutions and government agencies, and professional and branch organizations, that as stakeholders collaborated in providing time, finances and moral support to make the project possible.

We also appreciate the support we have received from the Transforming Chaplaincy series editors, not only in their role in this publication, but also in their interest in the project at earlier stages, their roles in previous publications and gatherings,[12] and particularly their inspiration with regard to case studies research in chaplaincy care. The initiatives of George Fitchett and Steve Nolan were the starting point for the project. The editors also put

---

11. Körver, *Om en nabij Igny*.

12. Walton and Körver, "Dutch Case Studies Project"; Van Loenen et al., "Case Study of 'Moral Injury'"; Kruizinga et al., *Learning from Case Studies*.

us in touch with the publisher Wipf and Stock, that with clarity and preciseness has made the publication possible.

Our greatest indebtedness is finally to all those persons—patients, clients, residents, homeless people, students, prisoners, military personnel—who are present in the case studies as living human beings and as participants in their own care process and in the sharing of their stories and permission for the case studies. Whatever the attention paid in this book to articulating what chaplaincy is and how the case for chaplaincy can be developed,[13] the primary concern is to contribute to better care for all those who for whatever reason come into contact with chaplains.

REFERENCES

Boelsbjerg, Hanne Bess, and Carlo Leget. "Art of Spiritual Care: Implications for the Use of Instruments and Tools." *Tidsskrift for Forskning i Sygdom og Samfund* 20.38 (2023) 71–86.

Den Toom, Niels. *The Chaplain-Researcher: The Perceived Impact of Participation in a Dutch Research Project on Chaplains' Professionalism*. Utrecht: Eburon, 2022.

Fitchett, George. "Making Our Case(s)." *Journal of Health Care Chaplaincy* 17.1–2 (2011) 3–18.

Friedman, Michelle S. *The Art of Jewish Pastoral Counseling: A Guide for All Faiths*. London: Routledge, 2017.

Gladding, Samuel T. *Counseling as an Art: The Creative Arts in Counseling*. Alexandria: Pearson–Merrill Prentice Hall, 2006.

Hansen, David. *The Art of Pastoring: Ministry Without All the Answers*. Downers Grove: IVP, 2012.

Haythorn, Trace, and Jason Callahan. "A Commissioning." In *Chaplaincy and Spiritual Care in the Twenty-First Century. An Introduction*, edited by Wendy Cadge and Shelly Rambo, 258–66. Chapel Hill: University of North Carolina Press, 2022.

Körver, Jacques. *Om en nabij Igny. 2014–2018*, Eindhoven: private collection.

Kruizinga, Renske, et al, eds. *Learning from Case Studies in Chaplaincy: Towards Practice Based Evidence & Professionalism*. Utrecht: Eburon, 2020.

MacIntyre, Alisdair. *After Virtue: A Study in Moral Theory*. London: Bloomsbury, 1985.

Muthert, Hanneke. "OG GGZ: Daar aansluiten waar mensen niet willen zijn." In *Richting, Repertoire en Resultaat. Uitkomsten van het Nederlandse Case Studies Project Geestelijke Verzorging (2016–2021)*, edited by Jacques Körver, et al., 190–201. Utrecht: PThU–UCGV, 2023.

Ostrom, Vincent. "Artisanship and Artifact." *Public Administration Review* 40.4 (1980) 309.

Pembroke, Neil. *The Art of Listening : Dialogue, Shame and Pastoral Care*. London: T. & T. Clark–Handsel–Eerdmans, 2002.

Peterson, Eugene H. *The Contemplative Pastor: Returning to the Art of Spiritual Direction*. Grand Rapids: Eerdmans, 1993.

13. See Fitchett, "Making Our Case(s)"; Kruizinga, et al., *Learning from Case Studies*; den Toom, *The Chaplain-Researcher*.

Schön, Donald A. *Educating the Reflective Practitioner: Toward a New Design for Teaching and Learning in the Professions*. San Francisco: Jossey-Bass, 1990.

Snodgrass, Jill L., ed. *The Art of Spiritual Care Across Religious Difference*. Minneapolis: Fortress, 2024.

Stratford, Walter Blair. *Art of Interfaith Spiritual Care: Integration of Spirituality in Health Care Regardless of Religion or Beliefs*. Eugene, OR: Wipf & Stock, 2016.

Van der Meer, Tjeerd. "Is MacDonald's Freedom?" In *Learning from Case Studies in Chaplaincy: Towards Practice Based Evidence & Professionalism*, edited by Renske Kruizinga, et al., 147–52. Utrecht: Eburon, 2020.

Van Loenen, Guus, Jacques Körver, Martin Walton, and Reijer de Vries. "Case Study of 'Moral Injury': Format Dutch Case Studies Project." *Health and Social Care Chaplaincy* 5.2 (2018) 281–96.

Walton, Martin, and Jacques Körver. "Dutch Case Studies Project in Chaplaincy Care: A Description and Theoretical Explanation of the Format and Procedures." *Health and Social Care Chaplaincy* 5.2 (2018) 257–80.

Walton, Martin. "Test All Things Spiritual; Hold on to What is Concrete: Toward a Hermeneutics of Story and Statistics." In *Transforming Chaplaincy: The George Fitchett Reader*, edited by Steve Nolan and Annelieke Damen, 218–30. Transforming Chaplaincy Series. Eugene, OR: Pickwick Publications, 2021.

Willows, David. "Editorial: The Art of Pastoral Care." *Contact* 128.1 (1999) 1.

Part One

THE DUTCH CASE STUDIES PROJECT: BACKGROUND AND METHODOLOGY

1

Context and Objectives of the Case Studies Project
—Jacques Körver

"There are things in your life that only you will see, stories that only you will hear. If you don't tell them or write them down, . . . these things will not be heard."

Emmet Gowin[1]

A YOUNG PROFESSION WITH A SHORT RESEARCH TRADITION

CHAPLAINCY IS A YOUNG profession with a long tradition. Over the past hundred years, clergy with primarily Christian backgrounds have with increasing frequency become active in social institutions where people are forced to spend extended periods of time separated from their home and religious milieu. Priests, ministers, and other clerics were "dispatched" to the army, prison and care institutions to serve military personnel, prisoners, and the sick from their faith community and tradition. In the military, prisons, and care facilities, the chaplains functioned as extensions of the parish, congregation or other faith community. The emphasis was on holding worship services, offering prayer and other rituals, and catechesis. The

---

1. *Emmet Gowin*, 64.

goal was to keep and "serve" people, wherever they resided, within their own community and tradition.[2]

Chaplaincy has moved quite a way from the starting point briefly outlined above. It is against the background of these developments that the Dutch Case Studies Project in Chaplaincy Care (from here on: CSP) is presented. Through a number of circular movements in this chapter, we eventually arrive at the research questions and objectives of the CSP. In those circular movements, we will outline the development of chaplaincy as a profession and as a discipline. We will pay special attention to the situation in the Netherlands as the immediate context of the CSP, though that situation is in many ways similar to what is going on in other countries. Influential factors in recent developments in the Netherlands are the rise of a professional association and the contributions of specific forms of research.

Upon retirement from Princeton University in 2009, photographer Emmet Gowin concluded his valedictory address with the above words, which *avant la lettre* describe the program of the CSP. It is an exhortation to apprehend all those special moments witnessed by chaplains, whatever the context of their work, with an open, curious, and uninhibited mind. As a photographer, chaplains are to be aware of perspective, framing, and choice of subject, and in any case, mindful of the richness of images and realities that characterize life.

A Different Profession—from Supply to Demand

During the 1960s, at least in the Netherlands and other Western European countries, a new vision for clergy practice in the "outlying areas" of religious associations emerged. That process especially gained momentum within the health care sector.[3] Chaplaincy was increasingly challenged to make explicit what it added to the care provided by a hospital, rehabilitation center, psychiatric institution, or an institution for people with physical or mental disabilities. For chaplaincy the emphasis came to lie more on its contribution in patient care, that is, on the *questions* with which patients struggled in the context of their illness or disability and on the existential and spiritual

---

2. Cadge, *Paging God*, 18–50; De Groot, *Liquidation of the Church*, 115–28; Fitchett, et al., "Spiritual Care"; Orton, "Transforming Chaplaincy"; Stahl, "Chaplaincy in the United States."

3. See the literature in the previous note. And in addition: Doolaard, *Nieuw Handboek*, 23–100; Holmes, "Chaplaincy to Spiritual Care"; Nolan, et al., "Religious, Spiritual, Pastoral"; Peng-Keller, *Healthcare Chaplaincy as Specialised*, 51–66, 175–82; Schilderman, *Religion as a Profession*; Stifoss-Hanssen, et al., "Chaplaincy in Northern Europe"; Swift, et al., "Healthcare Chaplaincy."

upheaval they faced. The *services* of churches and religious associations, in the sense of ritual and catechesis, were no longer paramount. Chaplains—or pastors and ministers, as they were long called—sought integration into the care facility on the basis of their own professionalism. They also sought contact, consultation and cooperation among themselves, which in the Netherlands led via associations of Catholic and Protestant hospital chaplains to a professional association of chaplains in health care. That professional association is now open to chaplains of all worldview and religious backgrounds and all fields of work.[4]

While these developments provided a new impetus for chaplaincy in terms of self-understanding and positioning, they were not welcomed by all since one consequence was disengagement from church hierarchies and worldview tenets.[5] Also, the direct influence of theology and humanism began to recede. From the point of view of ministry and the sanctuary function of chaplaincy[6], therefore, distrust of professionalism prevailed.[7] The shifts in conceptions of professionalism and their consequences resulted for some in a sense of loss of identity and mourning.[8]

At the same time, a new perspective on chaplaincy in terms of contributing to care processes and care policies from the point of worldview, religion, and spirituality made it possible for humanistic, Jewish, Islamic, Hindu and Buddhist spiritual caregivers, in addition to Christian chaplains, to be seen as colleagues with the same professional domain and purpose. That development initiated significant shifts in the professional outlook, compared to that of the former clergyman, who represented his (!) own religious denomination in the military, prison or healthcare facility. Although the profession has older roots, chaplaincy in the present form is relatively young.

---

4. Cadge, "Healthcare Chaplaincy as a Companion Profession"; Zock, "Chaplaincy in the Netherlands."

5. MacLaren, "All Things to All People?"; Vlasblom, et al., "Developments in Healthcare Chaplaincy"; Zock, "Chaplaincy in the Netherlands."

6. The sanctuary function is the provision of a free space for patients in an institution for personal reflection and expression, for example, in speaking confidentially about one's situation or one's relation to treatment. The sanctuary function is based on the legal freedom to confess one's religion. See Mackor, "Standardization of spiritual care."

7. Den Toom, *The Chaplain-Researcher*, 215–48; Grefe, *Encounters for Change*; Schipani and Bueckert, *Interfaith Spiritual Care*.

8. Yih, "The Chaplain Grieves."

Global Process with Broad Spectrum of Outcomes

The processes described above have not occurred in the same way throughout the world, nor have they led to the same results everywhere. There are countries where the influence of the churches is still strong. In many places, chaplains have at most acquired a status of tolerance in the various organizations in which they work. Often they are only allowed to perform a ritual at the end of life or another tragic or pivotal moment. Frequently they have no access to the files of military personnel, prisoners or the sick. There are also countries where chaplains function almost independently of religious organizations, employed by the institutions concerned and integrated into care and counseling policies. It is not feasible to outline here the development in, for example, the US, Great Britain, Australia, the various Western European countries, Scandinavia, or Brazil. Sufficient information on this can be found elsewhere.[9]

A number of factors played a role in the shift in professional outlook. The particular constellations of these factors ultimately determined the outcomes. The situation in one country is not immediately comparable or transferable to another. However, the influence of the factors can be compared. The cultural, social, political and economic relations in each country, processes of de-churching and secularization, the separation of church and state, diversity in terms of worldview and religious denominations, the baseline and benchmark in the development into an independent profession, the attitude of the religious organizations toward social issues and professionalization, the role of science and research in society and health care, the level of education of chaplains, the presence of a professional association that supports the interests of chaplains, all those factors contributed to a professional profile of chaplaincy that is specific to each country. That includes the claim of a domain in which they want to operate, what it is they do there, what goals they pursue, and what they achieve through their actions.[10] And the domain and deployment of chaplaincy are also strongly determined by the expectations and perceptions of others, clients, professionals and administrators.[11] A common thread is the attempt to legitimate the position, distinct profile and recognized professionalism of chaplaincy within social institutions.

---

9. See among others: Fitchett and Nolan, *Spiritual Care*; Holmes, "Chaplaincy to Spiritual Care"; Orton, "Transforming Chaplaincy"; Vlasblom, et al., "Developments in Healthcare Chaplaincy"; Zock, "Chaplaincy in the Netherlands."

10. A good example is Wendy Cadge's description of the development of chaplaincy in the US: Cadge, "Healthcare Chaplaincy as a Companion Profession."

11. See for example: Flannelly, et al., "Department Directors' Perceptions."

The conclusion of Wendy Cadge's and Shelly Rambo's book on the necessary competencies of chaplains in the twenty-first century[12] fits seamlessly with the above considerations:

> The field of chaplaincy is defined by its paradoxical nature. It is centuries old, and yet it is only beginning to grow into its potential. It is historically tied to religious communities, traditions, and practices, but best practices today are embodied by those who serve people regardless of faith tradition or source of meaning. Much of this work is done in private moments of pain and grief, yet chaplaincy's public role is rarely understood. It has often been an area that administrators struggle to fund, and yet in the wake of pandemics it has never seemed more essential.[13]

Empirical Research as a Stimulating Factor

An important motive for empirical research on the practice of chaplaincy and its enhancement is the search for its own position, profile and professionalism. Attention to empirical research has been promoted worldwide for several decades, especially by professional associations that want to strengthen the empirical basis of chaplaincy and undergird its professionalization.[14] It is a phenomenon that provides status in society and in health care in particular due to the broad advocacy of evidence-based practice in Western societies. And chaplaincy in healthcare settings becomes better integrated and gains greater recognition when chaplains rely on or participate in research.[15]

Since the end of the previous century, the Netherlands has seen a sharp increase in empirical research on chaplaincy, conducted in part by chaplains themselves. Dozens of dissertations have been written in the field, and more and more research projects are being subsidized by government and private funds.[16] That is also true elsewhere. The literature cited here and in chapters that follow explicitly underscores that. This trend has manifested itself more

---

12. Cadge and Rambo, *Chaplaincy and Spiritual Care*.
13. Haythorn and Callahan, "A Commissioning," 258.
14. Handzo, et al., "Outcomes"; Kestenbaum, et al., "Taking Your Place"; Myers and Roberts, *An Invitation to Chaplaincy Research*; VandeCreek, *Professional Chaplaincy*.
15. Sinclair, et al., "What Are the Core Elements."
16. Some of these studies and dissertations are to be found on the website of the Dutch professional association of chaplains (VGVZ): https://vgvz.nl/kennisbank-gv/overzicht-onderzoek/. Many studies and dissertations are written in Dutch in order to be accessible to the chaplains themselves.

in health care than in military and prison chaplaincy. The latter likely has to do with the fact that chaplaincy in military and prison settings is still organized primarily on the basis of the concept of representation of traditional religious and worldview institutions. In that context, there was less need for empirical research, as the provision of chaplaincy was assumed to be familiar with a clear position, a recognized profile, and a defined professional input. In fact, research could raise questions about the underpinnings of those services. It might reveal that traditional religious and worldview stratification has lessened, that diversity of religious orientations has increased, that religiosity, spirituality and worldview have become fluid, and that ecclesial and theological assumptions have become less recognizable in practice.[17]

DESCRIPTION AND ANALYSIS OF THE PRACTICE OF CHAPLAINCY

The development process of chaplaincy in the Netherlands and elsewhere has not resulted in a uniform practice and a theoretical basis shared by all. The opposite is true. It is also questionable whether uniformity would be desirable. The diversity of interventions, methods, and theories used is great. That has to do with the diversity of fields in which chaplains work, the great variety of target groups, and the broad spectrum of themes and life events that can be addressed in care. The themes can also shift in focus depending on the subculture, social class or stage of life in which clients find themselves. Added to this is the religious and worldview diversity in society. Working in the context of deployment to a war zone with young soldiers most of whom have taken practical education and who hardly have any religious background, is quite different from providing guidance to an elderly resident who has lived in an institution for people with intellectual disabilities all her life and who is traditionally Catholic. With this wide and rich array of interventions, practices and tools, the question can be asked how they are interrelated and to what extent they refer to the same domain or profession. And do the interventions, practices and instruments rise above the personal professional intuition of an individual chaplain? A similar breadth and variety will be apparent in every country and context in which chaplains work.

---

17. See among others: Swift, et al., *Handbook of Chaplaincy Studies*, 327–35.

The Profile and Domain of Chaplaincy

In 2015, the Dutch professional association for spiritual caregivers VGVZ formulated a professional code and professional standard. The professional standard describes the profile of chaplaincy: "Spiritual care is professional support, guidance and consultancy regarding meaning and world views."[18] Four dimensions of meaning and worldview are distinguished: existential, spiritual, ethical and aesthetic dimensions.[19]

(a) The existential dimension pertains to a person's existence as it is experienced in its everyday reality and with its (contingent) experiences of horror and wonder and all things in between.

(b) The spiritual dimension pertains to transcendental meaning and experience.

(c) The ethical dimension pertains to values, standards and responsible conduct.

(d) The aesthetic dimension pertains to constitutive experiences of natural and cultural beauty.

The aim is to define the domain of spiritual care across fields and denominations. The professional association wants to do justice to the breadth, scope and richness of the practice of chaplaincy. Of course, choices have been made. Important is the emphasis on professionalism. Chaplaincy requires specific and recognized training, not only initial but also postgraduate and permanent. Traditional theological training that focuses on working in church settings is no longer adequate. Postgraduate training should account for the specific contexts of spiritual care. Since the previous century, an important impetus in this regard has come from Clinical Pastoral Education (CPE), which began in the US in the 1920s and developed in its own form in the Netherlands since the 1960s. CPE pointed attention to the client as a *living human document*[20] in a *living human web*,[21] with an eye for both the client's life story (diachronic) and the client's relationships and context (synchronic). That focus can be broadened and deepened by attention for the interaction between client and chaplains, the *living human encounter*.[22] The professional profile of spiritual caregivers includes,

---

18. VGVZ, *Professional Standard*, 4.
19. VGVZ, *Professional Standard*, 6.
20. Asquith, "Anton T. Boisen."
21. Miller-McLemore, "Living Human Web."
22. Walton, "Introduction."

therefore, content-oriented, process-oriented, and person-oriented competencies. Content-oriented competencies concern the domain of meaning and worldview. Process-oriented competencies concern the ability to work as a professional in organizational and social contexts. And person-oriented competencies provide a warrant for integrity and self-reflection.[23]

A second important aspect of the Dutch professional standard has to do with the connection made between meaning and worldview. Together the two terms define the domain of chaplaincy (spiritual care), by connecting existential questions (meaning) and religion and other philosophical orientations (worldview). The emphasis on what happens in interactions (living human encounter) needs more detailed exploration, but so does the relation between domain and diversity of practice. The domain description in the professional standard appears capable of bridging different fields of work and denominations, but it is not yet immediately clear how the abstract formulation can function in the context of highly differentiated practice.[24] In the CSP, it is precisely the interaction between the general domain formulation and the descriptions of the concrete practice of chaplaincy that has led to a rich result. The pendulum between domain description and concrete practice descriptions proved to be a fruitful framework for research, as later chapters will show.

From Intention to Intervention—an International Perspective

Against this background, George Fitchett's call to use qualitative research in the form of case studies to map the practice of chaplaincy came as welcome.[25] In 2015, Fitchett repeated his call at a conference in the Netherlands, which effectively sowed the seed for the CSP. Fitchett emphasized that we (both researchers and chaplains) have little insight into what is actually going on in the interaction between clients and chaplains. What do chaplains actually do, what goals do they pursue, what theories and models do they draw on, and what outcomes (effects, results) do they (and their clients) observe?

Fitchett's call challenges chaplains to observe carefully and then accurately describe what is happening (and why and to what end) in the interaction between them and their clients. That challenge demands various skills. (1) Chaplains should be able to openly and unbiasedly observe and

---

23. VGVZ, *Professional Standard*, 8–10. See also: Cadge and Rambo, *Chaplaincy and Spiritual Care*. They describe competencies in the domain of meaning making, interpersonal functioning, and organization.

24. De Groot, *Questions of Life*; Körver, "Das Tabu."

25. Fitchett, "Making Our Case(s)."

describe (their own part in) the interaction with their clients. (2) When observing and reporting, chaplains need to pay attention primarily to what is visible (behavior and interventions), not just to what the intention was. (3) Chaplains need to continually move back and forth (reflection) between the concrete practice description and the domain description of chaplaincy. And (4) they need to enter into dialogue on the basis of their observations, descriptions, and reflections with fellow chaplains, other professionals and administrators.[26]

The call has led to research projects based on case studies in several countries, and numerous publications have since appeared, describing and analyzing practice step by step.[27] In Chapter 2 we position the CSP methodologically in that international framework. In Chapter 3 we elaborate on what a case study is in the context of the CSP and how case studies are used elsewhere in chaplaincy research.

The Dutch Case Studies Project in Spiritual Care

Fitchett's call was well received in the Netherlands. Interest was high. After an initial call through the professional association, 150 interested chaplains came forward, about 10 percent of the professional group of registered chaplains in the Netherlands. Ultimately, over sixty chaplains participated. This great interest was, we believe, due to a number of factors.

1. Case studies as a research method is close to what chaplains know of and are able to do due to their initial and postgraduate training. CPE has greatly influenced not only postgraduate training in the Netherlands, but also initial training. Under the influence of CPE, interaction between practice and reflection has been integrated into initial training, especially during the internship period. During an internship, students are regularly required to submit case studies (sometimes *verbatim*) precisely to learn to properly observe and articulate and reflect on their practice and their own actions.[28]

2. Using one's own practice as subject of research situated the research close to practice. For many years, there was a certain suspicion of

26. Walton and Körver, "Dutch Case Studies Project."

27. See among others: Boeykens, "What Are Chaplains Learning"; Desmet, "Towards a Distinct Professional Identity"; Fitchett and Nolan, *Spiritual Care in Practice*; Fitchett and Nolan, *Special Issue*; Fitchett and Nolan, *Case Studies in Spiritual Care*; Höfler, *Wirksamkeit von Krankenhausseelsorge*; Kruizinga, et al., *Learning from Case Studies*; Wirpsa and Pugliese, *Chaplains as Partners*.

28. Asquith, *The Case Study Method*; Powell, *CPE: Fifty Years of Learning*.

research among chaplains. It was assumed that research could not do justice to the precarious and nuanced practice, in which clients and chaplains searched together for answers to existential questions. A case study, on the contrary, is able to move closer to that encounter and to what is difficult to put into words.

3. Chaplains were given an active role of their own in the project (agency), so that they did not feel at the mercy of academic questions that might seem far removed from practice.

4. The time was ripe for a more empirical approach to the profession, to move beyond all the discussions, indicated above, on identity, professionalism, worldview background and endorsement, sanctuary function, presence, diagnosis, *et cetera*.[29]

The project is a clear example of the turn toward a more empirical stance, where ideological assumptions that long defined internal discussions within the profession could be put under an empirical magnifying glass. Is it true that chaplains do not use (explicit or implicit) goals in their accompaniment? Is it true that chaplains should not cooperate, or at least as little as possible, with other professionals in order to guarantee a sanctuary function and confidentiality for the client? Is chaplaincy primarily about presence or do diagnostics and assessment also play a role? What are the meaning and value of the endorsement, and how do they play a role in practice? And is it true that chaplains should only bring up existential and religious or spiritual questions, when the client explicitly starts talking about them?

RESEARCH QUESTIONS AND OBJECTIVES OF THE CSP

The profession of chaplaincy is young and old at the same time. Old because it stems from the work of clergy who for centuries provided care for those who were forced to spend extended periods of time away from their homes and were confronted with profound life questions and events. Over the past decades, it became clear that existing chaplaincy services were poorly suited to the questions of persons in these special circumstances, the sick, the military, prisoners. That provided a great challenge and incentive for the profession to reflect on how it can contribute to supporting or resolving those life questions.

Chaplaincy is, therefore, a young profession, that may boast of old traditions but that at the same time must reinvent itself. In a sense, a new

---

29. Vlasblom, et al., *Developments in Healthcare Chaplaincy*.

conception of the profession has emerged, making of chaplaincy a hybrid profession that does not rely solely on the background sciences of theology and humanistic studies, but that also consults the humanities, social and behavioral sciences, organizational studies, medicine, and pedagogy, among others. At the same time, a great diversity of fields of work, target groups, existential themes and dilemmas, life events and life stages, cultural and social backgrounds, and religious and other worldview movements all lead to a broad spectrum of interventions, practices, and tools, based on a like diversity of theories and models. Very little was known and written about this multicolored practice in an empirical sense until recently, apart from a few anecdotal case studies. The space between the abstract and general domain description of chaplaincy on the one hand and the multicolored, diverse, and complex reality of chaplaincy practice on the other needs to be filled in.

Research Questions of the CSP

Fitchett's plea[30] to invest in research about the current situation of chaplaincy using case studies ("Making our case(s)") well fits the context. The CSP and case study research elsewhere focuses on opening the black box of chaplaincy.[31] On the one hand, there is a need to discover with what purposes and methods chaplains actually work. On the other hand, there is a need to use such an exploration and inventory to strengthen position, profile, and professionalism of chaplaincy. There is, in other words, a need to make the qualities of chaplaincy visible.[32]

A concise formulation of the research questions of the CSP is: "What do chaplains do, why and to what end?"[33] More broadly, the research questions read:

- What do chaplains do in direct accompaniment of clients, what interventions do they employ, and in what contexts and consultation situations?
- Why do chaplains do what they do, that is, in response to what questions and desired outcomes, on the basis of what goals and theoretical considerations, in what contexts and consultation situations?

30. Fitchett, "Making Our Case(s)."
31. Steve Nolan used another metaphor to describe the same goal: "lifting the lid." See: Nolan, "Lifting the Lid on Chaplaincy."
32. HealthCare Chaplaincy Network, *What Is Quality Spiritual Care*.
33. Körver, et al., *Richting, Repertoire en Resultaat*; Kruizinga, et al., *Learning from Case Studies*; Walton and Körver, "Dutch Case Studies Project."

- To what end do chaplains do what they do, that is, with what observable and reported outcomes and side effects?

The emphasis was on the direct accompaniment of clients, individually or in small groups, as it is impossible to describe the broad spectrum of the work of chaplains in a single study. The choice fell on what chaplains themselves, as well as others, consider the chaplains' basic handwork. The methodological interpretation of this choice is discussed in the next chapter. In the course of the study, a fourth research question was added that was addressed in a PhD trajectory that became part of the project.

- What effects has participation in the CSP had on the practice and professionalism of the participating chaplains?[34]

Objectives of the CSP

We formulated the objectives of the project as follows:

- Description of chaplaincy interventions and their effects in relation to existential well-being, recovery and coping with illness, disability, loss and end of life within the various fields of institutional care, primary health care and social care, in relation to coping with responsibility, guilt, punishment and reconciliation within the context of justice, and in relation to violence, war and peace within the armed forces.
- Description of the interaction of chaplains with other staff involved with a client, of the interaction with the surrounding organization, and of the effects on the accompaniment of clients.
- Selection of good practices of chaplaincy.
- Broadening and strengthening the empirical and theoretical basis of the chaplaincy profession.

The CSP as a research project can be characterized as phenomenological, hermeneutic, and participatory research. The CSP was not only about accurate and unbiased descriptions of what happens in interactions between clients and chaplains (phenomenological), but also about a clear and communicable interpretation of that interaction from the perspective of meaning and worldview (hermeneutical). At the same time, there was consultation with clients, other professionals involved in the case, and especially with fellow chaplains in the research communities (participatory).

---

34. This question is studied in Niels Den Toom's PhD: Den Toom, *The Chaplain-Researcher*. See the Chapters 17, 19, and 20 in this volume.

This threefold characterization of the CSP will be detailed in the next chapter.

REFERENCES

Asquith, Glenn H., Jr. "The Case Study Method of Anton T. Boisen." *Journal of Pastoral Care* 34.2 (1980) 84–94.
———. "Anton T. Boisen and the Study of 'Living Human Documents.'" *Journal of Presbyterian History* 60.3 (1982) 244–65.
Boeykens, Frida. "What Are Chaplains Learning by Producing Case Studies?" In *Learning from Case Studies in Chaplaincy. Towards Practice Based Evidence & Professionalism*, edited by Renske Kruizinga, et al., 191–97. Utrecht: Eburon, 2020.
Cadge, Wendy. *Paging God. Religion in the Halls of Medicine*. Chicago: University of Chicago Press, 2012.
———. "Healthcare Chaplaincy as a Companion Profession: Historical Developments." *Journal of Health Care Chaplaincy* 25.2 (2019) 45–60. https://doi.org/10.1080/08854726.2018.1463617.
Cadge, Wendy, and Shelly Rambo, eds. *Chaplaincy and Spiritual Care in the Twenty-First Century. An Introduction*. Chapel Hill: University of North Carolina Press, 2022.
De Groot, Kees. *The Liquidation of the Church*. Routledge New Critical Thinking in Religion, Theology and Biblical Studies. London: Routledge, 2018.
———. *Questions of Life: A Sociology of the Care of Souls*. Tilburg: Tilburg University, 2021.
Den Toom, Niels. *The Chaplain-Researcher. The Perceived Impact of Participation in a Dutch Research Project on Chaplains' Professionalism*. Utrecht: Eburon, 2022.
Desmet, Lindsy. "Towards a Distinct Professional Identity. What Chaplains Have Learned in Flanders Case Study Research." In *Learning from Case Studies in Chaplaincy. Towards Practice Based Evidence & Professionalism*, edited by Renske Kruizinga, et al., 182–90. Utrecht: Eburon, 2021.
Doolaard, Jaap J. A., ed. *Nieuw Handboek Geestelijke Verzorging*. Kampen: Kok, 2006.
Emmet Gowin. New York: Fundación Mapfre–Aperture, 2013.
Fitchett, George. "Making Our Case(s)." *Journal of Health Care Chaplaincy* 17.1–2 (2011) 3–18. https://doi.org/10.1080/08854726.2011.559829.
Fitchett, George, et al. "Spiritual Care: The Role of Health Care Chaplaincy." In *Spirituality, Religiousness and Health: From Research to Clinical Practice*, edited by Giancarlo Lucchetti, et al. Religion, Spirituality and Health: A Social Scientific Approach. 4, 183–206. Cham: Springer, 2019.
Fitchett, George, and Steve Nolan, eds. *Spiritual Care in Practice: Case Studies in Healthcare Chaplaincy*. London: Kingsley, 2015.
———, eds. *Special Issue: Chaplain Case Study Research* Vol. 5.2: *Health and Social Care Chaplaincy*, 2017.
———, eds. *Case Studies in Spiritual Care. Healthcare Chaplaincy Assessments, Interventions & Outcomes*. London: Kingsley, 2018.
Flannelly, Kevin J., et al. "Department Directors' Perceptions of the Roles and Functions of Hospital Chaplains: A National Survey." *Hospital Topics* 83.4 (2005) 19–28. https://doi.org/10.3200/HTPS.83.4.19-28.

Grefe, Dagmar. *Encounters for Change. Interreligious Cooperation in the Care of Individuals and Communities*. Eugene, OR: Wipf & Stock, 2011.

Handzo, George F., et al. "Outcomes for Professional Health Care Chaplaincy. An International Call to Action." *Journal of Health Care Chaplaincy* 20.2 (2014) 43–53. https://doi.org/10.1080/08854726.2014.902713.

Haythorn, Trace, and Jason Callahan. "A Commissioning." In *Chaplaincy and Spiritual Care in the Twenty-First Century. An Introduction*, edited by Wendy Cadge and Shelly Rambo, 258–66. Chapel Hill: University of North Carolina Press, 2022.

HealthCare Chaplaincy Network. *What Is Quality Spiritual Care in Health Care and How Do You Measure It?* HealthCare Chaplaincy Network (www.healthcarechaplaincy.org: 2020).

Höfler, Nika. *Wirksamkeit von Krankenhausseelsorge. Eine Qualitative Studie*. Arbeiten Zur Praktischen Theologie; Band 88. Leipzig: Evangelische Verlagsanstalt, 2022.

Holmes, Cheryl. "From Chaplaincy to Spiritual Care: Turning Points for an Emerging Health Profession." *Asia-Pacific Journal of Health Management* 16.4 (2021) 54–61. https://doi.org/0.24083/apjhm.v16i4.691.

Kestenbaum, Allison, et al. "'Taking Your Place at the Table.' An Autoethnographic Study of Chaplains' Participation on an Interdisciplinary Research Team." *BMC Palliative Care* 14.20 (2015). https://doi.org/10.1186/s12904-015-0006-2.

Körver, Jacques. "Das Tabu der Zielorientierung durchbrechen. Mit professioneller Intuition im Krankenhaus auf der Suche nach der Seele." *Wege zum Menschen* 74.4 (2022) 368–81. https://doi.org/10.13109/weme.2022.74.4.368.

Körver, Jacques, et al., eds. *Richting, Repertoire en Resultaat. Uitkomsten van het Nederlandse Case Studies Project Geestelijke Verzorging (2016—2021)*. Utrecht: PThU-UCGV, 2023.

Kruizinga, Renske, et al., eds. *Learning from Case Studies in Chaplaincy. Towards Practice Based Evidence & Professionalism*. Utrecht: Eburon, 2020.

Mackor, Anne Ruth. "Standardization of Spiritual Care in Healthcare Facilities in the Netherlands. Blessing of Curse?" *Ethics and Social Welfare* 3.2 (2009) 215–28. https://doi.org/10.1080/17496530902951996.

MacLaren, Duncan. "All Things to All People? The Integrity of Spiritual Care in a Plural Health Service." *Health and Social Care Chaplaincy* 9.1 (2021) 27–41. https://doi.org/10.1558/hscc.40568.

Miller-McLemore, Bonnie J. "The Living Human Web. A Twenty-Five Year Retrospective." *Pastoral Psychology* 67.3 (2018) 305–21. https://doi.org/10.1007/s11089-018-0811-7.

Myers, Gary E., and Stephen Roberts, eds. *An Invitation to Chaplaincy Research. Entering the Process*: John Templeton Foundation–Healthcare Chaplaincy Network, 2014.

Nolan, Steve. "Lifting the Lid on Chaplaincy: A First Look at Findings from Chaplains' Case Study Research." *Journal of Health Care Chaplaincy* 27.1 (2021) 1–23. https://doi.org/10.1080/08854726.2019.1603916.

Nolan, Steve, and Duncan MacLaren. "Religious, Spiritual, Pastoral ... And Secular? Where Next for Chaplaincy?" *Health and Social Care Chaplaincy* 9.1 (2021) 1–10. https://doi.org/10.1558/hscc.42735/.

Orton, Margaret J. "Transforming Chaplaincy: The Emergence of a Healthcare Pastoral Care for a Post-Modern World." *Journal of Health Care Chaplaincy* 15.2 (2008) 114–31. https://doi.org/10.1080/08854720903152513.

Peng-Keller, Simon. *Healthcare Chaplaincy as Specialised Spiritual Care. The Christian Call for Healing in a Global Health Context*. Translated by Simon Peng-Keller. Göttingen: Vandenhoeck & Ruprecht, 2024. [Klinikseelsorge als spezialisierte Spiritual Care. Der christliche Heilungsauftrag im Horizont globaler Gesundheit, 2021.]

Powell, Robert C. *CPE. Fifty Years of Learning through Supervised Encounter with Living Human Documents*. New York: Association for Clinical Pastoral Education, 1975.

Schilderman, Hans. *Religion as a Profession*. Empirical Studies in Theology. Vol. 12, Leiden: Brill, 2005.

Schipani, Daniel S., and Leah Dawn Bueckert, eds. *Interfaith Spiritual Care. Understanding and Practices*. Kitchener: Pandora Press, 2009.

Sinclair, Shane, et al. "What Are the Core Elements of Oncology Spiritual Care Programs?" *Palliative & Supportive Care* 7.4 (2009) 415–22. https://doi.org/10.1017/S1478951509990423.

Stahl, Ronit Y. "Chaplaincy in the United States. A Short History." In *Chaplaincy and Spiritual Care in the Twenty-First Century*, edited by Wendy Cadge and Shelly Rambo, 19–31. Chapel Hill: University of North Carolina Press, 2022.

Stifoss-Hanssen, Hans, et al. "Chaplaincy in Northern Europe. An Overview from Norway." *Tidsskrift for Praktisk Teologi* 36.2 (2019) 60–70. https://doi.org/https://doi.org/10.48626/tpt.v36i2.5355.

Swift, Chris, et al. "Healthcare Chaplaincy." In *Oxford Textbook of Spirituality in Healthcare*, edited by Mark Cobb, et al., 185–90. Oxford: Oxford University Press, 2012.

Swift, Christopher, et al., eds. *A Handbook of Chaplaincy Studies. Understanding Spiritual Care in Public Places*. Ashgate Contemporary Ecclesiology Series. Farnham: Ashgate, 2015.

VandeCreek, L. *Professional Chaplaincy and Clinical Pastoral Education Should Become More Scientific: Yes and No*. New York: Haworth, 2002.

VGVZ. *Professional Standard Spiritual Caregiver 2015*. VGVZ (Amsterdam: 2015). https://vgvz.nl/wp-content/uploads/2023/02/VGVZ_Professional_Standard_2015_Main_Text_EN_v03_WITH_APPENDICES.pdf/.

Vlasblom, Jan Piet, et al. "Developments in Healthcare Chaplaincy in the Netherlands and Scotland. A Content Analysis of Professional Journals." *Health and Social Care Chaplaincy* 2.2 (2014) 235–54. https://doi.org/10.1558/hscc.v2i2.20409.

Walton, Martin N. "Introduction. Researching Living Human Encounter." In *Learning from Case Studies in Chaplaincy. Towards Practice Based Evidence & Professionalism*, edited by Renske Kruizinga, et al., 9–17. Utrecht: Eburon, 2020.

Walton, Martin N., and Jacques Körver. "Dutch Case Studies Project in Chaplaincy Care. A Description and Theoretical Explanation of the Format and Procedures." *Health and Social Care Chaplaincy* 5.2 (2017) 257–80. https://doi.org/10.1558/hscc.34302.

Wirpsa, M. Jeanne, and Karen Pugliese, eds. *Chaplains as Partners in Medical Decision-Making: Case Studies in Healthcare Chaplaincy*. London: Kingsley, 2020.

Yih, Caroline. "The Chaplain Grieves in Silence: Marginalisation, Disenfranchised Grief, and Chaplaincy." *Practical Theology* 14.6 (2021) 570–79. https://doi.org/https://doi.org/10.1080/1756073X.2021.1967558.

Zock, Hetty. "Chaplaincy in the Netherlands. The Search for a Religious and a Professional Identity." *Tidsskrift for Praktisk Teologi* 36.2 (2019) 11–21.

2

Observing, Interpreting, and Participating
— Jacques Körver

"What will be needed, what goes unfelt, unsaid—what has been duplicated, redacted here, redacted there, altered to hide or disguise—words encoding the bodies they cover. And despite everything the body remains."

CLAUDIA RANKINE[1]

BASIC PRINCIPLES OF THE CSP

CHAPTER 1 ENDED WITH the characterization of the CSP as phenomenological, hermeneutic, and participatory research. In this chapter, we would like to further explain that from a methodological standpoint. In the above quote from her book *Citizen: An American Lyric*, Claudia Rankine argues for keen observation of what occurs between people. She has an eye for casual comments, slanted looks, implicit biases in human communication, and for "microaggressions" toward people of color. At the same time, that careful attention makes her aware of unconscious beliefs and ideologies that constantly play a role in interpreting another person's behavior, attitudes, and physical expressions. Her approach fits perfectly with what the CSP aimed at: sharp and detailed observations, awareness of one's own frames and interpretations, and mutual exchange on observations and interpretations.

---

1. Rankine, *Citizen*, 56.

In order to describe the method of the CSP, we will take a number of steps. First, we will present an argument for the choice of qualitative research and the use of case studies. Next, we will describe the various methodological choices we used to flesh out the three types of research: phenomenological, hermeneutic, and participatory. We will then discuss thematic analysis as an underlying method of the format we used in the project and the role it played in the secondary analysis of the case studies. Finally, we discuss practical and organizational difficulties that were evoked by the magnitude of the project. In that context, we will also discuss the ethical preconditions of the project.

QUALITATIVE RESEARCH USING CASE STUDIES

Chaplains have often been suspicious of research on their practice. Their concern is that the depth, uniqueness and mystery of the care contact will be lost in the context of research. The result might be that justice is not done to the precarious and intimate conversations on ethical and religious topics related to meaning-making and worldview. In part, the suspicion is due to cold feet. Chaplaincy has a limited tradition of empirical research, as we saw in Chapter 1. Much of the *modus operandi* of chaplains originates intuitively, based on an amalgam of theology, psychology, social science, humanities and wisdom literature and tested in their training and continuing education primarily in regard to their own authenticity. Values such as availability (presence), unconditional acceptance, recognition, reliability, and openness are central to their actions. In the perception of many chaplains, all that seems to be at odds with research. In another way, their suspicion is justified. For what they see of research around them in medical, psychological, criminological, or military fields is mostly of a quantitative nature, in which the nuance, complexity, and differentiation of practice are often lost and conceptual depth and clarity are regularly lacking. The original intent of evidence-based medicine, the fusion of the best available science, the patient's context, and the clinical experience of the care provider, is narrowed down to loose puzzle pieces of quantitative research.[2]

---

2. Raad voor Volksgezondheid en Samenleving, *No Evidence without Context;* Sackett, et al., "Evidence Based Medicine."

Revaluing Qualitative Research

In 2016, seventy-six experienced researchers from eleven countries sent an open letter to the publishers of *The British Medical Journal* (*The BMJ*). It was a plea to adjust the journal's policy on publishing articles based on qualitative research.[3] They opposed the perception that that type of research is of low priority, unlikely to be cited often, lacks practical value, and is of no interest to readers. It turns out that the readers of *The BMJ* actually highly value qualitative research because it brings them closer to the practice being studied and provides clear action alternatives.[4] It is striking that this reappraisal of qualitative research resonates in the context of medical research, the place where in recent decades quantitative research and especially the *randomized controlled trial* (RCT) has pre-eminently been seen as the gold standard.

In analyzing some of the misconceptions concerning qualitative research, the Danish researcher Bent Flyvbjerg demonstrates the power of qualitative research.[5] Over the past decades, the methodology of qualitative research has been described in ever more precise and varied manners, along with the quality standards this type of research should meet.[6] Qualitative research is capable of exploring and analyzing complex and multifaceted interaction practices, profound existential events, religious and spiritual experiences, and meaning-making practices. In the process, qualitative research also provides a necessary nuance to the context of the client and the reappraisal of the clinical experience of health care providers, thus restoring balance to precisely what was originally meant by *evidence-based medicine*. Qualitative research does not only have value as a preliminary phase of quantitative research, as is often assumed.[7] For that reason, chaplains and researchers should always ask themselves whether conducting quantitative research is the right instrument to answer a question. Is, for example, impact research possible in a context in which values and beliefs play a major role, such as youth care, education, and chaplaincy and spiritual care.[8]

In our research, we assume that qualitative research, that is, case study research, is not exclusively a preliminary phase of RCTs, but offers powerful perspectives of its own. For the CSP, the existential and phenomenological

---

3. Greenhalgh, et al., "Open Letter."
4. Payne, "Twenty Top Papers."
5. Flyvbjerg, "Five Misunderstandings."
6. Levitt, et al., "The Methodological Integrity"; Reischer and Cowan, "Quantity over Quality."
7. Rounsaville, et al., "Stage Model"; Veerman, "Researching Practices."
8. Biesta, *Educational Research*.

approaches in qualitative research proved especially relevant. Recently, American psychologist Scott D. Churchill aptly stated:

> doing psychology phenomenologically can be described as a process of starting with the meanings found within descriptions of situations lived through by our informants and working our way back to the latent intentionalities that 'made' those circumstances what they were for the participant ... When people find themselves in circumstances where they must make a choice or when they are living through emotional situations where they have lost their bearings, these experiences are well suited for analysis using existential phenomenological research.[9]

Case Study Research

In 1959, social psychologist Milton Rokeach brought together three patients at Ypsilanti State Hospital in Michigan who were all firmly convinced that they were Jesus Christ.[10] Rokeach was curious about the effect of this confrontation on the development of each person's identity. The experiment, which eventually lasted nearly two years, is meticulously described by Rokeach as a case study. Not only the behavior of the three men and the complications in the regular group discussions were recorded, but also the interventions of the therapists.[11] Leaving aside the question of whether from a therapeutic or ethical perspective such an experiment would still be possible in this day and age, this N=1 study offers a detailed insight into the method of treatment, into the behavior and development of the three patients, as well as important insights into what identity is.[12]

It is an example of a research tradition that from the early years of psychoanalysis has played an important role in the development of theories of human behavior and psychology. The Anna O. case study, for example, contributed fundamentally to the understanding of hysteria and helped to underpin the development of psychoanalysis.[13] That an intensive study of a single case can contribute to the development of a theory is also demonstrated by Ivan Petrovich Pavlov's study in which he demonstrated the

---

9. Churchill, *Essentials of Existential*, 21.

10. This section is a shortened adaptation of the first part of Körver, et al., "Fallgeschichten, Forschung, Seelsorge," 300–02.

11. Rokeach, *The Three Christs*.

12. Kazdin, *Single-Case Research Designs*.

13. Breuer and Freud, *Studies on Hysteria*.

principles of classical conditioning.[14] Burrhus Frederic Skinner who was a great advocate of the N=1 methodology put it this way: "instead of studying a thousand rats for one hour each, or a hundred rats for ten hours each, the investigator is likely to study one rat for a thousand hours."[15] The use of case studies is also familiar practice in the world of theology, pastoral ministry, and chaplaincy. The main emphasis is on their use in teaching, fueled in part by *Clinical Pastoral Education* (CPE) and pastoral supervision. Less well known is that one of the founders of the CPE, Anton Theophilus Boisen, meticulously described case studies out of scientific interest, focusing primarily on the possible relationship between religion and psychiatric disorders.[16]

Research using case studies is thus a recognized and successful strategy in numerous (humanities) sciences, that in addition to detailed descriptions and explorations has also led to numerous theoretical insights, as these and other examples make clear.[17] That case study research has by no means lost its value is shown, for example, by the online journal *Pragmatic Case Studies in Psychotherapy*, in which cases from psychotherapeutic practice are described and reflected upon in great detail, and in which existential and phenomenological approaches are extensively discussed.[18] In literature, the case study approach can also play a role, as the book by Rankine from the epigraph demonstrates.

CASE STUDIES IN THE CSP

Following George Fitchett's call,[19] numerous case studies have appeared internationally from a variety of fields of spiritual care.[20] Most have been drawn from chaplaincy and spiritual care in health care, fewer from other

---

14. Pavlov, *Conditioned Reflexes*.

15. Skinner, "Operant Behavior," 21.

16. Most known is Boisen's autobiography about his own experiences with psychiatric disorders: Boisen, *Out of the Depths*.

17. A particularly good example is the development of *Grounded Theory*, a kind of qualitative research based on the studies of Barney Glaser and Anselm Strauss: Glaser and Strauss, *Awareness of Dying*; Glaser and Strauss, *Discovery of Grounded Theory*.

18. This journal is freely available: https://pcsp.nationalregister.org/index.php/pcsp.

19. Fitchett, "Making Our Case(s)."

20. A significant number of these case studies are published in the following volumes: Fitchett and Nolan, *Spiritual Care in Practice*; Fitchett and Nolan, *Special Issue*; Fitchett and Nolan, *Case Studies in Spiritual Care*; Kruizinga, et al., *Learning from Case Studies*; Wirpsa and Pugliese, *Chaplains as Partners*. See also Chapter 3 "What Makes a Good Case?"

fields in which chaplains are active. For the purposes of the CSP, we have defined a case study as follows:

> A case study within the framework of the CSP on chaplaincy care is an informative story with methodical description and reflection in which the accompaniment process and the contribution of chaplaincy care are demonstrated and argued with the intent of identifying good practices."[21]

In addition to the publications of Fitchett and Nolan, we have been inspired by methodological publications in the field of case study research in the social sciences, including those of Gary Thomas and Robert K. Yin.[22] From Thomas's work we borrow the distinction between the *subject* and the *object* of a case study. The subject concerns the person, situation, event, or interaction being described, while the object concerns the analytical perspective.[23] A single or multiple case study can be examined from different analytical perspectives. The ritual acts that play a role within chaplaincy care or the forms of collaboration with other professionals are examples of possible perspectives.[24] In the context of the CSP, we focused primarily on what chaplains do concretely (behavior, interaction, intervention), on the basis of what considerations (intention, motivation, value, theory), for what purpose, and with what result (effect, outcome). In doing so, we considered a chaplain's practice as a network of observations, interactions, interventions, reflections, emotions, motivations, intentions, and effects.[25] The case study focuses not on a *living human document*[26] or a *living human web*[27], but on a *living human encounter*.[28]

What Do I See and What Do I Do? A Phenomenological Approach

In the design of the study, we chose to concentrate on individual accompaniment in providing care. Moreover, we chose to describe case studies based on a detailed format. Of course, it is true that chaplains do more than

---

21. Walton and Körver, "Dutch Case Studies Project," 260.
22. Thomas and Myers, *Anatomy Case Study*; Yin, *Case Study Research*.
23. Thomas, "A Typology for the Case Study," 513–15.
24. See "Chaplaincy in Context" (Chapter 13) and "Rituals in Chaplaincy" (Chapter 16).
25. Reckwitz, "Toward a Theory."
26. Boisen, *Exploration Inner World*.
27. Miller-McLemore, "Living Human Web."
28. Walton, "Introduction."

provide individual care. Chaplains are active on many levels within their organizations, often have a varied composition of tasks, and are widely employable. In addition, the different tasks are closely interrelated. A group discussion may turn into an individual contact, which could lead to a conversation with other professionals about ethical or treatment issues within the organization; and that conversation could lead to reflection on short- or long-term policy. There is something artificial about isolating a particular activity. At the same time, the concentration on individual care makes it possible to zoom in, to get a sharper picture of a part of the practice, and to avoid getting bogged down in the breadth of the work. The concentration also leads participating chaplains to repeatedly look at their practice from the same perspective, to develop experience in observing and articulating that part of the work that they themselves and others see as the heart of the profession. Such a prolonged joint concentration helps to bring prejudices and ideological assumptions into focus. Moreover, even this part of the work already has a vast range, given the broad spectrum of fields of work, contexts, target groups, life stages, life events, and religious or worldview backgrounds.

Chaplains are not unfamiliar with case studies. Initial and postgraduate training programs make frequent use of them, to teach how to observe and describe practice, to reflect on how theory and practice interact, and to examine how one's own actions and attitudes affect interaction. It is a method that is familiar, close to practice, and encourages a phenomenological gaze. The use of a comprehensive format for description and analysis explicitly helped in developing an inquisitive attitude, by repeating the same questions, continuingly following the same structure, and ingraining the same approach.[29] The format placed relatively more emphasis on the interventions than the intention of the chaplain. That helped in describing the behavioral aspects of the interaction. At the same time, the format focused on what the chaplain observed in the other person (behavior, attitude, physical expressions) and in oneself (motives for doing/not doing something, hesitations, decisions as the care process progressed). That can be considered a light form of what is called *stimulated recall* elsewhere in research and training.[30]

In Chapter 3, we look more at how the purpose and format of a case study in the CSP compares with what is common elsewhere in chaplaincy case study research. Here we point out that the CSP format is more detailed

---

29. See the case study format in Appendix B, and in Walton and Körver, "Dutch Case Studies Project."

30. Barrows, *Stimulated Recall*.

than is customary.[31] The set format makes case studies more comparable for the sake of analyzing multiple case studies. Another aspect of the format is the inclusion in the case study of discussion and analysis together with peers and researchers.[32]

How Do I Understand What I See and Do? A Hermeneutic Approach

It is not possible to completely (even if temporarily) renounce one's own conceptions of, relationship to, and ideals about chaplaincy. In order to assist the chaplains in thinking freely and openly about the interactions in the case studies, the goals that came up, the underlying theories and values, and the observed effects, some preconditions had to be met. That was particularly important for discussion and analysis in the research communities (RCs), that formed the heart of the CSP (see next section). First of all, an appreciative approach to the case studies was encouraged in the RCs. That approach assumes that each case study can contribute to the clarification and description of what chaplaincy is in a specific field of work, with a particular target group, or in view of a distinct life theme.[33] Participating chaplains and the chairpersons of the RCs were encouraged to suspend their own judgments about what constitutes good chaplaincy care. They were invited to reflect upon various questions. What is going on here? What intentions or purposes underlie an action? What theory or value might support the approach taken? What outcome or effect can be observed? We sought to probe the experiences and intentions in the interactions between client and chaplains and articulate them. We looked to see if there was a common ground where the horizons of experience of the client and of the chaplain might merge, as it were, without coinciding.[34]

    A second tool (precondition) was to describe and discuss the case study in the third person. "The chaplain . . ." "She has . . ." "He is now doing . . ." In that way, the overtly personal aspect (which in supervision or peer review is central) was somewhat filtered, shifting the primary focus

---

    31. This certainly applies to Fitchett's instructions for the design of a case study: Fitchett, "Making Our Case(s)," 12–14.

    32. This also is a different approach than Fitchett and Nolan have chosen in both of their collections of case studies, in which a chaplain and another professional provide their critical commentary for each group of case studies (for example in pediatrics, psychiatry, or palliative care): Fitchett and Nolan, *Spiritual Care in Practice*; Fitchett and Nolan, *Case Studies in Spiritual Care*.

    33. Bushe, "Appreciative Inquiry Model."

    34. Gadamer, *Truth and Method*.

from personal development to reflection on the profession, its clarification, and its development. In discussions on research in the humanities and in chaplaincy, there are different viewpoints on this matter of first and third person perspectives, mainly based on insights from autoethnography.[35] Our intention was to increase the reflective space in both authoring a case study and discussing it with others. It remained clear who the author was. And personal learning continued, of course, although with a different focus. The sole intention was to foster awareness—through the third person perspective—of one's own beliefs and stimulate open-minded discussion of everyone's work.

With the help of these two preconditions, the RCs reflected upon and analyzed the case studies, using a fixed and recurring structure from the format, just as was the case for description (see above). An important substantive point here was the use of the four-dimensional description of meaning and worldview from the Professional Standard of the Dutch Association of Chaplains[36] as *sensitizing concepts*, that is, as attentive and guiding concepts for reflection and analysis.[37] Each case study involved reflection on the existential, spiritual, ethical, and aesthetic aspects or qualities of the situation, theme, purpose, intervention, and outcome. The goal was continual interaction in the analysis phase between the very diverse and concrete descriptions of practice on the one hand and the more comprehensive abstract description of the professional domain on the other. That movement, we hypothesized, would connect the abstract description of the domain with the concreteness of practice, while lifting the descriptions of the concrete practice to a higher level of integration.[38]

How Do We Interpret Together What We See? A Participatory Approach

In two respects, the CSP was a participatory study, an approach that is currently receiving much attention in practical theology and other research traditions.[39] First, the case study format protocol included the (urgent) re-

---

35. Nolan, "Introduction"; Poulos, *Essentials of Autoethnography*.

36. The English translation of the Professional Standard can be accessed via: https://vgvz.nl/wp-content/uploads/2023/02/VGVZ_Professional_Standard_2015_Main_Text_EN_v03_WITH_APPENDICES.pdf.

37. The phrasing of *sensitizing concept* comes from Herbert Blumer: Blumer, "What Is Wrong." See also Bowen, "Sensitizing Concepts."

38. See Chapter 1 for the description of the domain.

39. Abma, et al., "Patients as Partners"; De Roest, *Collaborative Practical Theology*;

quest that, if possible, the chaplain submit the case description to the client or a legal representative. In research literature, that is known by the term *member check*.[40] The goal is to increase credibility—or as one would say in quantitative research, internal validity—by presenting respondents with the account of the contact. Moreover, the member check emphasizes the importance of the client's voice in research.[41] Though not always possible, the advantage of a member check was that it encouraged participating chaplains to bracket their own perceptions and check their report in light of the client's experiences and reflections, even if such a step might also represent a new intervention. Connected to that was the requirement to obtain written consent from clients (or their legal representatives) to make it clear that the case study is part of a research study. That requirement moved participating chaplains to handle the data with care and to consider clients as co-bearers of the study.[42]

A second form of collaboration involved analyzing case studies in a RC. Often in case study research, practitioners are invited to describe and submit one or more case studies to the researcher, who then conducts the analysis. Analyzing case studies together, over a period of four years, provided added value. Participating chaplains became co-researchers and co-responsible for the conduct of the study. Mutual differences in methodological approach, theoretical and religious or worldview background, and personal preferences came into clear focus. Despite the diversity, the opportunity arose for a clearer sense of the shared values that underpin the profession. The diversity induced a search for cohesion and integration. It encouraged the development of a common language across the boundaries of fields of work, denominations, and target groups.[43]

In addition to these forms of participation, from the beginning we included a number of researchers and chaplains who were not directly involved in the research. Together with the chairpersons of the RCs and the project leaders, they formed the *Research Collaboration Group* (RCG). The task of the RCG was to follow developments in the CSP in a critical manner, to provide comments and advice on the direction of the project, and especially to encourage the researchers themselves to reflect on their own position and possible biases.

Engelaar, et al., *Quality of Life in Oncology*; Visse, et al., "Relational Responsibilities."

40. Madill and Sullivan, "Mirrors, Portraits"; Motulsky, "Is Member Checking."

41. Thomas, et al., "Co-Creation in Citizen Social Science."

42. McCurdy and Fitchett, "Ethical Issues"; Timmerman, et al., "In Search of Good Care."

43. Den Toom, *The Chaplain-Researcher;* Den Toom, et al., "Professionalization of Chaplaincy."

ADDITIONAL METHODOLOGICAL, ORGANIZATIONAL, AND ETHICAL ASPECTS

Not only at the beginning but also during the process, the CSP faced multiple challenges, especially with regard to the analysis of multiple case studies, organizational difficulties, and ethical issues. We address these three issues below.

Thematic Analysis of Multiple Case Studies

The format for description and analysis of a case study in the CSP emerged in several steps. Initially, we started from the seven elements that Fitchett considered important for a good case study.[44] A next step was the distinction between intervention, goal, outcome, and the supporting theories in the description, a distinction that was also visible in the project's research questions. Gradually, further differentiation emerged with regard to background data, reason for the contact, communication, interventions, goals, and effects. A major step was the introduction of the four dimensions in the definition of meaning and worldview as sensitizing concepts.[45] All this can already be understood as a step towards thematic analysis, partly deductive and partly inductive. In the context of the CSP, we have drawn primarily upon the elaboration of thematic analysis by Virginia Braun and Victoria Clarke.

> Thematic analysis [is] a method for identifying, analyzing and reporting patterns (themes) within data. It minimally organizes and describes your data set in (rich) detail. However, frequently it goes further than this, and interprets various aspects of the research topic.[46]

Their approach has a constructionist perspective, in that the analysis of experiences and meanings takes place against the background of the context in which people live and work. The format developed within the CSP can be considered a deductive model. In addition, thematic analysis can also be inductive, or a combination of both approaches.[47]

---

44. Fitchett, "Making Our Case(s)," 12–14.
45. Chapter 1 and earlier in this chapter.
46. Braun and Clarke, "Using Thematic Analysis," 79.
47. Braun and Clarke, *Successful Qualitative Research*; Braun and Clarke, "Conceptual and Design Thinking."

During the analysis of case studies in the RCs, thematic analysis in a deductive form was employed. At the same time, especially during the repeated meetings, thematic patterns became visible in an inductive manner. Those patterns were named by the participants and received further elaboration by the chair-researchers of these groups in a variety of publications. One example is an analysis of thirteen case studies of chaplaincy in the armed forces using the *Framework Method*, a form of thematic analysis.[48] The analysis showed that chaplains contribute to the moral resilience of military personnel who face moral stress or moral injury in their work and environment.[49] Thematic analysis (in various forms) is a particularly manageable method for the comparative analysis of case studies.

Organization and Infrastructure

Following an initial call sent to the Dutch professional association, about 150 chaplains requested information about the project. Over sixty of them attended an information meeting in March 2016. Those interested came not only from different fields of institutional health care, but also from the fields of primary[50] and social care, justice, and defense. Fellow researchers from other universities also expressed interest. Initially, between fifty and sixty chaplains (and seven academic researchers who served as chairpersons of the RCs) made a commitment, meaning that it was no longer a small-scale project. The scale of the project raised the requirements for infrastructure, personnel, finances, data management, ethical review, and legal arrangements (such as agreements with the participants and their employers or supervisors).[51]

At the beginning of the project, a number of issues had not yet (properly) been settled. The methodological manual for the chairs of the RCs was in draft form, but required refinement. The coordination between the chairs (among other things regarding the process and the use of the format) took place mainly in writing and not by practicing with each other and exchanging on actual experiences. The recruitment of participating chaplains was based on work experience and interest in research and not explicitly on

48. Frazer, et al., "Applying the Framework Method"; Gale, et al., "Using the Framework Method."

49. Schuhmann, et al., "How Military Chaplains Strengthen."

50. Especially the collaboration with general practitioners and home care services including in the context of palliative care. See for example: Liefbroer et al., "A Spiritual Care Intervention."

51. To get an idea of the organizational aspects of the CSP, see the organogram in Appendix A.

research experience and competence. We let the chaplains begin writing case studies using the format immediately. Training in working with the format took place during the (initial) efforts and discussions.

It also took us some time to find a satisfactory solution for data management and administration. The supporting academic institutions[52] were not equipped to facilitate such an extensive project with collaboration agreements, employer contributions, external data users, and secure exchange of qualitative data on a large scale. The logistics were a greater challenge than the methodology.

The RCs were the heart of the project. In the end, we were able to start with six groups, five of which were based on fields of work (prisons, military, mental health, eldercare, and hospital) and one that mixed different fields (juvenile care, rehabilitation, disability care, university chaplaincy, homeless care, primary care, and hospital care). Over the course of the project, sixty-two professional chaplains participated. A few withdrew for various reasons; others joined during the course of the project. Generally, the composition of the groups remained very stable. The vast majority of the participating chaplains fulfilled their four year, in practice almost five-year, commitments to the project. Each RC was chaired by an academic researcher. All of the chairpersons had held positions in chaplaincy or pastoral ministry prior to their academic careers, generally in the field of their RC.

Ethical Aspects

An important aspect of empirical research concerns the protection of the respondents (clients) participating in the research. Guidelines in this area have become more stringent in recent years. (Inter)national legislation in the form of the *General Data Protection Regulation* and the *Dutch Code of Conduct on Scientific Integrity* impose clear and strict requirements on any research involving persons. The provision of information to and privacy of participants in research and the safe, careful, and sustainable management of research data are the main concerns. Internally within the university, there were reviews by faculty ethics committees.[53] Much of the data of the CSP came from health care institutions, that have their own forms of review. The research design of the CSP was reviewed by the MEC-U, the *Medical Research Ethics Committees United*, in which a number of major hospitals

---

52. The Protestant Theological University and the Tilburg School of Catholic Theology.

53. Given the fact that the research data are stored at Tilburg University, the internal assessment took place at the TST.

in the Netherlands collaborate.[54] The review committee was of the opinion that the research did not fall within the scope of the Dutch *Medical Research Involving Human Subjects Act* (registration number W18.064).[55] That judgement does not, however, release one from the obligation to provide correct information and protect the privacy of the respondents involved, as well as ensure safe and careful storage of the data.

In the CSP, not only clients but also the participating chaplains and researchers were object of research, each group in its own way. For each of these three different groups of participants, a separate information letter and informed consent was designed.[56] We realized in advance that seeking consent could become an additional bump in the contact between chaplains and clients. The requirement remained that a client (or a legal representative) be aware that data from the contact could be included in a study and possibly in publications. The protection of the client requires that one be accurately informed of the consequences of participation and of the rights and obligations to which consent is bound. Written agreements for participation and consent were also made with the chaplains and with the researchers involved. In cooperation with Tilburg University, arrangements were made for careful, secure, and anonymized storage of the data.

REFERENCES

Abma, Tineke A., et al. "Patients as Partners in Responsive Research. Methodological Notions for Collaborations in Mixed Research Teams." *Qualitative Health Research* 19.3 (2009) 401–15. https://doi.org/10.1177/1049732309331869.

Barrows, Howard S. *Stimulated Recall. Personalized Assessment of Clinical Reasoning.* Springfield: Southern Illinois University School of Medicine, 2000.

Biesta, Gert. *Educational Research. An Unorthodox Introduction.* London: Bloomsbury, 2020.

Blumer, Herbert. "What Is Wrong with Social Theory?" *American Sociological Review* 19.1 (1954) 3–10. https://doi.org/https://doi.org/10.2307/2088165.

Boisen, Anton Theophilus. *The Exploration of the Inner World.* Chicago: Willett, Clark, 1936.

———. *Out of the Depths. An Autobiographical Study of Mental Disorder and Religious Experience.* New York: Harper & Brothers, 1960.

Bowen, Glenn A. "Sensitizing Concepts." In *Sage Research Methods*, edited by Paul Atkinson, et al. Language and Qualitative Research. London: Sage, 2020.

---

54. https://www.mec-u.nl/.

55. For more information: https://www.mec-u.nl/wmo/niet-wmo-plichtig-onderzoek/.

56. See Appendix C for the text of the client information letter and informed consent form.

Braun, Virginia, and Victoria Clarke. "Using Thematic Analysis in Psychology." *Qualitative Research in Psychology* 3.2 (2006) 77–101. https://doi.org/10.1191/1478088706qp063oa.

———. *Successful Qualitative Research. A Practical Guide for Beginners.* Los Angeles etc.: Sage, 2013.

———. "Conceptual and Design Thinking for Thematic Analysis." *Qualitative Psychology* 9.1 (2022) 3–26. https://doi.org/10.1037/qup0000196.

Breuer, Josef, and Sigmund Freud. *Studies on Hysteria.* New York: Basic Books, 1957 [1895].

Bushe, Gervase. "Appreciative Inquiry Model." In *Encyclopedia of Management Theory* Volume 1, edited by Eric H. Kessler, 41–44. Thousand Oaks: Sage, 2013.

Churchill, Scott D. *Essentials of Existential Phenomenological Research.* Essentials of Qualitative Methods Series. Washington, DC: American Psychological Association, 2022. doi:10.1037/0000257-000.

De Roest, Henk. *Collaborative Practical Theology. Engaging Practitioners in Research on Christian Practices.* Leiden: Brill, 2020.

Den Toom, Niels. *The Chaplain-Researcher. The Perceived Impact of Participation in a Dutch Research Project on Chaplains' Professionalism.* Utrecht: Eburon, 2022.

Den Toom, Niels, et al. "The Professionalization of Chaplaincy. A Comparison of 1997 and 2017 Surveys in the Netherlands." *Journal of Health Care Chaplaincy* 29.1 (2023) 14–29. https://doi.org/10.1080/08854726.2021.1996810.

Engelaar, Merel, et al. *Quality of Life in Oncology: Measuring What Matters for Cancer Patients and Survivors in Europe: Handbook & Checklist.* Utrecht: Nivel–ECO, 2023.

Fitchett, George. "Making Our Case(s)." *Journal of Health Care Chaplaincy* 17.1–2 (2011) 3–18. https://doi.org/10.1080/08854726.2011.559829.

Fitchett, George, and Steve Nolan, eds. *Spiritual Care in Practice. Case Studies in Healthcare Chaplaincy.* London: Kingsley, 2015.

———, eds. *Special Issue: Chaplain Case Study Research* Vol. 5.2: *Health and Social Care Chaplaincy,* 2017.

———, eds. *Case Studies in Spiritual Care. Healthcare Chaplaincy Assessments, Interventions & Outcomes.* London: Kingsley, 2018.

Flyvbjerg, Bent. "Five Misunderstandings About Case-Study Research." *Qualitative Inquiry* 12.2 (2006) 219–45. https://doi.org/10.1177/1077800405284363.

Frazer, Imogen, et al. "Applying the Framework Method to Qualitative Psychological Research. Methodological Overview and Worked Example." *Qualitative Psychology* 10.1 (2023) 44–59. https://doi.org/10.1037/qup0000238.

Gadamer, Hans-Georg. *Truth and Method.* Translated by Joel C. Weinsheimer and Donald G. Marshall. Continuum Impacts. 2nd ed. London: Continuum, 2004.

Gale, Nicola, et al. "Using the Framework Method for the Analysis of Qualitative Data in Multi-Disciplinary Health Research." *BMC Medical Research Methodology* 13 (2013) 117. https://doi.org/10.1186/1471-2288-13-117.

Glaser, Barney G., and Anselm Leonard Strauss. *Awareness of Dying.* Observations. Chicago: Aldine, 1965.

———. *The Discovery of Grounded Theory. Strategies for Qualitative Research.* Observations. Chicago: Aldine, 1967.

Greenhalgh, Trisha, et al. "An Open Letter to the BMJ Editors on Qualitative Research." *The British Medical Journal* 352 (2016) i563. https://doi.org/10.1136/bmj.i563.

Kazdin, Alan E. *Single-Case Research Designs. Methods for Clinical and Applied Settings.* 3rd ed. Oxford: Oxford University Press, 2020.

Körver, Jacques, et al. "Fallgeschichten, Forschung, Seelsorge. Ein inspirirendes Trio." *Wege zum Menschen* 74.4 (2022) 300–13. https://doi.org/10.13109/weme.2022.74.4.300.

Kruizinga, Renske, et al., eds. *Learning from Case Studies in Chaplaincy. Towards Practice Based Evidence & Professionalism.* Utrecht: Eburon, 2020.

Levitt, Heidi M., et al. "The Methodological Integrity of Critical Qualitative Research. Principles to Support Design and Research Review." *Journal of Counseling Psychology* 68.3 (2021) 357–70. https://doi.org/http://dx.doi.org/10.1037/cou0000523.

Liefbroer, Anke I., et al. "A Spiritual Care Intervention for Chaplains in Home-Based Palliative Care: Design of a Mixed-Methods Study Investigating Effects on Patients' Spiritual Wellbeing." *Journal of Health Care Chaplaincy* 28.3 (2021) 328–41. https://doi.org/10.1080/08854726.2021.1894532.

Madill, Anna, and Paul Sullivan. "Mirrors, Portraits, and Member Checking: Managing Difficult Moments of Knowledge Exchange in the Social Sciences." *Qualitative Psychology* 5.3 (2018) 321–39. https://doi.org/10.1037/qup0000089.

McCurdy, David B., and George Fitchett. "Ethical Issues in Case Study Publication. 'Making Our Case(s)' Ethically." *Journal of Health Care Chaplaincy* 17.1–2 (2011) 55–74. https://doi.org/10.1080/08854726.2011.559855.

Miller-McLemore, Bonnie J. "The Living Human Web. A Twenty-Five Year Retrospective." *Pastoral Psychology* 67.3 (2018) 305–21. https://doi.org/10.1007/s11089-018-0811-7.

Motulsky, Sue L. "Is Member Checking the Gold Standard of Quality in Qualitative Research?" *Qualitative Psychology* 8.3 (2021) 389–406. https://doi.org/10.1037/qup0000215.

Nolan, Steve. "Introduction. Autoethnography in Chaplain Case Study Research." In *Case Studies in Spiritual Care. Healthcare Chaplaincy Assessments, Interventions & Outcomes*, edited by George Fitchett and Steve Nolan, 11–32. London: Kingsley, 2018.

Pavlov, Ivan Petrovich. *Conditioned Reflexes. An Investigation of Psychological Activity of the Cerebral Cortex.* London: Oxford University Press, 1927.

Payne, David. "Twenty Top Papers to Mark the BMJ's Two Digital Decades." *The British Medical Journal* 351 (2015) h3660. https://doi.org/10.1136/bmj.h3660.

Poulos, Christopher N. *Essentials of Autoethnography.* Washington: American Psychological Association, 2021.

Raad voor Volksgezondheid en Samenleving. *No Evidence without Context. About the Illusion of Evidence-Based Practice in Healthcare.* Den Haag: RVS, 2017.

Rankine, Claudia. *Citizen. An American Lyric.* Minneapolis: Graywolf, 2014.

Reckwitz, Andreas. "Toward a Theory of Social Practices. A Development in Culturalist Theorizing." *European Journal of Social Theory* 5.2 (2002) 243–63. https://doi.org/10.1177/13684310222225432.

Reischer, Hollen, and Henry R. Cowan. "Quantity over Quality? Reproducible Psychological Science from a Mixed Methods Perspective." *Collabra: Psychology* 6.1 (2020) 26. https://doi.org/https://doi.org/10.1525/collabra.284.

Rokeach, Milton. *The Three Christs of Ypsilanti. A Psychological Study.* New York: Alfred A. Knopf, 1964.

Rounsaville, Bruce J., et al. "A Stage Model of Behavioral Therapies Research: Getting Started and Moving on from Stage I." *Clinical Psychology: Science and Practice* 8.2 (2001) 133–42. https://doi.org/10.1093/clipsy.8.2.133.

Sackett, David L., et al. "Evidence Based Medicine: What It Is and What It Isn't." *British Medical Journal* 312.7023 (1996) 71–72.

Schuhmann, Carmen, et al. "How Military Chaplains Strengthen the Moral Resilience of Soldiers and Veterans: Results from a Case Studies Project in the Netherlands." *Pastoral Psychology* 72 (2023) 605–24. https://doi.org/10.1007/s11089-023-01097-5.

Skinner, Burrhus Frediric. "Operant Behavior." In *Operant Behavior: Areas of Research and Application*, edited by W.K. Honig, 12–32. New York: Appleton-Century-Crofts, 1966.

Thomas, Gary. "A Typology for the Case Study in Social Science Following a Review of Definition, Discourse, and Structure." *Qualitative Inquiry* 17.6 (2011) 511–21. https://doi.org/10.1177/1077800411409884.

Thomas, Gary, and Kevin Myers. *The Anatomy of the Case Study*. London: Sage, 2015.

Thomas, Stefan, et al. "Co-Creation in Citizen Social Science: The Research Forum as a Methodological Foundation for Communication and Participation." *Humanities & Social Sciences Communications* 8.244 (2021) 1–11. https://doi.org/https://doi.org/10.1057/s41599-021-00902-x.

Timmerman, Guus, et al. "In Search of Good Care. The Methodology of Phenomenological, Theory-Oriented 'N=N Case Studies' in Empirically Grounded Ethics of Care." *Medicine, Health Care and Philosophy* 22.4 (2019) 573–82. https://doi.org/10.1007/s11019-019-09892-9.

Veerman, Jan Willem. "Researching Practices. Lessons from Dutch Youth Care." In *Learning from Case Studies in Chaplaincy. Towards Practice Based Evidence & Professionalism*, edited by Renske Kruizinga, et al., 46–59. Utrecht: Eburon, 2020.

Visse, Merel, et al. "Relational Responsibilities in Responsive Evaluation." *Evaluation and Program Planning* 35.1 (2012) 97–104.

Walton, Martin N. "Introduction. Researching Living Human Encounter." In *Learning from Case Studies in Chaplaincy. Towards Practice Based Evidence & Professionalism*, edited by Renske Kruizinga, et al., 9–17. Utrecht: Eburon, 2020.

Walton, Martin N., and Jacques Körver. "Dutch Case Studies Project in Chaplaincy Care. A Description and Theoretical Explanation of the Format and Procedures." *Health and Social Care Chaplaincy* 5.2 (2017) 257–80. https://doi.org/10.1558/hscc.34302.

Wirpsa, M. Jeanne, and Karen Pugliese, eds. *Chaplains as Partners in Medical Decision-Making: Case Studies in Healthcare Chaplaincy*. London: Kingsley, 2020.

Yin, Robert K. *Case Study Research. Design and Methods*. 5th ed. Los Angeles: Sage, 2014.

3

What Makes a Good Case?
—Martin Walton

"Only what is precise becomes concrete."
Otl Aicher[1]

STORY AND CASE STUDY

One of the briefest chaplaincy encounters I know of (from oral history) takes place in the context of a military unit preparing for a foreign mission. The chaplain is passed by a young soldier who asks, "Chaplain, are you going with us on the mission." "Yes," the chaplain replies. "Good," is the response of the soldier, who, with what sounds like a sigh of relief, continues on his way.

The encounter consists of (1) a question that could be tentatively assessed in the context of the situation and interaction, (2) a reply that serves as a response if not an intervention, and (3) an outcome in an expression of positive evaluation and relief. As background information one would want to know more about the soldier and the chaplain and if they had had previous contacts or not. Also, it would be helpful to know if any direct encounters between the soldier and the chaplain followed, so that we might understand more of why it was good that the chaplain would accompany the unit on the mission. On the one hand, therefore, the story of the encounter includes specific elements of a case study, including verbatim and

---

1. Wolf, *Ein Tag im Jahr 1960–2000*, 842.

an observable effect, which is enough to assess it as a meaningful encounter. On the other hand, the story lacks sufficient information for a case study in the context of research. It tells us something about the significance of baseline chaplaincy care in the military,[2] but does not clarify why it is significant.

What is needed to turn a story into a case study? The key elements that George Fitchett has proposed (the point or story, contribution of the chaplain, background, chaplain–patient relationship, spiritual assessment, summary and theory or measurement) indicate why the brief story of the encounter with the military chaplain above is insufficient.[3] The format of the Case Studies Project (CSP) strives for more differentiation and structuring, in response to Fitchett's comment, "The general rule is the more detail the better."[4] In his proposals for writing case studies, Fitchett uses the word detail, or a variant, fourteen times. So how do we get the details we need?

The question "What makes a good case?" can have different meanings. (1) Why case studies are needed to make a good case for chaplaincy care is a question about how case studies fit into research. That has been addressed in Chapter 1. (2) What makes a case a good example of what good chaplaincy care is, is a research question as well. But the qualifier "good" in this instance also includes normative and ideological issues. What is good chaplaincy and who decides that on what basis? More will be said about that in Chapter 22. (3) The question we address in this chapter is what criteria we set for a case study within the framework of the CSP in relation to the context of the broader development of case study research. We ask, what does a case study seek to communicate and clarify? What is the vocabulary and what are the analytical frames at work in the case study? How are various case studies with various intentions comparable?

USES OF CASE STUDIES IN RESEARCH

About fifty case studies in chaplaincy have appeared in scholarly publications in English, depending on where one looks and how one counts. In a review of case studies from 2011 to 2018, Steve Nolan lists 28.[5] Nolan focusses on a new generation of case studies written and gathered explicitly for the purpose of developing a descriptive base for research in line with the research agenda Fitchett set in 2011.[6] (See Appendix D for the journals

2. Pleizier and Schuhmann, "How the Military Context."
3. Fitchett, "Making Our Case(s)." See also Chapter 2.
4. Fitchett, "Making Our Case(s)," 13.
5. Nolan, "Lifting the Lid on Chaplaincy."
6. Fitchett, "Making Our Case(s)."

and volumes with case studies we looked at and the list we came up with for what follows.)

Fitchett points to earlier case studies that serve various purposes. From a case study published in 1989, James Gibbons and Sherry Miller derive eleven "features" of the chaplain, some of them activities, some dispositions, some expertise.[7] Thomas O'Connor and Elizabeth Meakes use a case to describe phases in the practice of "evidence based pastoral care": encounter with a client, [setting a goal,] consulting relevant research literature, appraising the research evidence, implementing the relevant evidence and evaluating the outcome.[8] In both case studies the contribution to research is indirect, in developing the self-understanding of chaplains or in demonstrating a procedure for a research informed practice.

An illustrative use is made of three case studies in the *Journal of Pastoral Care and Counseling*, to demonstrate a particular methodology of outcome-oriented chaplaincy, "The Discipline."[9] Fitchett understands the case studies in his book on the 7 x 7 assessment model[10] in a similar light, noting that they do not provide detailed information about the chaplaincy care or its outcomes. An older case study on marital therapy, not in a chaplaincy setting but at a counseling center, is used to illustrate a dialogical and systemic approach based on Buber and Nagy.[11]

A series of case studies edited by Jeanne Wirpsa and Karen Pugliese from chaplains involved in medical-decision making[12] tells us a lot about what chaplains do and with what outcomes, but the primary use is to substantiate and complement the roles of chaplains in medical decision making that were forthcoming from a survey among chaplains. In an individual case study Jeffrey Murphy makes a similar point: the chaplain as mediator.[13] The sequence in the study of Wirpsa and Pugliese is, however, of interest, in that case studies were not the starting point for gathering evidence, as in Fitchett's proposal, but used in a second step of triangulation. A thematic analysis guided the study.

Some recent case studies tend in the same direction, such as a study that demonstrates the use of reminiscence in group spiritual care among

---

7. Gibbons and Miller, "An Image of Contemporary Hospital Chaplaincy."
8. O'Connor and Meakes, "Hope in the Midst of Challenge."
9. Berger, "A Case Study"; Crane, "A Case Study"; Rodrigues Yim, "A Case Study of Jerry"; simultaneously published in book form in VandeCreek and Lucas, *The Discipline*.
10. Fitchett, *Assessing Spiritual Needs*.
11. Potts, "Martin Buber's 'Healing Dialogue.'"
12. Wirpsa and Pugliese, *Chaplains as Partners*.
13. Murphy, "Chaplain as the Mediator."

elderly persons[14] or spiritual care with persons with dementia.[15] Peter Heikkinen and Benjamin Roberts emphasize the "unique value" in care for a patient and the role of the chaplain in a transdisciplinary approach to palliative care.[16] Christina Shu is clear in her intentions to provide a case study that explores various roles that racial and patriarchal issues play where the patient is an African American and the chaplain a Chinese American.[17] The theoretical frame of alterity and collaboration[18] and the societal focus on racial justice in assessment and care are explicit. That focus is present in the "self-assessment" as well. These case studies advocate a particular kind of chaplaincy care.

Other points can also be made. David Glenister includes various first person reports of the patient, family members and other professionals, illustrating how a case can be constructed collaboratively, providing internal triangulation beyond the self-reporting of the chaplain.[19] Nolan provides a case where he demonstrates what he calls non-religious spiritual care.[20] Quite a different purpose is addressed by Nolan in a case study in which he examines his own over-identification with a client.[21] The primary concern is the self-reflexivity of the chaplain.

We mention here two publications in German, due to their proximity to the Dutch context. An early collection was provided by Hans Van der Geest, a Dutch pastor and supervisor who worked in Switzerland.[22] In 1981 Van der Geest published 27 cases with extensive verbatim sections, that he considered examples of efficacious pastoral care. The primary intention of his publication was to provide good examples for educational and training purposes. It had an influential role in clinical pastoral training in the German language.

More recently Nika Höfler included 39 case studies in an initial phase of research on the effectiveness of chaplaincy in a hospital setting.[23] A second phase consisted of interviews with patients, family and other

---

14. Timbers and Childers, "A Case Study in Group."
15. Reed, Lane, and Hirst, "Spiritual Care for Those with Dementia."
16. Heikkinen and Roberts, "I See You."
17. Shu, "I Need My Granddaughter."
18. Doehring, "Teaching an Intercultural Approach."
19. Glenister, "I Want to Make it Right."
20. Nolan, "He Needs to Talk!"
21. Nolan, "I'd Like You to Get to Know."
22. Van der Geest, *Unter vier Augen*.
23. Höfler, "Wirksamkeit von Krankenhausseelsorge"; Höfler, *Wirksamkeit von Krankenhausseelsorge*.

professionals. A third phase using quantitative instruments will follow. From her analysis with a grounded theory approach, Höfler identifies vulnerability as the core aspect in chaplaincy accompaniment. Höfler discerns physical conditions of chaplaincy with regard to place and resources, indicates that relational aspects of chaplaincy care foster trust (and also interdisciplinary cooperation) and notes that the spiritual dimension elicits an interruption of the situation of vulnerability.[24] The outcome of chaplaincy care is a changed or transformed relation to vulnerability and/or a more affirmative attitude towards life.

Case studies can thus be written for different reasons. That means that a case study written to demonstrate a particular method may tell us more about how chaplaincy care *could* be done than about how chaplaincy care *is* generally done. Or a case study written for a specific setting may prove relevant in another setting by its use of a more general narrative approach. A focus on the self-reflexivity of the chaplain may be more suitable for training and personal reflection than for the evaluation of specific interventions and their outcomes. The purpose shapes form and content of the case study. Helpful here is Gary Thomas's distinction between the subject and object of a case study. By the subject he means the person, situation, event or interaction being described, while the object concerns the analytical perspective. Thus, one or more case studies can be analyzed from more than one analytical perspective.[25]

The primary intention of the CSP was to gather case studies that describe what chaplains do. More precisely formulated, the focus of the CSP was on what chaplains do when they think they are providing good care, but description was the primary intent. An appreciative approach guided the work in the research communities. That did not mean that a case study met the (full) approval of colleagues as an example of good care, but that it was reviewed to identify effective elements in the care. If we see that care by a chaplain contributes to a positive outcome, then what is it that we see the chaplain doing well enough to make that outcome possible? What do we see the chaplain doing (or trying to do) that we recognize as part of chaplaincy, even if we might have done things somewhat differently ourselves?

---

24. Knoll, "Nika Höfler."
25. Thomas, "A Typology for the Case Study."

ANALYTICAL FRAMES

In an afterword to a collection of case studies, Fitchett states that it is important to take note of the diversity in the cases.[26] The diversity encompasses not only the situations chaplains encounter, but also religion, settings, systemic dynamics, approaches to care, interventions, interdisciplinary aspects, *et cetera*. Fitchett addresses two issues: outcomes of care and societal changes in religion and spirituality. He could easily have chosen more matters to discuss. Reading case studies on chaplaincy care is like reading through discussions of the major issues in chaplaincy debates.

How we evaluate case studies and what we think is a good case depends on the interpretive frames and views on chaplaincy that are written into them and that we bring with us when reading them. In an initial review of emergent publications of case studies Nolan situated his analysis in the discussions in chaplaincy on presence and outcomes, or presence versus outcomes and vice versa.[27] He proceeded to identify, on the one hand, common factors of chaplaincy, similar to psychotherapy: assessments, rapport, active listening, empathy, unconditional regard, use of self, *et cetera*, and on the other hand specific factors of chaplaincy: affirming transcendence, working with belief or life philosophy, ritual, presence and supporting the institution.

Two issues arise. The first issue has to do with the significance of the common factors for understanding chaplaincy. Nolan drew parallels with psychotherapy, but parallels to social case work and pastoral counselling could be drawn as well. Gerben Heitink once proposed a scheme for distinguishing similarity and difference with regard to social, medical, psychological and spiritual care approaches.[28] Common to all is the conversational method, colored in by each discipline in relation to context, motivations of the care provider and expectations of the other. A central aspect is the helping relation as a relation. Then there is an in between space in which each type of care becomes more characteristic of the discipline, although certain factors still overlap. Finally, there are the terrains peculiar to each type of care. For chaplaincy that is the meaning of life. At the same time the various approaches remain related and are strengthened by cooperation with each other.

Later on (in Chapter 22) we will make some proposals for the difficult task of ordering the elements of chaplaincy that Nolan has begun. How,

---

26. Fitchett and Nolan, *Case Studies in Spiritual Care*.
27. Nolan, "Lifting the Lid on Chaplaincy."
28. Heitink, *Pastoraat als hulpverlening*.

for example, do working with life philosophy and presence relate to each other, or ritual and supporting the institution? In what follows in this chapter we will provide some observations on case studies (and responses to them) mentioned in the publications above. The comments on aspects of case studies in no way imply a judgement on the quality of chaplaincy care that was actually provided. The point here is not whether good care was provided or not, but how the care is described conceptually, that is, how the care is framed. The point is not to evaluate the published case studies, but to point to some issues that arise in reading the case studies and that also played a role in the CSP. The hope is to clarify the perspectives and concepts that were used in the CSP. We focus here on three matters that have also played a role in discussions on chaplaincy in the Netherlands: (1) the relation between being and doing in chaplaincy, especially the notion of presence, (2) method in chaplaincy, and (3) concepts concerning religiosity and the secular[29] in relation to the domain of chaplaincy.

Being and Doing

Chaplains are very good at listening.[30] Empathy and presence are crucial to their work. Even a quick reading of recent case studies shows that presence and relation play a central role. The question here is what that role is and how it can be described in case studies.

In a case study on end-of-life-care Lynn Bassett states that although care is often about "doing something," spiritual care also involves the capacity to simply "be" in the presence of another human being.[31] "By actively "doing nothing" but "being with" the other person in the spiritual care relationship, that person may be enabled to respond to their own spiritual needs." Bassett considers this approach a "contemplative" and an "apophatic dimension" of chaplaincy. Apophatic refers to a negative way of knowing in theology that acknowledges the limitation of language to describe God. We can only say what God is not. Similarly, in chaplaincy there is a recognition of the value of "non-speaking" and "staying-in a place of uncertainty and vulnerability with another person." For the initial research question of the CSP "What do chaplains do?" Bassett's comments represent a challenge. If we focus on doing, do we miss the being?

---

29. Stenmark, "Worldview Studies." Stenmark prefers the term "secular" to the term "non-religious" as the former is not determined by a negation.

30. Walton, *Hoe waait de wind?*

31. Bassett, "Space, Time and Shared Humanity," 200–201, 207.

There is a cluster of terms that in chaplaincy literature are often used in proximity to each other and that circle around the aspect of being: presence, relationship, companionship, faithfulness, empathy, listening, friendship. An example can be found in a passage in Stephen King's reflection on what made the difference in the patient-chaplaincy encounters in his case with regard to the outcome.[32]

> The whole of the care Esther received in relationship to me—addressing spiritual-religious struggle, emotional pain, isolation, religious needs, end of life issues, and relational issues—may be described using various terminologies, for example, "spiritual companionship," "ministry of presence," "faithful care and compassion," and "faithful companioning."

It may be the intention of King to place all of the specific interventions in the context of an overriding approach of companionship (see also the comments by Richard Maddox[33]). However, a side effect is that the significance and effect of specific interventions recedes to the background. The interconnectedness of "attitude, method and presence" that King advocates[34] dissipates rather than it being explicated.

In an introduction to a case study in palliative care in *Spiritual Care in Practice*,[35] Nolan points to the term "deep listening" that the chaplain uses, to indicate a way of paying "attention to what is present in a person that has not yet been spoken."[36] Nolan distinguishes passive and active (or directed) listening[37] and relates deep listening to advanced empathy. Similar is Nolan's reflection on a case study of his own.[38]

> My work with Den and his family represents an episode of nonreligious spiritual care. Nonetheless, I would argue the work responded to their religious/spiritual instincts. Such instincts are often expressed in nonrational, "I–Thou" communication, the unconscious connection that transcends objective rationality and communicates without words in the subjective and

---

32. King, "Facing Fears and Counting Blessings," 19. King refers for the term "faithful care and compassion" to his own publication King, *Trust the Process*, and for the term "faithful companioning" to Schlauch, *Faithful Companioning*. No page numbers.
33. Maddox, "The Chaplain as Faithful Companion," 36.
34. King, "Facing Fears and Counting Blessings," 20.
35. Nolan, "Palliative Case Studies," 196.
36. Huth and Roberts, "I Need to Do the Right Thing," 215.
37. Autton, *The Pastoral Care of the Dying*.
38. Nolan, "He Needs to Talk!"

immediate. Some chaplains call this presence and regard it as a key and distinctive aspect of their spiritual care.

Earlier in the case study Nolan indicated two moments in which such communication took place: in the exchange of a gaze and in the gentle squeeze of a hand and a response on the brink of death (cf. the smile and the kissing of the chaplain's hand by the resident and the chaplain holding the resident's hand or placing a hand on his shoulder in dementia care described by Reed[39]). The strength of what Nolan conveys lies in how he links presence in the case study with communication, not in words but in the use of the senses of seeing and touching. Presence becomes precise in the description of tactile and sense experiences. The chaplain is not "just being" in the act of presence with the other, but also doing things in responding with a gaze and squeezing a hand. And while Nolan relates his responses to instinct, his reflection on it tells us that it is also a response learned from experience and literature.

There is so much more to be said about presence. Nolan has written on it elsewhere[40] as well as on relationship.[41] In *The Art of Listening*, Neil Pembroke[42] appeals to Gabriel Marcel[43] and Martin Buber[44] and connects notions of availability, openness, fidelity and belonging to a grace of presence. In the Netherlands the presence theory of the sociologist Andries Baart has been very influential in chaplaincy circles.[45] The original setting from which Baart drew his observations on availability and honoring the agenda of the other was, however, not chaplaincy but urban mission dealing with social inequity. In the understandings of listening and availability the insights of Carl Rogers are also perceptible, especially the criteria for a therapeutic relationship in order to foster the personal development of the other: congruence, positive regard and empathy.[46] The sources of presence theories and approaches are, therefore, not only theological but also philosophical, psychological and sociological. They are empirical and reflective.

---

39. Reed, et al, "Spiritual Care for Those with Dementia."
40. Nolan, *Spiritual Care at the End of Life*.
41. Nolan, "Healthcare Chaplains Responding to Change."
42. Pembroke, *The Art of Listening*.
43. Marcel, *The Mystery of Being*.
44. Buber, *I and Thou*.
45. Baart, *Een theorie van de presentie*. Baart, "The Presence Approach"; Baart and Vosman, "Relationship based care and recognition."
46. Rogers, *The Therapeutic Relationship*; Rogers et al, *Client Centered Therapy*; Zwaan, *Een prachtige dans*.

However skilled chaplains are at listening and however crucial empathy and presence are to their work, those skills and dispositions are not, as the sources indicate, peculiar to chaplaincy. With Pembroke we can agree that compassionate availability is foundational to pastoral care (and to chaplaincy), but that holds for all sorts of care. Presence tells us (part of) what chaplaincy is built upon, but it tells us too little about what it is that chaplains build on that foundation and what their artisanship is. That artisanship is what we were looking for in the CSP.

In an early publication from the CSP, Myriam Braakhuis sought a balance between relational aspects of chaplaincy care (e.g. presence) and the content of that care.[47] She also pointed out several risks of too much emphasis on a relational attitude: not daring to confront, losing track of existential and spiritual themes, and crossing personal boundaries. In addition, one can lose sight of specific goals in care. She suggests using the term "professional proximity," which she defines as:

> A relationship in which the counselor is concerned with the client with attentiveness and empathy. In this relationship the autonomy of the client is acknowledged, and the client can manifest herself. Together, the counselor and the client determine key questions and objectives.[48]

Braakhuis thus emphasizes the need for examples of an optimal combination of a relational attitude with a focus on concrete goals.

In the CSP we refused for strategic research reasons to take presence as an answer. For some chaplains, the response "just being there" or "simply listening" had become their default answer to the question about what they had offered in their care. What we then did was to ask what was the posture when being present, in what acts did one prove faithful, how was empathy expressed and received. Verbatims were analyzed and interpretations were deconstructed in order to discover in what ways one was listening. The point was not in any way to question the depth of communication or the mystery of presence, but to seek to observe and recognize the interactions and means of communication, however small, by means of which a relationship is established and in which presence is experienced.[49] In the case studies in the following chapters such interactions will emerge in the hug that a veteran gives a chaplain after a ritual, in the rapport between the mother of a deceased soldier and the chaplain, in the attunement of a chaplain to a man

---

47. Braakhuis, "Professional Proximity."
48. Braakhuis, 115.
49. Walton, "Test All Things Spiritual."

with autism, and a woman with terminal cancer saying that contacts with the chaplain were like taking a hike through heather. But it is the description of the interaction and intention that helps us see how being is done.

Process and Method

What is the relation between method, process and outcome in chaplaincy care? The relation is not easy to trace.[50] The taxonomy of Kevin Massey, et al, shows how complex the matter is.[51] There are innumerable variables of biography, personality, values, context and interaction. And besides the chaplaincy care given, there are always many other influences and forces (positive and negative) at play. How could one show that a particular form of assessment, pointing toward a specific goal and care plan, leads to a specific outcome? Or that it could have the same outcome in another situation?

In their case study on transdisciplinary support in addressing total pain mentioned above, Heikkinen and Roberts provide chart notes on the context of their visit, assessment, interventions, outcomes, and plan of care.[52] What is striking in the case study is the methodical arrangement in the chart notes and the (matter of fact) combination of technical terms (PC–7 for assessment of spiritual concerns, Personal Existential Analysis (PEA), ego integrity), formal descriptions (processing and gestalt movement), metaphors (spiritual journey, holistic), chaplaincy approaches (ministry of presence), and more or less everyday language (partnering, finding peace), often within the same sentence. Another combination is made in the assertion that "the progression of PEA fits into Emmanuel Lartey's pastoral functions of healing, sustaining, guiding, reconciling, nurturing, liberating, and empowering [and] inform this chaplain's interventions."[53] The case study thus describes a "state of the art" care process in chaplaincy that is methodical and research oriented while integrating language from everyday use, personal development and chaplaincy and illustrating interdisciplinary collaboration.

While the complexity of the case study is its strength, it challenges the reader to discern what came from what. The relationship of conversational to more instrumental approaches is not reflected upon. Outcomes in the chart are largely process outcomes: "Pt responded to the chaplain by sharing in life review . . ." and "Pt shared a more resolved outlook to focus . . ." A

50. Biesta, *Educational Research*.
51. Massey et al, "What Do I Do?"
52. Heikkinen and Roberts, "I See You."
53. Lartey, *In Living Color*. Cited by Heikkinen and Robert, 417.

patient reported outcome, "Thanks for coming by and giving me a chance to work through all this. I feel at peace about it all. I just needed to see what is important," is found in a verbatim context.[54] What influence did the tools that the chaplain employed have on that outcome? The more the chaplain knows and the more the chaplain integrates skillful counseling, multiple tools of assessment, intervention and analysis (or as King put it: attitude, method and presence), the more complex the care becomes and the more it is difficult to relate outcomes to the interactions and interventions. The tables that Rhonda Cooper, King and others include in their case studies with needs, interventions and outcomes are helpful but exemplify the same complexity.[55]

Fitchett has suggested that "Having five or ten published case studies of chaplains' work with advanced cancer patients would provide information about the salient components of the chaplain's care."[56] A number of the case studies published to date are, in fact, from oncology and palliative care, but the diversity in the issues, methods and approach may yet be too diverse to say much about effective methods and interventions. At the same time, the use of a singular method such as life review in very different settings could show great similarity in method and outcome. In his comment on case studies in pediatric care, Alister Bull notes that there is not "an agreed collective approach to assessment" and that "in each case there is an internalized assessment that is strongly relational and subjective."[57] What also becomes apparent is that there are few agreed upon relationships between assessments and interventions and too little evidence from case studies for (direct) relationships between interventions and outcomes, especially when the reported outcomes are expressed in terms of intention or process, as Fitchett has noted.[58] Observing outcomes, as Fitchett calls it, does not seem to come naturally to chaplains.

What some readers will notice in the case studies in the following chapters is that little explicit use is made of assessment tools, as has been advocated above and in other literature.[59] The approach in the Dutch case

---

54. Heikkinen and Roberts, "I See You." Quotes are on pages 411, 413, and 416, respectively.

55. Cooper, "Case Study"; King, "Facing Fears and Counting Blessings."

56. Fitchett, "Introduction," 12.

57. Bull, "Critical Response to Pediatric Case Studies," 92.

58. Fitchett, "Afterword. Case Studies and Chaplaincy Research."

59. See, e.g. Anandarajah and Hight, "Spirituality and Medical Practice"; Fitchett, *Assessing Spiritual Needs*; LaRocca-Pitts, "FACT. A Chaplain's Tool"; Shields, et al, "Spiritual AIM." For the Netherlands see: Bouwer, "Pastorale Diagnostiek"; Bouwer, "Levensbeschouwelijke diagnostiek."

studies is varied, sometimes narrative, sometimes a stepped process of observance and attentiveness, discernment of concerns, junctures or crises in the life orientation of the other, exploring and interpreting what is of meaning and value for the person, what their (re)sources might be and seeking a pursuable path, at times with the aid of a specific (methodic or ritual) intervention. The "analysis" of the situation is often a process of simultaneously mapping the situation and providing care. An iterative process of presence, observation, interpretation, analysis and intervention is often part of a continual and differentiated course of care. In our summary answer to the research question in Chapter 22, we will say more about the interactions, methods and outcomes. The nine case studies in the coming chapters were chosen not only to illustrate the style of description and analysis in the CSP, but also because we think that each case offers a well-described relation between the apprehended needs (analysis and assessment), goals that emerge, the form and content of care (interactions, interventions and methods), and observable or verifiable effects (outcomes). In other words, what has the chaplain done, why and with what effects?

The Religious and the Secular

How do we describe the domain of chaplaincy? And how can chaplains deal with the societal changes in religion and spirituality, to which Fitchett refers, especially with regard to the religious roots of chaplaincy and the secularity of many clients and the secular context of the work?

In comments on Nolan's case study on non-religious chaplaincy care, Barbara Pesut states "that the loss of a shared religious language has created a liminal space for chaplains" but that turning to meaning making, to which social workers and nurses also contribute, will "fail to fully capture the uniqueness of the chaplain's contribution to care." She goes on to suggest that "the way out of liminal spaces may lie not in the adoption of a spirituality, broadly defined, but in reclaiming the contributions that religion makes to the societal dilemmas we all face."[60] The point Pesut makes may be illustrated with a reflection by Alice Hildebrand on her case study on care for a mother of a small child with cancer. "My goal was to get religion out of the way so that spiritual care could begin." In her next sentence Hildebrand states that she "never doubted that Erica's sense of connection to a loving, powerful and wise God was vivid and real, and helpful to her."[61] Here we see

---

60. Pesut, "Recovering Religious Voice and Imagination," 30.
61. Hildebrand, "I Can Tell You This," 67.

that the notions "religion" and the "spiritual" are constructed in ways that religion and spirituality can get in each other's way.

Pesut's comments are nevertheless striking in light of Nolan's own comment on his non-religious spiritual care (quoted above) that it responded to the client's "religious/spiritual instincts."[62] At another place, in his analysis of case studies from 2021, Nolan states: "As chaplains, we know that religion is to spirituality as painting or poetry or music is to the arts: it is one expression and there are more ways to be spiritual than the religious way."[63] Instead of retreating to meaning making or letting religion and spirituality get in each other's way, Nolan takes a leap forward with his understanding of the more fundamental spiritual nature of human needs and chaplaincy care. Speaking of a religious/spiritual instinct reveals not only an understanding of chaplaincy but also certain anthropological assumptions.

The formulations put us right in the middle of contemporary developments and discussions with regard to religion, spirituality and worldview.[64] But more important in this context is the way in which the domain of chaplaincy and the worldview identity of chaplains is framed. If case studies are to contribute to a better case for chaplaincy, then they need to include a clear expression of the domain of chaplaincy. Our reading of the case study literature suggests that, along with the key elements that Fitchett has proposed, a domain description is an essential aspect. Elsewhere we have assessed the way the concept of spirituality is framed and constructed in chaplaincy and health care[65] and proposed an alternate conceptualization of the domain of chaplaincy as has taken shape in the professional standard of Dutch chaplaincy.[66] In the following we briefly present our motivation for a conceptualization in terms of meaning and worldview and indicate how the four dimensions enabled a more differentiated analysis of the cases in the CSP.

The term "worldview" translates the Dutch *levensbeschouwing*, literally "life view," that one could also translate as "life philosophy." It includes both religions and secular perspectives on life, such as humanism and Buddhism. It has become a common term in Dutch chaplaincy literature for reasons of inclusion,[67] as has also been proposed in studies from philosophy

---

62. Nolan, "He Needs to Talk!" 14.

63. Nolan, "Lifting the Lid on Chaplaincy," 19.

64. Pargament and Zinnbauer, "Religiousness and Spirituality"; Bregman, *The Ecology of Spirituality*; Stenmark, "Worldview Studies."

65. Walton, "Assessing the Construction of Spirituality."

66. VGVZ, "Professional Standard"; Den Toom et al., "Rearranging the Domain." See Chapter 1.

67. Smeets, *Spiritual Care in a Hospital Setting*.

and the social sciences.⁶⁸ Along with worldview we use the term "meaning" because chaplains encounter all sorts of ways in which persons seek to find meaning in the midst of existential situations. In Dutch literature the distinction is sometimes made between everyday meaning and ultimate meaning,⁶⁹ similar to the distinction by Park between situational and global meaning,⁷⁰ or a distinction between meaning in life and meaning of life, but all such distinctions are fluid.

We follow the Dutch professional standard of chaplaincy in understanding the domain of chaplaincy as meaning and worldview. "The two terms are complementary, related concepts that cover various aspects of the quest for meaning and religious practice: formal and informal, passive and active, communal and individual, related to both process and content."⁷¹ The motivation for using the two terms together is both practical and strategic. Practical because chaplains deal with meaning making in all sorts of ways and draw specifically upon religious and other worldview sources in meaning making processes. And religions, whatever else they are, are meaning making enterprises. The use of the terms together is also strategic because it is important to share the realm of meaning making with other disciplines but not fully surrender it to them, while at the same time recognizing the roots and resources of chaplaincy in religious and other worldview traditions. In our conceptualization, the term "spirituality" is understood as a dimension of meaning and worldview (see next paragraph) and of the domain of chaplaincy, but not an overriding term, as it fails to express the richness and complexity of religion and worldview.⁷²

More important than the summary concepts of meaning and worldview for the evaluation of the case studies were the four dimensions: existential, spiritual, ethical and aesthetic. The use of multiple terms allowed for differentiation in the analysis of the case studies, more particularly of the needs of the client and of the care by the chaplain. And it allowed for differentiation in the naming of outcomes. A dilemma of a young woman who has promised to follow her best girlfriend into suicide is addressed by the chaplain in a method of moral counseling with as outcome the decision to go on living.⁷³ While one could frame the young woman's concerns (and the outcome) in general spiritual terms (purpose and connectedness),

---

68. Hijmans, *Je moet er het beste van maken*; Stenmark, "Worldview Studies."
69. Ter Borg, *Waarom geestelijke verzorging?*
70. Park, "Making Sense of the Meaning Literature."
71. VGVZ, "Professional Standard Spiritual Caregiver," 7.
72. Cadge, *Paging God*.
73. Muthert et al., "Re-Evaluating a Suicide Pact."

existentially there is also the simultaneity of her friendship and fear. Ethically speaking there is a dilemma between life and solidarity to be clarified. That allows for a more precise analysis of what was going on and what came of it.

CASE STUDIES FROM THE CSP

In the coming Chapters (4–12), we present nine case studies from the CSP in which the matters discussed above become more evident. In different ways and in different settings they also exemplify (and combine) the criteria for case studies that we derived from literature.[74]

Representative case for the client group

Paradigmatic case for the way the chaplain generally works

Unusual case that brings something to light due to its special character

Critical case that is a test for the usual way of working or understanding

The case study "Energy *and* Inspiration" (Chapter 4) is the story of care of a woman seeking inspiration to keep going in the face of recurring breast cancer. It is a *representative* situation on an oncology ward in a general hospital. The introduction of the term inspiration by the chaplain is *paradigmatic* for the way the chaplain generally works with patients. It is *unusual* in the effort the chaplain had to make to find acceptance in the interdisciplinary team for the term "inspiration."

"The Enigma of a Day" (Chapter 5) is *representative* and *paradigmatic* in the care of the chaplain in a general hospital, exploring themes in end-of-life-care with a woman when cancer treatment has reached its limits. *Unusual* is the specific role of aesthetic elements (a reproduction, a poem) in the case.

"Exposure?" (Chapter 6) is *representative* and *paradigmatic* for the work of a chaplain in mental health care with a woman with suicidal tendencies. A *critical* aspect is the manner in which the chaplaincy care evolves into a kind of exposure therapy, when exposure in psychiatric treatment stagnates.

"I Do It My Way" (Chapter 7) is *paradigmatic* for the way the chaplain works with a narrative model of meaning, but it has a *critical* edge in the situation of the client who has both intellectual disabilities and psychological issues.

---

74. Flyvbjerg, "Five Misunderstandings About Case-Study Research"; Thomas, *How to Do Your Case Study*; Yin, *Case Study Research*.

"Reiteration of Ritual" (Chapter 8) relates *representative* care for a woman with dementia who suffers the loss of a daughter but in contacts with the chaplain relives childhood traumas. *Critical* is the way in which a transitional ritual has to be repeated.

"A Church for Charly" (Chapter 9) is *unusual* in the role the chaplain takes upon herself to vicariously bring the church to the room of a man with severe autism. The ritual performed in his room has an observable therapeutic effect.

"Wounded Warrior" (Chapter 10) was the pilot case study of the CSP and is reprinted here.[75] Although it is *paradigmatic* in the bringing together of conversations, religious resources and ritual, it was for the chaplain a *critical* case in the interaction with a veteran with moral injury.

"To Honor and Confirm" (Chapter 11) includes a number of *representative* aspects of military chaplaincy, dealing with soldiers and their officers, relating to soldiers who have been suspended and interacting with family of a deceased soldier, but all in one day of a military ceremony. In the physical positioning of the chaplain and in the varieties of her interactions she makes *unusually* clear what "baseline" chaplaincy care (as a variation on presence) is.

"From Slumped to Upright" (Chapter 12) relates *paradigmatically* how a Buddhist prison chaplain works with mindfulness with a detainee whose physical bearing starkly expresses his mindset.

All of the case studies have multiple authors in the following sequence: chaplain, chairperson(s) of the RC, coordinators of the CSP, others who commented. In a note attached to the names of the authors, the names are added of all the members of the RC in which the case study was reviewed.[76] In the presentation of the case studies the initial summary and reflection by the chaplain and the subsequent summary and reflection by the RC, have been integrated. The case studies in these chapters have for publication purposes been reduced in length, but we hope that they still include enough detail and precision to contribute to the case of chaplaincy.

REFERENCES

Anandarajah, G., and E. Hight. "Spirituality and Medical Practice: Using the HOPE Questions as a Practical Tool for Spiritual Assessment." *American Family Physician* 63.1 (2001) 81–89.

Autton, Norman. *The Pastoral Care of the Dying*. London: S.P.C.K., 1969.

75. Van Loenen et al., "Case Study of 'Moral Injury.'"

76. One exception is the case study "Wounded Warrior" that as a pilot case study was reviewed with the author by the coordinators of the CSP and one other chairperson.

Baart, Andries J. *Een theorie van de presentie.* Den Haag: Boom, 2001.

———. *The Presence Approach: An Introductory Sketch of a Practice.* Utrecht: Stichting Presentie, 2002. https://www.presentie.nl/kennisbank/the-presence-approach-an-introductory-sketch-of-a-practice/.

Baart, Andries J., and Frans Vosman. "Relationship Based Care and Recognition: Part One: Sketching good care from the theory of presence and five entries." In *Care, Compassion and Recognition: An Ethical Discussion,* edited by Carlo Leget, et al., 201–27. Leuven: Peeters, 2011.

Bassett, Lynn. "Space, Time and Shared Humanity: A Case Study Demonstrating a Chaplain's Role in End-of-Life Care." *Health and Social Care Chaplaincy* 5.2 (2018) 194–208.

Berger, Julie Allen. "A Case Study: Linda." *Journal of Health Care Chaplaincy* 10.2 (2000) 35–43.

Biesta, Gert J. J. *Educational Research: An Unorthodox Introduction.* London: Bloomsbury Academic, 2020.

Bouwer, J. "Levensbeschouwelijke diagnostiek—een substantiële benadering." *Tijdschrift Geestelijke Verzorging* 3.14 (1999) 35–44.

———. "Pastorale Diagnostiek." *Tijdschrift Geestelijke Verzorging* 2.4 (1997) 22–27.

Braakhuis, M. "Professional Proximity: Seeking a Balance between Relation and Content in Spiritual Counseling." In *Learning from Case Studies in Chaplaincy: Towards Practice Based Evidence & Professionalism,* edited by Renske Kruizinga, et al., 112–17. Utrecht: Eburon, 2020.

Bregman, Lucy. *The Ecology of Spirituality: Meanings, Virtues, and Practices in a Post-Religious Age.* Waco: Baylor University Press, 2014.

Buber, M. *I and Thou.* Edinburgh: T&T Clark, 1958.

Bull, Alister W. "Critical Response to Pediatric Case Studies. A Chaplain's Response." In *Spiritual Care in Practice: Case Studies in Healthcare Chaplaincy,* edited by George Fitchett and Steve Nolan, 90–97. London: Kingsley, 2015.

Cadge, Wendy. *Paging God: Religion in the Halls of Medicine.* Chicago: University of Chicago Press, 2012.

Cooper, Rhonda S. "Case Study of a Chaplain's Spiritual Care for a Patient with Advanced Metastatic Breast Cancer." *Journal of Health Care Chaplaincy* 17.1–2 (2011) 19–37.

Crane, Janet R. "A Case Study Using 'The Discipline' with a Clinical Team." *Journal of Health Care Chaplaincy* 10.2 (2000) 57–68.

Den Toom, Niels, et al. "Rearranging the Domain: Spiritual Care in Multiple Dimensions." *Health and Social Care Chaplaincy* 9.1 (2021) 42–59.

Doehring, Carrie. "Teaching an Intercultural Approach to Spiritual Care." *Journal of Pastoral Theology* 22.2 (2012) 2.1–2.24.

Fitchett, George. "Afterword. Case Studies and Chaplaincy Research." In *Case Studies in Spiritual Care,* edited by George Fitchett and Steve Nolan, 259–71. London: Kingsley, 2018.

———. *Assessing Spiritual Needs: A Guide for Caregivers.* Lima: Academic Renewal Press, 2002.

———. "Introduction." In *Spiritual Care in Practice: Case Studies in Healthcare Chaplaincy,* edited by George Fitchett and Steve Nolan, 11–24. London: Kingsley, 2015.

———. "Making Our Case(s)." *Journal of Health Care Chaplaincy* 17, nr. 1–2 (2011) 3–18.

Fitchett, George, and Steve Nolan, eds. *Case Studies in Spiritual Care*. London: Kingsley, 2018.

Flyvbjerg, Bent. "Five Misunderstandings About Case-Study Research." *Qualitative Inquiry* 12,.2 (2006) 219–45.

Gibbons, James L., and Sherry L. Miller. "An Image of Contemporary Hospital Chaplaincy." *Journal of Pastoral Care* 43.4 (1989) 355–61.

Glenister, David. "'I Want to Make it Right'—A 46 Year-old Woman with End Stage Renal Disease and Her Australian Aboriginal Partner Make Significant Choices." *Health and Social Care Chaplaincy* 5.2 (2018) 224–40.

Heikkinen, Peter J., and Benjamin Roberts. "'I See You.' A Chaplain Case Study on Existential Distress and Transdisciplinary Support." *Journal of Health Care Chaplaincy* 29.4 (2023) 406–23.

Heitink, Gerben. *Pastoraat als hulpverlening: inleiding in de pastorale theologie en psychologie*. Kampen: Kok, 1984.

Hijmans, Ellen J. *Je moet er het beste van maken: een empirisch onderzoek naar hedendaagse zingevingssystemen*. Nijmegen: Instituut voor Toegepaste Sociale Wetenschappen, 1994.

Hildebrand, Alice. "'I can tell *you* this, but not everyone understands'—Erica, mother of a 2-year-old girl with cancer." In *Spiritual Care in Practice: Case Studies in Healthcare Chaplaincy*, edited by George Fitchett and Steve Nolan, 51–68. London: Kingsley, 2015.

Höfler, Nika. "Wirksamkeit von Krankenhausseelsorge: Ein Projekt zur Entwicklung von Kenngrößen zur Messung der Wirksamkeit von Krankenhausseelsorge." *Wege zum Menschen* 72.6 (2020) 536–47.

———. *Wirksamkeit von Krankenhausseelsorge: eine qualitative Studie*. Leipzig: Evangelische Verlagsanstalt, 2022.

Huth, Jim, and Wes Roberts. "'I need to do the right thing for him'—Andrew a Canadian veteran at the end of his life, and his daughter Lee." In *Spiritual Care in Practice: Case Studies in Healthcare Chaplaincy*, edited by George Fitchett and Steve Nolan, 201–22. London: Kingsley, 2015.

King, Stephen D. W. "Facing Fears and Counting Blessings: A Case Study of a Chaplain's Faithful Companioning a Cancer Patient." *Journal of Health Care Chaplaincy* 18.1–2 (2012) 3–22.

———. *Trust the Process: A History of Clinical Pastoral Education as Theological Education*. Lanham: University Press of America, 2007.

Knoll, Franziskus. "Nika Höfler (2022) Wirksamkeit Der Krankenhausseelsorge. Eine Qualitative Studie. Leipzig: Evangelische Verlagsanstalt." *Spiritual Care* 12.4 (2023) 395–96.

LaRocca-Pitts, Mark. "FACT, A Chaplain's Tool for Assessing Spiritual Needs in an Acute Care Setting." *Chaplaincy Today* 28.1 (2012) 25–32.

Lartey, Emmanuel Y. *In Living Color: An Intercultural Approach to Pastoral Care and Counseling*. 2nd ed. London: Kingsley, 2003.

Maddox, Richard T. "The Chaplain as Faithful Companion: A Response to King's Case Study." *Journal of Health Care Chaplaincy* 18.1–2 (2012) 33–42.

Marcel, Gabriel. *The Mystery of Being*. South Bend: St. Augustine's, 2001.

Massey, Kevin, et al. "What do I do? Developing a Taxonomy of Chaplaincy Activities and Interventions for Spiritual Care in Intensive Care Unit Palliative Care." *BMC Palliative Care* 14.1 (2015) 10.

Murphy, Jeffery. "Chaplain as the Mediator Between the Patient and the Interdisciplinary Team in Ethical Decision Making: A Chaplaincy Case Study Involving a Quadriplegic Patient." *Health and Social Care Chaplaincy* 5.2 (2018) 241–56.

Muthert, J. K, et al. "Re-Evaluating a Suicide Pact. Embodied Moral Counselling in a Dutch Case Study of Mental Healthcare Chaplaincy." *Tidsskrift for Praktisk Teologi*, 15 (2019) 81–89.

Nolan, Steve. "'He Needs to Talk!' A Chaplain's Case Study of Nonreligious Spiritual Care." *Journal of Health Care Chaplaincy* 22.1 (2016) 1–16.

———. "Healthcare Chaplains Responding to Change: Embracing Outcomes or Reaffirming Relationships?" *Health and Social Care Chaplaincy* 3.2 (2015) 93–109.

———. "'I'd Like You to Get to Know about Me'—Kristof, a 50-Year-Old Atheist Academic Admitted to a Hospice for Palliative Symptom Control." In *Case Studies in Spiritual Care*, edited by George Fitchett and Steve Nolan, 223–45. London: Kingsley, 2018.

———. "Lifting the Lid on Chaplaincy: A First Look at Findings from Chaplains' Case Study Research." *Journal of Health Care Chaplaincy* 27.1 (2021) 1–23.

———. "Palliative Case Studies." In *Spiritual Care in Practice: Case Studies in Healthcare Chaplaincy*, edited by George Fitchett and Steve Nolan, 195–200. London: Kingsley, 2015.

———. *Spiritual Care at the End of Life: The Chaplain as a "Hopeful presence."* London: Kingsley, 2012.

O'Connor, Thomas St James, and Elizabeth Meakes. "Hope in the Midst of Challenge: Evidence-Based Pastoral Care." *Journal of Pastoral Care* 52.4 (1998) 359–67.

Pargament, K. I., and B. J. Zinnbauer. "Religiousness and Spirituality." In *Handbook of the Psychology of Religion and Spirituality*, edited by Raymond F. Paloutzian and Crystal L. Park, 21–42. New York: Guilford, 2005.

Park, Crystal L. "Making Sense of the Meaning Literature: An Integrative Review of Meaning Making and Its Effects on Adjustment to Stressful Life Events." *Psychological Bulletin* 136.2 (2010) 257.

Pembroke, Neil. *The Art of Listening: Dialogue, Shame and Pastoral Care.* London: T. & T. Clark-Eerdmans, 2002.

Pesut, Barbara. "Recovering Religious Voice and Imagination: A Response to Nolan's Case Study 'He Needs to Talk!'" *Journal of Health Care Chaplaincy* 22.1 (2016) 28–39.

Pleizier, Theo, and Carmen Schuhmann. "How the Military Context Shapes Spiritual Care Interventions by Military Chaplains." *Journal of Pastoral Care & Counseling: Advancing Theory and Professional Practice through Scholarly and Reflective Publications* 76.1 (2022) 4–14.

Potts, Kenneth. "Martin Buber's 'Healing Dialogue' in Marital Therapy: A Case Study." *Journal of Pastoral Care* 48.4 (1994) 325–38.

Reed, Marlette B., et al. "Spiritual Care for Those with Dementia: A Case Study." *Journal of Religion, Spirituality & Aging* 28.4 (2016) 338–48.

Rodrigues Yim, Robert J. "A Case Study of Jerry: Emphasizing Team Communication Through Use of 'The Discipline.'" *Journal of Health Care Chaplaincy* 10.2 (2000) 45–56.

Rogers, Carl R. *The Therapeutic Relationship and Its Impact. A Study of Psychotherapy with Schizophrenics.* Madison: University of Wisconsin Press, 1967.

Rogers, Carl R., et al. *Client Centered Therapy: Its Current Practice, Implications and Theory.* 1951. Reprint, London: Robinson, 2015.

Schlauch, Chris R. *Faithful Companioning: How Pastoral Care Counseling Heals.* Minneapolis: Fortress, 1995.

Shields, M., et al. "Spiritual AIM and the Work of the Chaplain: A Model for Assessing Spiritual Needs and Outcomes in Relationship." *Palliative & Supportive Care* 13.1 (2015) 75–89.

Shu, Christina. "'I Need My Granddaughter to Know Who I Am!' A Case Study of a 67-Year-Old African American Man and His Spiritual Legacy." *Journal of Health Care Chaplaincy* 29.3 (2023) 256–68.

Smeets, Wim. *Spiritual Care in a Hospital Setting: An Empirical-Theological Exploration.* Leiden: Brill, 2006.

Stenmark, Mikael. "Worldview Studies." *Religious Studies* 58.3 (2022) 564–82.

Ter Borg, M. B. *Waarom geestelijke verzorging? Zingeving en geestelijke verzorging in de moderne maatschappij.* Nijmegen: KSGV, 2000.

Thomas, Gary. "A Typology for the Case Study in Social Science Following a Review of Definition, Discourse, and Structure." *Qualitative Inquiry* 17.6 (2011) 511–21.

———. *How To Do Your Case Study.* 3rd ed. Los Angeles: Sage, 2021.

Timbers, Veronica L., and Melanie Childers. "A Case Study in Group Spiritual Care for Residents of a Post-Acute Care Facility." *Journal of Religion, Spirituality & Aging* 33.1 (2021) 86–96.

Van der Geest, Hans. *Unter vier Augen: Beispiele gelungener Seelsorge.* Zürich: Theologischer Verlag, 1981 [2010].

Van Loenen, Guus, et al. "Case Study of 'Moral Injury': Format Dutch Case Studies Project." *Health and Social Care Chaplaincy* 5.2 (2018) 281–96.

VandeCreek, Larry, and Arthur M. Lucas, eds. *The Discipline for Pastoral Care Giving: Foundations for Outcome Oriented Chaplaincy.* New York: Haworth Pastoral, 2001.

VGVZ. "Professional Standard Spiritual Caregiver 2015." Amsterdam: Vereniging van Geestelijk Verzorgers, 2015. https://vgvz.nl/wp-content/uploads/2023/02/VGVZ_Professional_Standard_2015_Main_Text_EN_v03_WITH_APPENDICES.pdf.

Walton, Martin "Assessing the Construction of Spirituality: Conceptualizing Spirituality in Health Care Settings." *Journal of Pastoral Care & Counseling* 66.3 (2012) 1–16.

———. *Hoe waait de wind? Interpretatie van geestelijke verzorging door cliënten in de ggz.* Tilburg: KSGV, 2014.

———. "Test All Things Spiritual; Hold on to What is Concrete: Toward a Hermeneutics of Story and Statistics." In *Transforming Chaplaincy: The George Fitchett Reader*, edited by Steve Nolan and Annelieke Damen, 218–30. Transforming Chaplaincy Series. Eugene, OR: Pickwick Publications, 2021.

Wirpsa, M. Jeanne, and Karen Pugliese, eds. *Chaplains as Partners in Medical Decision-Making: Case Studies in Healthcare Chaplaincy.* London: Kingsley, 2020.

Wolf, Christa. *Ein Tag im Jahr 1960–2000.* Munich: Suhrkamp, 2003.

Yin, Robert K. *Case Study Research: Design and Methods.* 5th ed. Los Angeles: Sage, 2014.

Zwaan, Barbara. *Een prachtige dans: De therapeutische afstemming van afstand en nabijheid in het werk van Carl Rogers, Martin Buber en Henri Nouwen.* Tilburg: KSGV, 2017.

Part Two

EXEMPLARY CASE STUDIES

4

Energy *and* Inspiration
Case Study from Oncological Rehab
—Jowien van der Zaag, Jacques Körver,
Martin Walton[1]

SYNOPSIS

In an oncological rehab setting a chaplain is referred to a woman who has been treated for breast cancer and suffers among other things from a severe lack of energy. The chaplain introduces the term inspiration as an issue in her struggle. The chaplain then invites the patient to bring with her a representation of her soul. The material and metaphor that are part of that provide direction for the woman's recovery and healing. The chaplain also introduces the term inspiration in the interdisciplinary team. After initial resistance, working on inspiration becomes part of the treatment plan.[2]

BACKGROUND & SETTING

Setting and Occasion

A physician assistant on an oncological rehab ward refers a woman, Mrs. Francis (pseudonym), to a chaplain with the indication "spiritual emptiness."

---

1. Co-researchers in the RC Hospital: Loes Berkhout, Hilde Boekeloo, Eric Bras, Frans Broekhoff, Gabriëlle Gies, Karen van Huisstede, Jolanda Jacobs, Mirjam Krabbenborg, Joep Roding, Margot van Veen, and Henry Wolterink.
2. Previously published as Van der Zaag, et al., "Energie én bezieling."

For the third time breast cancer has been diagnosed. Following treatment consisting of chemotherapy and radiotherapy, the woman experiences severe physical and mental fatigue. The meetings with the chaplain take place in a consulting room in a newly opened Center for Quality of Life at the Oncological Hospital, that offers multidisciplinary support in cases of physical, psychological, social, and/or spiritual limitations. In the consulting room there is a desk with a computer and a round table with four chairs. The walls are in pastel tints.

Client

Mrs. Francis is a sixty-six-year-old woman, married for a second time, with a son from her first marriage. Her present husband lives in another country where she often resides. She is now retired, having studied and worked in the field of pedagogy. She practices yoga and is an accomplished weaver. Raised a Catholic, she considers herself spiritual in a broad sense. Her regular church attendance offered her, as she indicated to the doctor, the experience of "something larger than myself" and of being borne up. Since her third bout of breast cancer that feeling has disappeared.

Twenty years ago, the doctor adds in the referral, Mrs. Francis underwent treatment for breast cancer for the first time. At that time no rehab programs were available. It took her twenty years to "flatten out the dents." She cannot imagine fighting for another ten years. In the face of mental exhaustion, her question is, "How can I build up my energy?"

Chaplain

The chaplain is a woman, fifty-nine-years-old, Protestant minister, with fifteen years of experience as a hospital chaplain. Formerly she spent four years with her husband and children in an ecumenical center in Israel. She finds inspiration in the works of Viktor Frankl and Jonathan Sacks, among others. She takes the life and faith stories of the other as her starting point and pays special attention to experiences of vulnerability and displacement. She seeks to provide a space in which the other can express oneself and experience being heard, seen and recognized. The chaplain has access to digital patient charts and in this case checked the patient history and the distress thermometer[3] in the patient's chart before the first contact.

---

3. Ownby, "Use of the Distress Thermometer."

Others Involved

A physician assistant refers Mrs. Francis to the chaplain. Twice during the chaplaincy care trajectory of five conversations in four months, the situation is discussed in the multidisciplinary team. The chaplain and a medical-social worker synchronize their respective efforts.

ACCOMPANIMENT PROCESS

Initial Contact

The chaplain sees a woman enter the room with a friendly, open face, colorfully dressed, and a bit tense. The chaplain goes to fetch coffee. When she returns, Mrs. Francis has laid a note book and pen on the table. The chaplain introduces herself and indicates that the first conversation is for making acquaintance and exploring what Mrs. Francis's questions and concerns are with regard to faith and spirituality. Mrs. Francis indicates that she feels somewhat tense and has never talked with anyone about these things before. Expressing that seems to relieve some of the tension, so that Mrs. Francis begins to tell her story.

 A year ago, a primary tumor was discovered in her breast, for the third time in twenty years. She thought she was familiar with the whole process and with how to deal with the effects of treatment, but this time she finds herself in a deep valley with intense fatigue. Spiritually she feels worn out and no longer sustained: "I don't feel anything anymore." The chaplain asks her how spirituality has played a role in her life and offers her the opportunity to express what she misses, what her longing is, and where her questions lie.

 Mrs. Francis lived as a child in a foreign country where her father worked. The family was Roman Catholic. At the age of fourteen she returned to the Netherlands for schooling, where she and her older sister lived with her aunt. Her aunt was for her a kindred spirit with whom she talked about faith and new ideas. A new religious world opened up to her. When her parents returned to the Netherlands, the family rejoined and lived in a part of the country with a conservative religious climate. At the age of nineteen she left the church, much to the sorrow of her mother whom she considered "a kind of saint."

 Mrs. Francis's first husband had no interest in his (or her) religious background. Through her second husband she became acquainted with the Lutheran liturgy and that opened something up inside her. At the same time, she got the feeling that the form overruled the content. What she misses is quietness and serenity. The personification of God she finds difficult. "Everyone seems to think it's clear, but I don't, and I feel alone in that." She no longer knows where she can find strength.

In response, the chaplain proposes talking the next time about inspiration (Dutch: "bezieling") and checks that with Mrs. Francis. Mrs. Francis gestures with her hand in a fist that she presses against her abdomen. "That's where my soul (Dutch: "ziel") is now, somewhere in my stomach. My soul used to always enfold me." She then sways her arm wide. "That's where I want to go back to." For the next appointment, two weeks later, the chaplain asks Mrs. Francis to bring something with her that represents her soul. (In the chaplain's experience texts or images that clients take with them can deepen the communication and foster healing.) Mrs. Francis gladly agrees and writes it down in her notebook. She adds that the conversation is freeing, that she feels less tense. The chaplain senses that Mrs. Francis is eager, even hungry to work on the topic.

Second Conversation

As an image for her soul, Mrs. Francis has brought a text and a photograph with her. The text is from the writer and comedian Kees van Kooten. "I don't have time infinitely." When reading it, Mrs. Francis cries. Then she shows the chaplain a photo of a large wall tapestry with segments in which a large bird has been woven. "This is the very first tapestry I wove. It had to be a bird. When I was nine, I wanted to be a bird. An uncle wrote a poem for me, 'Free as a Bird.'" Again, she cries. "The bird is my inward self, my soul ... With heart and soul, I wove this. It's a kind of inspiration that I haven't felt for a long time."

Conversation continues on the metaphor, and what the bird would now look like, wounded. The cancer has returned. That makes Mrs. Francis feel lame and fearful. She is again confronted with her finitude. Expressing that in words seems to relieve her. It offers recognition for the pain and sorrow regarding the cancer, pain, and sorrow that she does not find time to pay attention to. She also mentions her concerns about her husband that have become too much for her. A couple of times he has tried to stop drinking, but he keeps starting again.

Subsequent Conversations

At the beginning of each conversation Mrs. Francis lays her notebook on the table, sometimes quoting from it or writing something down. The term inspiration leads to her telling about experiences of helping others and of feeling displaced and vulnerable. Taking time for those things, at moments in silence, is a conscious choice of the chaplain, inasmuch as Mrs. Francis has not previously granted herself the rest to do so. During the initial contact, the chaplain had observed that Mrs. Francis was tense, speaking rapidly and quietly, breathing high, carefully choosing words, or searching for them. Gradually more calmness arises, and there is room for laughs.

Multidisciplinary Team

On a weekly basis the Medical Specialist Rehab Team convenes for a multidisciplinary review of patient status. In one of the meetings the chaplain explains that in her care she is paying attention to Mrs. Francis's longing for inspiration, as a spiritual complement to her need for more energy, on which the physical and occupational therapists and the dietician are working. Some of the colleagues chuckle and say, "That's too vague and fluttery to do anything with."

The chaplain holds on to the notion of inspiration because it indicates precisely what Mrs. Francis longs for. The chaplain explains that for Mrs. Francis the term "inspiration" stands for a renewed motivation, in a religious sense as well, to live—and weave—with heart and soul. That is the well from which she has always drawn. Now, however, as a result of another confrontation with the fragility of her existence, of the uncertainties concerning her care for her husband, and of a lack of self-care, the well has dried up.

The rehab physician picks the term up and includes it in the summary of the key problem. "Due to a lack of energy / inspiration and inadequate coping the patient does not get around to activities that she likes and considers to be valuable to her." The terms "inspiration" and "valuable" have been added. With her colleague, the medical-social worker, the chaplain discusses the types of care each will provide. The colleague will focus on the family Mrs. Francis comes from, her restlessness from a life in two countries and her fear of recidivism. The chaplain will focus on her spiritual journey. At a subsequent sitting of the multidisciplinary team the suggestion is made to offer Mrs. Francis creative therapy to help her get closer to her emotions.

COMMUNICATION AND FEEDBACK

In an evaluation at the end of the rehab trajectory, Mrs. Francis tells the physician that she has gained a lot of insight into managing her energy, thanks to the care on a physical, psychosocial, and spiritual level. In an email to the chaplain she writes, "I cannot emphasize enough how important it was for my recovery to have support from different disciplines under one roof. Twenty years ago, I also went to a physical therapist, had psychological help, did yoga, took long hikes, and had haptotherapy[4]. But they were all loose pieces. Now I experienced the opportunity to reflect on the impact of cancer in my daily life, and to work through acceptance, regain some self-esteem, and share my questions concerning spiritual issues."

Regarding the conversations with the chaplain, she writes: "It's really very difficult to explain what happened in our conversations, because it is so enwrapped in intimacy, in listening and being heard, in the atmosphere ... being permitted, encouraged, and enabled to express doubts, fears, and searchings ... I believe that it was that, that was so healing." The term "healing" that the patient herself employs is noticeable, as it is often difficult to describe.

SUMMARY

What Does the Chaplain Do?

The chaplain observes and listens to the patient. She invites and encourages the patient to tell her story and to openly express her concerns, fears and needs. She invites the patient to bring a text or image that represents her soul. She elaborates with the patient on the metaphor of the bird (as a symbol of both longing and woundedness) and introduces a term to summarize a key spiritual issue for the patient, "inspiration" (and the lack of it), as a complement to the treatment of the lack of energy. In the conversations the chaplain provides space and time and silence to reflect on emotions and concerns that the patient had not gotten around to expressing or pondering.

In the multidisciplinary team the chaplain introduces the term "inspiration" and overcomes initial resistance to the term by explaining its significance for the patient. To that purpose she employs a metaphor of a well that has dried up. She sees how the rehab physician takes on to the term and includes the words "inspiration" and "valuable" in a description of the key

---

4. Haptotherapy addresses issues in physical posture and affective relationships by working with human demeanor and touch. See https://haptotherapy.com.

issues for the patient. She consults with the medical-social worker regarding which of them will provide what form of care.

For What Reasons?

With the term inspiration the chaplain seeks to provide an appropriate focus for working on the motivational and religious struggles of the patient. The chaplain's experience is that working with the patient's own text or images deepens communication and fosters healing. She senses that the patient needs time and space to express her concerns and desires in ways she has not yet been able to do.

The chaplain is convinced that the medical focus on (physical) energy needs to be complemented with a focus on inspiration and spiritual sources of strength.

With What Results?

There is in the patient an observable reduction of tension, particularly attributable to her getting closer to her emotions and being able to express her concerns. The introduction of the notion of inspiration and soul unlock a strong emotional response from the patient. The patient eagerly welcomes the opportunity to bring along something that represents her soul and provides a metaphor that is fruitfully explored. The patient attributes her recovery to the wholistic care, including spiritual care, under one roof. In the chaplaincy care she has experienced intimacy and the space and freedom to express her concerns and emotions. She calls that experience "healing," with moments for reflection and to stop and give things a thought instead of just pushing on.

With the introduction of the terms "inspiration" and "valuable," the language of spirituality and meaning is included in the treatment summary as a compliment to the focus on energy.

REFLECTIONS

Existentially the patient is for the third time in twenty years confronted with a life-threatening illness (finitude) and treatment that is severe and burdensome. She has deep concerns about her husband. In the background a sense of restlessness from her childhood years plays a role, but also the religious (*spiritual*) world that was opened for her in conversations with her aunt.

She experiences woundedness, sorrow, fear, *and* a deep longing to again be as a bird. *Spiritually* she has lost her sense of basic (religious) trust and feels dried up. The use of *aesthetic means* of her own choosing—the self-woven tapestry and the poem by her uncle—seem to foster a direction for the care process. The use of symbolic language proves helpful, as in her own metaphor of the bird for the patient herself and of the chaplain's image of a dried up well for the multidisciplinary team. From an *ethical* point of view, the invitation to the patient to bring a text or image of her own choosing has not only an emotional and expressive but also an empowering effect, strengthening her agency and subjectivity, among other things by reflecting her own artistry.

The use of worldview language plays a major role in the case. That is clear in the concreteness of the metaphors bird and well that are often employed in religious settings, but also in the use of what is otherwise a more abstract but for the patient recognizable term, "inspiration," of which the Dutch original is related to the word for soul. That term, which is closely related to domain descriptions of chaplaincy, and the metaphor of the well clarify the longing of the patient and the care concerns of the chaplain for the multidisciplinary team. The setting of the case is a Center for Quality of Life at an Oncological Hospital, care that provides multidisciplinary support in cases of physical, psychological, social, and/or spiritual limitations. This case demonstrates in a very direct way how both care for spiritual aspects and a specifically spiritual term like inspiration can be effective in a multidisciplinary setting.

In addition to understanding the care of the chaplain from the perspective of language, one might also point out the impact of the use of imagination in the case. The chaplain as "an imaginative professional"[5] appeals to the imagination of the patient, who introduces the metaphors. The impact of the term inspiration and of working with metaphors has a healing effect. That is in keeping with Stephen Asma's understanding that the core value of religion lies in its emotionally therapeutic power.[6]

REFERENCES

Alma, Hans. *De kunst van pelgrimeren. De geestelijk verzorger als verbeeldingsprofessional.* Utrecht: Eburon, 2024.
Asma, Stephen T. *Why We Need Religion.* New York: Oxford University Press, 2018.

5. Alma, *De kunst van pelgrimeren.*
6. Asma, *Why We Need Religion.*

Ownby, Kristin. "Use of the Distress Thermometer in Clinical Practice." *Journal of the Advanced Practitioner in Oncology* 10.2 (2019) 175–179.

Van der Zaag, et al. "Energie én bezieling: Geestelijke verzorging en oncologische revalidatie." *Handelingen* 46.2 (2019) 27–31.

5

The Enigma of a Day
Case Study from an Oncological and a Palliative Ward of a General Hospital

—Rob Vos, Martin Walton, Jacques Körver[1]

SYNOPSIS

A WOMAN, SIXTY-EIGHT YEARS old, has been diagnosed with ovary cancer and metastasis. In response to her restlessness and despondency, the chaplain seeks to help her relate to her situation, a world becoming smaller and a body losing its beauty and strength, as well as to her felt need to have control and to care for her family. Besides letting his care be guided by models on the art of dying and existential psychology, the chaplain makes use of aesthetic materials (visual and poetic) in keeping with the woman's aesthetic way of experiencing the world. During an accompaniment process that lasts, intermittently, two years, the woman is able to confront the enigma of death, to let go of what she cannot control, and peacefully depart from her loved ones. Before her death she speaks of chaplaincy as a gift.[2]

---

1. Co-researchers in the RC Mixed Fields: Hub van den Bosch, Joke de Koeijer, Tjeerd van der Meer, Maurice van der Put, Marieke Termeer, Rob Vos, Frans van Oosten, José de Groot, Riekje van Osnabrugge, and Myriam Braakhuis.

2. Vos, et al., "Het raadsel van de dag."

BACKGROUND & SETTING

Setting and Occasion

Marianne (pseudonym) has been admitted to an oncological ward of a general hospital due to ovary cancer with metastasis. A nurse on the ward observes that Marianne is restless and despondent and suggests calling upon the chaplain to come to see her. The nurse indicates that Marianne has things she would like to tell. During a period of two years the chaplain speaks with Marianne fifteen times during various hospital stays. The focus below is on the last several conversations.

Client

Marianne is sixty-eight years old, is married and has children and grandchildren. She speaks with tenderness about caring for her grandchildren and feels responsible for her family. She worked previously in administrative positions. She likes to read, regularly visits museums and enjoys nature. She appreciates moments of unexpected beauty that she can describe with great expression. She and her husband like being on the go. She is now frustrated that her activities are becoming limited and her world smaller.

Chaplain

The chaplain, fifty years old, took his training at the University of Humanistic Studies, has worked in mental health care, and serves now in a general hospital. Prior to becoming a chaplain, he worked for ten years as a visual artist. He has a particular interest in aesthetic ideas and practices in humanism. His approach to chaplaincy is narrative and hermeneutic and draws upon existential philosophy and psychology.

Others Involved

Marianne's husband Pieter (pseudonym) and her son Marco (pseudonym) are present during some of the conversations. Pieter worked for an art institute. The children and grandchildren play a significant role in the background.

ACCOMPANIMENT PROCESS

Initial Contacts

Marianne speaks with a soft voice and has clear diction. She sits straight up and actively seeks eye contact. Marianne indicates that the diagnosis is such a burden because she feels so full of life, as if there are still things for her to do. She hopes the chemotherapy will allow her some time to fill in the last part of her life in a satisfactory manner. She wrestles with the pressure to arrange things around the end of her life and has difficulty making decisions. At times she appears restless. She speaks associatively and moves from one subject to another.

In all of the care conversations Marianne expresses her concern about how things will be for her children and grandchildren. She is also concerned about her own quality of life and about missing the things she enjoys. That everything costs more energy frustrates her. The chaplain explores with Marianne what her sources of strength (family, nature, and art) mean to her. Managing things in the last phase and dealing with the limits of time are important topics of conversation. Questions about life and death gradually become sharper.

Goals of the Chaplaincy Care

The chaplain formulates three goals. The first is to help order Marianne's life story in order to help her get a grip on the numerous thoughts, associations and feelings of disquiet. The second is "treasure hunting" to find sources of inspiration or strength that might help Marianne. The third and more encompassing goal is to foster a greater sense of inner space for Marianne, so that she can more freely relate to her situation.

Tenth Conversation

The chaplain comes in shortly after a medical consult with the family. Marianne seems despondent. The decision has been made to no longer offer any life-prolonging treatment. In the previous months Marianne underwent her last palliative treatment with chemotherapy. She had hoped to win more time. In a night in which she slept poorly she had a dream she tells about.

> Marianne: "It was warm. I wasn't lying well. I was short of breath. I got up and walked through the hallways. It was a strange experience. It was so quiet. There was no one else . . . an empty

> hall, dead silence. As if I was walking between the buildings in a world that had been hit by a nuclear disaster and I was the only one left . . . the last. Completely alone . . . so strange."
>
> Chaplain: "How did you feel?"
>
> Marianne: "Lonely. It was a lonely experience. I felt completely abandoned. It was terrible, and the feeling came back that we have talked about before, that there is still something I have to do. A finger pointing at me and saying, 'You have no time to lose.'"

The chaplain speaks with her about the dream, about losing her grip on minor and major things, and about the frustration that her world keeps getting smaller. She then says that there are also moments of happiness.

> Marianne: "Speaking of that, we were downstairs [in the meditation room] the other day. That poem is so beautiful . . . So wonderful. Pieter thought so, too. We both thought it was beautiful, inciting, a bit provocative, but that's good. It makes you think."
>
> Chaplain quotes from the poem: "The art is to live in a way that it comes over you."
>
> Marianne: "Right. Beautiful."

Later that day the chaplain comes by with a reproduction of the painting *L'Enigma di una Giornata* (1914, *The Enigma of a Day*) by Giorgio de Chirico and tells her that he thought of it when she told about her dream. On the backside he printed the poem by Martin Bril, that expresses a desire for lucidity and clarity, rare moments that can hardly be sought for themselves, but can be received when they occur.[3]

Eleventh Conversation

The chaplain walks in to the hospital room and greets Marianne. She thanks him for the reproduction. She appears restless and excited, so that the chaplain suggests talking about the painting later and first exploring how she is feeling. She says that she is thinking a lot about death. She has been asked about her wishes with regard to resuscitation. She is not worried about dying, as she has confidence that the pain can be taken care of. It is the phenomenon of death itself that she is thinking about.

---

3. Bril, *Verzameld werk*.

> Marianne: "It's such a strange idea that in a little bit, I just will not be here. What's comes after that?"
>
> Chaplain: "Do you mean what comes after death?"
>
> Marianne: "Yes, perhaps. But also, how can life just stop? That's what I've been thinking about recently. How can it be that I am no longer with them, that it stops? And what is it that stops? Where will I be then? You may think that these are silly questions. It's so strange."

The chaplain explains to her that a lot of people have such thoughts at the end of their life, both religious and non-religious persons. For the chaplain they are liminal questions that touch upon the "enigma of existence." That phrase resonates with what Marianne is thinking and feeling. The chaplain suggests to her that her bond with her family seems to reach beyond the limits of death for her.

> Marianne: "Yes, that's true. Somehow I will still be there . . . Maybe it's a little egoistic, I guess, the idea that I cannot imagine not being there. I know it's not right, but I have lived so well. Healthy. That plays a role, too."
>
> Chaplain: "Do you sometimes ask: Why you? Is that what you mean?"
>
> Marianne: "Yes, I guess that's silly. I know it doesn't work that way, but sometimes you still think it."

During the last part of this conversation Marianne returns to the painting by De Chirico. The chaplain looks at the reproduction with her and she expresses that the atmosphere of emptiness and abandonment in it well mirrors her dream.

Thirteenth Conversation

A month later the chaplain again finds Marianne on the nursing ward. She tells him how nice it was to have been able to work in her garden at home in the sun. When she returned to the ward, the nurses did not recognize her from her photo. Her situation has worsened and she feels even weaker.

> "That photo is not so pretty. It was made too quickly. But I think my hair is pretty. I'm a bit idle, I guess, but I use to look good. And now, it startles me. I've lost a lot of weight."

Marianne has often indicated that her appearance is very important to her. Now she can no longer pay much attention to that. She tells again about a recent dream that expresses her present situation.

> Marianne: "Pieter and the children were standing beside my bed with the oncologist. The oncologist said that nothing more could be done. 'I'm powerless,' he said. But they all slowly disappeared, became unclear like in a fog."
>
> Chaplain: "Was it a pleasant feeling or just the opposite?"
>
> Marianne: "In a sense it was. It's a double feeling. It was strange, but that may be the way it's going to happen, that they slowly disappear in the fog. That would be good. That's what I saw with my mother. That was the image I had of the end . . . She was lying quietly in bed."

Unconsciously at first, Marianne describes here her ideal way of dying. It confronts her again with her restlessness and the things she still wants to do. She tells about the woman who laid next to her during her previous hospital stay. That woman, unlike Marianne, had already arranged everything. Her relaxation and acceptance were very confronting.

Fourteenth Conversation

When the chaplain arrives at bedside a couple of days later, he is startled. Marianne is much weaker, looks pale and thin. She lies sleeping with an oxygen tube inserted. When she awakes, she says that she has indicated that she wants to die. The pain and the exhaustion are just too much. The morphine causes anxious dreams and hallucinations. She is wondering if her desire to die is not egoistic in relation to her family. The chaplain responds that there are times when things become overwhelming. She says that she feels at peace about it. She has arranged everything that is important and she can leave the rest to others. Her voice has become softer, the sentences shorter and the silences longer.

It is September and the temperature above seventy degrees (Fahrenheit). Marianne tells how much she and Pieter could enjoy the seasons together. Then she says that she is tired and the conversation ends. In the afternoon the chaplain passes by and talks briefly with Pieter. A couple of days later palliative sedation is started and shortly thereafter Marianne passes away.

Use of Theory

In the accompaniment process the chaplain makes use of three theoretical models. The first is the STEM-model that explores ways in which clients and caregivers relate to death and dying and how they can relate to each other.[4] Marianne's s response can be characterized as more or less *proactive*: fearful of becoming dependent, placing great importance upon her dignity, and seeking to maintain control, although Marianne did not always follow through.

A second theoretical approach is provided by the *Ars Moriendi* (Art of Dying) Model of Carlo Leget.[5] The ultimate aim of the model is to increase one's inner space. Inner space is understood as the disposition in which a person can relate freely and calmly to the emotions and relations that play a role in dying. Particularly five fields of possible tension are addressed: I—the other; doing—undergoing; holding on—letting go; remembering—forgetting; and believing—knowing. The tension doing—undergoing manifests itself in Marianne's feeling, expressed in various ways, that she has something more to do. Finally, the balance shifts from seeking control of the situation to allowing things to be (abstaining from further treatment and wanting to die at the end), and from holding on to her loved ones and to precious moments to letting go and leaving things to others. The chaplain consciously explores the concerns of believing and knowing in relation to Marianne's explicit concern about death and her anxiety with regards to no longer being with her loved ones. The chaplain indicates that that is a liminal experience and introduces the term "enigma of existence." That offers Marianne words and recognition for what is incomprehensible to her and consequently more inner space in her thoughts and feelings.

In the third place, the Dimensions of Human Experience Model (DHEM)[6] is helpful. Emmy Van Deurzen's DHEM model is directed towards a realistic perspective in the tension between the ideal of a rich cultured life and the threat of illness and decline. Marianne wants to remain in the midst of life but is increasingly hindered by illness and weakness. Time becomes an urgent matter for her. In early conversations the chaplain speaks with her

---

4. STEM, which is the word for voice in Dutch, stands for *Sterven op je Eigen Manier,* Dying in Your Own Way. STEM differentiates five profiles of responding to death and dying: proactive, social, candid, trusting, and rational. See https://www.medischcontact.nl/actueel/laatste-nieuws/artikel/vijf-visies-op-sterven, consulted August 22, 2023, and https://stichtingstem.info, consulted August 22, 2023.

5. Leget, *Art of Living, Art of Dying.* See also Chapter 22.

6. Van Deurzen, *Existential Counselling & Psychotherapy.*

about living in a smaller world to enable her to rediscover her sources of inspiration within the limits of what she can do.

The use of visual and poetical materials fits in with the worldview background of the chaplain. The painting is used as an intervention to mirror the existential loneliness that Marianne experiences in the hospital hallway. It is related to the expression "enigma of existence" which well fits Marianne's perceptions. In the poem a "moment of happiness" resonates, enabling her to see that such moments are still present. Both interventions connect Marianne to the aesthetic dimension that is so important to her.

Communication and Feedback

During the accompaniment process the chaplain reports on his contacts with Marianne in the electronic health records. He also participated in palliative team meetings on the ward. The nurse who refers Marianne to the chaplain indicates that the talks with the chaplain help reduce the anxiety Marianne felt about her situation. An oncologist and a palliative team nurse report that Marianna is intensely concerned about her life ending and that she experiences significant support from the talks with the chaplain. After Marianne has passed away, Pieter and Marco both tell the chaplain that the contacts with him helped Marianne find more peace and quiet, create more order in her thoughts and feelings, and find more clarity. In her last conversation with the chaplain, Marianne tells him that the conversations with him were very supportive in reflecting upon the last phase of her life. She calls the encounters with the chaplain "a gift." Previously she had said that the conversations were like "reading a good book or a nice hike across fields of heather."

SUMMARY

What Does the Chaplain Do?

The chaplain listens to what Marianne tells about her struggles. On the basis of what she tells him, he sets three goals: help Marianne order her life story, help her to reconnect to her sources of strength and inspiration, and foster a sense of inner space so that she can more freely relate to her situation. The chaplain recognizes in Marianne a proactive (STEM-model) style of seeking to maintain control and dignity. The chaplain talks with Marianne about letting go of things, finding trust in her relation to her loved ones, even when she will no longer be there with them, and reflecting on death and the enigmas of life (*Ars Moriendi*). The chaplain addresses Marianne's sense of urgency and the discrepancies she experiences between her aesthetic perception of life and of herself on the one hand and on the other hand the limits due to illness and the changes in her body and appearance (DHEM). The chaplain makes use of Marianne's aesthetic sensitivities (sources of inspiration) by presenting her with a reproduction of a painting and responding to her thoughts on the poem. He introduces a worldview term "enigma of existence" that enables her to relate to what is incomprehensible to her, that is, death and no longer being among her loved ones.

For What Reasons?

The chaplain responds to a referral by a nurse and addresses in multiple conversations with Marianne her anxiety and restlessness. He is both informed and guided in his interactions by theoretical models of death and dying (STEM, *Ars Moriendi*) and on existential experience (DHEM). He feels affinity, personally and professionally, with her aesthetic approach to life and makes use of that. The encompassing goal is to foster a sense of inner space in her relation to her illness and its effects upon her, to death itself, and to her loved ones.

With What Results?

Marianne moves from a sense of having too little time and too little control to being able to let things go and leave things to others. She is able to focus more on what is of significance to her and feel less concerned about appearance and how others will go on without her. Her anxiety and restlessness decrease visibly, as is confirmed by several others. She gains a sense of clarity, as her husband and son report. She experiences chaplaincy as a gift, a good book, and a hike across heather fields. Together those results indicate that she gained a sense of inner space.

REFLECTIONS

There is an interesting interconnection between the goals the chaplain sets and the models he employs in response to what Marianne tells him. The models are used to address Marianne's needs and concerns, but they had already made the chaplain alert to needs that could be present. They structure to a lesser or greater degree his listening and his formulation of the goals. The theoretical and practical frameworks shape the sensitivity of the chaplain (though not exclusively), who then formulates goals in terms of the conceptual frameworks he is familiar with and considers fruitful, and subsequently he employs the models as strategies and methodologies for addressing her needs and pursuing the (shared) goals. In other words, the models have become incorporated in the professional awareness of the chaplain and guide his listening and response. Finally, when the models prove appropriate and things work out more or less as hoped, the results are formulated in terms of the same models. To put it more briefly, the models shape the assessment, the care process and the goals, and they are used to interpret the results. That may seem circular, but the circle can only be completed (or the spiral only continued), because the models fit the situation and actually do help to adequately address and meet Marianne's needs. Also, fostering inner space seems to ask of the chaplain a like inner space and non-anxious presence.[7] That is, of course, to a great extent a disposition gained in training and maturity, but it seems in the present case to be fostered by the access to methodical or analytical tools (models) with the help of which the terrain of death and dying can be negotiated.

Of particular interest in this case is the use of aesthetic means (visual and poetic). There lies an indication for their employment in Marianne's *aesthetic* manner of experiencing the world. One might even speak of an aesthetic meaning system. To be sure there are *existential* issues of illness and death, *spiritual* issues on the nature of death and existence, and *ethical* issues of her relation and responsibilities towards her loved ones, but the aesthetics of Marianne's experience of her own body, of a world becoming smaller, of not being able to imagine her loved ones without her being there, *et cetera*, is quite prevalent. In response the chaplain makes use of his own background in art and aesthetics to share the reproduction and elaborate on the poem. Those interventions engender a resonance, not only with regard to how Marianne experiences her present situation, but also in keeping with the way she has experienced the world in her life. Something similar seems to happen earlier when the chaplain introduces the phrase "enigma of existence." While the phrase has an existential reference and spiritual intention, the formulation also has an aesthetic impact, as a concise and illuminating act of language that resonates, not only with the dilemmas and paradoxes Marianne is facing, but also with her own conscious use of language.

The use of aesthetic means is notable for another reason as well. The case study speaks of a series of fifteen conversations with Marianne. The

---

7. Friedman, *Generation to Generation*; Friedman, *The Art of Jewish Pastoral Counseling*.

family indicates that the conversations helped Marianne. In light of the content one might also say fifteen dialogues. From the viewpoint of form the conversations include non-verbal interactions and non-conversational manners of communication between Marianne and the chaplain, for example, besides the painting and the poem, the photograph of Marianne. And in the conversations, there is attention to aesthetic aspects such as appearance, nature, the seasons, and a hike across heather fields. In fact, the aesthetic aspects play a key role in the accompaniment process and in Marianne's development during the care process. The introduction of the painting and the elaboration on the poem play a role that is not unlike that of conversational counseling techniques: mirroring, offering recognition, reframing, and adding depth. That observation led the research community to frame the term "aesthetic counseling" for those interventions, as they fulfill the same functions that might otherwise have been offered in verbal interactions. The use of aesthetic means, however, strengthens the relation, or attunement between form and content, which in turn facilitates the accessibility and affects the impact.[8] In that sense, the conversations are not just conversations, but encounters.

REFERENCES

Alma, Hans. "Art and Religion as Invitation. An Exploration Based on John Dewey's Theory of Experience and Imagination." *Perichoresis* 18.3 (2020) 33–45.
Bril, Martin. *Verzameld werk: gedichten*. Amsterdam: Uitgeverij 521, 2002.
Friedman, Edwin H. *Generation to Generation: Family Process in Church and Synagogue*. New York: Guilford, 1985.
Friedman, Michelle S. *The Art of Jewish Pastoral Counseling: A Guide for All Faiths*. Psyche and Soul 1. London: Routledge, 2017.
Gladding, Samuel T. *Counseling as an Art: The Creative Arts in Counseling*. 3rd ed. Alexandria: Pearson-Merrill Prentice Hall, 2006.
Leget, Carlo. *Art of Living, Art of Dying: Spiritual Care for a Good Death*. London: Kingsley, 2017.
Murphy, Alice. "Form and Content: A Defense of Aesthetic Value in Science." *Philosophy of Science* 90.3 (2023) 669–85.
Van Deurzen, Emmy. *Existential Counselling & Psychotherapy in Practice*. 3rd ed. Los Angeles: Sage, 2012.
Vos, Rob, et al. "Het raadsel van de dag. Esthetisch counselen in het ziekenhuis." *Tijdschrift Geestelijke Verzorging* 23.100 (2022) 40–45.

---

8. Alma, "Art and Religion as Invitation"; Gladding, *Counseling as an Art*; Murphy, "Form and Content."

6

Exposure?
Case Study from Mental Health Care
—Marie-José van Bolhuis, Hanneke Muthert, Jacques Körver, Martin Walton[1]

SYNOPSIS

A YOUNG WOMAN IS referred to a chaplain after exposure treatment has been stopped. Central issues are her severe fear of death and lack of trust. The chaplain uses imagery to enable the woman to face her fears. She then accompanies the woman through various dealings with her fear of death in the form of music, reading, conversations, and visiting compline prayers at a monastery. The woman is gradually able to develop trust and face her fears. The question arises if the chaplaincy care was perhaps an alternative form of exposure.[2]

---

1. Co-researchers in the RC Mental Health: Monique van Hoof, Ruud Jellema, Berthilde van de Loosdrecht, Arnoud van der Mheen, Thea Sprangers, and Jacqueline Weeda-Hageman.

2. Previously published in Dutch as Van Bolhuis, et al. "Dus toch exposure?"

BACKGROUND & SETTING

Setting and Occasion

Anne (pseudonym) follows psychiatric group treatment in the form of exposure in a large mental health care institution. Under accompaniment of a psychiatric nurse and a psychologist, clients are gradually exposed to situations that arouse their fear. Anne refuses to participate in exercises that deal with death. After she withdraws from the exposure treatment and as a result of a reorganization in the institution, time passes without any treatment. An adequate follow up is blocked by her refusal of additional diagnostic examination. She is referred by a psychologist to a chaplain, who begins weekly conversations that are gradually decreased in frequency. After the initial meeting, the conversations take place in the office of the chaplain.

Client

Anne is a woman, twenty-five years old. She lives together with her friend. Her appearance is friendly, brisk and even cheerful. She talks freely and easily makes contact. She indicates that under her demeanor fears and uncertainties rage. Inside she feels sad and does not know what to do with her life. Compulsive behavior and thoughts cost her a lot of time and energy. Her life is dominated by questions and fears regarding death. Since a year she is on sick leave from her work with burn-out. Her plan to go back to school is falling through. She was baptized a Catholic and was administered first communion, but is not religiously active or part of a church community.

Chaplain

The chaplain is a woman, sixty-one years old, and Catholic. She has worked for seventeen years in mental health care. The principles of Carl Rogers—congruency, unconditional regard and empathy—are for her the basis of every contact.[3] She sometimes departs from the non-directive listening approach of Rogers in order to ask questions and introduce experiences of others. Her style of work is hermeneutic in the use of (biblical) stories, songs, anonymous experiences of clients, or her own experience in order to shed (a different) light on the story of the client. Although religion seldom plays an explicit role in much of her work, she finds inspiration in the Christian tradition.

---

3. Rogers et al. *Client Centered Therapy*; Zwaan, *Een prachtige dans*.

Others Involved

There is the treatment team by whom Anne is referred to the chaplain when participation in group therapy is ended and no alternative is in sight. Anne's friend offers support and reassurance. During the course of Anne's contacts with the chaplain, the grandmother of the friend passes away.

ACCOMPANIMENT PROCESS

Initial Contact

After a brief introduction and mention of the referral, the chaplain says, "Well, tell me . . ." Anne tells the chaplain that she is burdened by compulsive behavior, like checking twenty times to see if a door is closed or a faucet is turned off. She has compulsive thoughts regarding food. All of that is accompanied by major fears. Only when her friend says that things are alright, does she calm down. She trusts him.

Anne sees two possible connections. After her parents divorced when she was young, she felt a large responsibility for household matters. That was (and is) for her too great of a burden.

In addition, she associates her compulsive behavior with her fear of death. If she does not carry out the compulsive acts, she might just die. And thinking about death like that also seems dangerous to her. During exposure treatment she repeatedly had suicidal thoughts that frightened her terribly.

Anne wants to know what happens when you die. She wants to be certain that there is life after death. She asks everyone about it, including the chaplain. But whom should she believe? She seeks an answer in religion, "because that deals with life after death." Then she remembers, "I was once baptized and did first confirmation. Why not begin with Christianity?" She asks the chaplain if she should start reading the Bible to find an answer. The chaplain asks, "Is that what you want?" "No," is Anne's answer.

The chaplain suggests first looking at her questions more closely and then to look at some religious texts when possible and desirable. The chaplain also suggests distinguishing two things. The compulsive behavior will be left to the psychiatric treatment. The chaplain offers to help Anne look more closely at her thoughts on and fear of death. They plan three meetings, after which they can evaluate.

The chaplain says that "trust" seems to be a key word. She has heard Anne use the word several times. She understands Anne's refusal to participate in exposure treatment as a lack of trust. She does trust her friend. If he says things are alright, she becomes calmer. Could it be that Anne wants to learn to have trust that things will be okay after death? Could that give her trust to go on living. If her sense of trust and self-confidence could grow, then she might not always have a feeling that she has to control things. The notions of "trust" and "faith/belief," the chaplain explains, are closely related (cf. *pistis* in New Testament Greek). Both terms belong to the domain of the chaplain.

After thinking for a moment, Anne heartily says, "Yes, it has to do with trust. Can we work on that?" They agree to do so and to examine together if and how reflecting on death might help Anne. The chaplain shares with Anne a motto, "If you think there is a ghost under your bed, then it's good to have a look." Since Anne is worrying about death so much, it would be handy to start thinking and talking about it. Doing it together could be less scary. Does Anne dare to do that? "Yes," Anne answers.

Second Conversation

Anne says that her friend is on vacation and that things are extra difficult. She would like to just live her life and not concern herself with death, but death keeps coming at her. How should she live her life? The chaplain tells how she herself combines *memento mori* (remember that you will die) and *carpe diem* (pluck the day). She suggests that the two are like two legs. If you are only concerned with plucking the day, then death can surprise you. "I wanted to still do this or that. Give me another chance." If you only think of death, then you do not come to life. "Balance is found in using both legs. That way you can ride a bike." The chaplain moves her legs as if biking.

The chaplain then asks Anne what her sources of inspiration are for plucking the day. It is the chaplain's experience that self-chosen texts or images can deepen the communication and have a healing effect. Anne replies that music is a source of inspiration. As homework, could Anne, the chaplain asks, look up five songs about death. Then they can listen to the songs the next time and talk about them. Would that be possible? Anne dares to do so.

Third Conversation

Anne comes in enthusiastically. She is happy with the conversations. "Finally, something is happening." All the time she was in the treatment group, she had the feeling she was not getting anywhere, but now she does. The compulsive disorder is not over. She still walks back to check the door. But now she realizes that she does not have to do so and that creates space. She has found five songs about death and she plays them for the chaplain on her telephone. She feels she has been courageous in doing it. It was not easy but she did it.

Anne then shows the chaplain two books she found in the library, both about death. She asks if it is dangerous to read them. "Do you want to read them?" the chaplain asks. "Yes," Anne replies. They decide to choose one of the books with the title (translated) *Living without fear of death*,[4] in which the author, after the loss of his partner, realizes that he is also mortal. He is almost unable to live with that insight. He leads the reader through his own searchings in philosophy and religion for an answer to the question: How can one live without fear of death?

Further Encounters

Anne reads one chapter at a time, makes notes and formulates questions, that are dealt with at each next appointment. At first there is a lot of recognition in what she reads. Later she has to wrestle with the thoughts of the philosophers. Some passages she has to read three times, but she finds them interesting.

In the perception of the chaplain the path being pursued offers Anne hope that in the near future things will be better. That seems to provide her with a sense of calmness. She takes initiative, is willing to learn, and is curious with regard to her own religiosity. She connects with the things she reads. She writes things down, reflects upon them and reads them out loud. She seeks knowledge and a sense of meaningfulness. By reading the testimony of another person, the acuteness of her own story seems to recede to some extent. That reduces the fear and enlarges the space in which she can live.

"Are there other ways of pondering death?" Anne asks. The chaplain tells about the compline prayers at the monastery she regularly visits. Every evening there is a prayer, ". . . and may all who come to you this night find rest to die in your love." That arouses Anne's interest. Anne and the chaplain make an appointment to visit the compline. Anne asks for a children's Bible, because she finds the Bible too complex, but wants to know more. The chaplain lends her a Bible.[5] Shortly after that Anne and the chaplain visit the monastery for the compline, which Anne experiences with a bit of apprehension but with contentment.

4. Kind, *Leven zonder angst*.
5. Eykman and Bouman, *Woord voor woord*.

Communication and Feedback

Anne's friend sees the benefit of the conversations of Anne with the chaplain. When the grandmother of Anne's friend passes away, she is able to accompany him. Via Anne the chaplain hears that the psychologist reflects that Anne stopped with the exposure treatment and consequently undergoes exposure in chaplaincy care.

SUMMARY

What Does the Chaplain Do?

The chaplain offers Anne the space to tell her story, listens closely, and distills from what Anne says the aspect of "trust" as a crucial issue and links the word trust to faith. The chaplain reaches agreement with Anne to have a closer look at her fear of death while leaving her compulsive behavior and thinking to psychiatric treatment. With the help of a metaphor (motto), the chaplain motivates Anne to look at her fear of death. The chaplain introduces and physically demonstrates an image of two legs, one representing the recognition of death (*memento mori*) and one representing the choice to live (*carpe diem*). The chaplain asks about Anne's sources of inspiration and invites Anne subsequently to examine the matter of death through songs of her own choosing. The chaplain discusses the songs with Anne and also accompanies Anne's reading of literature on the fear of death. The chaplain accompanies Anne to the monastery for compline in response to Anne's question if there is another way of dealing with the issue of death.

For What Reasons?

The chaplain seems guided by the notion of trust in carefully gaining Anne's trust, in identifying trust as a key issue, and in engendering in Anne the trust that she can face her own fears. The chaplain shares her own perspectives of looking under the bed, of combining *memento mori* and *carpe diem*, and of visiting the compline. The whole time the chaplain carefully checks what Anne wants and how much she is able to handle.

With What Results?

Anne learns to speak more readily about death, read about it, confront her own thoughts on death and is less avoidant of everything that has to do with death (she accompanies her friend at his grandmother's death). She develops a learning attitude and shows herself capable of reading literature on the fear of death, wrestling with it, and positively applying it to her situation. She gains some distance from her compulsive thoughts. The compulsive behavior is less prevalent though not absent. She gradually learns to seek a balance between accepting death and living a meaningful life as a result. Anne has a stronger sense of trust and self-confidence.

REFLECTIONS

With empathy, regard, and close listening the chaplain responds to what Anne tells her and identifies key issues. The chaplain then follows the procedures of spiritual guidance,[6] not directly answering requests for advice or seeking to solve problems, but aiding the other in pursuing her path. Anne introduces literature herself, asks the questions that are important to her, and indicates the direction she wants to go. When the chaplain is more directive her hermeneutic approach works well, in the use of imagery, of sayings (*memento mori* and *carpe diem*), and of ritual (compline), by drawing upon both tradition and her own experience or perspective.[7] All that offers Anne more precise formulations, recognition, confirmation, and change. It engenders alternative behavior.

Existentially the focus is upon the fear of death. The compulsive behavior is left to other settings (as is the possible influence of the divorce of her parents on her bonding and fear of death[8]), but functions on the background and may have been partially alleviated by addressing the fear of death. On a *spiritual* level Anne is curious about what answers religion might provide her on the issue of death and investigates that with the help of the chaplain in her readings. The "answer" is not certainty about life after death, but the ability to relate to death and her fear of it. On a spiritual but also an *ethical* level the issue of trust plays an essential role. Along with her cognitive wrestling with the issue of death the *aesthetic* use of music (songs) and of ritual (compline) is helpful to Anne in dealing with death and living her life. Noteworthy is the comment of the psychologist that the

---

6. Andriessen, *Oorspronkelijk bestaan*.
7. Caldwell, *Pastoral Hermeneutics*; Heitink, "Geestelijk verzorger."
8. Zuccala, et al. "The Role of Death Fears."

chaplaincy care provided a form of exposure.[9] The primary precondition of the chaplaincy exposure seems to have been the issue of trust. Of further interest would be how the method and form of the exposure provided in chaplaincy care was similar to and/or different from the exposure offered in psychological treatment.

REFERENCES

Andriessen, Herman C. I. *Oorspronkelijk bestaan: Geestelijke begeleiding in onze tijd.* Baarn: Gooi en Sticht, 1996.

Caldwell, Charles F. *Pastoral Hermeneutics: A Quest for a Method.* Indiana: Notre Dame, 1978.

Canada, Andrea L. "A Psychologist's Response to the Case Study. Application of Theory and Measurement." *Journal of Health Care Chaplaincy* 17.1–2 (2011) 46–54.

Eykman, Karel, and Bert Bouman. *Woord voor woord: Kinderbijbel Oude en Nieuwe Testament.* Utrecht: Zomer & Keuning, 1984.

Heitink, Gerben. "Geestelijk verzorger. Over ambt en ambacht, over identiteit en pluraliteit." *Tijdschrift Geestelijke Verzorging* 6.28 (2003) 31–38.

Kind, Gerard. *Leven zonder angst voor de dood.* Kampen: Ten Have, 2009.

Rogers, Carl R., et al. *Client Centered Therapy: Its Current Practice, Implications and Theory.* 1951. Reprint, London: Robinson, 2015.

Van Bolhuis, Marie-José, et al. "Dus toch exposure? Geestelijke zorg bij het leren leven met angst voor de dood." *Tijdschrift Geestelijke Verzorging* 23.98 (2020) 50–55.

Zuccala, Matteo, et al. "The Role of Death Fears and Attachment Processes in Social Anxiety: A Novel Hypothesis Explored." *Australian Journal of Psychology* 73.3 (2021) 381–91.

Zwaan, Barbara. *Een prachtige dans. De therapeutische afstemming van afstand en nabijheid in het werk van Carl Rogers, Martin Buber en Henri Nouwen,* Tilburg: KSGV, 2017.

---

9. Canada, "A Psychologist's Response."

7

I Do It My Way
Case Study from Mental Health Care

—Irene Plaatsman, Hanneke Muthert, Martin Walton, Jacques Körver[1]

SYNOPSIS

A WOMAN, FORTY-TWO YEARS old, lives with the consequences of a brain tumor as a child. She wrestles with her dependency and a sense of meaningless. Following treatment in a psychiatric clinic, she is referred to a chaplain. In response to the woman's story the chaplain proposes working on themes on the meaning of life using objects and visual materials, focusing on the themes of agency and communion. Due to the woman's memory impairment, the chaplain documents each session in a logbook. The chaplain is also able to use psychological theory (transitional space) and philosophical insights from Kierkegaard to strengthen the woman's sense of self and understand the need of a balance between imaginary world and real world, between being alone and being with others. Sharing the logbook with family and care providers deepens their understanding of the woman.[2]

---

1. Co-researchers in the RC Mental Health Care: Marie-José van Bolhuis, Monique van Hoof, Ruud Jellema, Berthilde van de Loosdrecht, Arnoud van der Mheen, Thea Sprangers, and Jacqueline Weeda-Hageman.

2. Portions of this case study were previously published in: Plaatsman and Muthert, "Levensverhalen zinvol verteld."

BACKGROUND & SETTING

Setting and Occasion

Franka (pseudonym) is referred to the chaplain by a psychiatric nurse specialist from outpatient treatment in a mental health care center following treatment for depression. Franka previously made an appointment with a chaplain, but then cancelled it because of her nearing discharge. When the nurse asks if Franka would still like to talk with a chaplain, Franka responds positively and the nurse makes a referral. The mental health care chaplain visits Franka in an apartment in a residential setting where twenty-four persons with disabilities live, most of them with intellectual disabilities.

Client

Franka is a woman, forty-two years old, the third daughter in a family of four children. She has regular contact with her parents and other family members. At the age of nine, Franka suffered a brain tumor with severe consequences for her further life. Her spine was damaged resulting in abnormal growth. From her sixteenth year on she has lived in various institutions for her schooling. In her present residence she feels at home, but different from the other residents and therefore lonely at times. She had bad experiences in a previous residential situation for persons with acquired brain damage. Due to brain damage she has memory impairments. Four days a week she has daytime activities, but often she cannot remember what she has done there. She wishes that she could live on her own and lead a "normal" life, but household chores, cooking, and managing finances are too difficult for her. That makes her sad and causes her to sometimes feel like her life is meaningless.

Chaplain

The chaplain is a woman, fifty-nine years old, who has been working in mental health care for eleven years. She has completed two master studies, in religion and in chaplaincy care, with majors in philosophy. She works in a team of five chaplains, but relatively independently in a large region in outpatient treatment, day care, assisted living, eldercare, and community care. She also works in child and juvenile psychiatric care, where she uses her earlier experience in education and works with material objects and symbols as an aid in conversation. She is member of the sector of the Dutch chaplaincy association for chaplains with no affiliation with a particular worldview body.

Others Involved

The chaplain lets the nurse specialist know that she will keep her informed about the care process. When the chaplain decides to describe the care process in a case study, she informs the nurse who agrees to offer feedback upon completion. The care providers of the resident setting are aware of Franka's contact with the chaplain. Franka has provided permission for the case description and eventual publication under a pseudonym.

ACCOMPANIMENT PROCESS

Initial Contact

Franka has looked forward to contact with the chaplain. She readily tells the chaplain about her life, the tumor, her problems with memory, her grief that she is unable to live on her own, and how she feels about her present situation. Franka says she wants to talk about "deep things." When the chaplain asks what she means by that, Franka answers that she wants to talk about herself and matters of life. Because it is difficult for Franka to articulate what she wants to talk about, the chaplain proposes working with a method called "My Way."[3]

"My Way" is a practical and creative way to interact on themes on the meaning of life. There is a case full of objects around the theme "inspiration"; pictures of plants that symbolize "my place under the sun"; photographs with images of "my way in life"; and a collection of cards with values. Topics like letting go, desires, and personal qualities are also included. Close attention is paid to the personal significance of the themes. "So actually, my way through life," Franka says. "Nice, then you know what you are talking about." Because of Franka's memory impairment, the chaplain offers to write down the key elements of what Franka tells about her life in a logbook. Franka agrees. In that way a document is made that can be reread and shared with others. Franka responds enthusiastically to the chaplain's proposal.

---

3. "My Way" was developed by the chaplain (the first author of the case study) for working with individuals or groups with diverse backgrounds and combines life stories with themes on the meaning of life. The materials described below are often combined with stories, songs, pieces of art, video films, *et cetera*.

Theoretical Framework

Inspired by the "Life Story Model of Identity" of the American psychologist Dan McAdams,[4] the chaplain sees "agency" and "communion" as important pointers for conversation. For McAdams both notions represent needs that have or have not been fulfilled and that subsequently become theme's in every life story. He understands agency as self-actualization and individuation, the human need to be who you are and to distinguish yourself from others. Communion is about connectedness with others, the desire for intimacy in the form of warm, firm, and loving relations. The quality of the relations is the central aspect. In a religious or spiritual sense, it can also refer to connectedness with what is transcendent. Both needs contribute to the degree in which people experience their life as meaningful. "The Life Story Model of Identity" offers no solutions but helps to clarify and understand what plays a role in the life of persons. Using the thematic approach "My Way" offers various reflections on how both needs play a role in Franka's life.

Subsequent Contacts

Franka is always eagerly waiting when the chaplain comes. If the chaplain is late, Franka asks a care provider to call to see if the chaplain is still coming. The chaplain feels very welcome. When she is let in to the resident setting by a care provider, she is usually told, "Franka will be happy that you are here." The chaplain comes every three weeks, at the end of a day, after daytime activities. The visits go on for a year. Franka makes frequent eye contact, is open, and talks easily and lively. The chaplain has to speak loudly, because of Franka's hearing impairment.

Talking about Life, Deep Things: The Need for Self-Actualization

In the conversations with the chaplain it becomes clear that Franka has a great desire to be by herself. She indicates that she wants to be left alone more, in peace and quiet. That comes up in relation to almost every theme that is addressed, for example, the theme "independence."

> *Franka*: "Independence is important to me. I don't want to always be dependent on others. I really want to lead my own life. I sort of keep to myself. I stay in my room a lot and do my own

---

4. McAdams, "Self and Story."

things. I like to be alone. I really would like to live somewhere alone, but I can't. I know that and that's really hard."

Then Franka chooses the quality "honest." She says that she is honest but that she sometimes puts on a mask. Wearing a cheerful mask, even when she is not cheerful, means that she cannot always be herself.

> *Franka:* "People want you to always be cheerful and fun. So I put on my mask and do as if I am cheerful. You can't show what you feel to just anyone. So I act like I am doing better than I feel."

For the theme "life path" Franka chooses a picture with a sign "Private Road" (Dutch: "Eigen Weg" = "Own Way"). She explains that her life will never be all her own because of her handicaps. She also chooses a path through woods that is so overgrown that the path is hardly visible.

> *Franka:* "If there's too much going on, I can't see the path anymore. Then I don't see where it leads. You have to do this and you have to do that."

The feeling that there are a lot of things she has to do, is also clear from her choice for the word "rest" on the theme "desire."

> *Franka:* "I would like to be left alone more, have more rest, and not be interrupted by others. I have the feeling that I am constantly being interrupted: four times a day for medicine, for meals, and when the carers just walk in. Especially on days when I am home. Then I want to do my own things, like watching TV or doing things on the computer, and I don't want to be interrupted."

On the theme "desire" she also chooses "freedom": "Freedom to be able to be who I am."

Talking about Life, Deep Things: The Need for Connectedness.

The need for communion also plays a major role. In order to feel connected to others, it is important for Franka to feel that she is being taken seriously. It is important that her family and the care providers at the residence and at daytime activities really listen to her. On the theme "inspiration" she chooses from the case with objects an empty picture frame that symbolizes someone who is a source of inspiration for her. That is her father.

> *Franka:* "My mother use to be first, but now it's my father. If you talk to someone, then you hope—how should I say that?—that the person understands you. My father just listens. He's patient."

Later Franka says that her mother, though she means well, often tries to soothe her right away by saying that things are going well and that where she lives is nice. Franka also tries to connect with the others in the residence where she is living. She invites other residents to her room and can have fun with them, but she misses a real companion. That is evident from the heart she also chooses from the inspiration case.

> *Franka:* "I would really like to have a good friend, someone to do fun things with, just a companion."

At one point, Franka points to a card with Mary and child in the case. She says that she has some faith but does not give it much attention. When the chaplain asks about that, Franka says that she experiences faith in her own way and that it is positive. But when she is depressed, she has less trust that there is a God. The chaplain explains that depression can be so pervasive that you can feel lonely and disconnected. That holds for faith as well. Franka recognizes that, and she hopes that life after death is better, because her life now is not always easy. But for the rest, Franka makes clear that she believes in her own manner.

Connectedness is something that Franka misses in her surroundings, but that she experiences in her play with dolls. She calls them "my children." On the theme "desire" she chooses "stillness."

> *Franka:* "The stillness is restful for me. I talk with my children, my dolls in the stillness. It has a lot to do with imagination. I'm very good at imagining things . . . It's an imaginary life next to my own real life. It makes my usual life more worthwhile. I need the imaginary world. Life is too barren for me without the imaginary world."

When Franka tells about her dolls, she indicates that it irritates her that she is interrupted so often when playing with them. The chaplain asks her if playing with the dolls helps her. Franka says it does. The chaplain senses that Franka looks a bit uncertain when talking about her dolls and asks if that is true. It is and Franka is relieved that the chaplain does not think that playing with dolls is silly. The chaplain then asks Franka more precisely, if in her playing with dolls, she is working through the things that she experiences or that come from the world around her. Franka affirms that. "Yes, I think that's true. I can deal with life better that way."

The chaplain's question is related to the thoughts of Donald Winnicott on "transitional space."[5] Winnicott uses the term for the space between what is going on in the inner world of the subject (in this case, Franka) and the outside world, the object-world (what she goes through). In the transitional space the subject uses imagination to develop a relationship to the object-world, experiment with and incorporate new behavior. According to Winnicott the process of becoming a self takes place in continual interaction between a subject and the object-world. An open and creative interaction between the two contributes positively to the experience of meaning.

For Franka her play creates the space to deal with what comes upon her from the world around her. That interpretation helps her to formulate what it is that she experiences in her playing with dolls and why it is so important to her to do that and not be interrupted. That diminishes the barrenness that she says she sometimes experiences in life. Her strong need for imaginary play leads the chaplain to tell Franka in simplified form something about the Danish philosopher Søren Kierkegaard. One of his pseudonyms was "Anti-Climacus."[6] According to Anti-Climacus a person can lose oneself in an endless, limitless imaginary world. One then flees from reality and becomes a fantasy of oneself. One then loses oneself and reality becomes more and more remote. Franka recognizes that immediately and understands why the chaplain is telling her about it.

> *Franka:* "Yes, that's true. I need to just keep doing things. Even if I don't feel like doing it, I need to go to daytime activities. I have to stay in the world."

According to Anti-Climacus people need imagination to envision new possibilities. People who do not use their fantasy or imagination, do not see their possibilities either. They do not try out new things or take risks. They say in advance: "Never mind." "There's no point." "I can't do it." It is the challenge for each person to try to find a balance, to remain firmly planted in reality, accepting what cannot be changed, while continuing to look for new possibilities. Franka thinks that Anti-Climacus put it well. She also thinks that she herself has found a good balance. Four days a week she goes to daytime activities. That provides her with structure and keeps her firmly planted. But when she is at home, she wants to be by herself and not be interrupted in her own world.

---

5. Winnicott, *Playing and Reality*; Ogden, "Reading Winnicott."
6. Kierkegaard and Hannay, *The Sickness unto Death*.

Résumé

Agency

As a consequence of the brain tumor as a child Franka was unable to finish school and live independently. That grieves her. Because people like her to be nice and cheerful, she regularly puts on a cheerful mask, even though she does not feel cheerful. But that gives her a feeling that she is not herself. There is no place for her real feelings. In every encounter with the chaplain Franka expresses that she needs more time at home for herself. Four days of daytime activities, all the meals with others, and interruptions by care providers who regularly come to her room do not leave her enough time to be alone. She needs time to play with her dolls without interruption, withdraw into her inner world and participate in another, imaginary world, so that she be more herself and find meaning and satisfaction in her life.

Communion

Franka gains more insight into her needs for connectedness with others. It means a lot to her when people take her seriously and really listen to her. It is clear that she misses a companion. She does feel connectedness in her play with dolls. It is a relief to hear that making use of fantasy and imagination can be positive ways of dealing with the things you experience. If, and that is where Anti-Climacus contributes, if you find a good balance and keep in contact with reality.

Communication and Feedback

Franka expresses that it has helped her to tell her story and work with the materials. "You discover things about yourself that you didn't know yet." At the end of the trajectory she lets her parents and some of the care providers read the logbook. Franka also tells the chaplain that she is going to join peer group sessions for persons with acquired brain damage. "Something has been started and I'm going to go on with it." Later Franka also reads the case study and says that it is "good." She is proud that her story can be part of research.

The parents and a sister of Franka read the logbook and respond positively. They have the feeling that they have gotten to know Franka better. The primary care providers have a similar experience. The psychiatric nurse practitioner, who referred Franka to the chaplain, responds to the logbook the chaplain sent to her. "So nice to read what the two of you worked on for a year. It's a wonderful and clear overview. I well recognize Franka in it." Later the nurse responds to the case study. "I think you have written a very clear report in which you have followed the chronology, so that it's nice to read. You show all the different facets of the patient without any judgement in any form. You have done so in a dignified and respectful manner. You are able to tell a moving story that, despite some hurt at the edges, shows the patient in her full glory."

SUMMARY

What Does the Chaplain Do?

The chaplain listens to the client's story and her feelings of grief and meaninglessness. The chaplain proposes using concrete materials (method "My Way") with themes on the meaning of life to explore two primary themes, agency and communion ("Life Story Model"). The chaplain documents what Franka says and discovers about herself in a logbook, so that Franka can reread what they have talked about and share it with others. The chaplain helps Franka understand the impact of depression on all aspects of her life, including faith. The chaplain helps Franka positively understand the significance and meaning of playing with dolls as an imaginary world in learning to deal with things in life (transitional space). At the same time, she helps Franka understand that a balance is needed between imagination and fantasy on the one hand and contact with reality on the other hand ("Anti-Climacus").

For What Reasons?

Franka indicates at the beginning that she wants to talk about "deep things," that is, about herself and matters of life. The chaplain realizes that it is very important for Franka to be seen and really listened to, but that it is not easy for Franka to articulate things (hence the concrete materials) or to remember things (hence the logbook). The chaplain takes the matters of agency and communion and their relation (and possible tension) as a framework for working with Franka. The chaplain notices that it is with reticence that Franka talks about playing with dolls and that a different understanding of what the imaginary world means can be of help to her.

With What Results?

Franka actively and eagerly participates in the search for her own path in life, "My Way." It strengthens her self-understanding and sense of self ("You discover things about yourself"). She is happy with the logbook and shares it later with others, who in turn understand her better. She learns to understand relations between her inner life and her outward life: cheerful mask and feelings of grief and loneliness, imaginary world and real world, being alone and being with others. She becomes more capable of dealing with both her limits and possibilities, in the present and with an eye to the future. She looks forward to continuing her journey in sessions with peers. Franka is happy to be a participant in research.

REFLECTIONS

The Dutch "eigen weg," which literally means "own way," does not translate easily into English. The equivalent on a posted sign is "private road." But both meanings play a role: the need to do things in her own way and the need to have more privacy so that she can do things in her own. The way is also a personal way, that is, her own personal ways of withdrawing into an imaginary world, of believing, and of seeking to maintain her own sense of dignity despite her dependence. And Frank Sinatra resonates in this, "I did it my way."

The *existential* dimension is present in the client's life story, including the consequences of the brain tumor, her grief, loneliness, and sense of meaninglessness. The consequences of the handicaps are more an (explicit) issue than the handicaps themselves. The search for meaning is structured by the chaplain in the use of themes, particularly agency and communion. The *spiritual* dimension is present in the longing for connectedness and the experience of the imaginary world. The chaplain is able to help the client positively value her imaginary world, and be aware of the balance between being alone and being with others and between imagination and reality. *Ethically* the chaplain contributes to the agency of the client who can express her need to be alone and at the same time understand the need for balance. *Aesthetically* the chaplain adjusts herself to the tempo and communicative capabilities of the client. The use of materials and the writing of a physical document caters to the issues of limits in expression and memory.

With structured attention to life story and to existential themes (meaning of life) the chaplain helps the client understand herself better and develop a more realistic and nuanced view of her needs for agency (time alone) and communion (companionship) and her behavior (imaginary world as transitional space). The exploration of themes from the meaning of life is combined with and motivated by psychological approaches and philosophical insights. That helps the client find words and images for the core experiences in her life,[7] which in turn increases her sense of self and agency. Although no direct relation to the earlier depression is made, the general outlook of the client seems to have significantly improved.

REFERENCES

Kierkegaard, Søren, and Alastair Hannay. *The Sickness unto Death: A Christian Psychological Exposition for Edification and Awakening by Anti-Climacus*. 1989. Reprint, London: Penguin, 2004.

McAdams, Dan. "Self and Story." In *Approaches to Understanding Lives*. Perspectives in Personality—A Research Annual Volume 3b, edited by Robert Hogan, et al., 133–59. London: Kingsley, 1991.

Muthert, Hanneke. *Ruimte voor verlies: geestelijke verzorging in de psychiatrie*. Tilburg: KSGV, 2012.

———. "Meaningful Mourning." In *Recovery: The Interface between Psychiatry and Spiritual Care*. edited by Erik Olsman, et al, 113–32. Utrecht: Eburon, 2023.

Ogden, Thomas H. "Reading Winnicott." *Psychoanalytic Quarterly* 70.2 (2001) 299–323.

Plaatsman, Irene, and Hanneke Muthert. "Levensverhalen zinvol verteld en opgetekend in de GGZ." *GGzet Wetenschappelijk* 24.2 (2020) 13–22.

Winnicott, Donald W. *Playing and Reality*. 1971. Reprint, London: Routledge, 2005.

---

7. Muthert, *Ruimte voor verlies*; Muthert, "Meaningful Mourning."

8

Reiteration of Ritual
Case Study from Eldercare for Dementia

—Joke Zuidema, Martin Walton, Jacques Körver[1]

SYNOPSIS

A woman, eighty-five years old and a widow, resides as a result of dementia on a psychogeriatric ward in a nursing facility. When told that her only daughter has passed away, she expresses severe grief and restlessness. The chaplain, new to the job, is asked to visit her. In the contact with the chaplain it is not the loss of her daughter but a trauma from her youth that comes to be the central concern. The chaplain performs a ritual with the woman to confront the trauma. The ritual helps but contrary to the original intention (of a rite of passage), the ritual needs to be repeated in order to reiterate the effect. While demonstrating a conscientious accompaniment process by the chaplain, the case also contributes to ritual theory.[2]

---

1. Co-researchers in the RC Eldercare: Karin Derks-Hanff, Brechtje Hallo-van Bekkum, Mualla Kaya, Eva Kersbergen-Kummerow, José Krijnen, Wendy Perez Herrera-van der Geugten, and Annemarie Roding-Schilt.

2. Zuidema, et al., "Wordt vervolgd."

BACKGROUND & SETTING

Setting and Occasion

Mrs. Bremer (pseudonym) lives on a locked psychogeriatric unit of a nursing home. During an introductory conversation with the chaplain, who has just started on the job, the ward manager draws attention to the situation of Mrs. Bremer. The daughter and only child of Mrs. Bremer has recently passed away. At first the family does not want to inform Mrs. Bremer, but on the insistence of the nursing staff the family agrees to letting one of the nurses inform her. When Mrs. Bremer is told, she expresses severe grief. The chaplain has no prior knowledge of or acquaintance with Mrs. Bremer.

Client

Mrs. Bremer is a widow, eighty-five years old. She comes from a family with five children in a village where she lived all of her life, before entering the nursing home in an adjacent village. She had one child, who recently passed away after a period of illness. Mrs. Bremer has Alzheimer, but she is not aware of that. On the ward she is a calm and satisfied woman who enjoys company. She is a practicing Roman Catholic, but lives in a region where faith is more a matter of doing (that is, ritual) than something to talk about. She shares with the chaplain a story she has not shared with other care providers. The presence of the chaplain evokes her telling and retelling the story time and again.

Chaplain

The chaplain is a woman, fifty-five years old. She is a Protestant, ecumenical in understanding, who studied theology later in life. She first served as a congregational minister in a predominantly Roman Catholic region. She also worked as a hospital chaplain, where she at times performed an anointing of the sick. She later served as a pastor for the elderly in a neighboring congregation. For the last five years she has been working as a chaplain in the care organization of which the nursing facility is a part. Most of the residents are Roman Catholic. One day a week she is present on the ward where Mrs. Bremer lives.

Others involved

The ward manager, a woman, who refers the chaplain to Mrs. Bremer, maintains contact regarding Mrs. Bremer with the care coordinator and the various care providers. The fourth time the ritual is performed, Mrs. Bremer's brother is present. Informed consent is provided by a granddaughter after reading the case study.

ACCOMPANIMENT PROCESS

Initial Contact. *Autumn*

A week after referral the chaplain enters the ward for the first time. In the sitting area she meets Mrs. Bremer who is sitting alone in the sitting area and glad to converse. She tells about growing up in a small village nearby, where her mother also had grown up. Her father came from a city and always looked down upon her mother. Her father spent most of the family money on drinking. He regularly battered her mother and the children. Her younger years were arduous, including trying to protect her younger brothers, a sister and one older brother. She sometimes attempted to protect her mother by moving in front of her, which only led to her getting hit as well. Mrs. Bremer tells her story extensively and eagerly. Periodically she interrupts herself, as if surprised, "That's a coincidence. I thought about that just yesterday."

Mrs. Bremer does not speak about her daughter. The chaplain chooses not to bring up the daughter, though that was the reason for referral. The chaplain responds (on the basis of validation theory[3]) to what is said and done in the moment. She observes that a different cause of grief plays a predominant role.

Subsequent Visits

Each time the chaplain comes, Mrs. Bremer tells and retells the same story about her father. Whenever she talks about him, she makes a fist and is clearly angry. From the moment she left home to work in a household elsewhere, her life became better. Her marriage was good. Her daughter and the death of her daughter are never mentioned, nor does she talk about it with the care providers.

---

3. Feil, "Validation: An Empathetic Approach."

The chaplain chooses to deal with the grief that Mrs. Bremer talks about. She suspects that traumatization plays a role. After five months the chaplain decides that something might be done in order to alleviate the trauma. From her knowledge of bereavement theory, she knows that rituals can help one to put things behind. She asks Mrs. Bremer if she thinks it would be a good idea to go together to the chapel, light some candles and try to alleviate the grief. Mrs. Bremer thinks it would be a good idea. The chaplain informs the care coordinator that the ritual will take place the next week, so that if necessary extra care can be provided.

Ritual. *Spring*

The chaplain chooses a ritual form in which written letters are burned. She knows that the use of basic elements (water, air, earth, and fire) in rituals can have a powerful effect. Early on the appointed day the chaplain comes to the sitting room, where Mrs. Bremer is always one of the first to be present. She is no longer aware of the appointment, but she willingly goes along. In the chapel the chaplain has set a low table with two chairs, a fire-resistant dish with a lid nearby, a number of small candles, a writing tablet and a pen.

Seated at the table, the chaplain explains why they are present. "You have told me a lot about your experiences as a young girl. Now we are here to put that behind you, to bring it before God, so that it is less of a burden for you." Mrs. Bremer nods and says, "My father, who . . . " while making a gesture of drinking. "And my mother got hit. And . . . " Mrs. Bremer tells again, what she has often told about her experiences as a child. The chaplain proposes that Mrs. Bremer light a candle for each of the persons involved. She agrees to that. First a candle for herself, then for her mother, her father, her older brother, and her younger brothers and sister. She calls them all by name.

The chaplain then helps Mrs. Bremer to write a little letter to each person. To her mother she writes: "You had a difficult life. You deserved better." Although the chaplain does the writing and has to assist Mrs. Bremer in finding suitable formulations, Mrs. Bremer is well able to indicate what her intention is. For her father she quickly formulates, "You are a scoundrel." For that she uses a derogatory word from her dialect and expresses great satisfaction in speaking the word out loud. She practically shines. Nothing more needs to be added to the letter. To her brothers and sister, she writes that she loves them and that life at home did not treat them well. The precise formulation of these letters seems less important, but it is clear that her brothers and sisters are important to her. A letter is written to each of them.

After writing all of the letters, the chaplain explains that they will burn the letters in order to release what has been written and place it before God. Mrs. Bremer agrees immediately and burns all of the letters herself, with conviction. She is clearly present and engaged in the performance. After the burning, the chaplain prays the Lord's Prayer and a Hail Mary. Mrs. Bremer joins into the prayer but displays no affect. The chaplain has brought a hymn in large type with her, "Abide with Me." Mrs. Bremer says she cannot sing, but appreciates it being sung for her. The chaplain sings two verses. Then she extinguishes the candles and they leave the chapel. Mrs. Bremer looks satisfied and restfully takes her seat in the sitting area. The chaplain informs the care providers that there has been an intensive moment for Mrs. Bremer, in order to alleviate a trauma from her younger years. She asks the care providers to be attentive to Mrs. Bremer, because it is not clear what might come of it.

Conversations after the Ritual.

In the period following the ritual the chaplain visits Mrs. Bremer weekly. There is a remarkable difference with the previous conversations. Mrs. Bremer no longer speaks about her father, nor about the situation in her childhood home. She only says that things are fine, tells about her knitting or about things around her. After a month and a half, the stories about her childhood begin to return, and after three months the stories are as frequent, extensive, and intensive as prior to the ritual. Because the ritual had seemed so "successful," the chaplain is at first disappointed. Eventually, however, she decides to repeat the ritual. Mrs. Bremer seems to recall the initial ritual and willingly responds to the proposal to go to the chapel again to light candles, write letters, and burn them.

Second Ritual Performance. *Early Summer*

The steps of the initial ritual are repeated. The chaplain goes with Mrs. Bremer to the chapel. They light candles for her, her father and mother and all her brothers and sisters. They write letters in more or less the same words. Mrs. Bremer tells a bit more than the previous time. She again burns the letters, one by one. They pray and sing the hymn as before. Mrs. Bremer indicates that she is very pleased. The chaplain returns with Mrs. Bremer to the ward and receives a kiss as farewell. Mrs. Bremer keeps the paper with the hymn with her. When a co-resident wants to read it, she responds angrily, "That's mine."

In the period following the second ritual talk about her father and her childhood is absent. Again, that lasts about a month and a half. When it returns, the chaplain suggests, sooner than on the previous occasion, to go to the chapel for the familiar ritual. Mrs. Bremer wants to do just that.

Third Ritual Performance. *Late Summer*

The third performance of the ritual takes place two months after the second. It is a repetition of the first and second rituals. Again, Mrs. Bremer expresses her satisfaction. From the point of view of ritual theory, the chaplain notes that the ritual that was initially intended as a rite of passage, now seems to function as a reiterative form of support.

The stories about her childhood are absent for a somewhat longer period, but after three months they return. Mrs. Bremer indicates herself that she would like to repeat the ritual, and the chaplain suggests including her older brother, Chris. Mrs. Bremer and her brother have gone through a lot together, and he regularly comes to visit her. Perhaps he can confirm what has happened in the past in a way that might offer more peace.

Fourth Ritual Performance. *Autumn*

During the fourth performance, Mrs. Bremer's brother is present. He has a lot to tell. That results in less attention to the ritual and less space for Mrs. Bremer to tell about things herself. The brother relates incidents of which she is no longer aware. She becomes silent, only confirming once and a while what her brother has to say. Conversation and ritual last two hours. Afterward, the chaplain asks the care providers to watch Mrs. Bremer, as the new information from her brother could cause unrest.

Following the fourth ritual, Mrs. Bremer talks now and then about her childhood memories. She remembers the conversation with her brother and the chaplain, but there is no indication that that conversation caused any intensified emotions. Mrs. Bremer seems restful and satisfied.

During renovation of the ward, Mrs. Bremer is moved with others to a temporary facility. That causes no noticeable distress. She seems to feel comfortable there. Her cognitive capacities, however, decrease. Aphasia develops. She has difficulty finding words for her thoughts. Once and a while she makes a fist while talking with the chaplain and says, "My father . . . " Sometimes she goes on, " . . . and my mother . . . and Chris . . . " The chaplain completes the row of names of her other brothers and her sister. Mrs. Bremer nods with satisfaction. She indicates that she wants to maintain contact.

One day when the chaplain comes, Mrs. Bremer is reading a magazine about royalty. She has difficulty expressing herself, but is finally able to do so. Remembrances of former queens are intertwined with her own memories. She shows no signs of sadness. Only two years after the fourth ritual is there again a sign of the pain from her childhood years. She says that she thinks about it a lot. It stays that way for a month. She goes with the chaplain to the chapel in the temporary quarters and lights a candle. Her gladness in doing so causes the chaplain to consider repeating the ritual.

Fifth Ritual Performance. *Winter, a Year Later*

The same ritual is performed, but this time in the office of the chaplain in the temporary nursing facility. The stories are different. What now bothers Mrs. Bremer is how people talked about her family when she was a child. The chaplain lets Mrs. Bremer find the words to express herself. "That's a child of . . . " she says, while making a drinking gesture. This concern is added to the letters that are written and burned.

During half a year the chaplain is on sick leave and does not see Mrs. Bremer. On the ward she still seems restful and satisfied. The entire ward moves back to the original facility, without noticeable problems for Mrs. Bremer. When the chaplain returns, Mrs. Bremer makes a good impression. She enjoys little things such as company with others and sitting in the sun. She now often sits with a doll on her lap, offering it care and attention, which seems to make her feel safe and satisfied. She indicates that she feels fine, once remarking, "No quarrels."

Two years later, worship services are held in the dining room of the nursing home, led once a month by the chaplain. Mrs. Bremer attends regularly, has a positive attitude, sings the hymns and pronounces the creeds and the prayers. A few months later the memories return. At times Mrs. Bremer sits with a wrinkled forehead. She can clearly indicate that she is thinking about her childhood years. Talking about it seems to relieve her. Because the chaplain is familiar with the situation, Mrs. Bremer needs only a few words to express herself. Understanding and sympathy are enough to provide comfort.

In Autumn, five years after the first contacts with Mrs. Bremer, the chaplain and a music therapist initiate a circle for residents on "Speaking Hands." The goal is to recall memories and draw strength from them. The central theme is all the things one's hands have done and brought about in life. Initially the chaplain does not invite Mrs. Bremer because of her difficulties in expressing herself. But the third time she is present and enjoys the interaction. She tries to sing everything, even the songs that are new for her. During a conversation on school, she tells about being allowed to go to school with her elder brother. When the chaplain nods in recognition, Mrs. Bremer nods back with satisfaction. Mrs. Bremer continues to visit the circle, assumes an active role and tries to find words to express herself. She is clearly glad to be present. At the end of the final session, she does not want to return to the ward and is angry when she is taken back, indicating how much she enjoyed the company, the music, the memories, and the atmosphere.

The most recent conversations that the chaplain has with Mrs. Bremer are very brief. When the chaplain asks how things are, Mrs. Bremer nods and laughs. "Fine." Sometimes she adds, "Very good."

Communication and Feedback

During the entire care process, up to the time of writing the case study, the contacts are recorded in the client records. Each conversation (longer than a greeting or remark), each performance of a ritual, each visit to the chapel services is reported. Orally the chaplain communicates with the care coordinator and the primary care provider about the plans and performances of the rituals. After each ritual the chaplain informs the care providers how the ritual has gone and what the consequences might be, especially after the fourth ritual. The chaplain consults Mrs. Bremer's brother and together they plan the brother's presence at one of the performances of the ritual, with the expectation that he could have a positive influence on Mrs. Bremer's dealing with her memories.

Mrs. Bremer is not capable of providing consent to share the case study. Permission is asked of the granddaughter as contact person. By email she replies that the description seems correct. She recognizes the stories about her grandfather (*great*-grandfather is probably meant), that she has often heard in her youth. It is striking to her that her grandmother does not talk about her deceased daughter, the mother of the granddaughter providing consent. She delivers written consent in person at the nursing home. The chaplain helps her understand the fact that Mrs. Bremer did not speak about her deceased daughter. Permission is also asked of Chris, because of his role at the fourth ritual. He indicates that he no longer has contact with his sister and does not want to concern himself with the matter. He entrusts consent to his niece who is the contact person.

The psychologist on the ward reads the case description and replies, "It is a nice report, in which Mrs. Bremer is described well, just like she is.

Perhaps I might add on the latter sections that Mrs. Bremer always takes her doll with her and cares well for it. That makes her feel more secure. I think that is something important for her." The primary care provider during most of the period described, reads the case and responds, "I thought it was quite recognizable. It was very important for Mrs. Bremer." Later she adds: "The case is well and clearly written. Mrs. Bremer did not talk much about her past on the ward, but it was really special that she could share her story with you. Afterwards she was always in a good mood. I am sure that this gave her a good feeling and that she again felt safe and secure on the ward. She expresses that with the doll. She never showed grief at the loss of her daughter and never spoke about it. I think it is really special that you performed the ritual in a beautiful manner with her."

SUMMARY

What Does the Chaplain Do?

The chaplain seeks contact with Mrs. Bremer upon referral regarding the loss of a daughter. When Mrs. Bremer only speaks about a major trauma from her childhood, the chaplain focuses on those stories. That leads to the design and performance of a ritual with writing and burning of letters, ritual prayers and a hymn. When the effects of the ritual, which was intended as a rite of passage, wane, the chaplain overcomes her disappointment and repeats the ritual with Mrs. Bremer, eventually another four times. The chaplain continues to regularly visit, observe, and converse with Mrs. Bremer, allowing her to share her daily experiences and feelings.

For What Reasons?

On the basis of validation theory, the chaplain chooses to focus on the stories of childhood trauma. When conversation does not sufficiently relieve the hurt and anger, the chaplain makes use of her knowledge of bereavement processes and the possible effects of ritual. When the effects of the ritual prove to be temporary, the chaplain, after initial disappointment, proposes repeating the ritual, shifting a rite of passage to a supportive reiterative process.

With What Results?

Mrs. Bremer takes an active part in the ritual. Each time the ritual is performed the intensity of anger and hurt subside, or are temporarily absent. Continued contacts and conversations provide Mrs. Bremer opportunity to express herself. She expresses explicit appreciation of the chaplain's visits and the rituals, including a kiss.

REFLECTIONS

The period of chaplaincy care covered more than five years and continued at the moment of writing. The most intensive accompaniment process was during the first year, during which the responses to the ritual was conspicuous. (The brother's presence during the fourth performance seems to have lessened the effect of the ritual.) The exact influence of dementia on the response of Mrs. Bremer to the ritual cannot be ascertained and needs further exploration in similar cases.

The original intention of the chaplain was to perform a rite of passage that might enable Mrs. Bremer to release the intense emotions associated with her childhood memories. The effect was manifest but temporary. However, the reiterative performance of the ritual had observable and repeated effects in easing the emotional burden of Mrs. Bremer's trauma and her preoccupation with it. Whitehouse differentiates various forms of (cognitive) transference of religiosity and corresponding one-time rituals (such as baptism) or repeated ritual forms (eucharist).[4] In the present case we see how what was initially a one-time ritual evolved into a repeated form. A characteristic of repeated rituals is that they step by step make an imprint on the life of a person, in contrast to one-time rituals (like initiation rituals) that have a strong emotional impact to last a lifetime. That suggests a complement or correction to the theory of Harvey Whitehouse, whereby the influence of dementia may have played a role.

It remains interesting that the chaplain was presented with and went on to address another issue in the life of the client than upon which the referral was based. That, however, is in keeping with the insight that a later event can reactivate a trauma, or bring it to consciousness again. The body remembers the trauma, or in the formulation by Bessel Van der Kolk, "The Body Keeps the Score."[5] Along with daring to talk about the trauma (saying "scoundrel" out loud), ritual can be an important way of dealing with

---

4. Whitehouse, *Modes of religiosity*.
5. Van der Kolk, *The Body Keeps the Score*.

trauma. The observation on the (Roman Catholic) religious background of the client where faith was more a matter of doing than something to talk about may further explain why the ritual was effective. The case study demonstrates how the chaplain was effectively able to address the systemic[6] and existential issues that plagued Mrs. Bremer by reiteration of a ritual, both tailored to the situation[7] and tied to the spiritual tradition of Mrs. Bremer.

REFERENCES

Feil, Naomi. "Validation: An Empathetic Approach to the Care of Dementia." *Clinical Gerontologist. The Journal of Aging and Mental Health* 8.3 (1989) 89–94.

Menken-Bekius, Corja. "Rituals in Individual Pastoral Care." In *Rituelen in het individuele pastoraat. Een praktisch theologisch onderzoek*. Kampen: Kok, 1998. Summary in English, 275–279.

Meulink-Korf, Hanneke, and Aat van Rhijn. *The Unexpected Third: Contextual Pastoral Care, Counselling and Ministry: An Introduction and Reflection*. Wellington: Christian Literature Fund, 2016.

Van der Kolk, Bessel A. *The Body Keeps the Score: Mind, Brain and Body in the Transformation of Trauma*. London: Penguin, 2015.

Whitehouse, Harvey. *Modes of Religiosity: A Cognitive Theory of Religious Transmission*. Walnut Creek: Alta Mira, 2004.

Zuidema, Joke, et al. "Wordt vervolgd. Een ritueel in de herhaling bij dementie." *Tijdschrift Geestelijke Verzorging* 22.95 (2019) 48–43.

---

6. Meulink-Korf en Rhijn, *The Unexpected Third*.
7. Menken-Bekius, "Rituals in individual pastoral care."

9

A Church for Charly
Case Study from Care for Persons with Intellectual and Developmental Disabilities

—Marieke Termeer, Martin Walton, Jacques Körver[1]

SYNOPSIS

THE MOTHER OF A sixty-five-year-old man, with autism and intellectual disabilities, had the wish for her son that he attend church. Because a church service confronts him with too many stimuli, once a month the chaplain offers him a ritual of "breaking and sharing" in his room, designed to meet the needs and fit the capacities of the client. The man has integrated the ritual into his expectations and experiential world as it offers him a sense of security and restfulness. On one occasion the ritual is recorded on video. The video-interaction-guidance practitioner observes how during the course of the ritual the man moves from a high level of tension to being relaxed.[2]

---

1. Co-researchers in the RC Mixed Fields: Hub van den Bosch, Joke de Koeijer, Tjeerd van der Meer, Maurice van der Put, Rob Vos, Frans van Oosten, José de Groot, Riekje van Osnabrugge, and Myriam Braakhuis.

2. Previously published in Dutch in Termeer, "De Plaatsbekleder" and Termeer, et al., "Kerk voor Cor."

BACKGROUND & SETTING

Setting and Occasion

Charly (pseudonym) resides in an institution for persons with intellectual and often multiple disabilities. He lives in a group setting with eight other residents and with care providers nearby. On the walls of his room there are pictures of family members. There is a large chest with a figure of Mary on top. His stereo is enclosed in a plexiglass cabinet, screwed tight. There is a table, a chair, a box with snips, a doll, and an adjacent bathroom. Once a month the chaplain comes for a ritual of "breaking and sharing." For the occasion there is a candle in a holder on the table.

Client

Charly is a man, sixty-five years old, Roman Catholic. He has severe intellectual disabilities and an autism spectrum syndrome. His level of social-emotional and cognitive development is that of a very young child. There is little emotional differentiation, mostly satisfaction and dissatisfaction. His body experience, adjusting to his surroundings and dealing with stimuli are his major level of functioning. How Charly experiences situations is not directly observable. There is sometimes eye contact, but it is unclear how much he sees.

Charly generally sits leaning to the right, with his faced turned left. He sways his head back and forth and waggles his legs when seeking to relate to his surroundings and find rest in what is unpredictable. In situations of tension he becomes compulsive, waving his hands and arms ("fluttering"). He can scream or become aggressive (hitting, kicking, or breaking things).

Chaplain

The chaplain is a woman, forty-four years old, with a Reformed Christian background, now Roman Catholic with an affinity for charismatic renewal. She has an academic education in chaplaincy studies and has followed multiple post-academic trainings in spiritual coping, rituals, and existential care. In her work she generally seeks a starting point in the personal interests of her clients, an approach that in the present case is hardly helpful.

Throughout the years the chaplain has learned to "read" Charly's behavior and see if he is comfortable. She is often able to calm Charly by making it clear that he need not be concerned. She at times offers her hand, but she lets Charly decide whether to make contact or not.

Others Involved

Ten years ago, Charly's mother initiated the process that led to the present ritual. She has since passed away. The resident care providers play a role in the background of the present case, providing support. The ritual performance that has been recorded on video is reviewed by a video-interaction-guidance (VIG)[3] practitioner with the chaplain. Much of the case report offered here reflects the perspective of the video recording.

ACCOMPANIMENT PROCESS

Initial Contact and Subsequent Developments

The ritual has been practiced regularly for a period of ten years. The original wish of Charly's mother was that he attend the church services at the institution. Because the services were too overwhelming for Charly, the alternative of a ritual in the office of the chaplain is initiated, to which Charly initially comes, accompanied by a care provider. Twice the chaplain's office is relocated, and both times Charly is agitated. When for a third time the chaplain's office is to be relocated, the decision is made to perform the ritual in Charly's own room. Charly often repeats that the chaplain has "Moved!" but has never visited the most recent office location.

It took some time to find the best form for the ritual. The initial request came in the first months that the chaplain came to work at the institution. Charly's mother indicated that once the eucharist had been celebrated in the church, Charly wanted to return home immediately. She felt that the moment of the eucharist was the core of Charly's religious experience. Rather than asking a priest from outside to come and share the elements, the mother requested a ritual in keeping with the church services in the institution.

The chaplain sought a form derived from the sharing of elements in the weekly service but adapted and simplified, somewhat by trial and error, to Charly's needs and capacities. The use of incense in the beginning, in the chaplain's office, was stopped, when Charly associated the burning with a fire. It became evident that the music must not last too long (maximum of three minutes). However, a piece of music has to be listened to to the very end. The music is played from the chaplain's smartphone, and when the chaplain once got a new phone, Charly was at first upset. Any distraction, any change causes restlessness.

---

3. Kennedy, *Video Interaction Guidance*. Maxwell and Rees, "Video Interaction Guidance."

Ritual Performance

On the day of the ritual described here, one thing is different. A camera has been placed in Charly's room. Video-registration is common in the institution, and Charly has been informed that the recording of the ritual is for only this one time. Charly and the chaplain enter the room together. Charly points to the camera and says, "Once?" The chaplain confirms that the camera is present this one time and says, "Nothing to be concerned about."

The chaplain moves the doll where she wants to sit to a chair near the camera. Charly says he needs to pee and goes into the bathroom without shutting the door. The chaplain closes the door behind him. The chaplain removes her coat, places the candle in the holder, and sets the pyx (container with hosts), the matches and the smartphone on the table.

When Charly returns, the chaplain says, "Shall we sit down?" Charly remains standing, comes close and grabs the chaplain's arm. He is tense and rather pushing. The chaplain again invites him to sit down, but Charly does not. He thinks the chaplain has come on the wrong day. The chaplain decides to go with Charly to the care providers to clarify the matter and then start over.

A few minutes later the chaplain and Charly enter the room again. This time Charly sits down and the ritual begins in the familiar form. The chaplain leads Charly through the ritual by saying, "First we light the candle. Look." She lights the candle and then holds the match for Charly to blow it out. Charly leans forward and blows the match out. He rocks back and forth in his chair.

The chaplain takes a singing bowl and a striker and hands the striker to Charly. Charly takes the striker and misses the first time. The chaplain says, "The last time you did it well. Try again." Charly tries again and strikes the bowl. The chaplain offers a compliment and waits for the singing to stop. "We wish each other the peace of Jesus." The chaplain and Charly shake hands. "Now we can pray and break and share together." Charly lays his hand in the chaplain's hand, who then prays, "Good Father God…" Charly says, "Everything?" The chaplain is unsure what Charly means and decides to continue, "Good Father God…" Charly: "Music?" Chaplain: "In a bit. First, we pray. Good Father God, …" Charly now begins to waggle his legs back and forth and to sway his head from left to right and slumps down a bit. That is usually a sign that things are alright.

The chaplain goes on with the prayer. "You are present for everyone on earth. You gave us warmth and love from people around us. They have taught us to love life and to love each other, each day, as Jesus showed us. In his name we have come together. We think of him with timeless words." The chaplain releases Charly's hand, takes the pyx, opens it and continues, "All who break this bread and share with one another, follow the way of Jesus, who broke and shared his life with others. Good Father God, let us share love for one another."

Charly sits up straight, takes hold of the armrest of the chair and then lays his hand on the arm of the chaplain. She responds by laying her hand on Charly's hand and praying the Lord's Prayer. Charly sways with his head and then joins the praying, as best he can, from the line, "Give us this day our daily bread." Then they pray the 'Hail Mary' in the wording of Charly. "Hail Mary, full of grace. The Lord with you. Blessed among women, fruit of your womb. Holy Mary, Mother of God, sinners, in the hour our death. Amen."

Charly breaths out slowly, several times. Since the movement with the hand to the mouth with a small piece of matzo is motorically difficult for Charly, the chaplain lays a piece of matzo on his tongue. She also takes a piece and they eat in silence. Then the chaplain takes her smartphone and turns on the music. They listen to 'Ubi Caritas'. Charly sways with the music and sits even straighter. When the music is done, Charly releases a long guttural sound.

The chaplain says, "Now we ask Good Father God for a blessing. Good Father God, thank you that we could be here together and break and share. We ask you to bless all people who are important to us, our family, the people with whom we live and the people who care for us, everyone dear to us. Good Father God, bless us on our way, today and every day."

Again, the chaplain takes the singing bowl and the striker. Charly misses three times before striking the bowl. When the singing stops, the chaplain asks Charly if he wants to blow out the candle. They stand and blow together. The chaplain asks if it was all right and says that she is going to pack things together. Charly watches and then says, "Filmed, off!" The chaplain responds, "Yes, I have to ask how to turn it off. Come with me." She offers Charly an arm and together they leave the room. As they exit Charly removes the pictogram with a church (symbol for chaplaincy services) from its hanging place next to the door and places it in a basket. Later a colleague from the residence turns off the camera, after which the chaplain gathers her belongings.

OBSERVATIONS VIDEO-INTERACTION GUIDANCE PRACTITIONER

With the agreement of family and care providers the chaplain asks a video-interaction practitioner to view the recording with her. The practitioner provides a micro-analysis of Charly's bearing and behavior in relation to the accompaniment by the chaplain. The practitioner sees that Charly is tense when he enters the room. He seeks contact but does not seem to really look with any focus. Then he goes into the bathroom. For some persons with autism that is a manner to seek a moment of quiet and reduce tension. Charly would not do so consciously, but that could be the effect. When Charly returns with a question which the chaplain does not understand, there is again tension. The chaplain maintains eye contact. The practitioner offers the tip to repeat what has been heard. That can be helpful.

Charly takes hold of the chaplains' arm and begins to flutter. When the chaplain indicates that there is no need for concern, Charly seems to be assured and stops immediately. The tension is less, but the question is still not answered. An intervention follows in which the chaplain offers Charly an arm in order to go to the care providers and solve the question. After that, the ritual begins. Charly follows the lead of the chaplain, but because he sways his head, he cannot always see her.

After the greeting of peace, there is eye contact. That seems to reassure Charly. He is being seen. Whether he sees the chaplain well, remains a question but the atmosphere changes. A recovery phase begins. That means for Charly finding rest amidst the threat of the surroundings. He seems to feel more secure. He places both feet on the ground and, although rocking back and forth, makes more eye contact. During the prayer Charly asks a question and lays his hand on the arm of the chaplain to gain her attention. The chaplain lays her hand on that of Charly and answers. Charly sits up straighter. There is focus.

During the Hail Mary it looks like Charly is letting off more steam by breathing out slowly. Then is it quiet and all of his sounds are absent. During the song Charly starts rocking again. The chaplain offers her hand, but it is not taken. Charly takes hold of the chair, sits up even straighter, and releases a guttural sound. According to the VIG-practitioner that is another way of relaxing.

The coach observes that within half an hour Charly moves from a high level of tension to practically being relaxed. That is the effect of the ritual with a clear pattern for Charly and the serenity of the chaplain who takes the lead and tunes into the client. The only commentary by the practitioner is for the chaplain to repeat a question from Charly so that Charly knows he has been heard. The observations of the VIG-practitioner coincide with the feedback through time from the primary care providers that the ritual seems to have a calming effect on Charly.

SUMMARY

What Does the Chaplain Do?

The chaplain performs a ritual with a clear pattern that has been attuned to the needs and capacities of the client and that reflects the religious tradition and wish of the client and his family. The chaplain adapts the location, ritual performance, and wordings as necessary to assure maximum calmness for the client. The chaplain provides the client clarity on each step taken in the ritual and responds to his behavior, which she has over a long period learned to read. The chaplain makes use of the support of the primary care providers. The chaplain has a video recording of the ritual made, asks and receives feedback from a VIG-practitioner.

For What Reasons?

The original reason to provide a ritual was the request by the client's mother to include Charly in church gatherings. The chaplain continues to offer the ritual also because of its calming effect on Charly and Charly's own expectations. From the prayers the chaplain formulates can be deduced that the performance of the ritual is also a manner to express inclusion of Charly in the religious and care communities to which he is proximate. The chaplain seeks feedback from another professional on her performance of the ritual and her accompaniment of the client.

With What Results?

The client experiences performatively a bond with the religious community and tradition of his upbringing. Charly actively participates in the greeting of peace and the formal prayers (Lord's Prayer and Hail Mary). On a behavioral level the client transitions from a high level of tension to almost relaxed. The calming effect has a duration beyond the limits of the ritual performance. The VIG-practitioner confirms the effects of the ritual and offers the chaplain a tip for communication with the client.

REFLECTIONS

The original "indication" for the performance of the ritual with Charly was a religious wish of the family. The religious aspect is actively confirmed by

Charly's participation in the ritual and expectation of its monthly performance. A secondary "indication" has arisen in the meantime in the calming effect of the ritual for Charly. The ritual offers him a (basic) sense of security, in a situation in which experiential and behavioral aspects as well as existential and spiritual dimensions can hardly be differentiated.

In this situation the chaplain and the performance of the ritual have (vicariously) become the church for Charly. That is strengthened by the long-standing contact and the constancy of the form of the ritual. There is no way of knowing whether another ritual (or another activity) could have the same effect. The performed ritual reflects, as confirmed by his mother, the core of Charly's religious experience. The familiarity of it and the constancy of the performance has a calming effect.

Can we say more about the nature of the ritual (and sacramental) effect? Does it, for example, meet the expectations of a "heterotopia" as a symbolic breech with recognizable elements from the life world of the person in question?[4] We do recognize aspects of contingency in the performance and effects of the ritual, in an experience that could have been otherwise, that is possible but not necessary.[5] Something *happens* in the experience of Charly during the performance of the ritual that can be fostered but not manipulated. It cannot be cognitively confirmed, but it is sensory and observable. The ritual elicits an observable effect that can be compared with the effects of rituals on others.[6]

We understand ritual to have both a symbolic and performative effect[7] of an aesthetic and spiritual character. Aesthetics is not understood here in the cognitive sense of Immanuel Kant as the (subjective) ability to discern and judge beauty[8], but in the (etymological) sense of sensory affect.[9] Hans Alma understands transcendence consequently in aesthetic terms as an intensification of experience that turns us to an "other" who elicits something in us. That perspective makes it possible to understand the experience of Charly, which is to a great degree of a somatic, sensory nature, in an aesthetic, ethical, and spiritual manner. His body indicates that the ritual experience is good for his well-being and that he can find rest in a greater whole.

---

4. Chauvet, *Symbol and Sacrament*.
5. Scherer-Rath, "Contingente en religieus-existentiële zorg."
6. Walton, "Blest Practices."
7. Quartier, "Symbolische en performatieve dimensies."
8. Kant et al., *Critique of the Power of Judgment*.
9. Alma, "Art and Religion as Invitation."

REFERENCES

Alma, Hans. "Art and Religion as Invitation. An Exploration Based on John Dewey's Theory of Experience and Imagination." *Perichoresis* 18.3 (2020) 33–45.

Chauvet, Louis-Marie. *Symbol and Sacrament: A Sacramental Reinterpretation of Christian Existence*. Collegeville: Liturgical Press, 1995.

Kant, Immanuel, et al. *Critique of the Power of Judgment*. Cambridge Edition of the Works of Immanuel Kant. Cambridge: Cambridge University Press, 2009.

Kennedy, Hilary, ed. *Video Interaction Guidance: A Relationship-Based Intervention to Promote Attunement, Empathy and Wellbeing*. London: Kingsley, 2011.

Maxwell, Nina, and Alyson Rees. "Video Interaction Guidance: A Return to Traditional Values and Relationship-Based Practice?" *The British Journal of Social Work* 49.6 (2019) 1415–33.

Quartier, Thomas. "Symbolische en performatieve dimensies van sacramentaliteit." *Tijdschrift voor Geestelijk Leven* 66 (2010) 59–70.

Scherer-Rath, Michel. "Contingente en religieus-existentiële zorg." *Tijdschrift Geestelijke Verzorging* 10.42 (2007) 28–36.

Termeer, Marieke. "De plaatsbekleder." In *De rituele competentie van geestelijk verzorgers*, edited by Jacques Körver, et al., 52–58. Utrecht: Eburon, 2021.

———, et al. "Kerk voor Cor. Anders kijken met video-interactie-begeleiding." *Tijdschrift Geestelijke Verzorging*, 24.103 (2021) 54–59.

Walton, Martin. "Blest Practices." Groningen: Protestant Theological University, 2019, https://martinwalton.nl/node/4. (Although the title is in English, the (farewell) lecture was in Dutch.)

10

Wounded Warrior
Case Study from Mental Health Care

—Guus van Loenen, Jacques Körver,
Martin Walton, Reijer de Vries[1]

SYNOPSIS

The case study traces care provided by a chaplain in a mental health institution to a former military sharpshooter. The veteran was in care at a specialized unit for military veterans with traumas, and he wants the chaplain to perform a ritual "to set things right with God." The case study traces the care provided in conversations, in the reading of Psalms, and in the development and performance of a ritual.[2]

BACKGROUND & SETTING

Setting and Occasion

Hans (name used with permission) is in treatment at a mental health care institution on a unit specialized in the treatment of war veterans with traumas and post-traumatic stress disorders. The night nurse sends an email to

---

1. The case study was written as a pilot application of the format of the Case Studies Project. It was not reviewed in a research community (RC) like the other case studies of the project but with three academic chairpersons of the RCs, who are co-authors.

2. Previously published as Van Loenen et al., "Case Study of 'Moral Injury.'"

the chaplain with a request to seek contact with the client, with no explanation why contact is desired. In the past, the chaplain has had sporadic contact with other clients and the staff of the ward and referral by an individual nurse is not unusual. The conversations with the chaplain take place in the single room where the client stays during admission. The chaplain had no previous knowledge of the client. Upon meeting him, the chaplain recognizes him from worship services in the hospital chapel that the client has visited. At no point does the chaplain have access to the client's dossier.

Client

Hans is a man in his early forties. He is divorced, the father of two children of elementary school age, who once a month spend a weekend with him. He has spent some time in detention before being transferred to the care unit for veterans. Recently he has obtained his own apartment, where he lives alone. His military training led him to become a sharpshooter. When his military service ended he worked for a while in construction and still has contact with his former employer. He may be able to return to that workplace. Hans was raised Roman Catholic, but until recently has not practiced his faith.

Chaplain

The chaplain is a man, sixty-one years old, with Roman Catholic academic theological training. For thirty-two years he has worked in mental health care, presently in a team with two other chaplains. Through the years, he has taken training in pastoral psychology, psychodynamic counseling, ethics, interculturalization, and supervision. In his work he focuses on questions of meaning with a special interest in the relationship between psychiatry and mysticism.[3]

Others Involved

At beginning and end of the care process the chaplain has contact with the psychiatrist. The first time the chaplain asks the psychiatrist whether a ritual is compatible with the treatment plan and if the psychiatrist has advice or concerns with which the chaplain can reckon. The second contact is at the

---

3. Van Loenen, *Voor de geest staan*.

ritual itself. Later the chaplain seeks contact with the psychiatrist to evaluate the case.

ACCOMPANIMENT PROCESS

Initial Contact

Upon receiving the nurse's email, the chaplain visits Hans in his room on the treatment unit. The chaplain is overwhelmed by the walls of Hans's room, filled with pictures of weapons and military scenes. The client himself is also overwhelming. As soon as the chaplain sits down, Hans tells of his service in a UN mission. As a sharpshooter, he killed thirty-seven people. Those thirty-seven people pursue him in his dreams. Fortunately, he recently received a new medicine that reduces the nightmares. In creative therapy he made thirty-seven figurines that he then buried. That ritual relieved him. Yet there is still something gnawing at him. He wants to set things right with God. He asks if the chaplain has a ritual for that. He hopes that it can be done on short term, because his planned date of discharge from the hospital is nearing.

Observations

In the perception of the chaplain, Hans treats his own question in the manner of a sharpshooter, taking aim at his goal. Detours seem unwanted. The chaplain prefers some detours and does not want to be pressured. In order to respond to Hans's request for help, the chaplain needs to know more about Hans's background: his (religious) development, his present situation, his family system, and his plans for the future. He lets Hans know that.

The confrontation with Hans disturbs the chaplain, who feels somewhat at a loss. The chaplain wonders what value a religious ritual would add to the ritual that Hans has already performed in creative therapy. Hans is unable to clearly formulate what the difference would be, but it is clear as daylight to him that there is a real difference. The chaplain then lets Hans know that he, the chaplain, needs to do some thinking and asks permission to consult Hans's psychiatrist. And the chaplain will need the opportunity to get to know Hans better so that he can offer Hans a ritual that fits the situation. Hans agrees.

Clarification

In the second contact Hans shows the chaplain an article with a term for his problem, "moral injury."[4] His war experiences have not only psychologically traumatized him, but they have also injured him morally. That is especially the case with regard to his actions as a sharpshooter. He is now thoroughly convinced that killing is not good. He can no longer even kill a fly. The psychiatrist confirms the moral dimension in the distress of the client and welcomes the attempt to relieve that distress by means of a ritual.

The term "moral injury" is helpful for the chaplain. The term helps him to start developing an appropriate religious ritual, distinct from what took place in creative therapy. His hypothesis is that the first ritual aided change in the realm of behavior and abilities, so that Hans is now less governed by his trauma, can relax more, and sleep better. The new medicine significantly strengthens the effect of that change. The request of a religious ritual is directed at healing of the wound that has been struck in the realm of identity and spirituality.[5] Hans wants to be able to love himself again and feel worthy of love from others. The religious ritual should address that need.

Conversations

Over a six-week period the chaplain and Hans have four extensive conversations. Hans tells that he was brought up as a traditional Catholic, but that faith did not play a major role during his youth. That changed through his war experiences. And during a period of detention, contacts with a (Protestant) chaplain deepened his religious interest. He now walks into the village church every day, preferably when no one else is present, and sits there quietly. That helps him feel better. Recently he has started reading the Bible daily. He asks the chaplain to suggest a text to him. The chaplain suggests Psalm 51, explaining that it is from the perspective of a person in a similar situation, someone who wants to come to terms with the death that is weighing upon his conscience. Even before the chaplain has departed, Hans has already looked up the text.

In the *second conversation*, when Hans introduces the term moral injury, the chaplain invites Hans to tell about the moral wound from his time of military duty. Hans begins with the story of the first time that he shot someone. He remembers as if it was yesterday how upset he was when he

---

4. Drescher et al., "An Exploration of the Viability"; Molendijk, et al., "Conflicting Notions on Violence."

5. Bateson, *Steps to an Ecology of Mind*. See the Reflections below.

returned to the base, and how his colleagues had laughed away his difficulties. Under peer pressure he gradually became more indifferent to shooting people. In addition, he felt lonely when deciding to shoot or not. The instructions were clear, but at the moment itself it was he and he alone who had to judge the situation. In retrospect, he doubts whether he always acted correctly, thinking he was sometimes wrong in shooting. He says that he is now bewildered at the fact that he did all those things, that he lost himself so completely.

Then he turns to Psalm 51. He is not sure what to think of it. The text seems heavy. The chaplain takes a piece of paper and sketches the various layers in the psalm: longing for purification (51:3–4); significance of one's misconduct (51:5–6); realization that evil is unfathomably woven into existence (51:7–8); but also the realization that there is a path that leads to healing (51:9–11); that from that process a magnanimous spirit can come forth enabling one to learn from the experience (51:12–15); on the condition that the speechless silence is lifted (51:16–17); and that recovery begins with the recognition of what has been destroyed (51:18–19). Immediately Hans asks if he can keep the paper. The explanation seems to help him recognize himself in the text. He also asks for another text for a more positive feeling. The chaplain suggests Psalm 139.

In a *third conversation,* the chaplain asks about the period after military service. Hans tells how his war experiences have been a burden with a detrimental effect on his life. When he returns to the circle of his family and friends, he is unable to relate to the issues that played a role there. Nor does he succeed in telling his family and friends about his experiences, in entrusting to them the horror of the memories that have become too powerful for him. In an attempt to escape, he starts drinking. The burden on his marriage becomes greater. The powerlessness on both sides becomes too much. His wife encourages him to leave his past behind him. He does not want to cause her sorrow by letting her know how much his past burdens him. The quarrels about his drinking become more severe. Finally, they divorce with a fight over the children.

For Hans, the different worlds get mixed up. He threatens with violence if he is not allowed to see his children. Because of his expertise with weapons, the threat is taken seriously. When an escalation occurs, he is arrested. Besides losing his children, he also loses his job. When Hans tells about all of that, he comments that in contact with the chaplain he experiences a lot of trust and connectedness and is able to get closer to his feelings.

In the *fourth conversation* Hans immediately expresses his dissatisfaction with his present situation. In the weekends he is at home, that he has furnished just like he wants it. During weekdays, he is required to be on the ward, which weighs heavy on him. Increasingly he has difficulty with all the rules on the ward and demands of the caregivers, such as the obligation to keep in contact with the probation officer after dismissal. The previous day it got to be too much, and he had an outburst against his personal mentor. All charged up he now claims that his treatment is done and that there is nothing more for him to do on the ward. He wants to leave.

The chaplain suggests taking a closer look at Hans's anger. Hans answers that his apartment is Psalm 139 and that the ward is Psalm 51. When the chaplain asks what that means, Hans replies that he has always thought that he deserved punishment for what he had done. He relates the ward to that conviction. He identifies the conditions on the ward with punishment. Psalm 139 enables him to see himself differently. It gives him the conviction that he deserves understanding and comfort for wat he has gone through. The symbol of that is his new apartment. The chaplain suggests the possibility of connecting the two. He points to the growth that Hans has gone through, the fruits of which he is now plucking. But he also points to the difficulties that Hans has had to overcome and that can still hinder him. He asks if Hans might be able to see the mentoring from the ward and later from the probation officer as a form of support, as an indication that people are looking after him and not abandoning him to his fate. The set of requirements can also be seen as the offer of a safety net upon which he can rely in difficult moments.

To the surprise of the chaplain, Hans immediately accepts that perspective. His face loses the dogged expression. He smiles. He says that he is going to set things right with his personal mentor the same day. At the end of the conversation a date is set for the ritual. Hans want to invite his psychiatrist to be present. Before the chaplain leaves, Hans sends a text message to the psychiatrist.

Ritual

Hans wants a ritual to set things right with God. Hans agrees to entrust the experiences that burden him and for which he seeks forgiveness to paper. For the rest, Hans does not want to know too much about what is going to happen. He expresses his trust in the chaplain and the wish to surrender himself to the ritual. His date of discharge from the ward will be the day after that of the ritual. It could not be better, as far as he is concerned.

The ritual takes place in the chapel of the psychiatric hospital with Hans, the psychiatrist and the chaplain present. Upon entering the chapel Hans walks directly to the altar. He asks if the ritual can take place there.

Three chairs are placed in a circle. The chaplain welcomes each person present and says something about the chapel. The size of the chapel makes using it no longer efficient, but the space does induce a powerful, inward influence on those present. The spaciousness of the chapel can help to experience an inner space when feeling oppressed. The chaplain also mentions the visits of Hans to the village church.

Then the chaplain explains that there are different layers in every person: a practical, a relational, an emotional, and a spiritual layer. In what Hans has gone through, all those layers have suffered harm. He then speaks directly to Hans. "In the past period you have worked hard to recover. And you have succeeded. The day of your discharge has come. But you also want to recover on a spiritual level. You want to set things right with God. You see yourself as morally wounded. You could consider this ritual to be a treatment of your moral wound. Just as in the treatment of a physical wound, three steps will be taken: cleansing the wound, binding the wound, and letting the wound heal."

The chaplain invites Hans to take the *first step*: letting the wound be seen so that it can be cleansed. He asks Hans to read the letter he has prepared with words for what burdens him morally. When Hans has done so, the chaplain asks him to set the letter away from him by laying it on the ground. Then the chaplain reads Psalm 51, emphasizing the desire to be cleansed. "Wash me and I shall be whiter than snow." (51:7) Then he explains that he is going to bless Hans with water. As the chaplain turns to get the holy water, Hans kneels down of his own accord. Spontaneously Hans utters a prayer, repeating what the letter said, but with more emotion in his voice. The chaplain blesses him and formulates a wish reflecting what Hans has prayed.

The chaplain introduces the *second step* on the binding of wounds. If a wound is clean, it is bandaged to prevent something from getting in to it and causing an infection. That also prevents one from scratching it open. As a treatment of a moral wound the ritual also includes that. The chaplain gives Hans a white cloth and asks him to lay it down on the ground on top of the letter. Then the chaplain reads Psalm 32:1–5 and says something about the interaction in the text between exposing and covering. If a person no longer hides his moral shortcoming, the Eternal will cover that shortcoming. Covering is not the same as neglecting, nor is it pretending that nothing has happened. Covering is letting the pain rest when all has been said. The aim of forgiveness is to put things to rest. Referring again to the imagery of treatment of a wound, the chaplain says that ultimately a phase commences in which we can do nothing more. The wound needs time to heal.

The chaplain explains the *third step*. It is about trusting one's inner, healing power and about creating space so that that power can do its work of healing. He reads the first part of Psalm 139. Hans utters, "I read that every day." The chaplain emphasizes the passage on light (139:11–12) and says, "There is light that penetrates even the deepest darkness. For that light, the divine light, there is no night. A spark of that light lives in every human being. Let your wound be healed by that light from inside. Let that light expel all that is dark for you." He then lights a candle and gives it to Hans. There is a period of silence. Then the chaplain asks Hans to set the candle on the cloth that lies over the letter. He offers Hans a choice. After the ritual he can take either the letter or the candle with him. Resolutely Hans chooses the candle. The chaplain offers the suggestion of lighting the candle at home at moments when life is not light for him. Finally, Hans, the psychiatrist, and the chaplain form a circle and give each other a hand. The chaplain proposes to Hans that he see this circle as a symbol of his return to the human community. He pronounces a blessing that Hans feel welcome and that the period of isolation has ended for him. By way of goodbye, Hans thanks the chaplain with a hug and says, "I never do this."

Results

During the chaplaincy care process, various changes in Hans become visible. He comes closer to his feelings, experiences more connectedness and trust, finds in the Psalms words to clarify and reinterpret his own situation, and is able in moments of anger to open himself to other interpretations. Gradually Hans removes the pictures of weapons and military scenes from the walls of his room, loosening himself from the images of his traumatic history. During a visit at Hans's home two months later, Hans explains to the chaplain that the most important change for him was effected by the ritual at the end of the chaplaincy care. Since then he no longer feels burdened by his conscience. He says, "I could go to the church on my own however many times, but I would sit there and cry. That helped me feel better, but I wasn't getting anywhere. It was only through the ritual that I got out of it and found rest." When the chaplain asks Hans to tell some more about the rest he has found, he says, "Through you I have gotten the idea that God understands what was going on in me as a soldier. I have done things which I should not have done and that I will never do again, but I believe that God understands why I did it. And the blessing with water took away the persistent hammering memory of it."

Communication and Feedback

During the accompaniment process, the chaplain discusses the care for Hans and his ideas for the ritual in the chaplaincy team and receives advice and support from his colleagues. He later shares the case study with them.

The chaplain consults the psychiatrist at the onset of the care trajectory. The psychiatrist is also present at the performance of the ritual and later reads the case study. The psychiatrist recognizes how meaning, moral recovery, and spirituality play an important role in the case. He expresses his intention to pay more attention to those aspects in contacts with other clients in the future and to refer to the chaplain more often. His perspective on his own role is surprising. He suggests that it was not so much as a psychiatrist that Hans invited him to be present at the ritual, but as a buddy or as a partner in fate. As a military doctor, he had also been on missions to war zones where he had suffered traumatic experiences. Hans knew that and it aroused a trust that he did not have in other caregivers.

A few weeks after discharge the chaplain receives an email from Hans in which he tells that things are well with him. The candle stands on the table, but has not been burned yet. During a concluding visit two months later, Hans points to the candle that has a prominent place in the apartment. He says emphatically, "That's never going away." He tells that he recently lighted the candle for the first time. He had broken his wrist. For the pain he had received extra medication from the doctor. That evening a friend called him. Because of his slow speech, the friend thought that Hans had been drinking again. The friend warned the police who came the same evening to his door. That had made Hans angry and anxious. For a moment he had thought, "Is the trouble starting all over again?" In that moment, he lit the candle. That kept him from doing anything impulsive.

SUMMARY

What Does the Chaplain Do?

The chaplain receives a referral and makes an appointment. In response to the initial encounter he allows himself to take time and consult others. He then invites the client to tell his story and welcomes the self-diagnosis ("moral injury") of the client. In response the chaplain offers source texts (Psalms) and (didactic) explanation for reflection, offers feedback and reframing on convictions of the client. The chaplain then designs and performs a ritual for the sake of healing the moral woundedness. He blesses the client and offers him the candle from the ritual as a reminder and continuing source of light. He provides follow up in a visit two months after the concluding ritual.

For What Reasons?

The chaplain recognizes his own sense of disturbance, feeling overwhelmed by the client and his question and feeling initially at a loss, but also realizing that he needs to get to know the client better to adequately address the request for a ritual. His Catholic background enables him to respond to Hans's religious practices by introducing the Psalms and developing a ritual in three steps. The chaplain becomes aware that there is a spiritual and moral dimension (a sense of identity and dignity) to what Hans needs that has not been addressed in treatment or in the ritual he performed in therapy.

With What Results?

Hans makes a transition from being overwhelmed by the remembrances of what he has done and what he has gone through, to being able to put them at a distance, as evidenced in the gradual removal of pictures of weapons and war scenes from the walls of his room. Alongside the conviction that he has committed wrong, he comes to think that he deserves understanding and comfort for what he has gone through. After the ritual the client no longer feels burdened by his conscience. The persistent hammering memory of his military past has been relieved (particularly by the blessing). He feels like God understands what he has gone through, so that he experiences a sense of reconciliation with God. The client makes use of the candle at moments of difficulty which helps him handle his (aggressive) impulses. The client is able (even before the ritual) to develop new behavior towards others, such as his mentor. At the end of the ritual the client hugs the chaplain. A "side effect" of the chaplaincy care is the intention expressed by the psychiatrist to pay more attention to issues of meaning, spirituality, and moral recovery.

REFLECTIONS

Care is provided step by step in four manners: conversational listening to storytelling, feedback and reframing (including didactive moments), use of source texts, and performance of a ritual. The "detour" the chaplain initially takes is also significant, but less clear is why the chaplain chose particular steps and texts, whatever their effectiveness. Although other forms of care (treatment) likely also contributed to the effects the client identifies, it seems clear that the whole of chaplaincy care fostered changes in the client's behavior and offered an anchor for future times. In the review of the case study, it became evident that the chaplain had wanted primarily to contribute to the client's (spiritual) healing in an encompassing sense, whereas the client's explicit question was focused on "settings things right with God" (reconciliation and later also forgiveness). In retrospect it seems that both goals were achieved, as the client got closer to his feelings, and recovered a sense of relationship with himself, others, and God.

The chaplain was aided in recognizing the spiritual dimension of the client's situation by a model of six logical levels of change of Bateson, including, convictions, identity, and spirituality, which had not yet adequately been addressed by treatment or a therapeutic ritual.[6] In retrospect the chaplain recognized the theoretical basis of the ritual he developed for the client: cleaning, binding, and healing.[7]

Existentially the trauma of the client was the issue that had to be addressed, but particularly in its *moral* (guilt and relations to others) and *spiritual* (relation to God and self) dimensions. The *aesthetic* dimension played a role in the initial care process (removal of posters), the performance of the ritual itself, and in the subsequent struggles of the client (candle). From an aesthetic viewpoint the juxtaposition of the two Psalms (51 and 139) by the client in relation to ward and apartment is noteworthy. The chaplain is able to help the client to bring them closer together so that the client is able to take a more nuanced moral and relational position.

The term moral injury plays a catalyzing role that is multi layered, both active and passive. Hans experiences guilt from his actions and decisions as a sharpshooter, but also feels that he himself was wronged by peer pressure and by the task he was given to perform. He seems, in other words, to feel dehumanized, in that both what he inflicted on others and what he himself underwent violated his own moral integrity. Through the conversations and the ritual Hans is enabled to reframe his experiences and reunderstand his

---

6. Bateson, *Steps to an Ecology of Mind*. Bateson distinguishes six levels with six corresponding questions: 1. Environment: Where am I? What is going on? 2. Behavior: What am I doing? 3. Capability and skills: Wat am I capable of? 4. Beliefs and Values: Why am I doing? What is important to me? 5. Identity: Who am I? and 6. Spirituality: With what do I feel connected? The model shows how a process of change effects each of the levels. Change at a lower level can lead to change at a higher level and changes at a higher level effect change at lower levels.

7. Van der Hart, *Rituals in Psychotherapy*.

narrative identity.[8] All of these aspects are addressed in the ritual, in which the aspect of woundedness in the term moral injury becomes an effective metaphor for the sake of moral and spiritual healing.

REFERENCES

Aviv, Rachel. *Strangers to Ourselves: Unsettled Minds and the Stories That Make Us*. New York: Farrar, Straus & Giroux, 2022.

Bateson, Gregory. *Steps to an Ecology of Mind*. Chicago: University of Chicago Press, 2000.

Drescher, Kent D., et al. "An Exploration of the Viability and Usefulness of the Construct of Moral Injury in War Veterans." *Traumatology* 17.1 (2011) 8–13.

McAdams, Dan P. "'First We Invented Stories, Then They Changed Us': The Evolution of Narrative Identity." *Evolutionary Studies in Imaginative Culture* 3.1 (2019) 1–18.

Molendijk, Tine, et al. "Conflicting Notions on Violence and PTSD in the Military: Institutional and Personal Narratives of Combat-Related Illness." *Culture, Medicine, and Psychiatry* 40.3 (2016) 338–60.

Van der Hart, Onno. *Rituals in Psychotherapy: Transition and Continuity*. New York: Irvington, 1983.

Van Loenen, Guus. *Voor de geest staan: zorg voor zingeving als taak van de geestelijke gezondheidszorg*. Tilburg: KSGV, 2005.

Van Loenen, Guus, et al. "Case Study of 'Moral Injury': Format Dutch Case Studies Project." *Health and Social Care Chaplaincy* 5.2 (2018) 281–96.

8. McAdams, "'First We Invented Stories'"; Aviv, *Strangers to Ourselves*.

11

To Honor and Confirm
Case Study from a Military Ritual

—Helga Knegt, Carmen Schuhmann,
  Theo Pleizier, Martin Walton, Jacques Körver[1]

SYNOPSIS

A RITUAL CALLED FLORAL salute is performed for a young man in the military who died in an accident during training. The ritual is a military tribute at the grave of the deceased and is combined with a visit to the family. The impact of the situation is complicated by a recently concluded investigation into the accident in which issues of guilt played a large role. The case shows how the performance of ritual is part of the chaplain's work and how the chaplain provides "baseline care" for all those involved.

BACKGROUND & SETTING

Setting and Occasion

A year after Luuk (pseudonym) died in an accident during military training for special forces, a floral salute has been planned. The floral salute is performed at the grave of the deceased, with a military tap, a minute of

---

1. Co-researchers in the RC Military: Harry Bols, Jan-Derk de Bruin, Stefan Dijkhuizen, Gert Jan Jorissen, Frank Kamp, Wouter-Johan Sintmaartensdijk, Ramaya Soe Agnie, Martijn Zwiers.

silence, and an honorary salute. A wreath is laid at the grave and a brief oration is held. Not only the special forces unit, but also the previous armored company of Luuk, with which he served on a foreign combat mission, are present, as is also the family. In the background, issues deriving from an investigation into the accident play a role, as does the presence of colleagues who are on suspension for a suspected substance offense. The case study focuses on the day of the floral salute that begins on a military base, continues with a drive across the country to Luuk's family home and the cemetery where he is buried, and concludes with a drive back to the base.

Persons Involved

There are many persons directly or indirectly involved or affected, including family, friends, and military personnel from various units. In the first place, *Luuk*, in his mid-twenties when he died, engaged to be married, still living at home at the time in a conservative Reformed, pious family. Previously he served with an armored company on a foreign combat mission. Afterwards he moved to a special forces unit (SFU) for which he was in training at the time of the accident.

The *family* consists of a father and mother in their early fifties, active in a conservative Reformed church. There are two brothers and two sisters of Luuk, all older, and their partners, with two children in the next generation. There is also Luuk's fiancé, in training as a nurse. Also present are any number of people from the village and church of Luuk's family.

From the *military* both the special forces unit and Luuk's previous company are represented. From the special forces unit, there is a senior officer who is responsible for the ceremony, the commander, a trumpet player, and another eight or so military. From the armored company, there is the sergeant major (CSM), a man in his forties with extensive experience. He has no specific religious affiliation, but is well disposed to chaplaincy and attentive to the needs of others. There is a lieutenant who roomed with Luuk on the foreign mission, in his early thirties. There are comrades from the company who have come from different parts of the country, in pairs or alone. They are part of an armored company of about one hundred soldiers, mostly in their twenties, for whom this ceremony is their first floral salute. About twenty men from the company travel to the salute. There is a driver and a driver's mate, both in their twenties. In addition, there are two servicemen in civilian dress who have been suspended during an investigation on trade in forbidden substances.

Chaplain

The chaplain is a woman, forty-two years old, with ministerial training in the Reformed tradition. She has worked as a minister and chaplain for fifteen years, with eleven years of experience in a psychogeriatric nursing home and three years in the military. She is a mother of three daughters. It is her first full day at work after a longer period of illness. She is the chaplain of the company with which Luuk was on a foreign mission. The chaplain has been in contact with a colleague, a Humanist chaplain, man, fifty-two years old. He went on the foreign mission with the unit, was present at the funeral, and a half year later performed a ritual when a memorial stone was placed.

ACCOMPANIMENT PROCESS

Previous Contacts and Context

It is October and a year has passed since the accident in which Luuk died. The funeral was led by a minister of the church of the family (not present at the floral salute). At that moment, the chaplain (who serves the company with which Luuk served on a foreign mission) was on leave and was represented by her Humanist colleague. It was the chaplain of the special forces unit, who at the time of the funeral had contact with the family.

The chaplain has good contacts with the company. The CSM keeps her informed about developments. He has acquired the name of "mother of the company." The chaplain has worked with the CSM in several formation training weeks, in which they have gotten to know several of the soldiers and their stories.

In May a memorial stone was placed on the military base. There was a brief ceremony with family and the unit of Luuk. The Humanist colleague who had accompanied the foreign mission spoke on the occasion. The colleague later shared the order for the ceremony and his address with the chaplain and conferred with her on the floral salute.

At the grave of Luuk near his place of birth, a brief ceremony has been planned a year after his death in the form of a floral salute, organized by the special forces unit. It is that unit's responsibility inasmuch as it was Luuk's last placement. The father of Luuk has requested that he be the only one to speak at the occasion.

A couple of weeks before the date the chaplain contacts the CSM of the armored company. He was the one who arranged things for the company at the time of the funeral (condolences, a place of commemoration with a photograph of Luuk, bus transportation to the funeral, *et cetera*). Initial contact is by email, as the CSM is temporarily on reconnaissance out of the country. The CSM appreciates that the chaplain offers to go with them to the floral salute. Since it will be a long drive cross country to the floral salute, the chaplain accepts the offer of the CSM to ride in the bus with them. In the coming weeks they regularly have contact by phone and then eventually meet to discuss matters. The CSM suspects that the family will appreciate it if the chaplain speaks a word at the ceremony. The chaplain writes up a brief reflection with some references to texts from the death announcement and the funeral service, but, as it turns out, the reflections are not spoken. With the company the chaplain has had several moments of contact. Especially during exercises, the chaplain was present and talked, at times extensively, with various persons.

The Day of the Floral Salute.

The chaplain arrives at 5.30 a.m. at the base and puts on her uniform. She chooses the variant with a skirt, in keeping with the dress custom for women in the conservative Reformed church to which Luuk's family belongs. At 6.15 a.m. she goes to the office of the CSM. The CSM has made coffee. There is some general talk with those arriving, packing their backpacks, visiting the toilets, and preparing for departure. Then there are technical problems with the bus, so that departure is delayed for forty-five minutes.

Outside the base two other servicemen in civilian dress are picked up. They have been suspended in relation to a military police investigation into trade with forbidden substances. A total of eight persons from the unit were arrested. The chaplain knows their names but has not been able to have contact with any of them. Nor has she had an opportunity to talk confidentially with the CSM about the situation. The two others ride in a different vehicle behind the bus. Because there is a delay, there is no time to stop and greet them. One of the men, whom the chaplain knows well, waves emphatically to her as the bus passes their car.

As highest-ranking military, the CSM sits at the front of the bus. The chaplain sits in the back with others. The radio is turned on, and most of the passengers close their eyes. Until about eight o'clock little is said. The chaplain seeks to tune in to the situation. A news item on the radio regarding measures to alleviate climate change is met with skepticism by the soldier next to her, but the chaplain lets it pass. It is too early for discussion. The music is turned up higher. "Good song." Gradually small talk develops.

Backpacks are opened for sandwiches and drinks. The chaplain gets several looks since she has no backpack, a silent sign that others notice that she might not have anything with her. She takes a health bar from her purse, and the looks turn away.

There is another news item about people who do not dare to go to the toilet at work for a bowel movement. That leads to hilarious reactions. "Imagine being on exercise for a long time together. That wouldn't work." Stories about portable toilets on exercise are exchanged, including the toilet that fell over in a curve and emptied out next to the base camp. The chaplain begins to feel like part of the group. A half hour later the driver stops at a roadside park. The chaplain remarks as a hint, "The toilets are closed." The others respond, "Oh, we don't need one." She does, however, but lets it pass, so as not to emphasize her difference as a woman.

The bus waits for the other car in order to arrive at the same time at the house of Luuk's family. The bus for the SFU joins them as well. An officer of the SFU informs the chaplain that the family does not want anyone but the father to speak at the ceremony. "Don't take it personally. The people are a bit stiff. A woman minister won't fit in." Back in the bus, the CSM says, "They would really be quite open to you. They're fine people. But their experience with your colleague was not a good one."

The bus parks at the house of Luuk's parents, a freestanding house outside the village. At the same time Luuk's fiancé arrives. There are greetings with hugs and kisses between her and Luuk's mates. On the way to the house the chaplain introduces herself as the minister of the unit. The family awaits the group inside. There is a warm welcome with coffee and cake. The sixty persons present are spread out through the living room, kitchen, pantry, and garden, with the smokers outside. All of Luuk's brothers and sisters are present, with Luuk's parents and the parents of his fiancé. When the chaplain introduces herself to Luuk's mother, the mother sighs, "You look so nice. So different from your colleague from the SFU who came in his jeans and old sweater. Do you have children?" When the chaplain answers that she has three daughters, Luuk's mother starts talking about Luuk, his brothers and sisters.

A short time later all leave to go to the cemetery. The chaplain attempts to step into the bus elegantly, but her skirt is a bit tight. Three newcomers who came with their own cars laugh at that. "My compliments for your attempt to step in elegantly," says a lieutenant who roomed with Luuk and whom the chaplain knows. It is a last laugh and relaxed moment, before the solemnity of the cemetery.

On the parking lot of the cemetery a briefing on the ceremony is given. The SFU will stand on one side of the grave, the company unit on the other, and the family in between facing the gravestone. In silence they take their places. The master of ceremonies of the SFU opens the ceremony and states the purpose. Those of the military give an honorary salute and stand for one minute in silence until the trumpeter plays taps. The father of Luuk speaks briefly. He talks about the grief, the pride he feels, and Luuk's faith, with a tear in his voice. He thanks all those who are present. (The chaplain notices that many others, persons from the village and the church as she learns later, have joined the ceremony.) One for one all of the military again give an honorary salute at the grave. The gravestone has an engraved photograph of Luuk on it, from a photograph on the fireplace mantle in the house. Many of the men struggle to hold in their tears. The chaplain waits until her turn at the end of the line, before joining the others at the bus.

At the bus the group waits for the family. Everyone is quiet. Luuk's mother goes directly to the lieutenant and says, "That was beautiful." "Yes," he replies but is unable to say anything more. The mother sees that and turns to the chaplain, looking for words. The chaplain comments, "What a beautiful grave stone, with Luuk's photo on it." "Yes, do you think so?" his mother replies. "I was uncertain about it. . . . The stone was only placed a couple of days ago." She tells how difficult it was to find something for her own son, for whom one does not want to have to look for such a thing. The men around the mother and the chaplain respond by nodding their heads and confirming that they think the likeness of Luuk on the gravestone is good. "I'm so glad," the mother says, "that you came all the way across the country to be here. You are Luuk's real mates. He felt at home with you. . . . I guess you'll come with us now for some soup."

In the bus on the way back to the family's home, there are comments like, "Last year the weather was different. Really cold." Soup is waiting in the house. Everyone is served a bowl of soup and a thick slice of bread.

The chaplain finds a seat near Luuk's father, who is sitting apart from the rest, and says to him "It was good what you said." "Yeah, it was hard, but I had to say something." A conversation follows about bereavement, about how partners grieve differently and at different paces, about family and communities who offer support and how lonely one can feel in sorrow. Part of the differences between the parents in responding to the loss of Luuk had to do with the nature of the accident and the subsequent investigation. It does the father well that the chaplain can follow and speak his language of faith. Father and chaplain touch base in a form of piety that many Reformed traditions share. The chaplain tells something about moments of reflection that the chaplain holds during exercises or on a mission. The father recognizes in that something that was important for Luuk. "It was not important for him to go to church, but his faith always went with him. God can be found everywhere. And he could open the Bible anywhere, if he felt the need." Between the lines the father expresses a great appreciation for what the chaplain stands for: the presence or representation of everything that has to do with faith in the world of the armed forces, and therefore, for his son. When a grandchild asks Luuk's father to come look at what he has made for Luuk, the (grand)father gets up and follows his grandson.

The chaplain makes eye contact with Luuk's fiancé, moves to sit next to her and asks how she is doing. She talks about her schooling, internship, and work. After she has spoken extensively about that, the chaplain states that it must be hard work. The fiancé answers, "Yeah, but at least I have control of it. At the least I can work hard at it. Other things just happen to you." She then tells how if things had gone different, she and Luuk would now be married. She tells about the plans they had.

Then the chaplain rolls into another conversation with one of Luuk's sisters. She tells about Luuk's passion for military service, his big dream of joining special forces, of never giving up. Even as a little boy he never wanted to give up and that became fatal for him. She relates several details of the accident. She sees how her father and mother respond differently to the situation, different also from her response. She talks about how empty it is, about missing her brother and expecting him at the back door any moment. When they take leave of each other, the fiancé wishes the chaplain success with "her men" and gives her a wink.

The chaplain sees the colleagues from special forces on the other side and goes over to them. Several short conversations follow, mostly about the ceremony, before the CSM gives a sign that it is time to leave. The chaplain shakes hands with all of the family members and thanks them for their hospitality. Several thank the chaplain emphatically for her presence. The men of the unit are waved out just as warmly.

There are some things to arrange about work and leave before getting back on the bus. In the meantime, the chaplain stands between the two men in civilian dress, the suspended servicemen, who are smoking. She asks the man who waved in the morning how he is doing. He immediately starts to explain that it is all a misunderstanding and that he expects to be back in the barracks next week. The chaplain attempts to carefully say that investigations sometimes last a long time and that he might prepare himself for that. She also asks if he has a lawyer, and if she might be of help. He holds that off. The other man is conspicuously silent during the conversation. The chaplain assures the first man that the chaplain is the only person in the military who is obligated to keep things confidential and who provides a sanctuary in such situations. That leads to eye contact with the other man. In the meantime, things are settled and everyone gets on the bus.

Right away the stories about Luuk begin. Like how he had landed on the other side of the country in the unit and felt at home. The fact he once drove home from an exercise for a party and returned in time for roll call the next morning seems even more poignant as the bus ride takes them on the same journey. The stories continue and the fact that a good dude has passed makes the emotions audible. The stories about keeping watch in the hospital after the accident are shared with detail and emotion, especially the feelings of powerlessness while keeping watch.

Later conversation turns to a future training for explosive ordnance disposal (EOD). The major question is if you can keep your head cool in the protective clothing at the moment you have something to deal with. More than thirty percent of the trainees fail because of that. There is a vulnerable and unnerving question to ask of yourself before starting the training. How well do you know yourself? The chaplain talks with several others about it in the back of the bus.

The conversation falls silent and is then resumed with a more or less ritual complaint about the military and problems with trainings, career mobility, and personal development. Having to wait a long time for a training with nothing really meaningful to do in the meantime is really frustrating. And the training often has worthless components as well. During the last part of the trip things get quiet, apart from a few random remarks. Smartphones are regularly consulted.

The end of the trip is a bit messy. The driver stops to fill the tank. The chaplain gets a call. When the chaplain gets off the bus and heads towards her office, several of the men wave to her. In the looks on their faces she reads appreciation for her presence on this day. Exhausted from a very intensive day, the chaplain walks to her office and changes again into her jeans.

Communication and Feedback

The chaplain shares her experiences with the Humanist chaplain who had been involved earlier. She later encounters casual remarks in the company. A week later she runs into the CSM who says that it was a good day. There is no contact with the colleague from special forces.

SUMMARY

What Does the Chaplain Do?

In a complex situation, the chaplain seeks to tune into the situation: prior consultation with CSM and Humanist colleague, choice of clothing, faith language of family, interaction with servicemen and introductions to family members. Her abilities to observe and respond, and make eye contact, constantly play a role. She engages in conversation about whatever issues present themselves: bereavement and faith with the father, children and the gravestone with the mother, bearing through things and the future with the fiancé, the person Luuk was and the emptiness in his absence with a sister, seeking (confidential) help with the suspended servicemen, and emotions regarding Luuk and knowledge of oneself with the soldiers on the bus. She serves as a go between, making connection with the other unit and with the suspended servicemen, and offering a response to the mother when the commander is at a loss for words. She keeps the speech that she has prepared in her pocket.

For What Reasons?

The chaplain is aware of her sensitive and unique position, not wanting to press matters but responding to openings with the family and the soldiers, aware of but also making use of her gender (especially with Luuk's mother, sister, and fiancé), and using her affinity with the faith of the family (conversation with father). She employs her power of observation and situational awareness, with a good antenna for what is going on. She offers what may be called "baseline care," a gentle but active presence, responding to what comes up, knowing that she in her function represents a dimension of faith and existential issues and that she can open up conversations on those matters. Not explicit, but of influence in her perceptions are insights from Contextual (systemic) Pastoral Care with regard to intergenerational issues and multi-partisanship.[2] In that way she seeks to confirm each person in one's position and perspective and so bring honor not only to the deceased but also to all those present.

With What Results?

Appreciation is expressed by both family and members of the military that the chaplain was present, in words, handshakes, and in the waving of hands. An opportunity has been given to family members to express things, that is well received, in which the fact that the chaplain is a woman at times plays a facilitating role. There is a remark in which the presence, dress, and

2. 'Multi-partisanship' is a term from system therapy, familiar to the chaplain through Contextual Pastoral Care (See Meulink-Korf and Van Rhijn, *The Unexpected Third*), and refers to the ability of the pastor to appreciate and work with the perspectives of various persons in the system at the same time without identifying with one of them.

demeanor of the chaplain is appreciated, in contrast with that of a colleague a year previous. There is the negotiation of the situation when another is at a loss for words. There is the connection that occurs as a result of serving as a go between.

REFLECTIONS

In the complex situation of the floral salute, issues of death, guilt, connectedness, past and future, faith and self-understanding, gender, and military context play a role. The whole pallet of spiritual, existential, ethical, and aesthetic dimensions is at play, but in a differentiated manner: whereas at one moment *spiritual* issues (faith and piety) are spoken of, more *existential* matters (bereavement, motherhood, the future, self-understanding) are addressed at another moment. The *ethical* plays an influential but more implicit role (investigation of the accident, suspension on substance abuse, the hospitality of the family) as does the *aesthetic* (clothing, inside/outside the base, cemetery, military context).

In that complexity the chaplain is recognized and accepted in her position, traditional and archetypal, of the one who presents or represents matters of existence and faith.[3] The chaplain responds from different positions such as general chaplain and Reformed pastor, woman and mother, and fulfills different roles: go between, companion, counselor, and advisor. In the conscientious and careful manner in which the chaplain chooses her positions, makes her moves, and communicates with the various parties she is an effective liaison. For the RC her contribution in this case is illustrative of what arises out of baseline care (presence) that chaplains in the military offer. The term "baseline care" is taken from an analysis by Theo Pleizier and Carmen Schuhmann of thirteen cases in the RC Military.

> In structuring pastoral availability, chaplains demonstrate conscious presence. The choice to be here at this moment with these soldiers. This kind of presence consists of a delicate balance between passive receptivity, a nonjudgmental attitude of being open for contact, and active awareness by noticing changes in group dynamics, in nonverbal behavior or extraordinary circumstances. The attitude of "active awareness" belongs to baseline care in the Dutch military (Dutch: "nuldelijnszorg"). Baseline care is of a preventive nature and is distinguished from "primary care." Pastoral availability is thus structured as preventive spiritual care.[4]

3. Dittes, *Pastoral Counseling*, 53–59.
4. Pleizier and Schuhmann, "How the Military Context Shapes Spiritual Care," 9.

For the present case one might add that the care is unassuming and light footed, responsive and to the point.

REFERENCES

Dittes, James E. *Pastoral Counseling: The Basics*. Louisville: Westminster John Knox, 1999.

Meulink-Korf, Hanneke, and Aat Van Rhijn. *The Unexpected Third: Contextual Pastoral Care, Counselling and Ministry: An Introduction and Reflection*. Wellington: Christian Literature Fund, 2016.

Pleizier, Theo, and Carmen Schuhmann. "How the Military Context Shapes Spiritual Care Interventions by Military Chaplains." *Journal of Pastoral Care & Counseling* 76.1 (2022) 4–14.

12

From Slumped to Upright
Case Study from a Psychiatric Penitentiary Center

—Bart van den Bosse, Reijer de Vries,
Jacques Körver, Martin Walton[1]

SYNOPSIS

A MAN IN HIS fifties is in treatment in a psychiatric penitentiary center. He does not cooperate with therapy. He is referred to the Buddhist chaplain for mindfulness training in relation to depression. He is unkempt, insecure, slouched down and makes little eye contact. The chaplain listens to the man's story and teaches him a mindfulness training (body scan) to help him relate to his issues. Results are slow in coming, but the man continues practice of the body scan and regular contacts with the chaplain. In the first year, hardly any results are visible. In a second phase the man is open to addressing his issues explicitly and responds to the encouragement of the chaplain to participate in therapy. In a third phase in which therapy and chaplaincy care complement each other, the man walks upright, demonstrates responsibility and initiative in his behavior, and develops a sense of worthiness.

---

1. Co-researchers in the RC Prison: Ron Colin, Jacqueline van Heel, Aryeh Leib Heintz, Martin van Hemert, Soerish Jaggan, Geerhard Kloppenburg, Jan Kraaijeveld, and Marja Went.

BACKGROUND AND SETTING

Setting and Occasion

Simon (pseudonym) is presently serving a sentence of two years, plus forensic commitment to treatment, in a psychiatric penitentiary center on a ward with twelve others. His diagnosis, previously borderline personality disorder, is now anxiety disorder and chronic Post Traumatic Stress Disorder (PTSD) and mentally unsound. He has a history of psychosis. At the time of contact with the chaplain he is severely depressed with signs of self-injury. He refuses treatment. A treatment coordinator asks the chaplain to contact Simon with the thought that mindfulness training might aid Simon in dealing with his depression.

Client

Simon is a Dutch man in his fifties. He has been convicted of attempted murder of his partner. He is appealing the sentence. With his partner he has a ten-year-old daughter and from a previous relation a twenty-year-old son. His daughter has perhaps been abused by his son, her half-brother. Until the age of thirty-two Simon did administrative work, then became a heating and electrical repairman. In the last six years he has been on disability pay due to somatic and mental issues. His Catholic upbringing plays no significant role in the present.

The chaplain learns from Simon that his upbringing was strict. His parents were very judgmental and always saw him as the guilty one, even for the behavior of his older sister. As a child he was violently sexually abused by older children in his neighborhood. He seems of average intelligence. He is a music fan and once played bass guitar in a band. He rides a motorcycle, accompanied with long hair, a beard and tattoos. He considers himself a friendly person who helps others. In his relationships he has been dependent and self-effacing.

Chaplain

The chaplain is a Dutch man, forty-two years old, working as a Buddhist chaplain with a degree in religious studies. He originally worked in the Zen tradition, has since followed training in mindfulness of the Western-Theravada tradition (MBSR)[2] and in acceptance and commitment therapy

---

2. Mindfulness and mindfulness training is embedded in the Buddhist tradition

(ACT).³ He has experience in working with persons with intellectual disabilities and as a teacher.

Others Involved

During the first months of contact with Simon, the chaplain regularly lets the coordinator know by mail, with Simon's permission, how Simon seems to be doing. Informally there are contacts with psychologists (assertivity training) and physical therapists (running therapy).

ACCOMPANIMENT PROCESS

Initial Contact

The chaplain goes to Simon in his cell and finds him lying on his bed. The chaplain introduces himself and his reason for coming. Simon says he has heard positive things about the Buddhist chaplain from other patients. Simon agrees to walk with the chaplain to the chapel to talk there and become acquainted. The chapel serves as a common room for the chaplaincy service where one can speak openly and quietly. The chaplain asks how Simon is doing and what he would like to talk about. Simon tells about his situation, the negative thoughts that overcome him, and his fear of the future, since he can no longer return home. He distrusts the prison workers. After Simon has told about his situation, the chaplain lets Simon become acquainted with mindfulness by offering a body scan to reduce stress and fretting, by means of a friendly exploration of physical sensations (MBSR).⁴ The chaplain explains how mindfulness works and together they reflect on Simon's experience with the body scan.

---

and was secularized and popularized by Jon Kabat-Zinn in 1979 as a eight week program (MBSR), initially for patients with chronic pain. The function of mindfulness is to help shift from automatic reactivity to responsiveness, and from avoidance patterns to a genuine willingness to meet present-moment experience as it is. See Feldman and Kuyken, *Mindfulness*.

3. Acceptance and Commitment Therapy (ACT) is a contextual-behavioral approach to psychotherapy and other behavioral health concerns that has progressively attracted attention from both researchers and clinicians. See Assaz et al., "Cognitive Defusion in Acceptance."

4. Cultivating mindfulness of the body is the basis for much of the experiential learning in mindfulness practice. That can be challenging because we have a paradoxical relationship to the body where we are prone to both overly identify with it and dissociate from it. Both patterns hold within them both potential for causing distress and potential for learning. See Feldman and Kuyken, *Mindfulness*.

Observations

Simon has difficulty telling a coherent story. However, he makes a willing impression on the chaplain, though very uncertain, anxious, depressive, somewhat confused, and unkempt. He moves slowly and has difficulty with eye contact, mostly looking down. He appears desperate and disoriented, but gentle, and open to having contact, in fact very much wanting to receive help.

Plan

The chaplain gives Simon a CD with the body scan and a book with more information on mindfulness training.[5] They agree to meet weekly. On Thursday mornings at 9 a.m. the chaplain goes to the cell, where Simon is usually found lying on his bed, often sleeping. They then walk to the chapel, drink something, talk for about twenty minutes, and spend half an hour doing a body scan. What follows can best be described in three phases: *1. Slumped* during which no improvement with regard to Simon's complaints is observed; *2. Half upright* in which a change begins to develop; and *3. Upright* when a significant reduction of symptoms becomes evident, as well as general improvement in Simon's situation.

Phase 1. Slumped

The first year of contacts produces no visible results with regard to Simon's symptoms. What does develop is a healthy relation with the chaplain, in which Simon opens up, tells a lot about himself, and learns to feel secure with the chaplain. Simon contrasts that with his resistance to therapy. The asylum function of chaplaincy is recognized and used by Simon in this respect. What Simon tells are often the same stories about misuse, about missing his children, and about problematic relations with his parents and his (ex)partners. He also talks about the evening of his criminal offence and his desperation about his situation, though he does not seem to have concrete suicidal plans.

A result that the chaplain does see, though it is not recognized by Simon, is the fact that Simon continues to do the body scan daily in his cell. Even though Simon seemingly does not experience any change for the better, the intention to continue the training remains. Simon speaks proudly

---

5. Maex, *Mindfulness*.

of it, "I do it every day," and seems to derive some structure and support from continuing the practice. That in turn seems to allow Simon to attain some inner distance from his general situation. Briefly the chaplain tries out another mindfulness practice with Simon, breath-sitting meditation, but Simon's fretting then increases to a degree that the chaplain reverts to the body scan.[6] There are also some contacts in which Simon and the chaplain only converse. Special attention is paid to the negative thoughts that repeatedly overcome Simon and to the patience and trust that are needed to deal with them. Though Simon's situation hardly changes, the chaplain sees no reason for extra concern, nor to stop with the mindfulness training, inasmuch as mindfulness does not aim at providing a "quick fix" but at engendering a transformation in how one relates to oneself, others, or matters of concern. The transformation cannot be forced but can only ripen by practice.

At one point the chaplain asks Simon if he might want to have contact with the Roman Catholic chaplain, thinking that Simon's background might have something to offer him. Simon, however, declines more than once, and the chaplain leaves it at that.

Phase 2. Half Upright

In a second phase, that lasts about a year and a half, Simon's situation gradually shows some improvement. When asked how he is doing, he no longer answers, "Bad," or "Very bad," but "I don't know," or "It differs." A lot of conversation with the chaplain is still devoted to Simon's troubles, but lighter matters like music and motorcycles are also talked about. The chaplain observes changes in Simon's demeanor, sometimes a smile or twinkle in his eye, more eye contact, and walking at times upright. He seldom is found lying in bed during the day. The symptoms, and his suffering, seem to decline. No longer does he express desperation. He continues doing the body scan in his cell, but they talk less often about it.

A change also comes about in Simon's relation to therapy. The chaplain plays a supportive and initiating role in that, by pointing out positive examples of following therapy among other prisoners and subsequently providing Simon the opportunity (a free space) to reflect on his experiences with various forms of therapy. Simon finally decides to do an intake and

---

6. The mindfulness practice of breath-sitting meditation starts with awareness of body sensations, moods, feelings, and thoughts and culminates in anchoring awareness in the sensations of breathing. In the case of posttraumatic stress, practitioners of mindfulness can end up outside their "window of tolerance," which can lead to both hyper- or hypo-arousal. Paying mindful attention then is troublesome, if not impossible. See Treleaven, *Trauma-Sensitive Mindfulness*.

participate in therapy. Gradually Simon gains more understanding of himself, insight into his own habits, with less fretting, and generally a better feeling about himself as a result.

With an eye to the Simon's insecurity and tendency to try to please others, the chaplain sometimes shares with Simon a little tale or parable like the following (a variation of an Aesop fable).

> Every day a father walks with his son ten kilometers to another village for work, with a donkey on which some of their things are loaded. One day the father walks while his boy rides the donkey. When they pass a well, some people there say, "Look at that boy. Isn't it awful how he lets his father walk while he lazily sits up on the donkey."
>
> The next day father, son and donkey pass the well again, but this time the boy walks and the father rides the donkey. This time some people say, "Look at that man who lets his son walk while he rides the donkey. What a bad father he must be."
>
> The third day they pass the well, both walking, with the donkey only bearing their things. Some people laugh and say, "Look at those silly people, both of them walking, whereas one of them could easily ride on the donkey."

The story has a major impact on Simon, who in turn shares it with his therapists and other prisoners and also reflects about how people talk about others and what that means for his pleasing behavior. Simon becomes able to look at himself from a distance, similar to the notion of decentering from mindfulness training.[7] In the initial phase, the chaplain had focused on the body scan primarily as a means for Simon to relate to his fretting and to his perceptions of self. Now Simon is able to examine the perceptions themselves, talk about them with the chaplain, and consider his alternatives, for example in his relations to his children. Simon indicates that he no longer wants to just accept things as they are but "struggle" to make things better. Instead of staying caught up in his past, he starts to look at his future. He develops a sense of resilience, assertiveness, and, consequently, freedom.

The chaplain encourages all of this, among other things by reminding Simon of his intention to continue the "struggle." A talk about courage, whether in opening oneself for inner feelings or in making conscious decisions, helps Simon to write some post cards to his son and daughter. In the meantime, Simon is assigned the (paid) task of cleaning the unit, a

---

7. Decentering is a way of becoming conscious of thoughts, feelings, bodily sensations, and volitions as processes that take place in one's mind and body, without identifying with them. See Segal, et al., *Mindfulness en cognitieve therapie*.

responsibility that strengthens his self-confidence and allows him to practice his assertiveness. The weekly contacts between Simon and the chaplain are changed to every other week. Not only have the chaplain's work hours been reduced, but Simon's situation has also improved.

Phase 3. Upright

Because of the improvement in his situation, Simon is moved to a less restricted unit. The transition is not smooth. Promises that have been made with regard to therapy and cleaning work (with pay) are not honored. The chaplain, like one of the therapists, suggests to Simon that the disappointments are a good opportunity to practice being constructive and assertive. Simon accepts the challenge, grudgingly but with a smile. In a multidisciplinary consult Simon is able to effectively express his dissatisfaction with the way he has been treated, among other things by the new treatment coordinator. From his mentor he receives a compliment on how he handled the situation. That further strengthens Simon's self-confidence.

On the new unit Simon makes friends with Richard (pseudonym), who is Buddhist. They watch Buddhist television programs together. Richard has some of the same problems as Simon, and Simon is sometimes able to offer Richard advice. Although Simon and the chaplain seldom talk explicitly about the content of Buddhism, Simon tips the chaplain about upcoming programs and laughs when it turns out the chaplain has missed them. This active, giving role strengthens Simon's sense of worth.

Although he lost the CD when moving to the new unit, Simon continues to do the body scan, even if not daily. When the chaplain offers Simon a new CD, Simon says that he no longer has a CD player, but that it is alright like it is. The role of the body scan has evolved from a ritual handhold in the initial phase to a conscious and casual use in the third phase.

When the chaplain expresses his joy that things are going better for Simon, Simon no longer denies it, as in the second phase, but assents without reservation. For the first time Simon forgets one of their appointments. The chaplain smiles and suggests that that may be a good sign. Simon tells the chaplain about what he has learned in Schema Therapy,[8] about how one can respond from different modes or roles. He then also picks up the book he had received from the chaplain about MBSR and talks about the similarities.

---

8. Schema therapy is a type of therapy that targets *schemas*, a term used clinically to describe maladaptive patterns of thinking that could cause someone to engage in unhealthy behavior, or to struggle to maintain adult relationships. See Bamelis et al., "Results of a Multicenter RCT"; and Taylor, et al., "Does Schema Therapy Change."

One of the prison workers complements Simon that he has never seen a prisoner who worked so consciously on his therapy, which can be seen, among other things, on the lists and texts on Simon's bulletin board. One is a card that the chaplain had given Simon on the previous unit with the text, "Life is not about waiting for the storm to pass, but about learning how to dance in the rain." Simon indicates that he now better understands what that means, one of many instances in which Simon refers to texts from books about mindfulness that the chaplain has provided, including a glossy with quotes and pictures.

In the third phase Simon has become more independent. He takes initiative and works actively on himself and his situation. He writes another letter to his son and sends his daughter a card. Simon talks about his legal situation, saying the decision not to seek a different lawyer was a result of avoiding confrontations. With his psychologist he explores the possibility of treatment elsewhere, conditionally rather than coerced. Although he is still uncertain about it, he is able to talk about the future with the chaplain. He is happy that he has become unit cleaner again. He walks around upright, straight, often with a smile on his face.

In a period of three years Simon has moved from being a broken man to a so-called model prisoner. In the first phase he was often literally laid out with depression in bed. He rose up halfway in the second phase moving about with difficulty, often bent over. In the third phase he has taken on an active posture, steady and with raised chest. His facial expression has opened up with a brighter look in his eyes.

Communication and Feedback

There was no documented reporting on the case. In the initial period the chaplain shared some information with the treatment coordinator by email, and the coordinator let the chaplain know that she was pleased with the chaplain's contact with Simon. In the second and third phases, unit workers and therapists responded informally that they were pleased with Simon's progression and attributed it to the mindfulness training.

Simon himself regularly reported on his continued practice of mindfulness (body scan). He indicated also what particular insights from mindfulness and from the story of father and son meant for him, directly in conversation with the chaplain, but also indirectly in sharing insights with others. He consciously drew parallels between the ways he was working on things with mindfulness and in (schema) therapy.

SUMMARY

What Does the Chaplain Do?

The chaplain establishes a relation of trust with Simon, among other things by listening and re-listening to his story. He offers Simon a training in mindfulness (body scan, MBSR) that they do together once a week and that Simon can do daily in his cell. Another technique is tried but laid aside. Once Simon is better able to relate to his situation, the chaplain converses with him about his various issues, at one time offering a tale on the issue of trying to please others. The chaplain allows for a long-term trajectory with mindfulness and conversations so that behavior and attitude can gradually be transformed. The chaplain encourages Simon to engage more in therapy. The chaplain offers Simon complementary feedback on his more open, more active attitude and encourages him to continue the "struggle." The chaplain observes how Simon moves, literally and figuratively, from an insecure, slumping posture to upright and confident stance.

For What Reasons?

The chaplain offers the body scan technique in order to help Simon relate to his issues and relax (reduction of stress and fretting). Although mindfulness is directed towards change, paradoxically the first step is practicing acceptance and friendliness towards one's inner thoughts and experience. The chaplain is aware that the continued practice of new behavior (body scan) can provide a basis for new attitudes and a transformed perception of self. The repeated routine of the ritual is a key to the result.[9] Later when Simon becomes more restful, the chaplain sees that there is an opportunity to address the fretting and self-perceptions of Simon more directly, though one of the means is indirect through the telling of a tale. Somewhat indirect is also the way in which the chaplain points out the advantages of therapy to Simon. The chaplain is always careful about giving advice and seeks to approach Simon with friendliness (mindfulness) and encouragement (empowerment).

With What Results?

The physical change in Simon's posture from slumping to upright, from looking down and avoiding eye contact to open facial expressions, is also a

---

9. Whitehouse, *Modes of Religiosity*.

metaphor for his change from always seeking to please others to discovering different modes of response, from insecure to confident, from despondency to making decisions, from inertia to taking initiative. One of the first signs of change is the discipline with which Simon continues his practice of the body scan. Although the changes in Simon are attributable to multiple sources, the chaplain plays an initiating and complementary role. Significant is the change in Simon's attitude towards therapy, from resistant to diligent participant, which is facilitated by the chaplain.

REFLECTIONS

There is a parallel between mindfulness and schema therapy with regards to developing new modes of response and behavior, as Simon himself noted. In retrospect the chaplain realizes that ACT played an implicit role in the exploration of alternatives for behavior in the second phase. ACT focuses, more than MBSR, on value orientations and commitments and resultant behavior. One might speak of complementary approaches, whereby in this case the interventions of the chaplain open the way for therapy. The chaplain also sees a parallel between mindfulness and presence theory with regard to the three tenets of the Zen Peacemakers: not knowing, bearing witness, and taking action.[10] The latter led to the chaplain continuing contacts with Simon, even when results were slow in coming. The chaplain maintained the Buddhist trust in healing as a potential that people naturally possess. That is related to the narrative approach of the chaplain, inspired by Paul Ricoeur's thinking on narrative identity, listening and re-listening to another's story and enabling the other to re-write one's life story.[11]

As indicated, the changes in Simon are also attributable to the various therapies (running, schema, assertivity, *et cetera*) in which he participated. That does not lessen the significance of the role of the chaplain. The referral to the chaplain for mindfulness training was intended to address Simon's depression. At the same time Simon is resistant to therapy and distrustful of the prison workers. The chaplain makes contact and introduces the body scan that Simon practices with discipline. Subsequently, in a following phase, the chaplain takes initiative in encouraging Simon to reconsider

---

10. The three tenets: (1) not knowing, (2) bearing witness, and (3) taking action (or loving action) were first formulated by Zen teacher Roshi Bernie Glassman in 1994 and refer to (1) letting go of fixed ideas about yourself, others and the universe, (2) an openness to the joy and suffering of the world, and (3) the necessary action that arises from not knowing and bearing witness. See Nakao, "The Three Tenets."

11. Ricœur, *Oneself as Another*.

participating in therapy. In addition, the chaplain continues to help Simon to relate not only to the issues that are addressed in therapy, but also to how Simon experiences therapy as such and relates to it. Especially noteworthy is how Simon himself sees complementary parallels in what he is learning in therapy and in what the chaplain has offered him in the form of mindfulness, tales, and sayings. There are, therefore, several aspects of the accompaniment by the chaplain that directly contribute to the changes in Simon: making contact and offering care when Simon is resistant to therapy, facilitating Simon's participation in therapy, helping Simon to relate to therapy, and complementing the work of therapy through conversational interactions and mindfulness training.[12]

The *existential* conditions of the case are manifold: emotional and sexual abuse as a child, conviction for attempted murder of his partner, problematic relations with his children, somatic and mental issues leading to work disability, depression and other acute mental health issues, conflicts with therapists, and a general lack of self-confidence. The role of mindfulness in the case is *existential* in the confrontation with present moment experience, *spiritual* in the practice of acceptance and friendliness towards that experience and in the transformation in the relation to self, *ethical* in the non-judgmental approach and *aesthetic* in the means of body scan at quiet moments. Conversation contributes *existentially* in encouraging Simon to continue the struggle, *spiritually* in helping him reflect on his relation to self and dignity and *ethically* in the encouragement to start therapy again and relate to others. The *aesthetic* outcomes, from slumped to upright, from unkempt to groomed, from a downward gaze to an open face, hold in both a literal and a figurative sense.

REFERENCES

Assaz, Daniel A., et al. "Cognitive Defusion in Acceptance and Commitment Therapy: What Are the Basic Processes of Change?" *The Psychological Record* 68.4 (2018) 405–18.

Bamelis, Lotte L. M., et al. "Results of a Multicenter Randomized Controlled Trial of the Clinical Effectiveness of Schema Therapy for Personality Disorders." *American Journal of Psychiatry* 171.3 (2014) 305–22.

Feldman, Christina, and Willem Kuyken. *Mindfulness: Ancient Wisdom Meets Modern Psychology*. New York: The Guilford, 2019.

Maex, Edel. *Mindfulness: in de maalstroom van je leven*. Tielt: Lannoo, 2014.

Nakao, Roshi E. "The Three Tenets." https://zenpeacemakers.org/the-three-tenets/.

Ricœur, Paul. *Oneself as Another*. Chicago: University of Chicago Press, 2008.

---

12. For various relations of chaplaincy to treatment, see Chapter 18.

Segal, Zindel V., et al. *Mindfulness en cognitieve therapie bij depressie.* 2nd ed. Amsterdam: Nieuwezijds, 2022.

Taylor, Christopher D. J., et al. "Does Schema Therapy Change Schemas and Symptoms? A Systematic Review across Mental Health Disorders." *Psychology and Psychotherapy: Theory, Research and Practice* 90.3 (2017) 456–79.

Treleaven, David A. *Trauma-Sensitive Mindfulness: Practices for Safe and Transformative Healing.* New York: Norton & Company, 2018.

Whitehouse, Harvey. *Modes of Religiosity: A Cognitive Theory of Religious Transmission.* Walnut Creek: AltaMira, 2004.

Part Three

EMERGING THEMES

13

Chaplaincy in Context

—Jacques Körver

"But usually deeper experiences of trust are more informal, as when people learn on whom they can rely when given a difficult or impossible task. Such social bonds take time to develop, slowly rooting into the cracks and crevices of institutions."

Richard Sennett[1]

NO ISLAND

For chaplains, working in an organization or social institution is often a blind spot. At least, it is not in the spotlight. Although they have a room in the building, are given a key, receive a salary, and perform their work among other professionals and supporting services, this organizational and institutional context rarely comes to the forefront, nor does the way in which chaplains respond to it consciously or unconsciously.[2] Little has been written and even less research has been done on how chaplains deal with the organizational and institutional context. However, the competencies that they need in order to work in an organization such as a hospital or other health care facility, in corrections, or in the armed forces have recently been

---

1. Sennett, *The Corrosion of Character*, 24.
2. Cadge, "God on the Fly?"; Klitzman, et al., "Hospital Chaplains' Communication"; Kruizinga, et al., "Enhancing the Integration."

pointed out more often.³ The conclusion of those studies is clear: chaplains do not work on an island.

In this chapter, we provide an initial analysis of the relationship of chaplains to the organization where they work. There are at least two aspects to this. On the one hand, the relation may involve numerous formal and informal forms of cooperation with others in the organization in question.⁴ Cooperation does not, therefore, refer exclusively to the extensive exchange regarding a client between chaplains and other professionals. A brief interested conversation with a guard in prison demonstrates cooperation just as much as participation in a multidisciplinary consultation in a hospital, but at a different level. Having a name badge, a meditation center or chapel, access to (digital) information systems, and being recognized by other staff indicate cooperation and (partial) integration. On the other hand, the relationship of chaplains to the organization includes how the target group, purpose, policy, and work systems as "context" affect the content of chaplaincy.⁵ The themes addressed in the military are different from those in eldercare, for example. Working with homeless people who also suffer from addiction problems requires different methods and competencies than working with students at universities or colleges who get stuck in their studies. The cultures of institutions or fields of work also differ dramatically. Working in a prison where everything is directed towards security, control, and restricting freedom is different from working in a rehabilitation center where everything is directed at care and recovery, even though both institutions are aimed, to a greater or lesser degree, at the client's reintegration into society.

An initial scan of all the CSP case studies found that two thirds of them involve some form of cooperation. The term cooperation was understood broadly here, from a brief informal chat in the hallway about how a particular client has been doing over the past few days to a protocol-based multidisciplinary consultation in which the contribution of all professionals involved is discussed against the background of a client's care policy.

Cooperation is least common or least reported in the fields of detention and the military, but cooperation is not absent there. In health care institutions, cooperation seems to be much more self-evident, because health care institutions, in the terms of organizational expert Henry Mintzberg,

---

3. See, for example, the Dutch professional standard on spiritual care: VGVZ, *Professional Standard*. Another example is the publication regarding the state of the art of spiritual care in the twenty-first century: Cadge and Rambo, *Chaplaincy and Spiritual Care*.

4. Barker Scott and Manning, "Designing the Collaborative Organization."

5. Hofstede, et al., *Cultures and Organizations*.

are professional organizations where cooperation is indispensable in view of the goal to be achieved for the clients.[6] In the following section, we describe some patterns that emerge from a thematic analysis of the case studies, in which collaboration appears as a differentiated phenomenon that takes place at many levels and in many forms. In the section that follows, we describe from some fields of work (hospital, detention, the military) the distinct character that chaplaincy takes on in that context or culture due to the institution's own focus and specific target group. Both analyses show that chaplaincy is more intertwined with an institution or organization than chaplains often think. The concluding section offers some reflections on the above, as well as suggestions for further research.

Even when chaplains emphasize their sanctuary function within the organization, it is impossible to avoid the work context. They unavoidably become aware of their institutional and organizational embeddedness and distinguish different aspects and levels within it. It is precisely then that the awareness of mutual loyalty and commitment arises "slowly rooting into the cracks and crevices of institutions," as Richard Sennett so eloquently puts it in the opening quote to this chapter.

PATTERNS OF CHAPLAINS' COLLABORATION

The format for describing a case study in the CSP includes some questions related to the organizational bedding of chaplaincy care. Questions are asked about the type of organization where the care took place, the size of the institution, and the size and composition of the team. There are also questions about who was involved in the care process, in what way, and how, if at all, consultation, coordination, evaluation, and reporting occurred.[7] Based on the thematic analysis, three patterns or types of collaboration between chaplains and other staff in the organization can be discerned in the case studies: (1) aligning care and evaluating with each other, (2) knowing about and acknowledging each other, and (3) operating separately from each other. The three types or scenarios are located on a continuum of forms of cooperation. In no institution can those three types be unambiguously identified to a full extent. The types serve as landmarks on a continuum. Moreover, different types within the same institution may function side by side or one after the other, and the same chaplain may use different scenarios according

---

6. See Mintzberg, *Mintzberg on Management*; Mintzberg, *Understanding Organizations*.

7. Version 20 of the format involves questions 1J, 1K, 1L, 2E, 4A, and 4B regarding the context of chaplaincy. See Appendix B.

to the client's question or need, the situation and context of the question, or the nature of the referral. Below we describe the three types.

Aligning the Care and Evaluating with Each Other

In some cases, another professional refers a client to the chaplain, providing further information about the question or issue, and its background and context. Contact may also be established through the client or client system, or at the initiative of the chaplain. The latter happens more often in cases of readmission. There are regular consultations with other involved professionals, during which information about the background and context is also shared (sometimes at the client's request). The frequency can vary greatly. The consultation sometimes takes place in a multidisciplinary consultation (in a healthcare facility), in a team of attention officers (in the justice system), or in a social medical team (in the armed forces). Consultations can also take place in direct response to the client and/or to developments in the care process. The purpose of the consultation is to keep each other informed about goals, approach, important themes for the clients, and to coordinate care or guidance.

> A physician assistant refers Mrs. Francis to the chaplain. Twice during the chaplaincy care trajectory of five conversations and four months the situation is dealt with in the multidisciplinary team. The chaplain and a medical-social worker synchronize their respective focusses. ("Energy *and* Inspiration," Chapter 4)

The chaplains' input is incorporated into care policies and goals. The exchange focuses on the approach and goals, without the chaplain providing substantive, sensitive, or confidential information about the client, similar to the way other professionals report this. Technique can be used, such as Video Interaction Guidance.[8] At times a chaplain and another professional provide care accompaniment together.[9] The chaplain records and reports in the (electronic) file, where available, for which (oral) permission of the client is secured. Sometimes the chaplain reports to those directly involved only verbally and rather informally. Consultation may occur orally or via mail and telephone. At the end of a care process, an evaluation is held. Consultation and reporting may decrease in frequency and intensity in the course of a long-term care process, but be intensified again in the event of a crisis or new development. Sometimes the chaplain emphasizes

---

8. See, for example, "A Church for Charly" (Chapter 9).
9. An example is: Van Hoof, et al., "Agreement Is Agreement?"

the importance of attention by the client's supervisor, even when the accompaniment is completed (armed forces). The chaplains keep in touch with a client, even when others avoid the client.

> On a weekly basis the Medical Specialist Rehab Team convenes for a multidisciplinary review of patient status. In one of the meetings the chaplain explains that in her care she is paying attention to Mrs. Francis longing for inspiration, as a spiritual complement to her need for more energy, which the physical and occupational therapists are working on, along with the dietician. Some of the colleague's chuckle and say, "That's too vague and fluttery to do anything with." . . . The chaplain holds on to the term "inspiration" because it indicates precisely what Mrs. Francis longs for . . . The rehab physician picks the term up and includes it in the summary of the key problem. "Due to a lack of energy/inspiration and inadequate coping the patient does not get around to activities that she likes and considers to be valuable to her." The terms "inspiration" and "valuable" have been added. With her colleague, the medical-social worker, the chaplain discusses the types of care each will provide. ("Energy *and* Inspiration," Chapter 4)

The chaplain also makes his or her own notes, sometimes in the closed part of the electronic file, sometimes in one's own file or logbook. At other times, there is a summary note in the file after each contact in the form of general impressions. There are instances when a chaplain refers a client to another spiritual caregiver upon transfer, with a brief substantive report. Chaplains point out the importance of open, functional communication and the importance of cooperation with an eye to the client's well-being.

Knowing About and Acknowledging Each Other

In a second scenario or type of coordination, the client may initiate contact with a chaplain. Or the chaplain knows the client and/or family from previous contacts. Other staff members are aware of the contact, nothing more. It may also be that the referral comes about through another professional, where the question is briefly explained, but no information is provided about background and context. Nor does the chaplain request that information. The chaplain has a recognized position in the institution, has permission to contact clients, and also to take the client from a closed ward (to an office, chapel, or outdoors). Sometimes the line between chaplaincy and therapy is unclear, an issue that is only discussed informally outside the work context and not with other professionals in the institution.

> I knew Ralph for about a year before we sat down and talked. He suddenly said: "I would also like to go to McDonald's with you." I responded by planning an appointment in my diary. When allowed, I take young people to places outside the institution, for instance for a walk in the woods or a talk in a restaurant, of which McDonald's is their favorite.[10]

Occasionally (informal) consultations can occur in the corridors. No charting takes place, except sometimes in anonymized form, nor any reporting. If evaluation takes place at all, it is done informally, sometimes verbally by the client to other staff members, sometimes conveyed through the person who made the referral to other professionals involved. The focus of any consultation and coordination is on formal and practical aspects (space, time), or on the process side of the counseling, never on substantive issues. Sometimes reporting does not take place because the chaplain does not have access to the (electronic) file. Sometimes it is unclear whether there is feedback and/or evaluation.

> Anne's friend sees the benefit of the conversations of Anne with the chaplain. When the grandmother of Anne's friend passes away, she is able to accompany him. Via Anne the chaplain hears that the psychologist reflects that Anne stopped with the exposure treatment and consequently undergoes exposure in chaplaincy care. ("Exposure?," Chapter 6)

Operating Separately from Each Other

In the third scenario referral may be made by another professional or by a volunteer, without further information about question, background, and context. Or the client takes the initiative for contact with a chaplain. There is no consultation, registration, or reporting. Sometimes there is a brief evaluation of the contact, or the chaplains gives short instructions on how to approach the client. Sometimes the chaplain consults with a fellow chaplain as a peer. There is no formal evaluation at the end of the care process. If an evaluation takes place at all, it is only between the chaplain and the client. Chaplaincy is understood in terms of a sanctuary. Reporting rarely occurs, and more often is not necessary. Sometimes chaplains take brief notes for themselves, in key words. There may be a "light" anonymized form of

---

10. Van der Meer, "Is Macdonald's Freedom?," 147.

charting, for purposes of annual reporting and accountability to management. Sometimes referral to chaplaincy in the new institution is made upon transfer, but without details. The emphasis is primarily on the client's desire for chaplaincy care.

> The chaplain and Rick walk back to the unit and ask the guard Peter if it is possible to make a phone call. That is okay and they are allowed to sit in the consultation room . . . The chaplain says that it is only because the guard Peter told her that Rick was not feeling well. Rick is surprised that the guard noticed . . . The chaplain tells the guard that he made that possible and that she told Rick that, too. The guard seems to be surprised.[11]

INSTITUTION AND CONTENT OF CHAPLAINCY

Three work fields are discussed in this section. In addition to a characterization of hospital care, the fields of detention and the military are characterized. There are clear contrasts between these three fields that clarify how chaplains are confronted with different people, questions, and themes in each field of work and in every social institution. Working in a hospital is different from working during deployment with a military unit in a conflict zone. Working with elderly people with dementia is different from working for people with intellectual disabilities, although both groups deal with cognitive impairments. Different questions and themes present themselves when working in residential youth care than in student chaplaincy, even though the age of those involved is similar. It helps to focus sharply on all those different practices. What questions present themselves, what themes frequently arise? Analyses of multiple case studies helped to bring some of that into sharper focus, especially specific aspects of meaning and worldview that come up in the various fields of work. It is impossible to review all fields of work here. Elsewhere in this volume we refer to other fields, especially in Part II with the case studies.

Field of Work—Detention

In the field of detention, the chaplain encounters persons who have committed serious to very serious crimes.[12] Those include forms of assault, drug

---

11. De Vries, et al., "With an Open Mind," 143.

12. For the final report of the research community, see: De Vries, et al., "'Niet Zonder Ons.'" And for a case study: De Vries, et al., "With an Open Mind." Also the

crimes, murder (of the partner), abuse and other sex offenses. They are mostly men, usually between thirty and seventy years old, from very diverse cultural and religious backgrounds, often with mild intellectual disabilities combined with serious behavioral problems.[13]

That may sound obvious, but it is not, for it requires inner strength on the part of the chaplain to recognize on the one hand the seriousness of the act and not lose sight of it, and on the other hand to be open, empathetic, and compassionate in relation to the account and life story of the detainees. In addition, it is not always clear whether and to what extent detainees manipulate the exchange. It requires expertise to find a good balance between distance and proximity. Because chaplains in the judicial system do not usually consult with other professionals,[14] it requires a highly developed sense of discernment of what is credible.[15] The question of responsibility and culpability often remains in the background.

> By being present with an open mind, the chaplain offers prisoners the opportunity to share what they are concerned about. Sometimes there is much aggression or anger, that a short exchange can help bring de-escalation. That opens up a space to talk without violence.[16]

The prisoners' relationships mostly are complicated.[17] Nevertheless, prisoners are very often concerned about the well-being of their families, a concern that symbolizes the desire for a carefree and normal life and at the same time stands for the recognition of the consequences of one's own actions.[18] Recovery of relationships (partner, children, parents, friends) and a new life situation are obvious themes, just like the search for a new role in society (at least preparation for it) and the fear of quickly ending up back in the old environment with the possibility of recidivism. Faith and prayer appear to be important topics of conversation, in which the question of guilt might be present in the background.[19] The situation of the prisoners is further complicated by their isolation leading to loneliness, lethargy, and other

---

case study in "From Slumped to Upright" (Chapter 12).

13. Neimeijer, et al., "'Back Off Means Stay with Me.'"
14. De Vries, et al., "With an Open Mind," 146.
15. Stoesz, et al., *A Prison Chaplaincy Manual*.
16. De Vries, et al., "With an Open Mind," 145.
17. De Vries, et al., "'Niet Zonder Ons,'" 120–21.
18. For an approach to these issues from the family perspective: Hutton and Moran, *The Palgrave Handbook of Prison*.
19. As might be the case with the veteran who, before entering a psychiatric hospital, suffered a prison sentence. See "Wounded Warrior" (Chapter 10).

existential and spiritual issues. The experience of the judicial system and of the prison as a total institution can be traumatizing in itself. However, it also appears that posttraumatic growth can occur, with emotional support, religious coping, and the search for meaning being positive predictors.[20] Working on self-confidence and self-esteem is a recurring theme, as is working on learning to communicate better. That occasionally includes restorative mediation, where inmate and victim meet.[21]

> Chaplaincy work is recovery-oriented on multiple levels. Restoring relationships takes a big place, with the chaplain investing in making connections with partner and family, as well as with professionals in the facility. Integrated work is important in this context, because chaplaincy connects the individual approach with involvement in the community (group work, celebrations, meditation meetings, and contacts with community members outside the prison). Where possible, contact is made with victims. The contact is also focused on spiritual resources, one's own life story and tradition. Through volunteers and aftercare, sometimes through family, connection is made with the worldview or faith community outside the institution.[22]

Field of Work—Armed Forces

In the armed forces, chaplains deal with relatively young men and some women who often commit themselves to the armed forces for the rest of their working lives.[23] Through deployments abroad, these soldiers face serious conflicts and far-reaching events that can trigger trauma, PTSD and moral stress or injury.[24] The result can be physical, psychological, and/or existential problems, some of which may not manifest themselves until long after the events. The latter occurs with some regularity in the care of veterans. Questions of responsibility and guilt may arise, as well as existential

---

20. Vanhooren, *Loss of Meaning*.

21. For more background on restorative mediation and restorative justice: Claessen, *Forgiveness in Criminal Law*.

22. De Vries, et al., "'Niet zonder ons,'" 132. [Translation by JK]

23. Officially, conscription still exists in the Netherlands, but it was suspended in 1997. From then on, the Dutch army became a professional army. As long as the security situation does not require it, civilians do not have to do military service.

24. For further information see: Jorissen, et al., "You Can Remove"; Pleizier and Schuhmann, "How the Military Context"; Schuhmann, et al., "How Military Chaplains Strengthen." For two case studies, see "Wounded Warrior" (Chapter 10) and "To Honor and Confirm" (Chapter 11).

and spiritual questions through which the foundations of meaning and worldview may be affected, as well as the sense of justice and belief in the goodness of humankind and creation.[25]

> The fact that the chaplain is a representative of the military as well as of religious life is a condition for these outcomes [the veteran's openness about experiences in warfare]. A second condition is the time the chaplain takes, the fidelity with which he visits every couple of weeks. It is the chaplain's experience that a minimum of ten conversations is needed for the life story to come up. Stories around events about which silence has been kept for decades, and that are colored by guilt and shame, are not readily told.[26]

Often there are relational problems in the family sphere. The atmosphere of a military unit (hierarchical, totalitarian) is often not compatible with that of a relationship with a partner (equal, developing), family or relatives. Questions in relation to the development of one's own identity may arise, but also feelings of grief at the loss of a loved one or of a colleague. Some military personnel also become disappointed in their employer and in public opinion, feeling run down and useless, even though they have often identified fully with the armed forces and see their work as a kind of vocation.[27]

> It turned out, however, that, even though moral issues did play a central role in each of the cases selected by the chaplains, only a few of these were related to morally unsettling situations during deployment. In relation to some of the cases, the chaplains spoke about "moral ripples" rather than moral shock. Moral struggles that were described in the cases often had to do with relationships with family members, interactions with colleagues, or annoyance with the military organization.[28]

Chaplains try to create space so that military personnel can tell their stories, often in a low-threshold manner, in the corridors, during a deployment, on a ship, in a car. Most of those who serve in the military are secular, and if they have a religious or worldview background, it is not developed

---

25. Chaplains are frequently involved in the care of veterans dealing with psychological, existential, and spiritual problems: Nieuwsma, et al., "Chaplaincy and Mental Health."

26. Jorissen, et al., "You Can Remove," 163.

27. See further on this subject: Molendijk, "Moral Injury in Relation to Public Debates"; Molendijk, *Moral Injury and Soldiers in Conflict*.

28. Schuhmann, et al., "How Military Chaplains Strengthen," 606.

much or, on the contrary, rather strict in origin. It takes endurance and constant presence to inspire recognition and trust. Military personnel must feel that the chaplain is "one of them."[29]

> Our study suggests that sometimes, in relation to specific issues, it is important for soldiers that chaplains represent a religious tradition. However, the study also suggests that, generally, it is the "lived religion or worldview" of the chaplain that is crucial. It is through providing presence care that trust is built between soldiers and chaplains. As chaplains are present in the lifeworld of soldiers, the soldiers' sense whether chaplains "practice what they preach," that is, whether they embody a spiritual vision that allows them to look beyond "the soldier" and see "the human being." It seems worthwhile to include the perspective of "lived theology," or "lived worldview," and of embodiment in the discussion about the role of representation of religion and worldview in chaplaincy.[30]

Work Field—Hospital Care

Chaplaincy care in a hospital encompasses a great diversity and bandwidth in duration, frequency, themes, and forms of accompaniment.[31] It involves life-threatening conditions (cancer in various forms and phases, kidney rejection after transplantation, progressive degenerative disease, cerebral infarction, progressing dementia), serious complications after relatively simple operations and with a very poor prognosis, and serious consequences of prolonged admission to intensive care. In addition, there are physical conditions combined with psychiatric or social problems (loneliness, exclusion, misunderstanding) that intermingle with the disease process, complicated ethical questions in the context of treatment, or the struggle with decreased abilities and independence due to the disease, treatment or disability. Regularly, a patient's death has been mentioned, or is expected in the foreseeable future, without the patient having been properly informed. The sociologist Wendy Cadge regularly calls this the "dirty work" that chaplains

---

29. Schuhmann, et al., "How Military Chaplains Strengthen," 616–18.
30. Schuhmann, et al., "How Military Chaplains Strengthen," 621.
31. Regarding hospital chaplaincy, see the case studies "Energy *and* Inspiration" (Chapter 4) and "The Enigma of a Day" (Chapter 5). See further: Berkhout, "Interdisciplinary Work"; Körver, "Das Tabu"; Körver, "Wie neemt het initiatief."

take on, work that others do not want to do, and is not always considered "real work."[32]

> The analyses [of the case studies] showed that the chaplains were particularly well qualified to act in complex situations that were drastic for patients and their relatives and to respond to their wishes and needs ... They had rituals and symbolic skills as well as appropriate language and were therefore able to contribute in situations where others could no longer find the words. They did not avoid the fear of death, the confusion or the silence that can overcome patients, and their existential questions. They created a link between the systemic world of the hospital and the life world of those affected and their family and friends.[33]

In the "accumulation of problems" described above, complicated relationships of patients with partners, family members, acquaintances, and/or caregivers frequently play a role. Those relationships were already complicated prior to hospitalization or arose during the illness and hospitalization, and often can be explained from different ways of coping with the illness and differences in outlook or expectations regarding treatment. Patients and/or their loved ones often already have a complicated history, due to loss, illness, or disappointment in life. Sometimes that has led to deviant behavior, which can lead to complicated and irritated communication with health care providers, or even to social exclusion or stigmatization.[34]

At the same time, existential doubts and dilemmas arise, for example, feelings and questions of guilt, struggle with meaninglessness, fear of the end of life, loneliness, and isolation.[35] Like hospital care in general, chaplaincy care in a hospital is always based on the physical or medical condition. That condition determines the possibilities and limitations for communication, privacy, duration and intensity of contact, and cognitive abilities. That physical and medical condition is, to be sure, the reason patients are in the hospital. That is what demands their attention. And contact between patients and chaplains is always under time pressure: the average length of hospitalization is short, discharge is often sudden without the chaplain being informed, a patient's condition may suddenly deteriorate sharply so that

---

32. See, for example, the Chapter "Managing Death: The Personal and Institutional 'Dirty Work' of Chaplains," in: Cadge, *Paging God*, 171–90.

33. Körver, "Das Tabu," 373. [Translation by JK]

34. For further reflection on social exclusion or social redundancy in relation to care: Baart and Vosman, "Relationship Based Care."

35. In that description the four basic existential dilemmas formulated by Irvin Yalom can be discerned: Yalom, *Existential Psychotherapy*.

contact is hardly possible any longer. Within that context, chaplains act on numerous levels simultaneously. From the very beginning, the situation is complex.[36]

> ... a striking difference between the conversations of psychologists and social workers on the one hand and chaplains on the other hand, was the lack of a clear contract phase in the chaplains' conservations ... After a brief positioning, almost all conversations move quickly to the content level. Often, but by no means always, to a deeper level.[37]

Field and Frame

From these sketches from three different fields of work, emerges what we also saw in the final reports of the RCs. Every chaplain is in whatever setting both a generalist dealing with a great diversity of persons, worldview orientations and personal issues, and at the same time a specialist, working with existential issues characteristic of the setting, the organizational context, and approaches that are particularly helpful in that setting. The context, target population, themes, and dilemmas, and partly the methods are different in each field, but the perspective from which chaplains work does not change. The field changes but not the frame.

DIFFERENTIATION OF INSTITUTIONS, ORGANIZATIONS, AND FORMS OF COOPERATION

Based on an initial thematic analysis of the case studies in the CSP and the final reports of the project,[38] a number of findings regarding working in different contexts and organizations become visible, as described in the

---

36. When caregivers are open to the story of the patient or client, the complexity of life reveals itself. This was shown, for example, in research on ethical care questions in: Timmerman, et al., "In Search of Good Care." Another example is research based on autobiographies of men with prostate cancer: Van der Kamp, et al., "In Their Own Words." Chaplains have a keen eye for this complexity, and especially for the tragic elements in it.

37. Berkhout, "Interdisciplinary Work," 177.

38. The Dutch-language reports of all six RCs, preceded by a description and evaluation of the project, have been compiled in: Körver, et al., *Richting, Repertoire en Resultaat*. The report is available in digital form at this link: https://www.ucgv.nl/wp-content/uploads/2023/10/20230921-Eindrapport-CSP-Definitief.pdf.

previous sections. Following are some reflections, from the perspectives of collaboration, organization, and field of work or institution.

Collaboration and Integration

In the Netherlands, thinking about collaboration of chaplains with other staff in an organization received an important impetus from an article by practical theologian and organizational consultant Geert van Gerwen. He examined the practice of chaplains (in health care institutions) from the perspective of the organization on the basis of the degree of "integration."[39] He distinguished four levels of integration for chaplaincy: (1) In *tolerated integration* the institution allows chaplains to work in the setting but has no other involvement, whether substantive, managerial, or financial. The organizational basis lies outside the institution. (2) In *organizational integration* the institution facilitates chaplaincy care in an organizational sense: appointment, working conditions, workspace, chapel or meditation center, consultative structures, *et cetera*. However, there is no substantive involvement. (3) In *policy integration* the institution not only facilitates chaplaincy care but also incorporates it into institutional policy, contributing to the purpose of the institution. That requires consultation with management and alignment with other activities and professionals. (4) In *process integration* chaplaincy care is included in the primary process of the institution, for example through inclusion on an equal basis in treatment teams. The chaplain participates in the interdisciplinary conversation on the basis of the standards of chaplaincy.[40]

In the three patterns that emerge from the case studies (aligning and evaluating with each other; knowing about and acknowledging each other; and operating separately from each other), the levels of integration can be recognized in reverse order. It is striking that the patterns described occur in all fields of work. The first pattern is most evident in health care institutions, although it also occurs in fields such as detention, the military, and primary care. And conversely, the third pattern occurs most often in detention and military sectors, but is also observable in health care institutions. It also occurs that one and the same chaplain does not always operate according to the same pattern with all clients or in all departments of the organization. Apparently, different forms of collaboration are possible and

---

39. Van Gerwen, "Geestelijke verzorging." Unfortunately, the article is not available in English.

40. Van Gerwen, "Geestelijke verzorging," 469–71.

necessary within an organization, with reference to the issues at hand, the circumstances, and the care process.

Whereas Van Gerwen's model of four levels of integration was intended as an instrument for distinguishing and ordering patterns of integration and cooperation, it has come to function as a normative model. Process integration would be the pinnacle to which every chaplain should aspire in every context. The question, however, is whether that is necessary and possible in all situations and contexts. It would be good to first examine how the practice of collaboration actually works. Empirical research can clarify exactly how chaplains cooperate, at what level they coordinate their care with others, which patterns are best suited to what contexts, what the influence of protocols and of the culture of the organization are, to what extent the person and training of the chaplain play a role, and what the role of the other professionals, of support staff, and of management is. That could make evident what minimum level of collaboration and integration is necessary to gain recognition as a professional. Cooperation and integration are complex forms of social behavior that do not depend solely on the willingness of the chaplain. That requires focused research, in which ethnographic and ethological methods could play a role.[41]

Being Part of an Organization

Whether chaplains want to or not, they are part of an organization. The case studies and the emerging patterns of collaboration make that abundantly clear. There is formal and informal contact with staff at virtually all levels of an organization. Even if client contact is not discussed with other staff, some know about it. Even if, in Van Gerwen's terms,[42] there is a tolerance construction, an organization at least grants access, for example in the form of a key, a name badge, permission to visit clients, and/or a fee. That means that there are contacts, connections, and some form of integration, albeit partial which, for that matter, applies to any professional anywhere.[43]

---

41. A very interesting example of this kind of research is the observation of social behavior and interaction in a number of operating rooms in the US: Jones, et al., "Ethological Observations of Social Behavior." The observation used ethological methods, borrowed from the study of animal behavior.

42. Van Gerwen, "Geestelijke verzorging."

43. There is always partial identification in relation to an institution, worldview institution, party, or organization. This is true at the macro level of a country, but also for a workplace and even for a family of relatives. Partiality emphasizes that connection or dependence is a process, a process of identification and disengagement. For this sociological process at the macro level, see: Delmotte, "Identity, Identification, Habitus."

In general, although there is a vague realization among chaplains of working in an organization, there is little awareness of what that means and in what way the type of organization affects, for example, the position and recognition of a professional. In this regard, Mintzberg's organizational model and its various elaborations could be a help in reflecting on one's own position as a chaplain.[44] A hospital is a different type of organization than a prison, the military, or primary care. That seems like an open door, but Mintzberg's model shows how the possibilities and impossibilities of a professional vary by organizational type, and what the response might be. Research could also clarify whether the elements chaplains most relate to in their profession (sanctuary, confidentiality, collaboration as little as possible, a unique personal contact with the client) are considered elementary by other professionals, perhaps not in theory but in practice. Research could show how contacts are created, along what lines in what type of organization, how referral patterns emerge, and how procedures for contact with chaplaincy are supported or perhaps opposed by whom at what level or segment of the organization. It could also illumine the fact that once chaplains step over the threshold, they are part of the organization in question, evidenced simply by the adaptation of their working methods to the target group, the themes that resonate in their care, and the culture of the organization and institution.

Against this background, it is to be welcomed that in addition to meaning-making and interpersonal competencies, the book *Chaplaincy and Spiritual Care in the Twenty-First Century*[45] pays extensive attention to the organizational competencies of chaplains. The various authors emphasize that chaplains are inextricably linked to the organizations in which they work. Based on their world view or religious background, chaplains are tasked with representing a vision of healthy and just organizations as moral leaders and acting as change agents when fundamental human values are violated.[46] In this regard, it is of great importance that chaplaincy care is recognized as an integrated specialist discipline within (health care) organizations, as Swiss researcher Simon Peng-Keller, among others, convincingly demonstrates.[47]

---

44. Mintzberg, *Mintzberg on Management*; Mintzberg, *Understanding Organizations*.

45. Cadge and Rambo, *Chaplaincy and Spiritual Care*, 191–257.

46. See: McClure and Thiel, "Introduction to Organizational Competencies"; White, "Facilitating Resilience"; Pak, "Through a Multi-frame Lens"; Garrett-Cobbina, "The Emotional Undercurrents."

47. Peng-Keller, *Healthcare Chaplaincy as Specialised*, 139–73.

The Influence of Work Field and Institution

It has become evident that chaplaincy care adapts (and needs to adapt) in practices, interventions, and goals to the target group with which they deal. Examples of this have been given in the previous sections. It is also evident in the case studies described in Part II of this book. This fact emphasizes that chaplaincy must necessarily have a broad spectrum of methods and interventions adapted to the different target groups and contexts in which chaplains work. However, the question then arises as to what might be the supporting basis of all these forms and variants. Niels Den Toom's research clarified that in the CSP the constant interaction between the descriptions of very diverse concrete practice and the abstract domain description of chaplaincy from the Dutch professional standard helped the participating chaplains to see the coherence of their common profession in the midst of that diversity, a coherence that is at the same time supported by a number of founding values.[48]

In many ways, it has become evident that chaplains do not work on an island and that learning to discern the diversity of forms of collaboration, organization, and field of work contributes to the awareness of working on the mainland. This awareness might help to enhance, in a critical way, the loyalty and commitment to their organization.

REFERENCES

Baart, Andries, and Frans Vosman. "Relationship Based Care and Recognition: Part One: Sketching Good Care from the Theory of Presence and Five Entries." In *Care, Compassion and Recognition: An Ethical Discussion*, edited by Carlo Leget, et al., 183–200. Leuven: Peeters, 2011.

Barker Scott, Brenda A., and Michael R. Manning. "Designing the Collaborative Organization: A Framework for How Collaborative Work, Relationships, and Behaviors Generate Collaborative Capacity." *The Journal of Applied Behavioral Science* 60.1 (2022) 149–93. https://doi.org/10.1177/00218863221106245.

Berkhout, Loes. "Interdisciplinary Work in Chaplaincy Care." In *Learning Form Case Studies in Chaplaincy. Towards Practice Based Evidence & Professionalism*, edited by Renske Kruizinga, et al., 174–81. Utrecht: Eburon, 2020.

Cadge, Wendy. *Paging God. Religion in the Halls of Medicine*. Chicago: University of Chicago Press, 2012.

———. "God on the Fly? The Professional Mandates of Airport Chaplains." *Sociology of Religion* 78.4 (2017) 437–55. https://doi.org/10.1093/socrel/srx025.

---

48. For the description of the domain of chaplaincy according to the Dutch professional standard, see Chapter 2. For the results of Den Toom's research, see Chapters 17, 19, and 20.

Cadge, Wendy, and Shelly Rambo, eds. *Chaplaincy and Spiritual Care in the Twenty-First Century. An Introduction*. Chapel Hill: University of North Carolina Press, 2022.

Claessen, Jacques. *Forgiveness in Criminal Law through Incorporating Restorative Mediation*. Oisterwijk: Wolf Legal, 2017.

De Vries, Reijer, et al. "OG Justitie: 'Niet Zonder Ons.'" In *Richting, Repertoire en Resultaat. Uitkomsten van het Nederlandse Case Studies Project Geestelijke Verzorging (2016-2021)*, edited by Jacques Körver, et al., 116-33. Utrecht: PThU-UCGV, 2023.

De Vries, Reijer, et al. "With an Open Mind for the Unexpected. Prison Chaplaincy: A Case Study." In *Learning from Case Studies in Chaplaincy. Towards Practice Based Evidence & Professionalism*, edited by Renske Kruizinga, et al., 137-46. Utrecht: Eburon, 2020.

Delmotte, Florence. "Identity, Identification, Habitus. A Process Sociology Approach." In *The Palgrave Handbook of the History of Human Sciences*, edited by David McCallum, et al., 725-48. Singapore: Palgrave Macmillan, 2022.

Garrett-Cobbina, Laurie. "The Emotional Undercurrents of Organizations." In *Chaplaincy and Spiritual Care in the Twenty-First Century. An Introduction*, edited by Wendy Cadge and Shelly Rambo, 239-57. Chapel Hill: University of North Carolina Press, 2022.

Hofstede, Geert, et al. *Cultures and Organizations. Software of the Mind. Intercultural Cooperation and Its Importance for Survival*. 3rd ed. New York: McGraw-Hill, 2010.

Hutton, Marie, and Dominique Moran, eds. *The Palgrave Handbook of Prison and the Family*. Cham: Palgrave Macmillan, 2019.

Jones, Laura K., et al. "Ethological Observations of Social Behavior in the Operating Room." *PNAS* 115.29 (2018) 7575-80. https://doi.org/10.1073/pnas.1716883115.

Jorissen, Gertjan, et al. "You Can Remove a Person from the War, but Not the War from a Person." In *Learning from Case Studies in Chaplaincy. Towards Practice Based Evidence & Professionalism*, edited by Renske Kruizinga, et al., 159-64. Utrecht: Eburon, 2020.

Klitzman, Robert, et al. "Hospital Chaplains' Communication with Patients: Characteristics, Functions and Potential Benefits." *Patient Education and Counseling* 105.9 (2022) 2905-12. https://doi.org/10.1016/j.pec.2022.05.004.

Körver, Jacques. "Das Tabu der Zielorientierung durchbrechen. Mit professioneller Intuition im Krankenhaus auf der Suche nach der Seele." *Wege zum Menschen* 74.4 (2022) 368-81. https://doi.org/10.13109/weme.2022.74.4.368.

———. "OG Ziekenhuis: Wie neemt het initiatief, hoe, waarom en waartoe?" In *Richting, Repertoire en Resultaat. Uitkomsten van het Nederlandse Case Studies Project Geestelijke Verzorging (2016-2021)*, edited by Jacques Körver, et al., 145-67. Utrecht: PThU-UCGV, 2023.

Körver, Jacques, et al., eds. *Richting, Repertoire en Resultaat. Uitkomsten van het Nederlandse Case Studies Project Geestelijke Verzorging (2016-2021)*. Utrecht: PThU-UCGV, 2023.

Kruizinga, Renske, et al. "Enhancing the Integration of Chaplains within the Healthcare Team. A Qualitative Analysis of a Survey Study among Healthcare Chaplains." *Integrated Healthcare Journal* 4.1 (2023) e000138. https://doi.org/10.1136/ihj-2022-000138.

McClure, Barbara, and Mary Martha Thiel. "Introduction to Organizational Competencies." In *Chaplaincy and Spiritual Care in the Twenty-First Century. An Introduction*, edited by Wendy Cadge and Shelly Rambo, 193–200. Chapel Hill: University of North Carolina Press, 2022.

Mintzberg, Henry. *Mintzberg on Management. Inside Our Strange World of Organizations*. New York: The Free Press, 1989.

———. *Understanding Organizations . . . Finally. Structuring in Sevens*. Oakland: Berrett–Koehler, 2023.

Molendijk, Tine. "Moral Injury in Relation to Public Debates: The Role of Societal Misrecognition in Moral Conflict-Colored Trauma among Soldiers." *Social Science & Medicine* 211 (2018) 314–20. https://doi.org/10.1016/j.socscimed.2018.06.042.

———. *Moral Injury and Soldiers in Conflict: Political Practices and Public Perceptions*. Abingdon: Routledge, 2021.

Neimeijer, Elien, et al. "'Back Off Means Stay with Me'. Perceptions of Individuals with Mild Intellectual Disability or Borderline Intellectual Functioning About the Group Climate in a Secure Forensic Setting." *Journal of Intellectual Disabilities and Offending Behaviour* 12.1 (2021) 47–60. https://doi.org/10.1108/JIDOB-09-2020-0015.

Nieuwsma, Jason A., et al. "Chaplaincy and Mental Health in the Department of Veterans Affairs and Department of Defense." *Journal of Health Care Chaplaincy* 19.1 (2013) 3–21. https://doi.org/10.1080/08854726.2013.775820.

Pak, Su Yon. "Through a Multi-Frame Lens: Surviving, Thriving, and Leading Organizations." In *Chaplaincy and Spiritual Care in the Twenty-First Century. An Introduction*, edited by Wendy Cadge and Shelly Rambo, 219–38. Chapel Hill: University of North Carolina Press, 2022.

Peng-Keller, Simon. *Healthcare Chaplaincy as Specialised Spiritual Care. The Christian Call for Healing in a Global Health Context*. Göttingen: Vandenhoeck & Ruprecht, 2024.

Pleizier, Theo, and Carmen M. Schuhmann. "How the Military Context Shapes Spiritual Care Interventions by Military Chaplains." *Journal of Pastoral Care & Counseling* 76.1 (2022) 4–14. https://doi.org/10.1177/15423050221076462.

Schuhmann, Carmen, et al. "How Military Chaplains Strengthen the Moral Resilience of Soldiers and Veterans: Results from a Case Studies Project in the Netherlands." *Pastoral Psychology* 72 (2023) 605–24. https://doi.org/10.1007/s11089-023-01097-5.

Sennett, Richard. *The Corrosion of Character. The Personal Consequences of Work in the New Capitalism*. New York: Norton, 1998.

Stoesz, Donald B., et al. *A Prison Chaplaincy Manual. The Canadian Context*. Victoria: Friesen, 2020.

Timmerman, Guus, et al. "In Search of Good Care. The Methodology of Phenomenological, Theory-Oriented 'N=N Case Studies' in Empirically Grounded Ethics of Care." *Medicine, Health Care and Philosophy* 22.4 (2019) 573–82. https://doi.org/10.1007/s11019-019-09892-9.

Van der Kamp, Jill, et al. "In Their Own Words: A Narrative Analysis of Illness Memoirs Written by Men with Prostate Cancer." *Sociology of Health & Illness* 44.1 (2022) 236–52. https://doi.org/10.1111/1467-9566.13412.

Van der Meer, Tjeerd. "Is Macdonald's Freedom?" In *Learning from Case Studies in Chaplaincy. Towards Practice Based Evidence & Professionalism*, edited by R. Kruizinga, et al., 147–52. Utrecht: Eburon, 2020.

Van Gerwen, Geert T. "Geestelijke Verzorging in instellingen van gezondheidszorg." *Praktische Theologie* 19.5 (1992) 467–82.

Van Hoof, Monique, et al. "Agreement Is Agreement? Moral Counseling in a Life-Threatening Dilemma." In *Learning from Case Studies in Chaplaincy. Towards Practice Based Evidence & Professionalism*, edited by Renske Kruizinga, et al., 153–58. Utrecht: Eburon, 2020.

Vanhooren, Siebrecht. *Loss of Meaning, Meaning-Making Processes, and Posttraumatic Growth among Prisoners*. Leuven: Katholieke Universiteit Leuven, 2015. https://lirias.kuleuven.be/retrieve/341924.

VGVZ. *Professional Standard Spiritual Caregiver 2015*. VGVZ (Amsterdam: 2015). https://vgvz.nl/wp-content/uploads/2023/02/VGVZ_Professional_Standard_2015_Main_Text_EN_v03_WITH_APPENDICES.pdf.

White, Nathan H. "Facilitating Resilience: Chaplaincy as a Catalyst for Organizational Well-Being." In *Chaplaincy and Spiritual Care in the Twenty-First Century. An Introduction*, edited by Wendy Cadge and Shelly Rambo, 201–18. Chapel Hill: University of North Carolina Press, 2022.

Yalom, Irvin D. *Existential Psychotherapy*. New York: Basic Books, 1980.

14

Apprehending Goals
—Jacques Körver

"How can a sentient person of the modern age mistake photography for reality? All perception is selection... Photographs economize the truth; they are always moments more or less illusorily abducted from time's continuum."
Sally Mann[1]

IN SEARCH OF THE SOUL

IN THIS CHAPTER WE reflect on some observations and insights from the Research Community (RC) Hospital with regard to goals of chaplaincy. The first observation is that chaplains work much more purposefully than they realize, partly because they do so implicitly. A second observation is that they rarely explicitly bring up the domain of spiritual care to which we refer as meaning and worldview,[2] although that domain constantly functions, again often implicitly, as a focal point in their work. Both observations are related and have set in motion a learning process. More explicit goal-oriented action from the perspective of meaning and worldview requires, on the one hand, engagement with and attunement to the interlocutor and

---

1. Mann, *Hold Still*, 151.
2. As described in "Observing, Interpreting, and Participating" (Chapter 2) of this volume, the Dutch professional association (VGVZ) defines the domain of spiritual care with these two terms. The two terms are not separated but tied to each other in designating the domain of spiritual care. The domain includes four dimensions: existential, spiritual, ethical, and aesthetic. See: VGVZ, *Professional Standard*.

increases, on the other hand, professional self-awareness and job satisfaction. The development in the other RCs runs parallel to that of the RC Hospital in this respect.

Below we first describe the research process within the RC Hospital. Initially, the focus was on case studies from an intensive care unit (ICU). Later case studies were added that, according to the RC, reflected more "everyday" chaplaincy care. It is noteworthy that, although the second series arose by chance, they all had meaning and worldview as their focus. Next, we present the analysis of all the case studies from the perspective of the (implicit) goals that issued from the chaplains' actions. Again, the analysis shows that meaning and worldview is the focus.

In her autobiography *Hold Still: A Memoir in Photographs*,[3] Sally Mann describes the influences on her photographic work. Although she knew from an early age that she wanted to be a photographer and that she had a very distinctive view on style and technique, her subjects and her approach were not clear beforehand. They unfolded along the way. In her most recent book, *A Thousand Crossings*,[4] she brings together 115 photographs that testify to her career and her special intuition and outlook. Through everything shines the soul of the American South, whether they be landscapes, photographs of her young children and aging husband, twelve-year-old girls, or corpses given up to impermanence for forensic purposes. In the CSP, chaplains discovered the soul and purpose of their work in a similar way.

MORE THAN A RITUAL IN INTENSIVE CARE?

Most of the case studies covered in the first phase of the project took place, as indicated, in the ICU.[5] They always pertained to a matter of life or death. One case study involved a partner's question about whether her husband could receive the Anointing of the Sick after he was admitted to the ICU due to an acute deterioration in his condition.[6] The precise description reveals how the chaplain connects and communicates with all involved in the situation, "like a liaison officer," as he says himself. He is able to connect the lifeworld and the system. The system of the hospital maintains precise protocols, especially in an ICU. By informing and involving all professionals involved—nurses, doctors, paramedics—in the anointing of the sick and its meaning for the patient and his family, space is created, figuratively and

---

3. For an overview of her work see her website: https://www.sallymann.com/.
4. Mann, *A Thousand Crossings*.
5. This section is taken from and an abridged adaptation of Körver, "Das Tabu."
6. This case study was published as: Broekhoff and Körver, "Verbindingsofficier."

literally, for loss, and grief, and the ritual. Protocols suddenly turn out to be less strict than at first.[7]

A second case study describes how the chaplain explores the resilience of a patient who has undergone a kidney transplant, after which the donor kidney is rejected and the patient has to undergo weekly dialysis while waiting for another transplant. In doing so, the chaplain uses reframing[8] (e.g., asking if she sees a new transplant as the only option), employs humor for perspective, and discusses with her the meaning of a new tattoo with the words *luctor et emergo*.[9] A third case study shows step by step how the chaplain stimulates the patient exploring her worldview resources using imagination, including a cage with a mechanical bird, which is on her bedside table, and the only item of clothing in her room, a bright red wax raincoat hanging by the door. The patient is in the ICU, on life support, for an extended period of time, as a result of serious complications after simple surgery, with the question of whether she will ever come off life support.[10]

Because the format for describing a case study called for describing situations that chaplains believed to be good practices, the aforementioned examples were included. An important factor was that patients, their loved ones, and staff considered these situations to belong to the specific field of chaplaincy. In the analyses it became clear that chaplains are particularly competent to function in such complex situations with grave effects for patients and loved ones and to respond to the question or need. They appear to have a good eye for (the hitches in) the relationships involved, both between patient and loved ones and between patient and caregivers. They are attentive to social exclusion or redundancy. They have ritual and symbolic competence, and a sense of language, to still be able to say something in situations in which others have no words. They do not run away from the agony, confusion, or silence that can overwhelm patients, nor from the major existential themes. They form a link between the systemic world of the hospital and the life world of patients and their loved ones.

Step by step, in the RC the insight emerged that they work much more purposefully than they usually claim. And although they handle all these

---

7. See Habermas, *Lifeworld and System*.

8. Reframing, in combination with humor, in the context of chaplaincy is described by American practical theologian Donald Capps: Capps, *Reframing*; Capps, "Religion and Humor." This second case study is discussed in more detail in: Körver, et al., "Geestelijke verzorging onder de loep."

9. "I struggle and I emerge," the motto of one of the Dutch provinces to describe the struggle against the sea.

10. For the relationship between religion, art, and imagination in chaplaincy, see: Alma, "Art and Religion as Invitation"; Dodge-Peters Daiss, "Art at the Bedside."

situations well, often intuitively, and they are recognized in this situation by other caregivers, those situations simultaneously evoked a kind of dissatisfaction among the participants of the RC. Is this all that we are doing? Or does it create a skewed, overly classical image of chaplaincy? What about all those other contacts, where religious or worldview background, recognition of function, and existential or spiritual questions do not (seem to) play an explicit role?

STILL MEANING AND WORLDVIEW?

From then on, the RC focused on what the chaplains themselves called more "normal and everyday" situations. "Normal and everyday" means that the referral or question is much vaguer. "Would you like to talk to the lady sometime?" "This patient has no other contacts, maybe you could visit him?" "This man doesn't talk to us and yet something is going on. Will you have a look?" It is not immediately clear whether the referral to the chaplain is the best choice. In distinction to the situations described in the previous section, the role, content, and expectation of chaplaincy are less fixed. It is a kind of search process, together with the patient and with other professionals. Initially, there seem to be fewer scenarios available for their actions or functioning. However, the interactions do not appear to have fewer consequences, as some examples below show.

An example is a case study in which the chaplain is asked to counsel a woman whose breast cancer has recurred a third time. The accompaniment revolves around finding inspiration in life again, something the patient managed to do after the first two times. She is completely exhausted, physically, mentally, and spiritually. The care takes place as part of an oncology rehabilitation regimen, in which other health care providers (physical therapist, dietician, social worker, and physician) work to build energy, and the chaplain brings her own emphasis to that regimen, working on inspiration (see "Energy *and* Inspiration," Chapter 4). Another case study describes the first conversation on a Monday morning that a chaplain has with a woman about her partner who has an incurable form of cancer and about her concerns and fears in the process. She had been admitted urgently the night before with severe lung problems. During the conversation the photo album the woman is making about all they do together as husband and wife comes up, as does the knitting the woman is working on (a scarf, although outside temperatures are high). Photo album and knitting are ways for her to cope with the situation, on the one hand to recall good memories, on the other to find peace while waiting in all those waiting rooms in the hospital, or when she cannot sleep at night. Both activities are examples that contribute to increasing inner space, according to the chaplain.[11] It ended with this one conversation, as the woman was discharged from the hospital the following day.

A subsequent case study describes a chaplain's renewed contact with a very elderly patient, who a year earlier spent a long period in the hospital and nursing home following a major oncology procedure. She had been readmitted through the emergency room. As it turns out, she has metastases, about which nothing more can be done. The chaplain offers support in processing the bad news. The patient tends to talk a lot, keeping her feelings at bay. She prefers to keep the conversation as light-hearted as possible. By asking directly and explicitly about the meaning of the situation, the chaplain can occasionally break through the surface. It is a delicate balance between going along with the lightheartedness and focused probing. In the RC, that was called "diluted seriousness" or "homeopathic humor."

Even when the RC had planned to bring in the "first case on Monday morning," it turned out repeatedly that one of Irvin Yalom's four existential themes always came into play: the inevitability of death, dealing with freedom and responsibility, existential loneliness, and the tension between meaningfulness and meaninglessness in existence.[12] Although chaplains do not intend to address these themes in advance, they always come up. Is it because other caregivers implicitly refer in such situations? Or is it because patients have an almost archetypal image of the chaplain, with whom one talks about such topics? Or might it be because chaplains have learned in their training and professional socialization to be precisely attentive to these themes. It could also be because in a crisis situation the presence of a caregiver who is patient, interested, and non-judgmental is an incentive to bring up those existential issues. All of these possibilities (in different combinations) may play a role. In any case, reflecting on that led to two insights: chaplains are much more purposeful than they think, and their purposefulness is colored by the domain of meaning and worldview.

WHO INITIATES THE CONTACT AND FOR WHAT PURPOSE?

At the completion of the CSP, an analysis of all twenty-three case studies that had been described and jointly analyzed by the participants of the RC

---

11. The concept of *inner space* is derived from Carlo Leget's *ars moriendi*, or Diamond Model: Leget, *Art of Living*.

12. Yalom, *Existential Psychotherapy*.

Hospital was carried out.[13] Of the patients involved, seventeen were women and six were men. The average age was almost fifty-eight years, with a range of nineteen to eighty-three years. Of them, fifteen were married or cohabiting and sixteen of them had one or more children. Nine of them were disabled or retired, and seven were working in care or assistance. The background of seventeen of them was Christian, although for half of them the current orientation had shifted to non-Christian or secular.

In the thematic analysis,[14] aimed at the question of what interventions were addressed with what goal and with what result, three scenarios could be identified in the way the contact between patient and chaplains had been established: (1) at the initiative of the patient (or a loved one), (2) at the initiative of the chaplain, and (3) through referral by another health care provider. The analysis led to the description of the scenarios and the interventions, goals, and outcomes for each scenario.

Scenario 1—Patient's Initiative

If the patient or a loved one took the initiative, the questions were aligned with the professional content of the chaplain, to the extent present in the patient's or loved one's perception. On the one hand, they were requests for a ritual or sacramental act, such as a request for anointment or blessing of the sick in the ICU just before the patient's death, request of an already elderly expectant mother for the blessing of their child after the termination of pregnancy (with a diagnosed abnormality), and a request of a patient and his partner for regular prayer (far from home and uncertain about the outcome of treatment). On the other hand, there were requests to discuss fundamental ethical questions regarding the further treatment of a child with a congenital degenerative disease, for conversation from a religious perspective on coping with the imminent death of a partner, and for conversation about the religious experience and meaning of a serious illness and its impact on the patient's and partner's autonomy, work, and expectations about the future. Patients had a more or less clear idea of what to expect and ask from a chaplain. The contacts took place within a relatively short time frame (one day to a maximum of three weeks).

With a ritual, chaplains aimed to support perseverance during and coping with a pivotal moment in the life of the person(s) involved. They

---

13. Körver, "Wie neemt het initiatief." This section is an abbreviated version of that chapter from the CSP's final report.

14. Braun and Clarke, "Thematic Analysis"; Braun and Clarke, "Conceptual and Design Thinking."

wanted to embed that moment in the patients' religious or worldview background, in a larger story that could provide a framework for farewell and loss. The ritual provided space for the patient's story and focused on changing expectations for the future. As a marker in the discontinuity of existence, the ritual served as a bridge between the world of home, faith and cultural tradition, and the hospital. The ritual was given a place in the care process as a whole.

When discussing existential and ethical questions, chaplains first and foremost set themselves the goal of taking stock of what questions or topics were at hand, putting some order to them and possibly setting priorities for care, for the sake of overview and differentiation in (emotionally and existentially) complex and stacked problems. Implicit or explicit choices were made in the topics to be discussed. Next, the goal was to focus on the experience and meaning of illness and treatment, in connection with the patient's religious or worldview perspective. Chaplains offered words, stories, and images to become aware of in order to hold and nurture other perspectives. In some situations, the goal of chaplains was to be intermediaries between patient and ward for the purpose of (improving) mutual trust.

Scenario 2—Chaplain's Initiative

When chaplains took the initiative, two sub-scenarios occurred. In two case studies, chaplains visited the patient during readmission (after a signal from the electronic patient record) on the assumption that renewed contact would be necessary or desired. There was neither a concrete question nor a request for a consultation on the part of a caregiver. The assumption was that continued contact during a follow-up admission would contribute to the patient's well-being, as a form of an open supply and demand. In the second sub-scenario, the chaplain contacted the patient based on an intuitive impression from a nurse, just to see if there was a question at hand, which given the severity of the illness or the complexity of the situation was not unlikely. In both sub-scenarios, meaning and worldview were leading factors. The duration of contact was limited to a relatively short time frame of up to three weeks.

The chaplains emphasized fidelity and regularity of visits, almost as ends in themselves. They thereby countered the fleeting nature of most contacts with health care providers, who are often (re)identifiable only in their job title and not by name. They broke through the isolation that could occur when patients felt as if they were stuck with questions, insecurities, or fears. Chaplains sought to be an example to other caregivers on how to "look beyond" so-called deviant behaviors and on how person and profession can be compatible. They offered language, words, and images for existential experiences. Patients could distance themselves from those experiences, put some order to them, specify them, nuance them, put them into perspective, or reinterpret them. Agency and self-esteem, overview, and integration were offered an opportunity. In doing so, chaplains assessed the patient's abilities and limitations. They understood the patient's actual behavior, attitudes, and expressions as embodiments and gateways to the patient's personal attitude to life and faith. Through their implicit and explicit interest in meaning and worldview, they brought breadth and depth to the patient's account. The patient's story became multidimensional, and faith or worldview were activated. Implicitly, chaplains formed a kind of reminder of the transcendent, representing that world.

Scenario 3—Referral by a Health Care Provider

In more than half of the case studies, the contact came by referral from another health care provider. Sometimes the caregiver had spoken with the patient about possible referral to chaplaincy. Some of those consultation requests were not very sharply formulated. However, the wording did indicate major impact on the patient's well-being as a result of duration of admission, or of the complexity of the illness or treatment, issues that led to a sense of powerlessness or inadequacy on the part of the referring care providers. The formulations were variations on a theme. "The patient is (very) emotional, has been through a lot lately, is going through an admission that is longer or more intense than expected, is fretting, has doubts about the meaning of surgery, is difficult to gauge, is in a negative spiral, feels as if it is all becoming too much for her/him." The fact that caregivers chose a chaplain had to do with familiarity with the chaplain or a protocol about long stay patients.

There were also referrals that were more precisely tailored to the professional content of chaplaincy, at least from the perception of the referrer. They included the request to discuss the life-threatening situation or the increasing dependency in which the patient found herself, the caregiver's suspicion or very perception that faith might play a role in the disease process, or a patient history indicating that a question in the area of faith, church, or worldview had been raised by the illness. Thus, although the consultation requests were not always sharply tailored to the subject matter of chaplaincy, caregivers had at least a rough idea of relevant issues.[15] The picture was sharper the more often the chaplains entered into discussions

---

15. See for example: Damen, et al., "What Do Chaplains Do."

with other caregivers or was included in a protocol (for example, anamnesis or standard visits during complications, or ICU admission). Most of those contacts had a high frequency, often over a long to very long period of time (two to three months, even up to two years). The duration alone suggests that the problems were complex, involving serious medical complications, long-term care, or an accumulation of problems.

In short-term contacts, chaplains named the goal of faithful, undivided, and unconditional attention, a free space for telling about ups and downs. A goal was also to bring peace and inner space, to clarify awareness of time (in relation to life story) and place (hospital and social network). Chaplains wanted to provide space for (reordering) the story of profound experiences, as well as recognition of panic, grief, hopelessness, tragedy, and powerlessness. They recognized the ambivalences of hope and despair, faith and doubt, and defiance and resignation. Their aim was to help patients reflect on the consequences of illness or hospitalization. A goal was also to help patients be aware of their sources of strength, their familiar ways of coping, and their support from a social network. Moreover, chaplains aimed to activate a spiritual or religious perspective, affirming faith and trust in the face of fear and loneliness. In doing so, they regularly presented themselves, implicitly and explicitly, as representatives of the world of faith or worldview.

Those goals also played a role in long-term care processes. Added to that was that chaplains worked on the long term, represented continuity in the care process, and acted as confidants and points of recognition. An important goal was to find words and images for the experiences, promoting reflection on illness, treatment, and future, and on one's desires and self-confidence. Subsequent goals included ordering, reframing, and, if necessary, correcting choices and beliefs, taking stock of current and past experiences, and arriving at a coherent story. An important goal was to break through one-sided desires for control and autonomy and to help patients to relate those desires to experiences of uncertainty, powerlessness, vulnerability, and displacement. That integration also offered insight for the patients into their own spirituality, inspiration, and strength of mind. Usually chaplains did this with a certain sense of humor that helped to put things into perspective with a degree of lightness. In the long-term contacts, chaplains could also promote the concerns of the hospital. That could involve explaining medical information to patients, providing care personnel instructions for treating patients, or explicitly emphasizing spirituality as a goal or common thread in care and rehabilitation.

PURPOSEFULNESS OF CHAPLAINCY

"I have no goals in my chaplaincy care." In many variations, chaplains in the CSP made this known in advance. Thematic analysis, in the RC and in later review of the case studies, revealed that their standpoint did not correspond with their practice. One insight was that chaplains often have a mistaken idea of what constitutes a *goal* in a care process. Participants assumed that a goal is chosen independently of the interlocutor, prior to the contact. Moreover, they assumed that a goal works like an algorithm. There is a uniform solution for every situation as long as you follow the instructions. However, chaplaincy care, like all other forms of care, works on the basis of heuristic search schemes.[16] Implicit questions and goals are discovered and developed in the course of the accompaniment, based in part on search schemas that chaplains have internalized in their training and practice. As the project progressed, some of those mostly implicit heuristic search schemas became clear, and with them, the goals they have in mind, always in interaction with the other. Niels Den Toom refers to this as *labyrinthic purposiveness*. Even if the path seems to diverge, it eventually ends up in the center.[17] Often intuitively, chaplains are oriented toward worldview questions, such as "Where does the courage come from in patients who, despite all the hopelessness, try to seize the day?" or "What could all those drawings behind the bed, the figurine on the bedside table, or that conspicuous coat by the door have to do with someone's outlook on life?" or "What does that tattoo, obtained during the period of illness, mean for the process of dealing with the illness?" That is what their professional interest is, that is how they are socialized into the profession, and that was the orientation of their education. That is what they know and do.

In the context of the CSP and based on chaplaincy literature, Myriam Braakhuis observed that chaplains tend to work primarily on the basis of a relational attitude and that they formulate few or no goals in their care.[18] That conclusion from the literature was not confirmed in the practice described in the case studies. What chaplains regularly say about themselves does not always correspond to their practice. One of the participants put into words that he apparently draws from a "delta-like reservoir" of methods, models, and theories, a reservoir that has been fed during his training and professional experience from numerous sources, currents, and streams, from which he often draws intuitively, but whose origins he often can no

---

16. De Groot and Medendorp, "Signific Concept Analysis."

17. Den Toom, *The Chaplain-Researcher*, 225; also 158–60. For more on the research by Den Toom, see Chapters 17, 19, and 20 in this volume.

18. Braakhuis, "Professional Proximity."

longer precisely trace. In the reflection by the RC, the term *professional intuition* was introduced for this purpose.[19] A similar term, *professional body of knowledge,* was explored in the RC Mental Health. In this concept, formal professional knowledge, lived and embodied work and life experience, and concrete relational practice are intertwined.[20] Based on their professional intuition, chaplains get to work right away, as soon as they hear or read the first words of the referral and as soon as they set foot across the threshold. Impressions about referral, first contact, and further interaction activate aspects from that delta-like reservoir or from their *embodied knowledge,* activate heuristic search schemas, and focus listening and action on existential and spiritual questions or needs.

While analyzing the case study in which the chaplain asks about the patient's knitting and the photo album (see above), the chaplain discovered that she is always keen on the referential and symbolic value of seemingly mundane activities. She realized that her perception of them is *intuitively professionally oriented* because life experiences and questions are embodied in it. That realization was further supported by theory in this area. Something similar occurred in the case study in which the chaplain focused attention on the patient's new tattoo (*luctor et emergo*).[21]

Both the analyses in the RC and the later thematic analysis made chaplains more conscious of their *tacit knowledge.*[22] Theories are often congealed in action into self-evident *one-liners* that can be representations, on the one hand, of nuanced and differentiated theoretical knowledge but, on the other, also of fragments of essential elements of a theory or model. Becoming more aware of those premises leads to more nuanced or differentiated guidance in action and may also lead to correction of those premises through a renewed acquaintance with the full breadth of the theory. In any case, such reflections led to the awareness that chaplains work in a more purposeful manner than they imagined and that purposefulness is not to the detriment of the client, on the contrary. They realized that the very awareness (and possible adjustment) of theoretical models contributes to a more personalized

---

19. The term *professional intuition* originated in the world of education; see, among others: Claxton and Atkinson, *The Intuitive Practitioner.*

20. Muthert, et al., "Re-Evaluating a Suicide Pact," 82; Weeda and Muthert, "What Does Participation," 171. In his research, Den Toom describes the transition among participating chaplains from *embodied knowledge* to *body of knowledge*: Den Toom, *The Chaplain-Researcher,* 142–46.

21. A very recent dissertation that calls attention to what patients have at heart (in palliative care) and thus to the seemingly mundane comments that embody those very questions of life is: Van Meurs, *Spirituality in Healthcare.*

22. Polanyi, *The Tacit Dimension.* See also: Körver, "Ritual as a House," 117–18.

approach. At the same time, the reflection revealed that there is a discourse within chaplaincy in which goal orientation is considered less appropriate.[23] That discourse assumes that goal orientation typically belongs to therapy, is determined prior to the encounter or independently of the client, and ultimately leads to an almost protocol-based accompaniment process that threatens to put chaplaincy in a straitjacket of standardization.

Whichever way one turns it, chaplains have the existential or spiritual well-being of patients and clients in mind. They pursue that with *professional intuition*, with goals gradually emerging from the interactions with their clients. Those goals have to do with the domain of chaplaincy: meaning and worldview or religion.[24] Here it is important to point out a distinction between general goals of chaplaincy and specific goals in the concrete care process, that is made in the answer of the research questions of the CSP.[25]

TO CONCLUDE

During the course of the CSP a remarkable process of development occurred with the chaplains in the RCs. On the one hand they moved toward a more client-centered attitude in their practice that distanced them to some extent from more traditional, ecclesiastic positions on their role. And at the same time, they learned to recognize their own worldviews and their own religious expertise and identity more clearly, more *con amore*, and chose to work with it purposefully. A new professionalism of chaplaincy began to emerge, a new or renewed profession. By working with those simultaneous movements in an explicit, nuanced, deliberate, and detailed way, the CSP contributed to the development of the professional identity of the chaplains and their understanding of their profession. That served to bring not only the chaplains but, more importantly, also their patients, closer to their souls.[26]

---

23. Braakhuis, "Professional Proximity." See also Mackor, "Standardization of Spiritual Care."

24. See also the evaluations of some participating mental health professionals: Berkhout, "Interdisciplinary Work"; Weeda and Muthert, "What Does Participation."

25. See "Answering the Research Question" (Chapter 22).

26. A further elaboration of this development can be found in Den Toom's research that examined the impact of chaplains' participation in the CSP on their professionalism: Den Toom, *The Chaplain-Researcher*. See further Chapters 17, 19, and 20.

REFERENCES

Alma, Hans. "Art and Religion as Invitation. An Exploration Based on John Dewey's Theory of Experience and Imagination." *Perichoresis* 18.3 (2020) 33–45. https://doi.org/10.2478/perc-2020-0015.

Berkhout, Loes. "Interdisciplinary Work in Chaplaincy Care." In *Learning Form Case Studies in Chaplaincy. Towards Practice Based Evidence & Professionalism*, edited by Renske Kruizinga, et al., 174–81. Utrecht: Eburon, 2020.

Braakhuis, Myriam. "Professional Proximity. Seeking a Balance between Relation and Content in Spiritual Counseling." In *Learning from Case Studies in Chaplaincy. Towards Practice Based Evidence & Professionalism*, edited by Renske Kruizinga, et al., 112–17. Utrecht: Eburon, 2020.

Braun, Virginia, and Victoria Clarke. "Thematic Analysis." In *APA Handbook of Research Methods in Psychology, Volume 2: Research Designs: Quantitative, Qualitative, Neuropsychological, and Biological*, edited by Harris Cooper, et al. APA Handbooks in Psychology, 57–71. Washington: American Psychological Association, 2012.

———. "Conceptual and Design Thinking for Thematic Analysis." *Qualitative Psychology* 9.1 (2022) 3–26. https://doi.org/10.1037/qup0000196.

Broekhoff, Frans, and Jacques Körver. "Verbindingsofficier." In *Met lichaam en geest: De rituele competentie van geestelijk verzorgers*, edited by Jacques Körver, et al., 66–72. Utrecht: Eburon, 2021.

Capps, Donald. *Reframing: A New Method in Pastoral Care*. Minneapolis: Fortress, 1990.

———. "Religion and Humor. Estranged Bedfellows." *Pastoral Psychology* 54.5 (2006) 413–38. https://doi.org/10.1007/s11089-005-0008-8.

Claxton, Guy, and Terry Atkinson, eds. *The Intuitive Practitioner: On the Value of Not Always Knowing What One Is Doing*. Buckinghamshire: Open University Press, 2000.

Damen, Annelieke, et al. "What Do Chaplains Do: The Views of Palliative Care Physicians, Nurses, and Social Workers." *The American Journal of Hospice & Palliative Care* 36.5 (2019) 396–401. https://doi.org/10.1177/1049909118807123.

De Groot, Adrianus D., and Fester L Medendorp. "Signific Concept Analysis. A Modern Approach." *Methodology & Science* 21.4 (1988) 247–74.

Den Toom, Niels. *The Chaplain-Researcher. The Perceived Impact of Participation in a Dutch Research Project on Chaplains' Professionalism*. Utrecht: Eburon, 2022.

Dodge-Peters Daiss, Susan. "Art at the Bedside. Reflections on Use of Visual Imagery in Hospital Chaplaincy." *Journal of Pastoral Care & Counseling* 70.1 (2016) 70–79. https://doi.org/10.1177/1542305015618170.

Habermas, Jürgen. *Lifeworld and System. A Critique of Functionalist Reason. Volume 2: The Theory of Communicative Action*. Cambridge: Polity Press, 1987.

Körver, Jacques. "Ritual as a House with Many Mansions. Inspirations from Cultural Anthropology for Interreligious Cooperation." *Yearbook for Ritual and Liturgical Studies* 32 (2016) 105–23. https://ugp.rug.nl/jvlo/article/view/27209.

———. "Das Tabu der Zielorientierung durchbrechen. Mit professioneller Intuition im Krankenhaus auf der Suche nach der Seele." *Wege zum Menschen* 74.4 (2022) 368–81. https://doi.org/10.13109/weme.2022.74.4.368.

———. "OG Ziekenhuis: Wie neemt het initiatief, hoe, waarom en waartoe?" In *Richting, Repertoire en Resultaat. Uitkomsten van het Nederlandse Case Studies Project Geestelijke Verzorging (2016-2021)*, edited by Jacques Körver, et al., 145-67. Utrecht: PThU–UCGV, 2023.

Körver, Jacques, et al. "Geestelijke verzorging onder de loep. Elementen van zingeving en levensbeschouwing als aanknopingspunt voor de christelijke traditie?" In *Over de hardnekkige aanwezigheid van het Christendom*, edited by Sam Goyvaerts, et al. Utrechtse Studies, XXIII, 140-56. Almere: Parthenon, 2020.

Leget, Carlo. *Art of Living, Art of Dying. Spiritual Care for a Good Death*. Foreword by George Fitchett. London: Kingsley, 2017.

Mackor, Anne Ruth. "Standardization of Spiritual Care in Healthcare Facilities in the Netherlands. Blessing of Curse?" *Ethics and Social Welfare* 3.2 (2009) 215-28. https://doi.org/10.1080/17496530902951996.

Mann, Sally. *Hold Still. A Memoir with Photographs*. New York: Back Bay Books, 2016.

———. *A Thousand Crossings*. New York: Abrams, 2018.

Muthert, Hanneke, et al. "Re-Evaluating a Suicide Pact. Embodied Moral Counselling in a Dutch Case Study of Mental Healthcare Chaplaincy." *Tidsskrift for Praktisk Teologi* 36.2 (2019) 81-89. https://doi.org/https://doi.org/10.48626/tpt.v36i2.5357

Polanyi, Michael. *The Tacit Dimension*. New York: Doubleday, 1967.

Van Meurs, Jacqueline M. J. *Spirituality in Healthcare. Identifying, Exploring and Integrating into Care Provision What Matters Most to a Patient with Advanced Illness*. w.p.: published in-house, 2024.

VGVZ. *Professional Standard Spiritual Caregiver 2015*. VGVZ (Amsterdam: 2015). https://vgvz.nl/wp-content/uploads/2023/02/VGVZ_Professional_Standard_2015_Main_Text_EN_v03_WITH_APPENDICES.pdf.

Weeda, Jacqueline, and Hanneke Muthert. "What Does Participation in the Case Studies Project Mean for One's Professionalism? Preliminary Findings and Topics." In *Learning from Case Studies in Chaplaincy. Towards Practice Based Evidence & Professionalism*, edited by Renske Kruizinga, et al., 167-73. Utrecht: Eburon, 2020.

Yalom, Irvin D. *Existential Psychotherapy*. New York: Basic Books, 1980.

15

Aesthetic Counseling
— Martin Walton

"... not light that comes from the day,
nor light from the night,
but light with a luster of its own."

Rejzl Zychlinski[1]

COUNSELING AND MORE[2]

WHEN CHAPLAINS ARE ASKED to write down what they actually do in contacts with others, it is in no way surprising that conversation is a large part of the story, including verbatim reports on exchanges with others. Chaplaincy is a communicative activity, dealing with concerns and meanings, with perspectives and worldviews that are put into words and expressed. One does not need a case study project in order to establish the fact that conversation and the use of language play a major role in chaplaincy. In fact, conversation, counseling, and verbal communication provide more or less a dominant paradigm for chaplaincy, as is evident when other forms of communication are lumped together under the denominator "non-verbal communication" or one speaks of "body language." Communication by means of language and words seems to be an implicit norm, even in situations such

---

1. Excerpt from "I look into the eyes of Rembrandt." Brill, *Sprakeloos water*, 250–251. Translation by Martin Walton. Used with permission.

2. Portions of this article appeared previously in German in Walton, "Wie ein Spaziergang im Grünen."

as dementia, coma, severe handicaps, or hearing impairment, where verbal communication is limited or impossible and "other" or "alternate" forms of communication are sought.

Many of the chaplains in the Case Studies Project (CSP) indicated that they were well-trained in conversational and counseling techniques. Prevalent was the non-directive approach of Carl Rogers[3] but other forms of counseling such as motivational interviewing,[4] contemplative listening,[5] and moral counseling[6] were also named. The term "counseling" was employed (the English word is used untranslated in Dutch) to refer to various approaches and was at times more or less synonymous with a conversational approach or scheme. That indicates that the term counseling does possess an intentional focus, but that the meaning and method are not always clear or precise. In the Research Community (RC) Mixed Fields, the question arose whether the counseling by chaplains is in any way distinguishable from counseling in other psychological and social services. What does it mean when we say that chaplains offer counseling?

For the observations that follow two formal aspects of counseling are of importance. The first is the central place afforded to a person (client centeredness) to express or talk about one's own concerns or to tell one's story. The chaplain invites a person to express oneself and follows the direction or logic of what the other has to say. In the second place, support and encouragement to talk are offered by the chaplain through the use of specific techniques such as mirroring, offering recognition, summarizing, providing focus, naming ambivalences, reframing, and reflecting. In what follows we first explore the notion of counseling with regard to matters of meaning and worldview before turning more specifically to the notion of aesthetic counseling. The latter term arose during the review of a case in a research community (RC), in which aesthetic means were used in a manner similar to the function of verbal counseling.

WORLDVIEW COUNSELING

In a review of case studies produced in the RC Mixed Fields, the participants recognized that counseling by the chaplains did not distinguish itself in the use of technique, but in applying the techniques to clients' expressions with regard to meaning, values, and worldview. For example, in the context of

3. Rogers et al., *Client Centered Therapy*.
4. Miller and Rollnick, *Motivational Interviewing*.
5. Evers, "Contemplative Listening."
6. De Groot and Van Hoek, "Contemplative Listening in Moral Issues."

juvenile care, a chaplain listens to a young man's telling about his problems with his family.[7] The chaplain invites Richard to look at the situation from the position of his father, a fairly common approach in counseling. At one point the chaplain mirrors what Richard is saying about his family with the image of a roundabout without an exit, an image Richard finds helpful. The focus of the exchange shifts from relational issues to the reflection by the chaplain on what Richard says that indicate his desire for freedom. That the sense of confinement Richard experienced in his family is reproduced in the juvenile care setting and seems to reinforce Richard's suicidal thoughts, only complicates the matter. The chaplain further realizes how young people in juvenile care are pushed to decide what they want with their lives, while they simultaneously feel that they are not being listened to and not in a position to have real choices. As the chaplain often encounters such issues regarding a lack of freedom, he is sensitized in listening and responding to Richard's remarks. At the same time, freedom is an existential and ethical issue that belongs to the domain of meaning and worldview that defines chaplaincy.

The example shows how the listening and responding of chaplains are attuned to matters of meaning. They use their listening skills and employ counseling techniques to recognize, identify, and explore such issues. It is not the technique but the focus and content of their counseling that makes their counseling characteristic of the work of chaplains. That finding by the research community is paralleled by research in which clients in mental health care were interviewed on their experiences with chaplains.[8] The clients were very positive about the way in which chaplains listen and are capable of empathy, skills and qualities that are crucial to chaplaincy but not unique to it. A closer look at the interview material revealed that the positive evaluation of the listening and empathy of the chaplains usually stood in direct relation to the reflection, introduction, or focus on matters of meaning and worldview.

In the research community this understanding of counseling received the label "worldview counseling." The terminology requires some clarification.[9] "Worldview counseling" is congruent with the description of the goal of chaplaincy as "worldview communication" by Wim Smeets.[10] It is reminiscent of the term "worldview dialoguing," that Christa Anbeek employs in a slightly different context.[11] And the focus on meaning or worldview,

---

7. Van der Meer, "Is MacDonald's Freedom?"
8. Walton, *Hoe waait de wind?*
9. See the discussion of the term worldview in Chapter 3.
10. Smeets, *Spiritual Care in a Hospital.*
11. Anbeek, "World-viewing Dialogues."

especially religiosity, seems a logical consequence of the manner in which chaplaincy has emerged from pastoral counseling.[12]

In another context, however, Wendy Cadge, et al., speak of a "shift away from counseling and towards spiritual care and chaplaincy."[13] Their way of putting it seems to be a way of distinguishing chaplaincy and spiritual care as multifaith or interfaith endeavors from counseling in specifically ecclesial settings or with (Christian) pastoral attachments. What Cadge, et al., write about counseling does not seem to indicate a communicative art or conversational method, but its use in pastoral or religious settings. In the same article, however, the "enormous wisdom" of religious sources for facing suffering as a source for chaplaincy care is also emphasized, as well as the importance of theological reflection.

Our findings suggest that one could also speak of "chaplaincy counseling" or "spiritual care counseling," although we use the term "worldview counseling," as a conversational approach that employs techniques of counseling with a focus on matters of meaning, values, and wisdom and with the use of religious and worldview (re)sources. The technique and the client centeredness are for the communication and dialogue of utmost importance and helps chaplaincy conversations to be effective. The focus on meaning and resources of worldviews is for the content of utmost importance and make the counseling characteristic of chaplaincy. Together technique and focus define worldview counseling, as an essential element of chaplaincy (and of pastoral care, for that matter), though not an encompassing paradigm. For there is more to chaplaincy than conversation, as we will see below.

AESTHETIC COUNSELING

When taking a closer look at the interactions of chaplains in the case studies, the research community noticed not only conversations and ritual activities, but any number of interactions in which use was made of the surroundings or of sensory and artistic elements. The sensitivity to notice such interactions had been enlarged by the inclusion in the format of questions about the aesthetic dimension in the case studies.[14] Aesthetic was understood

---

12. See also: Schuhmann and Damen, "Representing the Good," who understand pastoral care as representing the Good, not dependent on a specific worldview. Fortuin, et al., "Worldview Commitment and Narrative," also speak of religious and non-religious worldviews as the background for life narratives.

13. Cadge et al., "Training Chaplains and Spiritual Caregivers," 194.

14. See Chapter 2.

partly in terms of beauty and art, of beauty (and ugliness) in culture and nature, but also in terms of the root meaning of the Greek word *aisthésis*,[15] as referring to the senses, sense perception, and affection. The sensitivity for the aesthetic directed attention to artistic and sensory means and physical instruments that chaplains employed in their contacts with others. To put it differently, not only their focus on questions of meaning but also their "peripheral vision" with regard to aesthetic means and the surroundings (what one might call "environmental factors") were seen to be essential to the chaplain's care.

In the final report of the RC Eldercare,[16] a palette of sensory perceptions, corporal and beautiful, presented themselves in the case studies, both from the perspective of chaplain interventions and from the perspective of residents.

a. Seeing light, candles, images, and objects.

b. Smelling flowers, food, and perfume in the course of a ritual or group encounter.

c. "Tasting," that is, taking in the atmosphere in a room (clinic, resident quarters, hallways), space (garden, area with sitting arrangement), and ritual or meditative setting (funeral, chapel).

d. Hearing music, voice quality, sounds from the surroundings (like a squeaking wheel chair), silence.

e. Feeling materials such as cards in a group conversation or objects during a symbolic transaction.

While in some instances the surroundings or sensory objects may be understood as accompanying or contributing factors, it is often possible to indicate a more primary function they fulfill. The way chairs are arranged in a chaplain's office not only provides comfort, but may also offer a client a certain spaciousness, a view of some aesthetic object, or a sense of reciprocity. The juvenile care chaplain, mentioned above, who takes a young person into a nature area or to a fast food restaurant, discovers that the surroundings not only help a person open up, but are also a trigger for other things: gaining a different perspective on things or a sense of freedom. When we asked what function sensory means fulfilled, we discovered that their function was often like that of counseling: mirroring, offering recognition, providing focus, reframing, and reflecting. That led to the name "aesthetic counseling" for the intentional use of physical surroundings and sensory

15. Meyer, "Introduction: From Imagined Communities."
16. De Groot, et al., "Van ambacht en kunst," 186.

material to actively contribute to the expression and self-understanding of the client.

The term aesthetic counseling first arose in the evaluation of a case study ("The Enigma of a Day," Chapter 5), in which a chaplain offers care to Marianne who has terminal cancer. Marianne's aesthetic style of living, seeking beauty, proportionality, and control, was encountered to help her deal with her situation. The most obvious aesthetic interaction was the use of a painting to reflect and provide recognition for the woman's feelings. Similar to the use of a metaphor, the image provides occasion for recognition and reminiscence.[17] That is strengthened by the title of the painting, "The Enigma of a Day," that parallels a verbal intervention of the chaplain speaking of "the enigma of existence." A metaphor such as balance (in "Exposure?," Chapter 6) or simply a term such as trust ("Exposure?") or "inspiration" ("Energy *and* Inspiration," Chapter 4) can itself have a performative effect and elicit a sensory response, similar to the aesthetic effect of a painting or artwork. The painting does not replace conversation, but is part of it as a complementary means of communication.

The effect of the poetry on Marianne is similar. Poetry uses language and puts things into words as do verbal forms of counseling. At the same time, a poem is a literary object of art, an aesthetic artefact, that in the constellation of wording, phrasing, spacing, rhythm, and imagery has a sensory, aesthetic effect. Similar to the effect of a ritual, poetry involves the body with its senses in the communication. The literary means serve to enrich the interaction with the other[18] and expand the imagination of the other.[19] In the case of Marianne the evaluation of the chaplaincy care is also expressed in aesthetic-metaphorical terms: like "reading a good book or taking a hike through heather" ("The Enigma of a Day," Chapter 5). That way of putting it fits well with her "aesthetic worldview" and accentuates the aesthetic aspects of the care.

USE OF CULTURAL-AESTHETIC SOURCES AND SURROUNDINGS

Once the term aesthetic counseling had been coined, the research community began to recognize more examples in which working with aesthetic material functioned in ways similar to counseling. In a conversation with a patient in the context of palliative home care the question arises what music

17. Cf. Dodge-Peters Daiss, "Art at the Bedside."
18. Burns, "My Story to be Told"; Ostrander, "The Chasing of Tales."
19. McClure, "Expanding the Psychological Imagination."

will be played at the funeral. At the next meeting, the chaplain offers a song that mirrors the needs of the patient as expressed in previous conversations. In another case study of home care with an elderly woman, reading of a Bible story and uttering a prayer have a double function. The story mirrors hermeneutically the self-understanding of the person and connects the person symbolically to the tradition from which she comes. In the words of the prayer the conversation is summarized and comes to a focus, providing recognition for the situation of the person, while also connecting the person to her experience of faith (or doubt) and with God.

With a client with a problematic understanding of heaven, a chaplain uses the intimate and benevolent experience of the client with prayer as a parable for gaining a different perspective on heaven. In other words, the experience with prayer is mirrored in order to enable a different relation to heaven. Listening together to music in the context of homeless care often mirrors what someone had just told, but also puts it in a new perspective, or is an occasion to talk about what participants hoped for their lives. In the case study "A Church for Charly" (Chapter 9) we see how the physical arrangement for the ritual, the abstinence with regard to sensory stimuli and the physical calmness of the chaplain provide a man not only a religious practice but also physical relaxation. What began as a religious practice at the request of the mother, has a positive effect on both the spiritual and physical wellbeing of the man.

Chaplains who care for persons with intellectual disabilities often make use of visual materials. In one case when a woman was unable to talk about her grief, the chaplain introduces a narrative method with the use of pictograms and photos to enable her to relate to her loss and understand her place in her family. Another chaplain uses pictograms to help a resident group of four persons see how they communicate with each other and how they might do otherwise. An image of two people talking at the same time mirrors their experience of a lot of talking going on and no one listening to another. With Franka, a client with acquired brain damage in "I Do It My Way" (Chapter 7), the chaplain likewise makes use of visual materials and objects to enable Franka to tell her story and express her values.

In almost all of the case studies some use is made of ritual, prayer, symbol, imagery, physical materials, or an aesthetic object, even if it is only the lighting of a candle or a metaphor. The introduction of cultural and worldview resources fulfills various roles at the same time, particularly due to their aesthetic character. They connect persons with religious traditions or with their personal perspectives on life. They function as non-verbal forms of counseling by mirroring, offering recognition, reframing, et cetera. And they often have a therapeutic effect, emotionally, physically, and/

or spiritually.[20] Hans Alma has recently written of chaplains as imaginative professionals, who use story, ritual, poetry, and other art forms in helping others deal with questions of life and meaning.[21]

The use of materials, imagery, and ritual is not the only way in which the aesthetic plays a role. That is clear from the way the RC Eldercare reports on tasting the atmosphere or feeling the space. That is clear from the way the chaplain in juvenile care carefully chooses the locations for his talks with young people, outside the juvenile center if possible, with a breath of fresh air or the smell of hamburgers and french fries. That is clear in the way a chaplain carefully arranges a ritual in the room of a man with autism. It becomes evident in the observation of a chaplain in mental health care that a traumatized veteran gradually removes the posters of warfare and weapons from the walls of his room ("Wounded Warrior," Chapter 10). It is also evident in the observation of a prison chaplain that a client has moved "From Slumped to Upright" (Chapter 12). A variation is found in the way a military chaplain observes and discerns the different physical positions of persons military and civilian, in active duty and suspended, *et cetera*, and moves around from one to another, choosing her position, reading the body language, making connections, bridging gaps ("To Honor and Confirm," Chapter 11). She speaks the "language" of the family not only in her familiarity with their reformed background but also in her careful choice of an appropriate uniform for the occasion.

INTERPRETING INTERACTIONS AESTHETICALLY

With a jest in the direction of the distinction between directive and non-directive counseling the RC Mixed Fields came up with the term "indirective counseling." The interactions parallel counseling interventions in the sense that they have functional similarity to verbal counseling techniques (mirroring, focusing), fulfill similar purposes (create space, enable reflection, reframe), and are complementary to verbal approaches (for example, in providing a palette or mirror in which one sees or senses what has not yet been verbalized). While the aesthetic or metaphoric interactions are in some ways more direct, that is, more experiential, more strongly felt, or more resonant, the term "indirective" points to the manner in which the interactions run, like in billiards, via the cushions of pictograms, art, poetry, thematic approaches, fast food, a walk, symbol, or metaphor. That lends the

20. Alma, "Imagination and Transcendence"; Alma, "Art and Religion as Invitation."
21. Alma, *De kunst van pelgrimeren*.

interactions a degree of indirectness that is similar to the use of an assessment tool or narrative instrument.

Hanneke Muthert has discussed a case (not from the CSP) in which a patient remembers a melody of what turns out to be a religious song. The chaplain recognizes the melody and uses it to offer the patient an alternative manner of dealing with her grief.[22] The aesthetic means or the pastoral instrument creates a sort of middle ground or in between space that furthers communication but is less confronting than direct conversation or questions. That creates a space, or dotted line, for the client to fill in as desired. For clients the indirectness can provide a degree of freedom in relating to the intervention and addressing their issues. The term "aesthetic distance"[23] is helpful here, not too close so that something becomes a re-experience, not too far away that it becomes merely factual. The metaphor of the cushion should not, however, suggest that the aesthetic interactions are always softer. The sensory stimulus may intensify their effect.

The labels "aesthetic counseling" and "indirective counseling" do not imply a new invention, but are an attempt to interpret the way aesthetics play a role in chaplaincy interactions. That interpretation is based on the recognition that religious and poetic texts, ritual, and art have always had an aesthetic effect and value of their own. In the present context of secularization, plurality, individualism, and multiple religious belonging, however, the center of gravity with regard to the use of a text, ritual, or image may shift from the traditional meaning it had to what its aesthetic effect on a person is. That is something for chaplains to be aware of. Aesthetics has a hermeneutic dynamic of its own. And an aesthetic viewpoint enriches the observation of the chaplain. Poetic listening, that is, being attentive to the poetic aspects of how others speak, can enrich the understanding by the chaplain of what is being said.[24]

The case studies indicate that such aesthetic interactions are characteristic of chaplaincy and closely related to the focus on and function of meaning and worldview in an embodied, sensory manner. A disadvantage of interpreting the interactions in terms of counseling remains the tendency to strengthen the notion that verbal conversation is the norm of chaplaincy, despite a richness of interactions with other than verbal means. The use of music with people with dementia is meaningful in itself and first of all a sensory experience. A ritual is often accompanied by an interpretation, but the explanation is generally secondary to the sensory and affective effect

---

22. Muthert, "Meaningful Mourning."
23. Scheff, *Catharsis in Healing*; Körver, "The Science of the Particular."
24. Walton, et al., "Poetic Listening in Pastoral Care."

and often only emerges during the ritual. That is the reason why it can have an integrative and bonding effect where words fall short.

This approach receives support from work by Kathleen Higgins on the value of aesthetics in relation to grief.[25] Higgins speaks of communication through aesthetic gestures and indicates that aesthetic practices facilitate the restoration of coherence in times of bereavement. Interestingly, Higgins takes care to emphasize that the notion of "aesthetic closure" is unrealistic and potentially harmful. Aesthetics do not serve closure in a strict sense, but containment of emotions and recovery, while serving as a catalyst for (re) connecting with others and the world and even as a sort of companion.[26]

PRACTICAL AESTHETICS IN CHAPLAINCY CARE

From the point of view of research, the term aesthetic functioned as a sensitizing concept[27] to point to and interpret dimensions of the case studies, both with regard to the issues confronting the client and the interventions of the chaplain. The connection with the question of the nature of counseling in chaplaincy led consequently to the formulation of "aesthetic counseling" as an intentional practice within the repertoire of chaplains.

Chaplains who participated as researchers in the CSP reported that they became more conscious of the aesthetic dimensions of their care practices.[28] That is not surprising, as it is a direct result of distinguishing four dimensions of meaning and worldview—existential, spiritual, ethical, and aesthetic—in the format, in concurrence with the Dutch professional standard. But to say that the chaplains became more conscious of the aesthetic is also an understatement. Paying attention to the aesthetic dimension proved eye opening, providing new and helpful perspectives on interactions that could more intentionally be put into practice. And the term aesthetic counseling was for many an occasion for renewing their (worldview) counseling techniques and practices in general. The chaplains learned to be more attentive to matters of meaning in worldview in conversational practice and counseling, both passively in listening to persons and actively in counseling with regard to matters of meaning and worldview. On the aesthetic level they learned to be more alert to factors in the surroundings, to non-verbal aspects of the communication, and to the opportunities that they provide for care practices. That led to paying attention to the use and function of

25. Higgins, "Aesthetics and the Containment of Grief."
26. Danto, "The Abuse of Beauty."
27. See Chapter 2.
28. See Chapter 20.

artistic and cultural resources in interactions with clients in order to employ various methods and materials. The value of the aesthetic does not just come into play where conversation reaches its limits, but is already part of chaplains' analysis and repertoire from the beginning in their care with regard to meaning and worldview.

REFERENCES

Alma, Hans. "Art and Religion as Invitation. An Exploration Based on John Dewey's Theory of Experience and Imagination." *Perichoresis* 18.3 (2020) 33–45.

———. *De kunst van pelgrimeren: de geestelijk verzorger als verbeeldingsprofessional.* Utrecht: Eburon, 2024.

———. "Imagination and Transcendence: The Transcendental Dimension in Art from a Psychological Point of View." In *Visual Arts and Religion*, edited by Hans Alma, et al., 109–23. Berlin: LIT, 2009.

Anbeek, Christa. "World-viewing Dialogues on Precarious Life: The Urgency of a New Existential, Spiritual, and Ethical Language in the Search for Meaning in Vulnerable life." *Essays in the Philosophy of Humanism* 25.2 (2017) 171–85.

APA. "Pastoral counseling." In *APA Dictionary of Psychology*, no date. https://dictionary.apa.org/pastoral-counseling.

Brill, Willy. *Sprakeloos water: spiegel van de moderne Jiddische poëzie.* Amsterdam: Meulenhoff, 2007.

Burns, Chanelle. "'My Story to Be Told': Explorations in Narrative Documentation with People from Refugee Backgrounds." *The International Journal of Narrative Therapy and Community Work* 4 (2015) 26–39.

Cadge, Wendy, et al. "Training Chaplains and Spiritual Caregivers: The Emergence and Growth of Chaplaincy Programs in Theological Education." *Pastoral Psychology* 69.3 (2020) 187–208.

Danto, Arthur C. "The Abuse of Beauty." *Daedalus* 131.4 (2002) 35–56.

De Groot, J., et al. "OG Ouderenzorg: Van ambacht en kunst tot specialisme." In *Richting, Repertoire en Resultaat. Uitkomsten van het Nederlandse Case Studies Project Geestelijke Verzorging (2016-2021)*, edited by J. Körver, et al., 180–89. Utrecht: PThU-UCGV, 2023.

De Groot, Jack, and Maria E. C. Van Hoek. "Contemplative Listening in Moral Issues: Moral Counseling Redefined in Principles and Method." *Journal of Pastoral Care & Counseling* 71.2 (2017) 106–13.

Dodge-Peters Daiss, Susan. "Art at the Bedside: Reflections on Use of Visual Imagery in Hospital Chaplaincy." *Journal of Pastoral Care & Counseling* 70.1 (2016) 70–79.

Evers, Hans. "Contemplative Listening: A Rhetorical-Critical Approach to Facilitate Internal Dialog." *Journal of Pastoral Care & Counseling* 71.2 (2017) 114–21.

Fortuin, Nienke P. M., et al. "Worldview Commitment and Narrative Foreclosure among Older Dutch Adults: Assessing the Importance of Grand Narratives." *Journal of Religion, Spirituality & Aging* 31.4 (2019) 338–59.

Higgins, Kathleen Marie. "Aesthetics and the Containment of Grief." *The Journal of Aesthetics and Art Criticism* 78.1 (2020) 9–20.

Körver, Jacques "The Science of the Particular." In *Learning from Case Studies in Chaplaincy. Towards Practice Based Evidence & Professionalism*, edited by Renske Kruizinga, et al., 71–81. Utrecht: Eburon, 2020.

McClure, Barbara J. "Expanding the Psychological Imagination in Pastoral Theology: Using Novels to Better Understand Underrepresented Persons and Groups." *Pastoral Psychology* 60.3 (2011) 323–37.

Meyer, Birgit. "Introduction: From Imagined Communities to Aesthetic Formations: Religious Mediations, Sensational Forms, and Styles of Binding." In *Aesthetic Formations: Media, Religion, and the Senses*, edited by Birgit Meyer, 5–11. New York: Palgrave Macmillan, 2009.

Miller, William R., and Stephen Rollnick. *Motivational Interviewing: Helping People Change and Grow*. 4 ed. New York: The Guilford Press, 2023.

Muthert, Hanneke. "Meaningful Mourning." In *Recovery: The Interface between Psychiatry and Spiritual Care*, edited by Erik Olsman, et al., 113–32. Utrecht: Eburon, 2023.

Ostrander, Carmen. "The Chasing of Tales: Poetic License with the Written Word in Narrative Practice." *International Journal of Narrative Therapy & Community Work* 2 (2017) 55–64.

Rogers, Carl R., et al. *Client Centered Therapy: Its Current Practice, Implications and Theory*. 1951. Reprint, London: Robinson, 2015.

Scheff, Thomas J. *Catharsis in Healing, Ritual, and Drama*. Lincoln, NE: Backinprint. com, 2001.

Schuhmann, Carmen, and Annelieke Damen. "Representing the Good: Pastoral Care in a Secular Age." *Pastoral Psychology* 67.4 (2018) 405–17.

Smeets, Wim. *Spiritual Care in a Hospital Setting: An Empirical-Theological Exploration*. Leiden; Brill, 2006.

Van der Meer, Tjeerd. "Is MacDonald's Freedom?" In *Learning from Case Studies in Chaplaincy: Towards Practice Based Evidence & Professionalism*, edited by Renske Kruizinga, et al., 147–52. Utrecht: Eburon, 2020.

Walton, M. *Hoe waait de wind? Interpretatie van geestelijke verzorging door cliënten in de ggz*. Tilburg: KSGV, 2014

Walton, Martin, et al. "Poetic Listening in Pastoral Care: Listening to the Poems That People Are." *International Journal of Practical Theology* 26.1 (2022) 19–38.

Walton, Martin N. "'Wie ein Spaziergang im Grünen.' Ästhetische Aspekte bei der Beratung durch *geestelijk verzorgers*." *Wege zum Menschen* 74.4 (2022) 357–67.

16

Rituals in Chaplaincy

—Jacques Körver

"The hour was approaching six, and up in the compound's solitary tree the sparrows began to call. Gustad listened to their chirping every morning while reciting his *kusti* prayers.

There was something reassuring about it. Always, the sparrows were first; the cawing of crows came later."

Rohinton Mistry[1]

INTRODUCTION—RESEARCH ON RITUALS IN CHAPLAINCY

The quote above comes from the opening sentences of the novel *Such a Long Journey* by the Indian-Canadian author Rohinton Mistry. The novel is set in 1971 in Mumbai, India, against the backdrop of the war with Pakistan and corruption scandals in Indira Ghandi's government. The protagonist, Gustad Noble, belongs to the Parsi minority in India, descendants of Persian refugees who adhered to Zoroastrianism, one of the oldest religious traditions in the world. Every morning he ties a sacred belt around his waist, the *kusti*, and prays to the supreme god Ahura Mazda, who stands for goodness, wisdom, light, and truth.[2]

    1. Mistry, *Such a Long Journey*, 1.
    2. For more information, see: https://en.wikipedia.org/wiki/Such_a_Long_Journey_(novel), https://en.wikipedia.org/wiki/Ahura_Mazda.org/wiki/Kushti (accessed

With the scene, the author immediately sets his book in a particular light. He introduces the main character in a ritual context. Features such as repetition, a more or less prescribed pattern, sacred objects, a specific time and place, accompanying texts: these are recognizable aspects of rituals. It is habitual and at the same time there exists room for improvisation. The story and perception of the protagonist become part of the ritual. This beginning of each morning provides a framework and perspective for Gustad Noble's communication and interaction with his environment and the events that come his way. The words and gestures each day are much the same but each day loaded with new meanings.

Rituals

Rituals play an important role in many areas of life, in both individual life and social contexts. In the view of anthropologist Roy Rappaport, ritual forms the bridge between public systems and the personal world of life. It is the basis of interaction par excellence.

> In attending to ritual's form, we must not lose sight of the fundamental nature of what it is that ritual does as a logically necessary outcome of its form. In enunciating, accepting and making conventions moral, ritual contains within itself not simply a symbolic representation of social contract, but tacit social contract itself. As such, ritual, which also establishes, guards, and bridges boundaries between public systems and private processes, is *the* basic social act.[3]

Ritual pertains to creating specific habits and "spaces" in which people can place their experiences and stories in an overarching context. That means that rituals are essential in all areas of life, but especially in the realm of religion and worldview.[4] The description of religion by anthropologist Clifford Geertz makes it clear that symbols and rituals are at the heart of religion.

> Without further ado, then, a religion is a system of symbols which acts to establish powerful, pervasive, and long-lasting moods and motivations in men by formulating conceptions of a

---

Feb. 9, 2024).

3. Rappaport, *Ritual and Religion*, 138.

4. Cf. Bell, *Ritual Theory, Ritual Practice*; Geertz, "Religion as a Cultural System"; Rappaport, *Ritual and Religion*. See also: Williams, "Embodied World Construction,'" 104.

general order of existence and clothing these conceptions with such an aura of factuality that the moods and motivations seem uniquely realistic.[5]

Research on Rituals in Chaplaincy Care

Rituals also play an important role in chaplaincy care. That is evident from published cases of chaplaincy around pivotal moments of existence, for example around birth, in which rituals are described from numerous religious backgrounds.[6] The case studies are instructive, providing a mirror for one's own practice. Research on rituals has taken place primarily from cultural anthropology. In recent decades, research on rituals from theology, humanism, and chaplaincy has gradually emerged in the Netherlands. The Dutch practical-theologian Corja Bekius conducted a study on how pastors, ministers, and chaplains use rituals in individual care in an increasingly pluralistic society from a worldview perspective. The study was a combination of conceptual and empirical research. The empirical part consisted of a survey and interviews with pastors and clients. There was a high response rate to the questionnaire in which great importance was attached to rituals.[7] Multidisciplinary research by Paul Post, a researcher in the field of ritual studies, points to the importance of all kinds of rituals in a broader cultural and social context.[8] Theologian Thomas Quartier researched Catholic funeral rites, rituals surrounding bereavement, and the role of chaplains in them.[9]

Social scientist Brenda Mathijssen researched the ritual practices and beliefs of people trying to give meaning to the death of a loved one.[10] Psychologist Joanna Wojtkowiak currently researches how chaplains can responsibly design new rituals and adapt old rituals to the present day demands and needs of people,[11] as well as how rituals can play a role in dealing with prolonged and traumatic grief.[12] In the context of palliative

---

5. Geertz, "Religion as a Cultural System," 90. See also: Körver, "Ritual as a House," 113–15.

6. Allen, "On Holy Ground"; Arshad, et al., "Pregnancy Loss"; Evans and Mitchell, "Exploring Midwives' Understanding"; Uçak-Ekinci, "Muslimische Krankenhausseelsorge bei Totgeburten."

7. Bekius, *Rituelen in het individuele pastoraat*. An English summary of this dissertation can be found at: https://ugp.rug.nl/jvlo/article/view/38187/35742.

8. Post, "Ritual Studies."

9. Quartier, "Bridging the Gaps"; Quartier, "Deathbed Rituals."

10. Mathijssen, *Making Sense of Death*.

11. Wojtkowiak, "Ritual (Re)Design."

12. Wojtkowiak, et al., "Ritual in Therapy."

care, anthropologist Kim Van der Weegen and colleagues have conducted research on the role of rituals with regard to spirituality and on the practice of old and new rituals.[13] As part of the growing interest within chaplaincy in rituals, attention has also arisen for ritual competence of chaplains. This is true both in the Netherlands, for example, where ritual competence has not thus far been explicitly mentioned in the professional standard of chaplains,[14] and in other countries such as the US, where, as part of an outline of what chaplaincy in the twenty-first century entails and should entail, a description is given of what ritual competence includes.[15]

Case Study Research on Rituals in Chaplaincy Care

An initial thrust of research into the practice of ritual in chaplaincy on the basis of case studies can be found in the second collection of case studies published by George Fitchett and Steve Nolan. The book features four case studies in which ritual plays a central role. Those case studies are drawn from care for a young psychiatric patient, care for a dying person in the palliative phase, care for an employee in a hospice and after her death for colleagues, and care for an elderly woman with advanced dementia, respectively. The four case studies are commented on by a practical theologian and a chaplain.[16] The importance of ritual and ritual competence for chaplaincy is already emphasized by devoting four case studies to the topic. Both commentaries also emphasize that importance while pointing out the need for good theoretical grounding and for chaplains to take their own critical view of the requests for ritual guidance directed to them.

Therefore, although there is increased attention among professionals and researchers for the ritual practice and competence of chaplains, two types of research are still needed. The first is a thorough empirical inventory and exploration of the ritual practice of chaplaincy care in all its facets. Not only the "visible" practice of larger ritual gatherings requires research, but also the more "invisible" practice of small rituals at a sickbed or in individual encounters. That entails identifying in what situations and for what clients chaplains use (or are asked to use) their ritual skills, what exactly they do, what goals they pursue in doing so, and what the outcomes of their actions are. It is also important to investigate to what extent chaplains make

---

13. Van der Weegen, et al., "Ritualization as Alternative Approach to the Spiritual"; Van der Weegen, et al., "Practices of Ritualization."
14. Körver, et al., *Met lichaam en geest*.
15. Robins and Tumminio Hansen, "Meaning Making through Ritual."
16. Fitchett and Nolan, *Case Studies in Spiritual Care*, 135–220.

use of traditional rituals or elements of them in their ritual practice, how they design a ritual adapted to the situation or request, or combine both (old and new) in a creative way. A second form of research that is needed is a solid theoretical foundation for ritual practice and competence. Here it is important to include anthropological insights, taking as a starting point that religion, worldview, and rituals are inextricably linked and that ritual competence is a core competence of chaplaincy.

In the remainder of this chapter, an initial inventory and an exploration of ritual practice of chaplains in the CSP are undertaken. The format for case description did not include a question about ritual practices. Spontaneously, participants regularly described larger or smaller rituals, occurring alone between client and chaplain or with multiple participants, classical in form or adapted. More often, a "smaller" ritual, such as a prayer, a scripture reading, or lighting a candle, was mentioned in a subordinate clause and not described in concrete terms. It was striking that many of the case studies involved a ritual act. This was as surprising to us as researchers as the very frequent use of aesthetic resources, as the previous chapter showed. A large proportion of the case studies included in this book involved ritual, sometimes very elaborate in nature and description, sometimes mentioned almost in passing and described very briefly. The inventory and exploration below offer an initial impetus that may give rise, on the one hand, to a secondary analysis of all the case studies in the project from the perspective of ritual action and, on the other hand, to the formulation of hypotheses regarding the content and form of the ritual action of chaplains.[17]

RITUAL ACTS IN THE PRACTICES DESCRIBED IN THE CSP

Based on an analysis of the seventy-five case studies from the CSP available at the time, spiritual care researcher Renske Kruizinga conducted an initial inventory of ritual acts.[18] Of those seventy-five case studies thirty-three (44 percent) involved ritual, spread across all fields of chaplaincy care but most frequently in the fields of detention and eldercare. The majority of both the clients and the chaplains had a Christian background, with the religious/worldview background of client and chaplain corresponding in half of the case studies. The rituals described or mentioned were categorized as follows: praying, lighting a candle, blessing, reading/reciting from the Bible or Qur'an, reading a poem or other text, singing or listening to religious music, offering a card with a special text, symbol or photograph, anointing

17. Veerman, "Researching Practices," 54–57.
18. Kruizinga, "Van reciteren tot mediteren."

or blessing the sick, mindfulness or meditation, offering a celebration (with communion) or memorial service.[19] In addition to these more or less familiar rituals from Christianity, Islam, and Buddhism, there were also new rituals, such as burning letters with a message for someone from the past.[20] The following goals of the rituals in the case studies were mentioned: strengthening faith or spirituality, creating space, relaxation or peace, offering strength or hope, processing loss, ordering experiences, acknowledging the situation, and reconnecting with the religious past. The outcomes of the rituals were mostly with regard to peace, relief, poignancy, sense of recognition, feeling accepted, mutual commitment, openness to the past or to one's own grief, fear and doubt, support and strength for the future, and connectedness in faith and with the divine.[21]

Rituals in the Hospital

Following the completion of the CSP, partly in response to the analysis described above, I conducted a new inventory and thematic analysis of the twenty-three case studies collected in the RC Hospital, focusing on the reported use of rituals (frequency, nature, context, purpose, and outcome). A table containing the inventory and analysis of those twenty-three case studies is included in Appendix F of this book.

In fifteen of the twenty-three case studies there is some form of ritual practice, that is, in about two thirds. Most ritual practices and actions are drawn from the Christian tradition. There are references to the Catholic sacraments (cases Z1, Z6, Z9), but they are adapted to the patient's request, the circumstances, and the authorization of the chaplain. The latter reflects the fact that in Catholic tradition, chaplains who are not priests are not officially allowed to perform sacraments. That means in practice that an anointment of the sick becomes a blessing of the sick, and a Eucharist becomes a celebration of prayers and communion. A baptism of a stillborn child is not allowed according to Catholic canon law; hence a blessing. In the picture of ritual action that emerges from the survey, it appears that chaplains always orient themselves to the question and circumstances of the patients and/or their loved ones, to the story of life and illness, and adjust their ritual action accordingly. Traditional elements are creatively and hermeneutically connected to the current situation. Nowhere is there a trace of a "ritualistic"

---

19. Kruizinga, "Van reciteren tot mediteren," 93.
20. See, for example, the case study "Reiteration of Ritual," Chapter 8.
21. Kruizinga, "Van reciteren tot mediteren," 91–99.

attitude, where the main concern would be to perform the ritual in a rigid manner without making use of the space that a ritual always offers.

Prominent among the rituals are blessings (with or without touching), praying together, reading from the Bible, visiting the chapel or sanctuary in the hospital, and lighting a candle on the spot. The lighting of a candle is sometimes done vicariously by the chaplain, or the chaplain encourages the patient to visit the chapel or meditation center and pray and/or light a candle there. Praying together regularly occurs using traditional prayers (such as the Lord's Prayer and the Hail Mary). In addition, chaplains often offer a free prayer that they adapt to their observations, to the patient's questions and vocabulary, and to the circumstances. Regularly, specific objects play a role in the performance of the ritual, such as a candle or lamp, a plant, a cloth, a rosary, holy water, a crucifix, or a Bible. Sometimes chaplains ask loved ones to participate in the performance of the ritual, such as in the laying on of hands as a blessing and the making of the sign of a cross on the forehead (with holy water).

Prayers, Bible texts, poems, and other texts offer another interpretive framework in which profound experiences (current or past) can be seen in a different light. There is frequent mention of blessings, either as part of a larger ritual or as a separate act, as a gesture of blessing in the air, sign of the cross on the forehead, or laying on of hands. The chaplain performing a blessing of the sick (Z1) explains the blessing as laying on of hands to those present as follows.

> The laying on of hands is a very ancient gesture, a sign that we want to pass God's power on. But it is also a gesture of comfort. When they [*the chaplain points to the children present*] are small and sorrowful, you can talk to them but that doesn't help. You have to hold them.[22]

The presence of a chapel or sanctuary in the hospital is significant. Chaplains regularly refer to that space where patients can go to rest and contemplate, whose furnishings include references to one or more religious traditions, where there is the possibility of prayer or lighting a candle, and where liturgical celebrations are sometimes held. However small or tucked away those spaces may be, they seem to provide a literal and figurative space for human needs in the hospital, or at the least for the patient's experiences.[23] Chaplaincy services offer that space, as a physical space similar to the symbolic space of prayers, texts, blessings, and other ritual acts.

22. In similar terms, Pruyser describes the anthropological basis of blessing, in Pruyser, "The Master Hand," 354–55.

23. This is also evidenced by Cadge's research in *Paging God*, 51–76, especially 59.

A few other things stand out in this context. (1) Sometimes chaplains act as substitutes, especially when it comes to lighting a candle in the chapel or saying a prayer for the patient. Against the background of what British sociologist of religion Abby Day says about the religious experience of young people, this substitution could be seen as an offer of "belonging" to a religious tradition and thus as an offer to understand one's own life story in relation to that tradition, something they themselves cannot express.[24] This action of chaplains can perhaps also be seen as an example of "vicarious religion," in which the religious involvement of a small group functions for the benefit of a larger group.[25] (2) In one of the case studies (Z10), the chaplain provides a Biblical text to interpret an image provided by the patient herself. This is not done in a ritual context, as in other case studies (e.g. Z3 and Z6), but in the course of conversation, where the chaplain does explicitly refer to the chapel. Perhaps ritual is involved here in a very rudimentary form. (3) Chaplains explicitly direct their attention to rituals that patients themselves provide (as in Z5, Z8 and Z12). Closing a door, a specific form of Marian devotion, a knitting work, and a photo album are given recognition within a different, broader scope, a more or less transcendent perspective. Those are not acts provided by the chaplain, but rather a recognition and reinterpretation of acts that patients themselves have developed. This reinterpretation allows patients to see their experiences in a new light and offers a connection to the religious background that the chaplain represents.

Finally (4), two different chaplains (Z7 and Z23) report silently praying what they call a "threshold prayer," standing at the door of the patient's room in preparation for conversation. An example is, "Eternal, give me the peace and space to be present for Mrs. . . . now" (Z7). Both chaplains thereby explicitly place their actions (at least for themselves) in a religious and ritual context. The question here is twofold: (a) do the chaplains themselves view their offerings explicitly from a religious perspective (and what does that mean for their actual actions), and (b) are the offerings and actions of a chaplain not in themselves a form of ritual action? The latter is consistent with the insight that numerous professional interactions have ritual elements, or even a ritual form altogether. Professional interactions consist of specific customs, make use of characteristic objects and furnishings, and are constructed in a patterned manner. This applies, for example, to (pastoral) supervision,[26] and also to visiting a doctor in a hospital.[27]

---

24. See Day, "Believing in Belonging."
25. Davie, "Vicarious Religion."
26. Bekius, "De rituele dimensie van supervisie."
27. The Dutch anthropologist Sjaak Van der Geest demonstrates this convincingly

RE-EVALUATION OF RITUALS IN CHAPLAINCY

An important result of the exploration and analysis of ritual acts of chaplains in the CSP is that ritual acts are much more frequent than both researchers and participating chaplains previously thought. More often, (minor) ritual acts are described in the margins, briefly and not concretely. Chaplains seem hesitant to name and describe that aspect of their practice. The hesitation seems to stem from concern not to be (too strongly) identified with traditional pastoral care. It could also have to do with the development that chaplaincy is identified primarily with meaning and spirituality and less and less with religion.[28] Moreover, there is a lack of theorizing about ritual action. What is and brings about a ritual? How is ritual action to be employed creatively and critically? In what context, to what end, and by what means are rituals performed?

The chaplains' concerns are countered by the perception of clients and staff that chaplaincy is concerned with performing rituals during pivotal or tragic moments in life or during special (holy) days.[29] The reluctance of chaplains to take ritual as a core theme for their work, at any rate in the description of their profession, calls to mind the plea of the Dutch-American pastoral psychologist Paul Pruyser in the 1960s and 1970s that chaplains should stick to their own trade and make more and better work of blessings, one of the possible ritual forms.[30] In that regard, chaplaincy textbooks are beginning to pay a little more attention to what the meaning of ritual is and what chaplains can contribute in it, although the attention is limited or rather anecdotal in the context of an example or case study.[31] It is hopeful that research is being conducted in which ritual is used as an intervention in specific situations, as an answer to or framework for certain life questions.[32] In doing so, the role of chaplains is also being redescribed from an anthropological perspective.[33] Ritual interventions can be helpful

in his article: Van der Geest, "'Sacraments' in the Hospital."

28. See also Chapter 1. Meaning and spirituality in this context are seen as open, free, and individual, while religion is seen as closed, unfree, and collective. See, among others: Salander, "Who Needs"; Zinnbauer and Pargament, "Religiousness and Spirituality."

29. Cf., among others: Best, et al., "Military Perspectives"; Cadge, et al., "What Do Chaplains Contribute"; Fisher, et al., "Church Services"; Heinke, et al., "Quality of Spiritual Care"; Piderman, et al., "Patients' Expectations of Hospital Chaplains."

30. Pruyser, "The Master Hand"; Pruyser, "The Use and Neglect."

31. Davies, "Ritual"; Nolan, "Case Study"; Stoesz, et al., *A Prison Chaplaincy Manual*.

32. Newitt, "Chaplaincy Support - Part 1"; Wierstra, et al., "Addressing Spiritual Needs."

33. Newitt, "Chaplaincy Support - Part 2."

not only for patients but also for staff members, especially when faced with severe distress, moral stress, and burnout, such as during the Covid-19 pandemic.[34] Moreover, research on rituals in chaplaincy received a strong impetus from the Covid-19 pandemic, especially as it was found that physical participation is essential to ritual and that ritual competence contributes to a clear role for chaplains.[35]

The ritual actions of chaplains deserve more empirical and theoretical research, as the inventories in this chapter and the examples in the case studies in Part II of this book make clear. This involves not only establishing the frequency, nature, and context of rituals, but also their core elements. What makes up a ritual? What is the relationship between tradition and new elements? What is the importance of the primal elements (water, fire, air, and earth) in rituals? Are there differences between ritual practices in different fields of work and what are they? What are the differences and similarities between ritual practices in different religious and worldview traditions? What are the constants? What is the consequence of the observation by various anthropologists and phenomenologists, that rituals and religion cannot be separated, that a ritual is not the expression of a pre-existing religious or worldview meaning, but that in the ritual meaning arises? Can ritual actually provide the connecting space for people with different religious backgrounds? In what way can (attention to) ritual performance strengthen the position and recognition of chaplains in all kinds of fields?[36] This is just a sampling of possible research questions.

All chaplaincy research in rituals should be concerned with how ritual affects the perception and experience of reality of those who experience ritual. This perspective was already addressed in the epigraph and introduction of this chapter. In the same vein this chapter concludes with a quote from an interview the ethnographer Saba Mahmood had with a certain Mona in her research into the ritual practice of believing Muslim women in Egypt. Mona said, "You will begin to notice if you say the morning prayer, it will also make your daily affairs easier, and if you don't pray it will make them hard."[37]

---

34. Farkas, "Spiritual Guidance"; Klitzman, et al., "How Hospital Chaplains Develop."

35. Desjardins, et al., "American Health Care Chaplains' Narrative Experiences"; Van Schaik and Wojtkowiak, "Disembodied Ritual."

36. Körver, "Ritual as a House."

37. Mahmood, *Politics of Piety*, 125.

REFERENCES

Allen, Katy Z. "On Holy Ground. Ritual for a Premature Jewish Baby Whose Death Is Imminent." *Chaplaincy Today* 19.2 (2003) 31–34. https://doi.org/10.1080/10999183.2003.10767238.

Arshad, Mohammed, et al. "Pregnancy Loss—the Islamic Perspective." *British Journal of Midwifery* 12.8 (2004) 481–85. https://doi.org/10.12968/bjom.2004.12.8.15272.

Bekius, Corja. *Rituelen in het individuele pastoraat. Een praktisch-theologisch onderzoek.* Kampen: Kok, 1998.

———. "De rituele dimensie van supervisie." In *Supervisie in Opleiding en Beroep. Verzameling Tijdschriftartikelen uit de periode 1982-2002*, edited by Willemine Regouin and Frans Siegers, 155–67. Houten: Bohn Stafleu van Loghum, 2005.

Bell, Catherine. *Ritual Theory, Ritual Practice.* New York–Oxford: Oxford University Press, 1992.

Best, Megan C., et al. "Military Perspectives on the Provision of Spiritual Care in the Australian Defence Force: A Cross-Sectional Study." *Journal of Religion and Health* 63 (2024) 289–308. https://doi.org/10.1007/s10943-023-01985-3.

Cadge, Wendy. *Paging God. Religion in the Halls of Medicine.* Chicago: University of Chicago Press, 2012.

Cadge, Wendy, et al. "What Do Chaplains Contribute to Large Academic Hospitals? The Perspectives of Pediatric Physicians and Chaplains." *Journal of Religion and Health* 50.2 (2011) 300–12. https://doi.org/10.1007/s10943-011-9474-8.

Davie, Grace. "Vicarious Religion: A Methodological Challenge." In *Everyday Religion: Observing Modern Religious Lives*, edited by Nancy T. Ammerman, 21–36. Oxford: Oxford University Press, 2007.

Davies, Douglas J. "Ritual." In *Oxford Textbook of Spirituality in Health Care*, edited by Mark Cobb et al., 163–68. Oxford: Oxford University Press, 2012.

Day, Abby. "Believing in Belonging: An Ethnography of Young People's Constructions of Belief." *Culture and Religion* 10.3 (2009) 263–78. http://www.informaworld.com/10.1080/14755610903279671.

Desjardins, Cate Michelle, et al. "American Health Care Chaplains' Narrative Experiences Serving During the Covid-19 Pandemic: A Phenomenological Hermeneutical Study." *Journal of Health Care Chaplaincy* 29.2 (2023) 229–44. https://doi.org/10.1080/08854726.2022.2087964.

Evans, Mark, and David Mitchell. "Exploring Midwives' Understanding of Spiritual Care and the Role of the Healthcare Chaplain within a Maternity Unit." *Health and Social Care Chaplaincy* 2.1 (2014) 79–97. https://doi.org/10.1558/hscc.v2i1.79.

Farkas, Edina A. "Spiritual Guidance of Patients, Families and Medical Staff During Paediatric End of Life Care." *Health and Social Care Chaplaincy* 5.1 (2017) 9–15. https://doi.org/10.1558/hscc.32146.

Fisher, Elizabeth, et al. "Church Services in a Complex Continuing Care Hospital: Why Bother?" *The Journal of Pastoral Care & Counseling* 71.4 (2017) 274–83. https://doi.org/10.1177/1542305017744492.

Fitchett, George, and Steve Nolan, eds. *Case Studies in Spiritual Care. Healthcare Chaplaincy Assessments, Interventions & Outcomes.* London: Kingsley, 2018.

Geertz, Clifford. "Religion as a Cultural System." In *The Interpretation of Cultures. Selected Essays*, edited by Clifford Geertz, 87–125. London: Fontana, 1993.

Heinke, Gary D., et al. "Quality of Spiritual Care at the End of Life: What the Family Expects for Their Loved One." *Journal of Health Care Chaplaincy* 26.4 (2020) 159–74. https://doi.org/10.1080/08854726.2019.1644816.

Klitzman, Robert, et al. "How Hospital Chaplains Develop and Use Rituals to Address Medical Staff Distress." *SSM - Qualitative Research in Health* 2 (2022) 100087. https://doi.org/10.1016/j.ssmqr.2022.100087.

Körver, Jacques. "Ritual as a House with Many Mansions: Inspirations from Cultural Anthropology for Interreligious Cooperation." *Yearbook for Ritual and Liturgical Studies* 32 (2016) 105–23. https://ugp.rug.nl/jvlo/article/view/27209.

Körver, Jacques, et al., eds. *Met lichaam en geest. De rituele competentie van geestelijk verzorgers*. Utrecht: Eburon, 2021.

Kruizinga, Renske. "Van reciteren tot mediteren. Analyse van rituele handelingen in casestudy's." In *Met lichaam en geest. De rituele competentie van geestelijk verzorgers*, edited by Jacques Körver, et al., 89–101. Utrecht: Eburon, 2021.

Mahmood, Saba. *Politics of Piety. The Islamic Revival and the Feminist Subject*. New Jersey: Princeton University Press, 2011. doi:10.1515/9781400839919.

Mathijssen, Brenda. *Making Sense of Death: Ritual Practices and Situational Beliefs of the Recently Bereaved in the Netherlands*. Death Studies. Nijmegen Studies in Thanatology, 5. Berlin: LIT, 2017.

Mistry, Rohinton. *Such a Long Journey*. London: Faber and Faber, 2006.

Newitt, Mark. "Chaplaincy Support to Bereaved Parents—Part 1." *Health and Social Care Chaplaincy* 2.2 (2014) 179–94. https://doi.org/10.1558/hscc.v2i2.20542.

———. "Chaplaincy Support to Bereaved Parents—Part 2." *Health and Social Care Chaplaincy* 3.1 (2015) 23–40. https://doi.org/10.1558/hscc.v3i1.20543.

Nolan, Steve. "Case Study." In *A Handbook of Chaplaincy Studies: Understanding Spiritual Care in Public Places*, edited by Christopher Swift, et al., 187–98. Farnham: Ashgate, 2015.

Piderman, Katherine M., et al. "Patients' Expectations of Hospital Chaplains." *Mayo Clinic Proceedings* 83.1 (2008) 58–65. https://doi.org/10.4065/83.1.58.

Post, Paul. "Ritual Studies." In *International Handbook of Practical Theology*, edited by Birgit Weyel, et al., 743–60. Berlin: De Gruyter, 2022.

Pruyser, Paul W. "The Master Hand: Psychological Notes on Pastoral Blessing." In *The New Shape of Pastoral Theology. Essays in Honor of Seward Hiltner*, edited by William B. Oglesby Jr, 352–65. Nashville: Abingdon, 1969.

———. "The Use and Neglect of Pastoral Resources." *Pastoral Psychology* 23.7 (1972) 5–17.

Quartier, Thomas. *Bridging the Gaps: An Empirical Study of Catholic Funeral Rites*. Empirische Theologie, edited by Johannes A. van der Ven, et al. Volume 17, Zürich–Münster: LIT Verlag, 2007.

———. "Deathbed Rituals. Roles of Spiritual Caregivers in Dutch Hospitals." *Mortality* 15.2 (2010) 107–21. https://doi.org/10.1080/13576275.2010.482769.

Rappaport, Roy A. *Ritual and Religion in the Making of Humanity*. Cambridge Studies in Social and Cultural Anthropology. Cambridge: Cambridge University Press, 1999.

Robins, Rochelle, and Danielle Tumminio Hansen. "Meaning Making through Ritual and Public Leadership." In *Chaplaincy and Spiritual Care in the Twenty-First Century. An Introduction*, edited by Wendy Cadge and Shelly Rambo, 110–25. Chapel Hill: University of North Carolina Press, 2022.

Salander, Pär. "Who Needs the Concept of 'Spirituality'?" *Psycho-Oncology* 15.7 (2006) 647–49. https://doi.org/10.1002/pon.1060.

Stoesz, Donald B., et al. *A Prison Chaplaincy Manual. The Canadian Context*. Victoria: Friesen, 2020.

Uçak-Ekinci, Dilek. "Muslimische Krankenhausseelsorge bei Totgeburten. Herausforderungen und Aufgabenvielfalt." *Spiritual Care* 12.4 (2023) 324–32. https://doi.org/doi:10.1515/spircare-2023-0047.

Van der Geest, Sjaak. "'Sacraments' in the Hospital. Exploring the Magic and Religion of Recovery." *Anthropology & Medicine* 12.2 (2005) 135–50. https://doi.org/10.1080/13648470500139957.

Van der Weegen, Kim, et al. "Ritualization as Alternative Approach to the Spiritual Dimension of Palliative Care: A Concept Analysis." *Journal of Religion and Health* 58.6 (2019) 2036–46. https://doi.org/10.1007/s10943-019-00792-z.

Van der Weegen, Kim, et al. "Practices of Ritualization in a Dutch Hospice Setting." *Religions* 11.11 (2020) 571. https://doi.org/10.3390/rel11110571.

Van Schaik, Tamara, and Joanna Wojtkowiak. "Disembodied Ritual: An Explorative Study on the Meanings of Physical Absence During Funerals by Bereaved in Times of Covid-19." *Death Studies* 47.7 (2023) 873–80. https://doi.org/10.1080/07481187.2022.2135047.

Veerman, Jan Willem. "Researching Practices. Lessons from Dutch Youth Care." In *Learning from Case Studies in Chaplaincy. Towards Practice Based Evidence & Professionalism*, edited by Renske Kruizinga, et al., 46–59. Utrecht: Eburon, 2020.

Wierstra, Iris R., et al. "Addressing Spiritual Needs in Palliative Care: Proposal for a Narrative and Interfaith Spiritual Care Intervention for Chaplaincy." *Journal of Health Care Chaplaincy* 29.1 (2023) 64–77. https://doi.org/10.1080/08854726.2021.2015055.

Williams, Jack. "Embodied World Construction: A Phenomenology of Ritual." *Religious Studies* 60.1 (2024) 103–22. https://doi.org/10.1017/S0034412523000033.

Wojtkowiak, Joanna. "Ritual (Re)Design. Towards a Framework for Professional Ritual Making in Postsecular Contexts." *Yearbook for Ritual and Liturgical Studies* 38 (2022) 108–23. https://doi.org/https://doi.org/10.21827/YRLS.38.108-123.

Wojtkowiak, Joanna, et al. "Ritual in Therapy for Prolonged Grief. A Scoping Review of Ritual Elements in Evidence-Informed Grief Interventions." *Frontiers in Psychiatry* 11 (2021) 623835. https://doi.org/10.3389/fpsyt.2020.623835.

Zinnbauer, Brian J., and Kenneth I. Pargament. "Religiousness and Spirituality." In *Handbook of the Psychology of Religion and Spirituality*, edited by Raymond F. Paloutzian and Crystal L. Park, 21–42. New York: Guilford, 2005.

17

Roles in Chaplaincy
—Niels Den Toom

"The nurse helps him to slide into his bath . . .
And each week, he is born again anew
and parted cruelly from his safe water-life
and every week he's destined to remain
a poor and fearful patient again."

M. Vasalis[1]

PROFESSIONALISM, PROFESSIONAL IDENTITY, AND ROLES

In seeking to open the black box of how chaplains provide spiritual care, various paths have been followed. One perspective is to focus on chaplains' interventions and methods. Massey et al. for instance developed a taxonomy of chaplains' interventions in a palliative setting, based on a study of literature, patient charts, focus group interviews with chaplains and self-observation of chaplains.[2] While the study shows the richness and variety of the profession, a review of these goals and interventions does not convincingly show how these interventions cohere and how chaplaincy is to

---

1. Excerpt from "De idioot in bad." Kingston, "M. Vasalis," 51. Translated by Maria Jacobs. In the original poem, the word "idiot" is used instead of patient. Due to the connotations of the word in English, it was changed into "patient." Used with permission.

2. Massey et al., "What Do I Do?"

be distinguished from other professions. One of the advantages of a case study is that it shows how various actions of a chaplain cohere and are embedded in an interactive context. Moreover, it also shows how chaplains perform certain actions in their own style. In the Dutch final report, we observed, based on the results of the Dutch Case Studies Project (CSP), that every chaplain has one's own style that characterizes the spiritual care they provide, influenced by their training, worldview, and personality.[3] In other words, methods, techniques, and interventions are never applied in isolation or clinically, but are always embedded in a context and colored by a personal style, that bears that person's signature of artisanship. Also, the various interventions and approaches are related in some way.

Earlier, I have argued that "professionalism" provides a good lens to look at the coherence of the practice of chaplaincy.[4] In a threefold model of professionalism, inspired by Eliot Freidson[5] and Ed De Jonge[6], three levels of professionalism can be distinguished: value-orientation, expertise, and positioning. Specifically, chaplains focus on their value-orientation, which includes both values that are central to the profession (e.g. human dignity, recognition, salvation) and concrete goals that guide chaplains in their practice. To pursue or even attain those goals and values, chaplains employ their expertise, including their knowledge, skills, methods, techniques, attitudes, *et cetera*. Their expertise is, however, always embedded in a professional context in a specific way. Ideally, chaplains have positioned themselves in such a way that they can employ their expertise in a manner guided by their value-orientation to pursue a greater good. Thus, professionalism is a way to understand the coherence of values, expertise, and positioning of a profession. The various ways in which professionals conduct professional behavior, how they have integrated their professionalism and how they understand themselves in relation to other professionals can be considered their professional identity.[7]

In relation to opening the black box of chaplaincy, it will help to analyze the rich case studies from the perspective of professionalism and professional identity. As concepts, however, the notions of professionalism and professional identity are too coarse for analyzing specific interactions of an individual chaplain in a particular situation. Therefore, we need a more

---

3. Körver et al., *Richting, Repertoire en Resultaat*, 138.
4. Den Toom, *The Chaplain-Researcher*, 18–19.
5. Freidson, *Professionalism, the Third Logic*.
6. De Jonge, *Beelden van de professional*.
7. Den Toom, *The Chaplain-Researcher*, 210.

refined concept to analyze the coherence of interactions, values and goals, knowledge and positioning. The concept of "roles" can help here.

ROLES

In the literature, one finds little on chaplaincy roles. "In keeping with other review findings, the bulk of the literature identified in relation to the chaplain's role was not empirically-based . . . Empirical research related to the role, skills, and competencies of healthcare chaplains was found to be very limited."[8] Indeed, much of what has been written about roles has to do with symbolic roles, such as the wounded healer,[9] the clown,[10] the welcoming guest,[11] et cetera. Those roles are also not empirically based but rather provide an ideal-typical role in which certain values are expressed: the values of vulnerability and healing in the wounded healer, of hospitality and modesty in the welcoming guest, and of disruption, vulnerability, and the liberating effect of humor in the clown. The roles do not prescribe precisely how chaplains should act and what expertise they need, but they express the attitude and style in which chaplains' expertise can be employed. There are also concepts of roles that refer to the CanMEDS model from the medical profession,[12] including roles of chaplain as theologian, ethicist, educator, researcher, et cetera.[13] Roles such as these are more closely related to certain competencies and thus to chaplains' expertise. As a consequence, the goals and values are more implicit in those roles. Therefore, a concept of roles is needed in which values, goals, and expertise are all included, as well as elements of positioning. Inspired by Hjalmar Súnden's interactional theory of roles,[14] I define a professional role as *a functional or symbolic designation of a coherent set of actions by which a person relates to others and integrates certain values, goals, expertise, and positioning in dynamic interaction with the context*. In line with Súnden's theory, those roles should not be understood to be static, remaining the same over time. Instead, a role presupposes reciprocity in the dynamic interaction with others, such as a client, and the interaction molds the role differently in every situation. Yet, one can speak

---

8. Timmins et al., "The Role of the Healthcare Chaplain," 99.
9. Nouwen, *The Wounded Healer*.
10. Faber, "Second Thoughts on the Minister as a Clown."
11. Walton, "The Welcoming Guest."
12. Herion et al., "Validating CanMEDS-Based Standards."
13. Spelt et al., *Rollen en competenties*.
14. Lindgren, "Hjalmar Sundén's Impact."

of a symbolic and/or functional designation in which goals and values, expertise, and positioning cohere.

To discover what such a concept of roles can mean for understanding chaplaincy, this chapter explores the various roles that can be identified in chaplaincy and reflects on what can be learned from the role perspective. As there may be many roles within chaplaincy, the current chapter aims to concretize and reflect on certain roles and does not pretend to provide a comprehensive overview of roles in chaplaincy.

METHODS

Thematic analysis[15] was conducted based on a convenience sample. Two sorts of documents were selected. The primary sources are the original and elaborate case studies that were presented in the previous chapters in an abbreviated version. Secondarily, the final reports from each research community of the CSP were analyzed, in which academic scholars answer the questions, "What do chaplains do, why, and with what results?"[16] The analysis was conducted using the qualitative data software Atlas.ti, version 23.

RESULTS

In the following, four roles will be described. That of the chaplains as a person of trust, as a representative of the good, as an intertextual interpreter and as a symbolizer of healing. The roles will be illustrated by quotations from the case studies within the present volume.

Person of Trust

The first role that can be identified in the case studies is that of the person of trust in a dual sense: a person whom can be trusted and a person whose expertise is about "trust." I will elaborate on both types of the person of trust.

First, in Dutch, a person of trust is generally someone within an organization who can be addressed when one encounters issues that require confidentiality (e.g., bullying, power abuse by a manager, *et cetera*). The idea of the person of trust is that within a certain context, confidentiality can be experienced with someone who is also acquainted with and connected to that context. The most obvious form in which this confidential role can

---

15. Clarke and Braun, "Using Thematic Analysis."
16. Körver et al., *Richting, Repertoire en Resultaat*.

be recognized is in the case study of Helga Knegt, "To Honor and Confirm" (Chapter 11). There, the chaplain speaks with some soldiers who have been suspended from duty, due to the suspicion of trafficking in prohibited substances. When talking to the soldiers, she notices the "silence" of one of them and seems to interpret that as a signal of a burden he is bearing. While talking to the group of soldiers in general, she emphasizes the role of the chaplain as a person of trust and makes eye contact. A similar example of confidentiality is the precondition for further spiritual care that can be found in the case study of Bart Van den Bosse ("From Slumped to Upright," Chapter 12). In that case study, the chaplain explains that he is bound to confidentiality as a precondition for their contact. The chaplain reports that the sanctuary he provides in that way, is "recognized and used" as Simon "learned to feel secure with the chaplain," as expressed by Simon when "his resistance to therapy" came up in the conversations.

Trust indeed is essential for coming to terms with questions or issues that are sensitive and existential. An example is acknowledging that one plays with dolls ("I Do It My Way," Chapter 7). While that trust sometimes requires formal guarantees within the organization, chaplains also aim to foster trust within the interaction with clients. In several case studies, we see indications of putting clients at ease and stimulating their trust. Chaplain Marie-José Van Bolhuis, for instance, wants to foster trust by inviting the client to think and speak about death and doing that together. "Doing it together could be less scary?" Does Anne dare to do that? 'Yes,' Anne answers." ("Exposure?," Chapter 6). While acknowledging that it can indeed be scary to talk about death, she also encourages her to take a leap of faith. The leap of faith is not taken individually by the client, but is mediated by the chaplain as a person who can be trusted. That can also be seen in the case study of Marieke Termeer, in which Charly, a mentally disabled man, starts to "flutter" in insecure situations. "When the chaplain indicates that there is no need for concern, Charly seems to be assured and stops immediately" ("A Church for Charly," Chapter 9). Here, not only the chaplains' words bring forth trust, but also the confident attitude of the chaplain. It goes without saying that the trust-fostering attitude of chaplains is only one side of the story. Trust only grows when the client attributes trust to the chaplain. In the examples mentioned above the chaplains show a vital reciprocal attitude.

So far, it can be said that trust is a necessary precondition for a person to discuss and participate in issues of meaning and worldview. One could argue that this might be the case for every social profession. Still, the legal base and practical function of chaplains' trust is often different from that of other social professionals. Where other professionals regard their confidentiality often as a shared confidentiality with all other professionals, chaplains are often more reserved or even opposed to sharing the contents of their conversations. Moreover, trust is not only a precondition, it is also an attitude in life, or perhaps even a virtue, that is stimulated by chaplains. That is what is indicated as the second meaning of "person of trust." The case study of Van Bolhuis illustrates this.

> The chaplain says that "trust" seems to be a key word. She has heard Anne use the word a couple of times. She understands Anne's refusal to participate in exposure treatment as a lack of trust. She does trust her friend. If he says things are alright, she becomes calmer. Could it be that Anne wants to learn to have trust that things will be okay after death? Could that give her trust to go on living. If her sense of trust and self-confidence could grow, then she might not always have a feeling that she has to control things. The notions of "trust" and "faith/belief," the chaplain explains, are closely related (cf. "*pistis*" in New Testament Greek). Both terms belong to the domain of the chaplain. ("Exposure?," Chapter 6)

Thus, trust is not only a precondition for spiritual care, but perhaps a precondition of the good life, or of life generally. Interestingly, the chaplain understands trust to be closely connected to the biblical word for faith or belief. Despite current associations with faith as "dogma" or things one should believe in, she emphasizes the emotional and spiritual attitude of trust. In other words, chaplains as persons of faith encourage people to have some faith and try to be faithful in helping clients discover that faith. Or, formulated differently, chaplains as persons of trust encourage others to have trust and they try to be trustworthy in helping clients discover that trust. It becomes clear that the role of "person of trust" includes both goals and values (a vision on the good life as a life characterized by trust), expertise (having knowledge about the relation between faith and trust), and positioning (having a particular, trusted position within the organization).

Representative of (the) Go(o)d

A second role that can be discerned in the case studies is the role of representative or embodiment of the good or of God. In some of the cases, the representation has a formal status within the organization. Here, again, the case studies of Van den Bosse and Knegt are taken together. In both prison and military organizations, chaplains are appointed and organized according to their worldview position. That means that chaplains are explicitly recognizable as Christian (Protestant or Roman-Catholic), Humanist,

Buddhist, Hindu, Muslim or Jewish chaplains. While the distribution of work is arranged differently within the two contexts, chaplains represent their worldview traditions and institutions within those settings. In the case study of Knegt, the chaplain represents the spiritual dimension within the military, more specifically she represents the Protestant tradition, or even God. When she enters the room with the family of the fallen soldier, she introduces herself as the minister, not as the chaplain, as the family is from a strict Protestant family. The chaplain writes in her case study that she chose to wear the uniform with a skirt, as women are accustomed to wearing skirts in that Protestant context. As such, she not only represents the spiritual dimension, the church, or God through her function, but also embodies that role so that the clients can attribute that role to her. Roles cannot be determined individually, but are constructed in a social interplay in which the chaplain adopts a role, in the hope that the other will attribute that role to her and adopt an appropriate complementary role (and vice versa). In this case, we see that her dress is appreciated by the mother and that the chaplain and mother connect. Later we see that the father of the fallen soldier speaks with the chaplain about grieving, his faith, and the faith of his son. The chaplain writes:

> It does the father well that the chaplain can follow and speak his language of faith. Father and chaplain touch base in a form of piety that many Reformed traditions share ... Between the lines the father expresses a great appreciation for what the chaplain stands for: the presence or representation of everything that has to do with faith in the world of the armed forces, and therefore for his son. ("To Honor and Confirm," Chapter 11)

Here we see that the rather formal role of chaplain as representative of the spiritual is embodied in clothing and language in a way that it serves to represent the good for the parents of the fallen soldier.

A second example of the representation of the good and God can be found in the case study of Termeer ("A Church for Charly," Chapter 9). Termeer describes in a beautiful way how she celebrates a communion ritual with Charly, a man with autism. In general, she writes, she is often addressed by the client not with her name, but with the word "church" or the word "praying," referring to the institutional context the chaplain represents. As a person, she represents the religious and the church. That is even more the case in the ritual she describes. Communion rituals are usually conducted within a community, but for Charly participation in such a ritual is too stressful. Therefore, the chaplain offers a specific ritual in Charly's own room, which provides him safety and security. "In this situation the chaplain and the performance of the ritual have (vicariously) become the church for Charly."

A final example is the language chaplains use to refer to a different perspective on life. In the case study of Jowien Van der Zaag ("Energy *and Inspiration*," Chapter 4) one of the vital points is the use of language that differs from that of the rest of the organization (inspiration instead of energy). With her language, the chaplain refers to a complementary image of human beings as not just physical beings (energy), but also spiritual beings (inspiration). She runs the risk that her language will not be understood by "the organization," but by explicitly using that language in the multidisciplinary meeting, she "represents" a different realm within the hospital setting. In the case study of Van Bolhuis, the chaplain uses the notion of "trust" instead of a psychological approach to anxiety. The case study of Guus Van Loenen speaks of moral guilt and moral injury alongside trauma or PTSS ("Wounded Warrior," Chapter 10). The chosen language serves to represent conceptions of the good life and as such has a culture-critical potential.[17]

The notion of representation is sometimes related to the religious sphere, and sometimes to the world of the good and the spiritual in broader terms. Even if people are not religious, the chaplains seem to be an archetype of the good and the spiritual. Chaplains are indeed committed to traditions and views on life (worldviews) that propagate a certain vision of what the good life entails. The counter-cultural potential of worldviews gives them a special position within an organization, providing the ability and freedom to criticize certain aspects of an organization.[18] How does the role of the representative function as a form of professionalism? The role of representative of the good and of the spiritual includes both goals and values (a vision on the good life as a spiritual life), expertise (having knowledge about ethics, spirituality, and specific worldview traditions, including embodied knowledge), and positioning (e.g., visible representation of the religious by a uniform, but also use of a different language).

Intertextual Interpreter

Traditionally many chaplains are trained to read, understand, and explain sacred texts and scriptures. In the case studies presented in this volume, the chaplains also work with texts in close interaction with their clients. The most traditional case may be that of Van Loenen, who closely reads and explains Psalm 51 to his client. They discuss the structure and the meaning

17. Den Toom, *The Chaplain-Researcher*, 218–22.
18. See Kruizinga, "Enhancing the Integration."

of the text. "The explanation seems to help him recognize himself in the text. He also asks for another text for a more positive feeling. The chaplain suggests Psalm 139" ("Wounded Warrior," Chapter 10). Interestingly, the focus of the conversation seems to be on the text *outside of* the client, but while discussing the text, they are discussing the client's situation. It seems that the client has appropriated the texts, as he later refers to the Psalms when speaking about his life.

> Hans answers that his apartment is Psalm 139 and that the ward is Psalm 51. When the chaplain asks what that means, Hans replies that he has always thought that he deserved punishment for what he had done. He relates the ward to that conviction. He identifies the conditions on the ward with punishment. Psalm 139 enables him to see himself differently. It gives him the conviction that he deserves understanding and comfort for what he has gone through. The symbol of that is his new apartment ("Wounded Warrior," Chapter 10).

The chaplain helps Hans to understand his feelings and situation and opens up the possibility of transformation by connecting both Psalms. In other words, the chaplain helps Hans in the interpretation of life by means of interpreting texts.

In other case studies, similar ways of working with texts can be found. In the case study of Van Bolhuis. we see the chaplain asking the client to bring along some song texts about death and to read a rather difficult book together. In the case study of Van den Bosse, the chaplain tells a story that has a significant impact on the prisoner. "The story has a major impact on Simon, who in turn shares it with his therapists and other prisoners and also reflects about how people talk about others and what that means for his pleasing behavior. Simon becomes able to look at himself from a distance (similar to the notion of decentering from mindfulness training)" ("From Slumped to Upright," Chapter 12).

The role of the intertextual interpreter is closely related to a hermeneutical approach to chaplaincy and Gerkin's characterization of pastoral care as reading a person as a "living human document."[19] Reading texts is one of the key characteristics of many chaplains' expertise, which is also used in the accompaniment of clients. Using texts, they aim to help clients understand themselves and their situations and to see their lives in a different light. That light may be understood transcendently, for example, the Light of God, or immanently as the light of the story. That light helps clients to discover and attribute meaning to their particular situation. The role of

---

19. Gerkin, *The Living Human Document*.

"intertextual interpreter" is a typical expertise-focused role, although it also touches on the value-orientation and positioning of chaplains. The role implicitly presupposes the idea that persons may become themselves and find their identity in relating their own stories to other stories. Knowing stories and being able to work with (sacred) stories and sources is one of the areas of chaplaincy expertise. That expertise has consequences for the positioning, as it indicates the specific contribution of the chaplain to the well-being of others. The role of intertextual interpreter thus distinguishes the chaplains from other professionals and their means.

Symbolizer of Healing

A striking characteristic of various case studies is the use of symbols. Most chaplains make use of symbols at some point in the care process. These symbols are sometimes expressed in a material way or a ritual, sometimes as a metaphor. In the case study of Van Loenen, a ritual is performed to enable the veteran to come to terms with his past, his actions, his guilt, and with God. The ritual can be regarded as a ritual of repentance and forgiveness. In the context of the psychiatric ward, this is described in words fitting that context: healing. The chaplain literally speaks of three steps in the ritual: "cleansing the wound, binding the wound, and letting the wound heal" ("Wounded Warrior," Chapter 10).

In the case study of Termeer the ritual seems to be an elementary form of a church service. However, the chaplain adapts the ritual to the perception and situation of Charly, and she lets him participate at moments. By performing the ritual together in the same way every time and being closely attuned to Charly's situation, the chaplain helps him go from a high level of tension to a virtually relaxed situation. Similar things can be said about the ritual in the case study of Joke Zuidema. The rituals all contribute to some form of recovery, healing, and well-being.

The case study of Van der Zaag deserves special attention in this regard. In the case study, the chaplain notices that her client experiences a lack of inspiration. To spark her inspiration again, she asks her client to take something with her that symbolizes the soul for her. "It is the chaplains' experience that self-chosen texts or images can deepen the communication and have a healing effect" ("Energy *and* Inspiration," Chapter 4). The woman brings a photo and a text to the next meeting which gives rise to several conversations on her experience of the loss of inspiration. Afterwards, the client writes:

> It's really very difficult to explain what happened in our conversations, because it is so enwrapped in intimacy, in listening and being heard, in the atmosphere, . . . being permitted, encouraged, and enabled to express doubts, fears, and searchings . . . I believe that it was that, that was so healing ("Energy *and* Inspiration," Chapter 4).

The symbols help clients to express themselves, where words do not suffice or cannot be found. Symbolizing what she both misses and longs for brings forth a healing experience. The chaplain combines here existential, spiritual, and aesthetic competencies to enable the client to express her experiences and have new experiences of a different nature. At the same time, as becomes clear in the case study of Irene Plaatsman, a balance is needed between the imaginary world and the real world. The encounter between chaplain and client may itself become a transitional phase in which the client "uses imagination to develop a relationship to the object-world, experiment with and incorporate new behavior" ("I Do It My Way," Chapter 7), thus becoming more oneself.

The role of symbolic healer has a clear value-orientation: healing. Although the way in which healing is understood varies, it seems to be closely related to the concept of existential recovery. In a review article, Mary Leamy et al. categorize five aspects of recovery with the acronym CHIME (Connectedness, Hope, Identity, Meaning, and Empowerment).[20] In an analysis of case studies from mental healthcare indications were found that chaplains contribute to those five aspects of recovery.[21] Besides this clear value-orientation, the role of symbolic healer also indicates chaplains' expertise in symbols, rituals, and worldview sources.[22] As symbols connect one world to the other, negotiating real and imaginary worlds, chaplains' positions themselves accordingly. On the one hand, they align with the institution's goals, in which healing and recovery are often shared goals. On the other hand, they intentionally use a different language ("Energy *and* Inspiration"),[23] place ("Wounded Warrior"),[24] materials ("I Do It My Way"),[25] or behavior ("A Church for Charly")[26] than is customary in that context, allowing clients to experience their life in a new way.

20. Leamy et al., "Recovery in Mental Health."
21. Rosie and Den Toom, "Spiritual Care and Recovery."
22. See Chapter 22, for more on chaplains' worldview sources.
23. See Chapter 4.
24. See Chapter 10.
25. See Chapter 7.
26. See Chapter 9.

THE CHAPLAIN AND THE BATH: A META-METAPHOR

In the previous sections, four roles of chaplains have been described that can be discerned in the case studies included in the present volume. In analyzing the roles, new designations were sought in addition to role descriptions such as that of clown, midwife, *et cetera*. Although the designated roles are not exhaustive of all possible roles within chaplaincy, their empirical base adds to their validity. Before reflecting on these roles, it has to be repeated that the focus of the chapter was on chaplains' actions, while roles in fact only function in a dynamic interplay between persons. In the descriptions of the roles, however, I have tried to account for the responses of the clients and the necessity of reciprocity. In this concluding section, some common characteristics of the various roles are highlighted and conclusions are drawn, using the poem about a patient being bathed.

First, roles integrate chaplains' values and goals, their expertise, and their positioning. That is an important observation as research of chaplaincy increasingly focuses on goals, interventions, and outcomes, which more or less isolates the interventions from the person who embodies those interventions. The same intervention might be used in various roles. To formulate it in terms of the bath, caregivers can put a patient in bath from the perspective of hygiene, from care, from the perspective of wellbeing and relaxation, *et cetera*. Each of those intentions affects the way the patient is bathed.

Second, roles are temporary and situational. Chaplains may play the roles frequently, and some may be part of their basic attitude, but they do not play a role with every client in every situation. As such, roles play an intermediating role, that is, fulfill a mediating function between generic values and goals, expertise, and positioning of chaplaincy and the concrete situations in which care is offered. Symbolizing those roles in a metaphor, as is done in the current chapter, might help chaplains to discern what role is most adequate in different situations. The meta-metaphor of the bath indicates that in each phase of the contact (bathing), different roles and interventions may be needed (hydrating, washing, rinsing, drying). In the Dutch context, Job Smit has elaborated upon the metaphor of the *mikve*, a ritual bath, to designate the basic method of chaplaincy.[27]

Third, all of the roles discussed above form a contrast in some way or another to the organizational culture. There is the chaplain who speaks of inspiration in a context in which one speaks of physical energy. Another chaplain uses religious and moral texts in a psychiatric context to contribute

---

27. Smit, *Responding to Life Itself*.

to the self-understanding of a client. A third chaplain is a person of trust in a context that is distrusted or experienced as frightening. Finally, there is a chaplain who embodies the good in a context of everyday life. As such, the bath of chaplaincy is an interruption of life in that specific context with potentially transformative power. Chaplaincy care as the water of the bath, can be experienced as safe water, where clients can quiet down and where old dreams are relived. Sometimes the "bliss" of the bath is more momentaneous for clients, while others experience a long-lasting effect. Those moments of bathing serve to help clients feel less like a patient and more like a human being.

REFERENCES

Clarke, Victoria, and Virginia Braun. "Using Thematic Analysis in Counselling and Psychotherapy Research: A Critical Reflection." *Counselling and Psychotherapy Research* 18.2 (2018) 107–10. https://doi.org/10.1002/capr.12165.

De Jonge, Ed. *Beelden van de professional: inspiratiebronnen voor professionalisering*. Utrecht: Eburon, 2015.

Den Toom, Niels. *The Chaplain-Researcher: The Perceived Impact of Participation in a Dutch Research Project on Chaplains' Professionalism*. Utrecht: Eburon, 2022.

Faber, Heije. "Second Thoughts on the Minister as a Clown." *Pastoral Psychology* 28.2 (1979) 132–37. https://doi.org/10.1007/BF01760447.

Freidson, Eliot. *Professionalism, the Third Logic: On the Practice of Knowledge*. Chicago : University of Chicago Press, 2001.

Gerkin, Charles V. *The Living Human Document: Re-Visioning Pastoral Counseling in a Hermeneutical Mode*. Nashville: Abingdon, 1984.

Herion, Christian, et al. "Validating International CanMEDS-Based Standards Defining Education and Safe Practice of Nurse Anesthetists." *International Nursing Review* 66.3 (2019) 404–15. https://doi.org/10.1111/inr.12503.

Kingston, Basil D. "M. Vasalis' De idioot in het bad: Five Versions and Some Comments." *Canadian Journal of Netherlandic Studies* IV.2 (1983) 50–53. Poem originally published in M. Vasalis, Verzamelde gedichten. Amsterdam: Van Oorschot, 2006.

Körver, Jacques, et al., eds. *Richting, Repertoire en Resultaat. Uitkomsten van het Nederlandse Case Studies Project Geestelijke Verzorging (2016–2021)*. Utrecht: PThU-UCGV, 2023.

Kruizinga, Renske, et al. "Enhancing the Integration of Chaplains within the Healthcare Team: A Qualitative Analysis of a Survey Study among Healthcare Chaplains." *Integrated Healthcare Journal* 4.1 (2023) e000138 .

Leamy, Mary, et al. "Conceptual Framework for Personal Recovery in Mental Health: Systematic Review and Narrative Synthesis." *The British Journal of Psychiatry* 199.6 (2011) 445–52.

Lindgren, Tomas. "Hjalmar Sundén's Impact on the Study of Religion in the Nordic Countries." *Temenos* 1 (2014) 39–62. https://doi.org/10.33356/temenos.46249.

Massey, Kevin, et al. "What Do I Do? Developing a Taxonomy of Chaplaincy Activities and Interventions for Spiritual Care in Intensive Care Unit Palliative Care." *BMC Palliative Care* 14.1 (2015) 10. https://doi.org/10.1186/s12904-015-0008-0.

Nouwen, Henri J. M. *The Wounded Healer: Ministry in Contemporary Society.* New York: Image Doubleday, 2010.

Rosie, Sujin, and Niels Den Toom. "Spiritual Care and Recovery in Mental Health Care: An Analysis of Spiritual Care According to CHIME." In *Recovery: The Interface Between Psychiatry and Spiritual Care*, edited by Erik Olsman, et al., 38–50. Utrecht: Eburon, 2023.

Smit, Job, et al. "Responding to Life Itself: A Proposed Understanding of Domain, Goal and Interventions for Chaplaincy in a Secular Age," *Journal of Pastoral Care and Counseling* 78.4 (2024) 188–95.

Spelt, Adri, et al. *Rollen en competenties van een geestelijk verzorger als expert levensbeschouwelijke zorgverlening.* Amsterdam: VGVZ, 2012.

Timmins, Fiona, et al. "The Role of the Healthcare Chaplain: A Literature Review." *Journal of Health Care Chaplaincy* 24.3 (2018) 87–106. https://doi.org/10.1080/08854726.2017.1338048.

Walton, Martin. "The Welcoming Guest. Practices of Mutual Hospitality in Chaplaincy." In *Encounter in Pastoral Care and Spiritual Healing. Towards an Integrative and Intercultural Approach*, edited by Daniel Louw, et al., 220–35. Pastoral Care and Spiritual Healing. Berlin: LIT, 2012.

18

Serving the Care Community
—Martin Walton

"In this universe we are given two gifts: the ability to love and the ability to ask questions. Which are, at the same time, the fires that warm us and the fires that scorch us."

Mary Oliver[1]

BONDS AND BURDENS

One of the concerns for further research that the Research Community (RC) Eldercare formulated was the question: "What does it mean for residents to involuntarily be part of a resident community that is not of their own choosing?"[2] That question was not part of the research focus of the CSP, as it focused primarily on direct care of clients, in this case residents, by a chaplain. It is, however, a question that is often indirectly addressed by chaplains in many settings in responding to what persons express with regard to other residents.

One of the expressions is new found friendships. A case study on moral counseling in a mental health care setting with regard to a suicide pact exemplifies two very different sides to that.[3] On the one hand there is the bond established on the ward of the treatment center between two young

---

1. Excerpt from Oliver, *Upstream*, 91.
2. De Groot et al, "Van ambacht en kunst," 186.
3. Muthert et al, "Re-Evaluating a Suicide Pact."

women who share a similar condition but also friendship. That friendship leads to a pact, one might say bondage, that if one commits suicide, the other will follow. When one of them does commit suicide, the pact that was meant to help prevent either from doing so, threatens to drive the one left behind into suicide as well. In carefully orchestrated moral counseling the chaplain helps the survivor to choose for life again.

Another form is the burden that people can be to each other, in hospital rooms, in a military barrack, prison ward, or resident group, a matter that is often neglected and under-researched.[4] One case study (unpublished) from the RC Mixed Fields documented the care a chaplain provided in a resident group of four persons with intellectual disabilities. Other care providers had signaled that there were often conflicts in the group because the four residents would compete to gain attention and be the one talking. The chaplain used pictograms to demonstrate rudimentary ways of responding to each other, including listening and waiting for the other to finish talking, and enable the group of residents to communicate better with each other and to live more peacefully together. The chaplain also coached the care providers in how to accompany the group and remind them of the rules of conduct that had been learned and agreed to. Not only did the atmosphere in the group improve substantially, the care providers were also able to function less as referees and more as care providers.

One of the questions that arose in the evaluation of the case study by the RC was whether having sessions to improve the communication in a resident group was to be reckoned as work for a chaplain. The response of the chaplain involved was that the staff knew no one else to ask. That he was familiar with the residents, respected by the care providers, and came from outside the immediate residential setting put him in a unique position to work with the group and the team. One can also imagine others, such as a teacher or social worker, doing the job, but in this particular case the opportunity fell to the chaplain. The decision of the chaplain to get involved was motivated from the viewpoint that he is not only called to provide good chaplaincy or spiritual care, but also to facilitate good care in a general sense wherever he can. The motivation to become involved was drawn by the chaplain from care ethics. The underlying existential issue of the residents was the need and desire to be heard, which was better fulfilled when they listened to each other. The means were aesthetic with pictograms and physical exercises in hearing, listening, and speaking. And the underlying

---

4. We did find: Bosman et al., "Multicultural Tensions in the Military?"; Clare et al., "The Experience of Living with Dementia."

concern was spiritual and ethical in the sense of what it means to be (or become) a community of residents together.

These examples indicate that settings of care, or of the military and detention, cause (or force) people to relate to each other, for better and for worse. People can experience others as a burden, but also as a source of support. At the best, those who find themselves in those settings, whether as clients or as care providers, can establish bonds or (temporary) friendship and in some cases form a (temporary or momentary) community.[5] In many ways, chaplains are involved in those events. We explore here additional examples that surfaced in the CSP and reflect on them.

THE CHAPLAIN AS GO BETWEEN

The case of a military ceremony in "To Honor and Confirm" (Chapter 11) describes how a chaplain throughout a day of travel, floral ceremony, and reception at the parental home of a deceased young soldier, positions herself in the bus, at the cemetery, and at the home and its garden, how she makes contacts with soldiers in regular duty and suspended soldiers in civilian clothing, how she positions herself in an encounter at the cemetery, and how she makes contact with various family members. Even her choice of uniform is part of being able to better relate to the family. In all of her positioning, speaking, and doing, she provides care for a particular person or persons. At the same time, she visibly "seeks the lost," that is, the suspended soldiers and makes connections that the commander or other soldiers cannot make. She provides distinct care for the mother and for the father in matters about which it is difficult for them to communicate with each other. The chaplain knows what to say and she know where to be. She steps in when the commander is at a loss for words. She serves as a go between for the military and the family. In and through the chaplain, connections are made, whatever the individual responses to her making contact might be. She becomes a point of contact in various relations, at times in vicarious ways, as a symbol of a larger story. She does what a good chaplain does, and in doing so does some things that others cannot do.

Speaking of the chaplain as a go between allows a link to a quite different setting, a case study on an intensive care unit in a general hospital that bears the title "Liaison."[6] When a man is taken acutely to surgery, from where he will go to the ICU, the wife of the man asks the nurse if there is

---

5. Stark and Walton, "Waarom de kring niet rond wordt."
6. Broekhoff and Körver, "Verbindingsofficier"; Körver, et al., *Richting, Repertoire en Resultaat*.

a priest available to administer last rites. The chaplain, who is not a priest, contacts the wife and lets her know that no priest is immediately available but that he can offer a blessing of the spouse. The wife consents, commenting that the chaplain surely knows what is best. The chaplain then negotiates with the ICU because of protocols and mediates between the "lifeworld" of the man and his partner and the "system" of the hospital.[7] The chaplain works to inform all of the professionals—nurses, doctors, and paramedics—and have them in touch with the blessing and its meaning for the man and his family. The application of the protocols becomes less strict than seemed at first sight and space is made, literally and figuratively, for the ritual and for loss and sorrow.[8] The case study received the title "Liaison" because of the manner in which the chaplain made connections and communicated with all involved. That coincides with the role of liaison or mediator we encountered in case studies on chaplaincy care on ICU's.[9]

Two case studies in juvenile care show not only how the chaplain can play a mediating role in relation to the systemic context (family) of young persons, but also how reflections on freedom can help young people understand their position in their social context. The chaplain further realizes how young people in juvenile care are pushed to decide what they want to do with their lives, while they have a sense of not being heard and not having real choices.[10] At a conversational level in contact with a young person, in dealing with care providers, and at a more analytical level, the notion of freedom plays a role. The chaplain mediates between persons but also negotiates concepts and values.

POSITION AND CONTRIBUTION OF CHAPLAINCY

The examples above show that every institution shapes the relationships of those involved. That holds for the formal procedures and protocols in the organization, but also for the life world that is created and that is an essential element of any organization.[11] That is especially true where people reside and are cared for, or are incarcerated, or live and work with each other as in the military. The question we address here is how the content of chaplaincy

---

7. Habermas et al., *Lifeworld and System*; Heath, "System and lifeworld"; De Roest, *Communicative Identity*.
8. See Chapter 16.
9. Wirpsa and Pugliese, *Chaplains as partners*; Murphy, "I'm Being Swallowed Up." See Chapter 3.
10. Van der Meer, "Is MacDonald's Freedom."
11. Sennett, *The Corrosion of Character*.

care can be understood in relation to the goals of an organization.[12] A subsequent question is what functions chaplains fulfill in those relations, not only in order to contribute to the wellbeing of clients, but also to the wellbeing and well-functioning of the organization as a life world.

The contribution of chaplains in a care setting will be different from that in a prison or in the military, different in a residential care setting from the position on a high-tech ward of a hospital with short-term patient stays. In the reflection on the case study "From Slumped to Upright" (Chapter 12), we noted:

> There are, therefore, several aspects of the accompaniment by the chaplain that directly contribute to the changes in Simon: making contact and offering care when Simon is resistant to therapy, facilitating Simon's participation in therapy, helping Simon to relate to therapy, and complementing the work of therapy through conversational interactions and mindfulness training.

Another example is provided by a case study from mental health care, "Wounded Warrior" (Chapter 10). There the chaplain fulfills several roles in regard to mental health care treatment. Those roles overlap and are interrelated, but they nevertheless can be distinguished. We do that with the help of five different relations of chaplaincy to therapy that were previously found in interviews with clients in mental health care on chaplaincy.[13]

a. *Chaplaincy as care of its own kind and with its own goals.* This is the starting point in the case study when Hans comes to the chaplain with the desire "to set things right with God." The chaplain adds for himself the goal of attaining spiritual healing. Both of these goals are part and parcel of the domain of chaplaincy itself. The means are ritual and religious texts.

b. *Chaplaincy as care in relating oneself to the illness, condition, or situation.* Hans is trying to understand what he has gone through and what that means to him. Is he a perpetrator or a victim or both?

c. *Chaplaincy as support in relating oneself to therapy, treatment, and its context and consequences.* Hans is regularly dissatisfied and upset about his treatment and feels confined. With the aid of the Psalms Hans has read, the chaplain reframes Hans's understanding of what is

---

12. Cf. "Chaplaincy in Context," Chapter 13.
13. Walton, *Hoe waait de wind?*

going on in treatment and motivates Hans to continue treatment (and apologize to a therapist).

d. *Chaplaincy as a complement to therapy.* Hans is in treatment for PTTS, but there is for him a need that has not been addressed. His discovery of the term "moral injury" and the way the chaplain helps Hans address that injury with the help of religious texts and a ritual, complement the treatment for PTTS.

e. *Chaplaincy as support of a treatment goal.* Hans is lined up for discharge from the hospital, but issues of aggression, dissatisfaction with supervision, and generally dealing with his situation are still at work. The support (coaching) of the chaplain, finally tangible in the candle that the chaplain lets Hans take with him after the ritual, facilitates his discharge and living in his own apartment.

Besides the five formal relations between goals of treatment and goals of chaplaincy care indicated above, we can also identify from the case studies a number of discerning and complementary functions that chaplains fulfill in those various relations to treatment and to the other professionals.

1. *Offering contact in disturbed care relations.* In the case study "Exposure?" (Chapter 6) the chaplain was able to establish a care relation that had not come about in the treatment setting. In other cases (unpublished) chaplains in general hospitals maintain contact with a patient where the communication with other care providers has stagnated or show how to deal with a patient with difficult behavior. The care of the chaplain is not only complementary but also provides an example of how care can be offered.

2. *Pedagogical input.* In "Energy and Inspiration" (Chapter 4) the chaplain is able to introduce, explain, and defend the introduction of the term "inspiration" in the care plan for the client. That the term "inspiration" shifts from a typical chaplaincy care issue to being a complement to treatment to becoming part of the goal of treatment is a result of the chaplain's input.

3. *Critical function.*[14] Related to the two above functions is critical reflection, as in the moral counseling of a young woman with a pact to commit suicide above.[15] When the therapist indicates that there is a need for control on the ward, due to another incident of suicide, the chaplain argues that what the client needs besides protection is

14. Sluijsmans, *Spanningsvol verbinden in een ziekenhuis.*
15. Muthert et al., "Re-Evaluating a Suicide Pact."

support and trust. Another instance is of a chaplain who with a patient writes a letter to the nurses and doctors about how she, the patient, feels when they talk about her in her presence while she is on oxygen.

4. *Liaison.* Broekhoff (in the case discussed above) provided chaplaincy care of its own kind (blessing of the sick), but the function of liaison is what made the blessing possible. In "To Honor and Confirm" (Chapter 11) the chaplain offers all sorts of care to family and military, but the striking feature is her function as go between.

5. *Mediation.* In an unpublished case study, a chaplain mediates between the parents of a child and medical personnel following a series of medical mistakes.[16]

6. *Link with the "world."* In "A Church for Charly" (Chapter 9) the chaplain links Charly vicariously to the religious community. In another case (unpublished) a chaplain cooperated with a local parish and a fund to provide diaconal care. A third instance is that of organizing a Memorial Day ceremony in a setting of residential care (see below).

7. *Excentric conversation partner.*[17] It is this function that the chaplain in juvenile care offered in the case study. In relation to treatment the chaplain can be experienced to help create an outer or *excentric* position from which the young men can reflect on themselves, their relations and future, and their dealings with treatment.

8. *Anchoring of a sense of dignity and humanity.* Many case studies indicate that the experience of being listened to and accompanied, generally in relation to questions of meaning, is reported by clients as a fundamental experience in which they could reappraise themselves and who they are ("Exposure?," Chapter 6; "From Slumped to Upright," Chapter 12), which they had not experienced or could not experience in the same way in treatment.

9. *Supporting staff.* In many case studies there were examples of chaplains responding to existential questions of other professionals or their dealing with life-work balance.

10. *Contributing to researched care.* In a case study from a rehab center (unpublished), the chaplain introduced a man with autism and depression

---

16. Unpublished case study.

17. Corveleyn, *De psycholoog kijkt*; Körver, "Excentriek of excentrisch?" Thus, not eccentric, but *excentric*, in other words, to the side of what are considered core treatment activities. The perceived outer position of the chaplain can fulfill a function, for example, in c. or d. of the relations to treatment described above.

to a spiritual coping scale. Not only was the man himself enthusiastic, but also the psychologist who had referred the man to the chaplain. And not only were the chaplain and the psychologist able to develop a care plan together, the psychologist suggested doing further research together on the use of the spiritual coping scale in the rehab center.

These functions are examples. Other functions and relations could be identified. The last example shows how a network of care emerged that involved the psychologist, the chaplain, and the man himself. Within the care organization, a care alliance developed. Together the examples show how chaplains take part in organizations and care communities and foster cooperation and community by their critical, complementary, and constructive participation. In other words, the chaplains contribute to persons being seen and heard, connected, and well cared for, so that a rudimentary sense of belonging can be engendered.[18]

A HORIZON OF COMMUNITY

In the case study of moral injury, it is significant that during the ritual performance the psychiatrist is also present, first more or less in the role of witness to what is going on, or, as he himself says, as a buddy or partner in fate (as he had previously served as a psychiatrist in the military, including a foreign mission). The psychiatrist is then invited to join Hans and the chaplain in forming a circle. "The chaplain proposes to Hans that he see this circle as a symbol of his return to the human community." Reminiscent of Jesus' words about a gathering of two or three, the circle vicariously represents a broader human community. In the setting of the chapel and the ritual, the religious community resonates as well. In the circle, in a momentary community created by the chaplain, both chaplaincy and treatment are present together with the client.

The aspect of community is explicitly named and embodied in the making of a circle by three persons. Such explicitness may be unusual, but the horizon of community is often present in the case studies. There is care for those close to the client in "To Honor and Confirm" (Chapter 11) and there is attention for the care others can offer the client (the friend of the young woman in "Exposure?" (Chapter 6). There are activities that bring clients together for sharing in "Reiteration of Ritual" (Chapter 8), music evenings in the care for homeless persons (unpublished), and the vicarious presence of the chaplain in "A Church for Charly" (Chapter 9).

18. Day, *Believing in Belonging*.

We encounter another form of community in a case study describing a Memorial Day gathering in an eldercare resident setting.[19] Besides the general awareness of the intense significance of war time experiences for many of the residents, the Humanist chaplain was triggered in a particular way to organize some activity. During a commemoration for the deceased in the period around All Soul's Day (November 2nd), one of the residents had expressed the wish to recite a familiar Dutch poem in remembrance of those who had died during World War II. The chaplain suggested reading the poem on Dutch Memorial Day (May 4th).

What did the chaplain then do? She enlisted the aid of an activity director, talked with care staff, and held a gathering in the early evening combining a flag ceremony, music, and poetry, and a national television broadcast. About twenty residents attended. For what reasons did she do this? The chaplain sought to offer the residents recognition for what they or those dear to them had experienced in times of war and to provide them an opportunity to express their grief and remembrances. The motivation by the chaplain for her involvement was to foster connectedness and make a humanizing contribution to the life sphere in the institution. What was the effect? First of all, residents simply thought it was important that there be such a gathering that they could be part of, partly to express grief, but also to show respect. For many the experience was intense and contributed to a sense of belonging. Although the ceremony was not religious, one of the participants commented, "Where two persons are, I am in their midst."

A horizon of community expresses itself in many ways in chaplaincy care, in the mediating roles chaplains fulfill,[20] in systemic approaches,[21] in community-based paradigms of chaplaincy care,[22] in understandings of spirituality in terms of connectedness[23] and reciprocity,[24] in serving as a catalyst to facilitate justice and resilience and promote values in organizations,[25] and in the relevance of care ethics with its emphases on relatedness and reciprocity for chaplaincy and health care in general.[26] When presence finds expression in availability, solidarity, and self-disclosure, the

---

19. Van der Geugten et al., "Opdat wij niet vergeten."
20. Wirpsa and Pugliese, *Chaplains as Partners*.
21. Meulink-Korf and Rhijn, *The Unexpected Third*.
22. Kelly and Swinton, *Chaplaincy and the Soul*.
23. Puchalski et al., "Improving the Quality."
24. Walton, "Discerning Lived Spirituality."
25. McClure and Thiel, "Introduction to Organizational Competencies"; White, "Facilitating Resilience"; Pak, "Through a Multi-frame Lens"; Garrett-Cobbina, "The Emotional Undercurrents." See Chapter 13.
26. Van Heijst and Caldwell, *Professional Loving Care*.

act of presence itself can create a sense of connectedness and community.[27] Chaplains fulfill roles in supporting other professionals in what motivates and inspires them[28] and in contributing to the ideals of health care institutions.[29] Embodied examples of all those perspectives are present in the case studies, in which chaplains attend to all concerned whether patient, family, or care provider, where they organize gatherings and vicariously represent communities, and where they facilitate good care.

People, both clients and personnel, come together in care settings, in prisons, and in the military, because they share some condition, situation, or mission or bear responsibility in those situations. They end up sharing space, time, and association, for better or for worse, in a hospital room, prison ward, or barrack. Their shared humanity and situation make it possible for them to share some form of bond, solidarity, or community with each other. The case studies show that chaplains can be instrumental in broadening horizons to include the perspective of community and that they are active in fostering cooperation and community.

Much of the work of chaplains is, to be sure, done individually. And contemporary chaplaincy must reckon with individualization of religion and worldview and shifts in the function of religion. That has, however, resulted in individual-oriented care rather than a community-based approach, as Barbara McClure[30] and Ewan Kelly and John Swinton[31] have pointed out. The same seems to be true for the (primary) focus of a significant portion of research on chaplaincy, as is the case with the CSP. The paradigms of chaplaincy care and the parameters of research on chaplaincy may be missing part of the story and lagging behind actual practice.

If persons are to be understood not only as living human documents, but as living human webs,[32] then not only is their personal background and social context of importance, but also their contextual and relational experiences within the care or organizational setting. The living human encounter of chaplaincy care takes place within a myriad of encounters and of supportive or absent relations with persons' contexts and communities. We need to understand more (1) what it means to persons to undergo similar things and share a similar condition or situation, including the loss of contexts, roles, and significant communities; (2) what it means to them to have

27. Baart, *Een theorie van de presentie*.
28. Giebner, *Gedeelde ruimte*.
29. Sluijsmans, *Spanningsvol verbinden in een ziekenhuis*.
30. McClure, *Moving beyond Individualism*.
31. Kelly and Swinton, *Chaplaincy and the Soul*.
32. See Chapter 2.

to participate, for better and for worse, passively and actively, voluntarily and involuntarily, in the collectivity of the care or organizational setting; and (3) what they might expect or experience in temporary or situational communities in those settings. We also need to ask whether our notions of chaplaincy and of people's search for meaning sufficiently reckon with processes of socialization in times of individualization and sufficiently appreciate the collective character of religion and worldview.

The case studies show that chaplains take responsibility for communal concerns in the settings where they work. That may stem from their location in religious and worldview communities and their knowledge of the benevolence of good communities. Their theological and philosophical background enables them to reflect not only on the good life of individuals but also on the *bonum commune*. There may be more community to it than we often realize, and more research to pursue on these questions.

REFERENCES

Baart, Andries J. *Een theorie van de presentie*. Den Haag: Boom, 2001.
Bosman, Femke, et al. "Multicultural Tensions in the Military? Evidence from the Netherlands Armed Forces." *International Journal of Intercultural Relations* 31.3 (2007) 339–61.
Broekhoff, Frans, and Jacques. Körver. "Verbindingsofficier. Ziekenzegen op de intensive care." In *Met lichaam en geest: De rituele competentie van geestelijk verzorgers*, edited by Jacques Körver, et al., 67–72. Utrecht: Eburon, 2021.
Clare, Linda, et al. "The Experience of Living with Dementia in Residential Care: An Interpretative Phenomenological Analysis." *The Gerontologist* 48.6 (2008) 711–20.
Corveleyn, Jozef. *De psycholoog kijkt niet in de ziel: Thema's uit de klinische godsdienstpsychologie*. Tilburg: KSGV, 2003.
Day, Abby. *Believing in Belonging: Belief and Social Identity in the Modern World*. Oxford: Oxford University Press, 2013.
De Groot, Jack, et al. "OG Ouderenzorg: Van ambacht en kunst tot specialisme." In *Richting, Repertoire en Resultaat. Uitkomsten van het Nederlandse Case Studies Project Geestelijke Verzorging (2016-2021).*, edited by Jacques Körver, et al., 180–89. Utrecht: PThU-UCGV, 2023.
De Roest, Henk P. *Communicative Identity: Habermas' Perspectives of Discourse as a Support for Practical Theology*. Kampen: Kok, 1998.
Garrett-Cobbina, Laurie. "The Emotional Undercurrents of Organizations." In *Chaplaincy and Spiritual Care in the Twenty-First Century. An Introduction*, edited by Wendy Cadge and Shelly Rambo, 239–57. Chapel Hill: University of North Carolina Press, 2022.
Giebner, Beate. *Gedeelde ruimte: de ontvankelijkheid van zorgverleners in patiëntencontacten*. Delft: Eburon, 2015.
Habermas, Jürgen, et al. *Lifeworld and System: A Critique of Functionalist Reason*. Boston: Beacon, 2005.

Heath, Joseph. "System and lifeworld." In *Jürgen Habermas*, edited by Barbara Fultner, 74–90. Stocksfield: Acumen, 2011.
Kelly, Ewan, and John Swinton. *Chaplaincy and the Soul of Health and Social Care: Fostering Spiritual Wellbeing in Emerging Paradigms of Care.* London: Kingsley, 2020.
Körver, Jacques. "Excentriek of excentrisch? Over de geestelijk verzorger in een zorginstelling." In *Zichtbare en onzichtbare religie: over de varianten van religieuze zin*, edited by Marinus van Uden and Rein Nauta, 139–54. Nijmegen: Valkhof Pers, 2009.
Körver, Jacques, et al. *Richting, Repertoire en Resultaat. Uitkomsten van het Nederlandse Case Studies Project Geestelijke Verzorging (2016-2021).* Utrecht: PThU–UCGV, 2023.
McClure, Barbara J. *Moving beyond Individualism in Pastoral Care and Counseling: Reflections on Theory, Theology, and Practice.* Eugene: Cascade Books, 2011.
McClure, Barbara, and Mary Martha Thiel. "Introduction to Organizational Competencies." In *Chaplaincy and Spiritual Care in the Twenty-First Century. An Introduction*, edited by Wendy Cadge and Shelly Rambo, 193–200. Chapel Hill: University of North Carolina Press, 2022.
Meulink-Korf, Hanneke, and Aat van Rhijn. *The Unexpected Third: Contextual Pastoral Care, Counselling and Ministry: An Introduction and Reflection.* Wellington: Christian Literature Fund, 2016.
Murphy, Karen. "'I'm Being Swallowed Up by This Illness, So Much Pain Deep Inside': Claire a 40 Year-old Woman with Cancer." *Health and Social Care Chaplaincy* 5.2 (2018) 209–23.
Muthert, Hanneke, et al. "Re-Evaluating a Suicide Pact. Embodied Moral Counselling in a Dutch Case Study of Mental Healthcare Chaplaincy." *Tidsskrift for Praktisk Teologi* 15 (2019) 81–89
Oliver, Mary. *Upstream: Selected Essays.* New York: Penguin, 2019.
Pak, Su Yon. "Through a Multi-Frame Lens: Surviving, Thriving, and Leading Organizations." In *Chaplaincy and Spiritual Care in the Twenty-First Century. An Introduction*, edited by Wendy Cadge and Shelly Rambo, 219–38. Chapel Hill: University of North Carolina Press, 2022.
Puchalski, Christina., et al. "Improving the Quality of Spiritual Care as a Dimension of Palliative Care: the Report of the Consensus Conference." *Journal of palliative medicine* 12.10 (2009) 885–904.
Sennett, Richard. *The Corrosion of Character: The Personal Consequences of Work in the New Capitalism.* New York: Norton, 1999.
Sluijsmans, Chantal. *Spanningsvol verbinden in een ziekenhuis: Menslievende zorg stimuleren door normatieve professionalisering.* Delft: Eburon, 2018.
Stark, Ciska, and Martin Walton. "Waarom de kring niet rond wordt. Lotgenoten—deelgenoten—bondgenoten." *Handelingen* 40.4 (2013) 59–66.
Van der Geugten, Wendy, et al. "Opdat wij niet vergeten: Een 4 mei-bijeenkomst in de ouderenzorg." *Tijdschrift Geestelijke Verzorging* 24.102 (2021) 48–53.
Van der Meer, Tjeerd. "Is MacDonald's Freedom?" In *Learning from Case Studies in Chaplaincy: Towards Practice Based Evidence & Professionalism*, edited by Renske Kruizinga, et al., 147–52. Utrecht: Eburon, 2020.
Van Heijst, Annelies, and Kay Caldwell. *Professional Loving Care: An Ethical View of the Healthcare Sector.* Leuven: Peeters, 2011.

Walton, Martin. "Discerning Lived Spirituality: The Reception of Otherness." *Journal of Pastoral Care & Counseling* 67.2 (2013) 1–10.

———. *Hoe waait de wind? Interpretatie van geestelijke verzorging door cliënten in de ggz.* Tilburg: KSGV, 2014.

White, Nathan H. "Facilitating Resilience: Chaplaincy as a Catalyst for Organizational Well-Being." In *Chaplaincy and Spiritual Care in the Twenty-First Century. An Introduction*, edited by Wendy Cadge and Shelly Rambo, 201–18. Chapel Hill: University of North Carolina Press, 2022.

Wirpsa, M. Jeanne, and Karen Pugliese, eds. *Chaplains as Partners in Medical Decision-Making: Case Studies in Healthcare Chaplaincy.* London: Kingsley, 2020.

Part Four

APPRAISAL

19

Consensus in the Research Communities
— Niels den Toom

"It is sometimes hard to grasp the difference between identifying with one's own roots, understanding people with other roots, and judging what is good or bad."

Umberto Eco[1]

BUILDING CONSENSUS IN THE CSP

Someone once said that chaplains work according to the Judges-principle from the Old Testament: "Everyone did what was right in one's own eyes" (Judges 17:5).[2] That characteristic verse not only indicates that chaplains work in very pluriform (and non-methodical) ways, but also that there is no consensus on what is "right" or good chaplaincy. Or to phrase it positively, many conceptions of the good are pursued and represented in chaplaincy.[3]

Those conceptions of the good have led to extended and ongoing discussions within the profession of chaplaincy in the Netherlands. The discussions often had an ideological character and a polarizing tendency, leading to dichotomous positions. One of those discussions concerned the question whether using diagnostics (spiritual assessments) is appropriate

---

1. Eco, "The Roots of Conflict."
2. Walton, *Bron, rivier, delta*.
3. Schuhmann and Damen, "Representing the Good"; Visser et al., "Goals of Chaplaincy Care."

for chaplains. As I described more extensively in my dissertation,[4] adherents of pastoral diagnostics and intervention and adherents of the theory of presence took opposing positions.[5] Another discussion regarded the question whether chaplains should be endorsed by a worldview institution or not. In that discussion, spirituality and professionalism became opposing terms, although one can argue that spirituality is part of chaplains' professionalism. Given the multitude of conceptions and the charged debates within the professional group, it is an audacious step to initiate an empirical, collaborative project on "good practices" of chaplaincy and include chaplains from various fields of work and various worldview backgrounds. Diversity seems to be the premise, consensus the exception.

Nevertheless, the Case Studies Project (CSP) sought descriptions of good practices and pursued consensus.[6] That gives rise to various questions. According to whom is an example of chaplaincy care considered to be a good practice? Do all members of a research community (RC) necessarily consent with the qualification "good"? And how good must the practice be, when obviously not perfect? In Chapter 3, the question what a "good" *case study* consists of from a research perspective was addressed. Here, I do not focus on the good case study, but on the good practice to which a case study attests.

Martin Walton and Jacques Körver explicitly aimed at "consensus building among chaplains and scholars as to what good practices in chaplaincy might be."[7] They define good practices as "examples of chaplaincy care that are demonstrably representative and effective, and that are backed up by theoretical reasoning . . . The Dutch CSP requires, in addition, confirmation by clients and other professionals, along with evaluation and recognition by experienced colleagues and researchers."[8] In other words, whether a case is *good* depends on its being *representative, effective, theoretically grounded*, on *confirmation* by clients and other professionals, and on the *evaluation* and *recognition* by experienced colleagues and researchers. The definition implies that a case can be effective and theoretically grounded, but still not regarded as "good" in the evaluation by other chaplains. In this chapter, the focus is on the last part of the definition, by describing the challenges, remedies, and outcomes of the search for consensus in the RCs of the CSP. First, the challenges in working with research communities will

---

4. Den Toom, *The Chaplain-Researcher*.
5. Vlasblom et al., "Developments in Healthcare Chaplaincy."
6. Walton and Körver, "Dutch Case Studies Project."
7. Walton and Körver, "Dutch Case Studies Project," 258.
8. Walton and Körver, "Dutch Case Studies Project," 261.

be discussed by further describing the pluriformity in the profession. Then, I point out what elements in the CSP's design stimulated consensus building despite the challenges. Finally, I describe how the process of building consensus was experienced by the chaplains-researchers.

PLURIFORMITY AS STARTING POINT

The various challenges chaplains face in working towards consensus can all be understood as the challenge of pluriformity.[9] A quick scan of chaplaincy handbooks reveals a great variety of conceptualizations and approaches in chaplaincy care.[10] First, the religious and worldview background of the chaplains is pluriform. Second, the contexts in which chaplains work differ. I will discuss both elements of the pluriform character of chaplaincy before elaborating on the notion of language.

Chaplains work from a variety of religious and worldview backgrounds. In the Netherlands chaplaincy finds itself situated in a society that can be characterized as a secularized, individualized, and highly pluriform religious landscape.[11] The worldviews of chaplains determine largely the orientation of chaplains, how they regard their clients, and how they provide their care.[12] While one's worldview always affects one's professional conduct, that is particularly the case with chaplains as their care expresses a *value rationality*.[13] The concept of value rationality, as developed by Max Weber,[14] indicates the inherent value of certain actions alongside its instrumental value. Value rationality is characteristic of a worldview and religious perspective. However, the fact that every worldview has its own values and understanding of values leads to a diversity of practices and a variety of norms on what a good practice is. In the CSP, that became apparent on a very elementary level in the RC Prison. The participating chaplain-researchers discussed the nomenclature for referring to their "clients." "Client" is generally used in healthcare settings, but is not customary in prisons. The Christian chaplains were inclined to speak of "pastoral care receiver" [Dutch: *pastorant*], but that was not a conversant term for chaplains from other worldviews. In the

---

9. See also Chapter 1, "Context and Objectives of the CSP."

10. See e.g., Cobb et al., *Oxford Textbook of Spirituality*; Swift et al., *Handbook of Chaplaincy Studies*; Fitchett et al., *Evidence-Based Healthcare Chaplaincy*.

11. Bernts and Berghuijs, *God in Nederland 1966–2015*; den Toom et al., "The Professionalization of Chaplaincy."

12. Den Toom, *The Chaplain-Researcher*.

13. Den Toom, *The Chaplain-Researcher*, 118–20.

14. Weber, *Wirtschaft und Gesellschaft*.

end, they decided to use the notion of "care receiver."[15] While this is only a formal form of consensus, it displays how the various worldviews lead to a variety of practices and norms.

In the RC Eldercare, a Muslim chaplain-researcher described a case in which the chaplain assumed that the client did not have feelings of anger, "because that was not possible according to their faith."[16] That led to a discussion in the research community on the normativity of the chaplain's regard of the client. In the specific case, it turned out that the chaplain was correct in the observation that *this* patient did not seem to be angry, but the presumption that Muslim patients do not feel anger about their situation raised critical questions in the research community.

Related to the diverse worldview backgrounds of chaplains is the diversity in their methods. Where one chaplain prefers to work from a presence approach, following the clients, trying to intervene as little as possible, others are more directive. In a survey from 2017, about one third did not report any theory that guided their care. Among those who did (consciously) use theory, the use was very diverse with a great variety of theories. The most prevalent theory, the Presence Approach,[17] was mentioned by only 22 percent of the respondents, underlining the great variety.[18] Where one chaplain takes on an explicit religious role, using religious language, other chaplains are more hesitant to use religious language. Where one chaplain stimulates the autonomy of the client, others emphasize the connectedness of all human beings.

Besides the values and practices of chaplains that affect their perspective on a case study, there is an influence from the context in which chaplains work. For instance, chaplains who work in the military hold a very different position in comparison with the position in a hospital. Military chaplains are part of the military, as they wear a uniform and their clients are staff members. Chaplains who work with people with dementia in an eldercare setting work more with nonverbal interventions compared to university chaplains. And it is not only the clients and their situation that affect chaplains' practices, but also the manner in which chaplaincy services are organized. In mental healthcare, chaplains are usually responsible for an entire resident setting or several wards, regardless of the clients' worldviews. In prisons, however, chaplaincy is organized along denominational lines so that chaplains in principle see clients from their own denomination.

15. Den Toom, *The Chaplain-Researcher*, 126.
16. Quotation from an interview transcript with one of the chaplain-researchers.
17. Baart, *The Presence Approach*.
18. Den Toom et al., "The Professionalization of Chaplaincy."

The differences in organizational forms and substantive themes between the contexts can make one wonder whether we can still speak of the same professional field. Yet, as we have seen, the domain of chaplaincy can be recognized in all contexts.[19]

Finally, there are differences in language. In a survey among all participants of the CSP, one respondent noted that "everyone has their own way of formulating" things, possibly due to "different worldview-related language."[20] Another chaplain suggested that it was the tenacity or idiosyncrasy of the profession which led to differences in language to describe the profession.

> The common thread [in the profession] is of course also a little pertinacity that one has. Which also means that we can name differently what is actually the same . . . For instance, one can speak of Gadamer and Levinas, and then I think, yes, of course, they have many differences, but . . . Gadamer is more about the method of entering into conversation, while Levinas states that one needs the conversation to become who one is. That lies in the same vein for me.[21]

The diverse practices and languages within chaplaincy, including its goals and values, make it hard to identify a common ground or shared perspective from which a practice can be assessed as a "good practice." This can be illustrated by an example.

> A chaplain in a nursing home meets a woman with dementia. The dementia causes difficulties in speaking (aphasia). The chaplain knows from experience that singing religious songs helps her in becoming more fluent in the conversation. For that reason, she starts the conversation by singing religious songs from the Protestant tradition. It appears to help the woman express herself and that results in a short conversation.[22]

In this example, the chaplain's intervention of singing a Psalm is effective in relation to the goal of communication and expression. The intervention is based on experience, but also informed by reminiscence theories (theoretical grounded). The increase in fluency of the lady's speech can be confirmed by other care professionals. In other words, the case can be considered a "good practice" in many respects. Still, one of the other chaplains may ask: Is

---

19. See Chapter 13, "Discerning Contexts."
20. Den Toom, *The Chaplain-Researcher*, 165.
21. Respondent "Maaike," as quoted in den Toom, *The Chaplain-Researcher*, 166.
22. This example is derived from an unpublished case study from the RC Eldercare.

it legitimate and ethical to use religious practices as Psalms, which address God, as a means of letting the woman express herself? Is this not an instrumentalization of religion? Thus, the worldview perspective of chaplains, the values they derive from that perspective, and the translation of those values in a specific context, play a significant role in the evaluation of a case study. Whereas one might regard it inappropriate to "use" a Psalm as a means to help the woman speak, another chaplain might consider it appropriate as a form of reminiscence.[23]

Although describing good practices is not as easy in a pluriform profession like chaplaincy, the process of describing one's own practices and discussing other chaplains' practices did lead to the development of the chaplains' professional identity. In a dual process of identification with and distinction from other chaplains, they positioned themselves in the field of chaplaincy. In Chapter 20, I will elaborate more on the chaplains' professional identity. Here, it is important to stress that along with the personal process of formation of professional identity, there is also a more collective aspect, which is the development of consensus. In light of pluriformity in the profession, how did the chaplain-researchers and academic researchers deal with the diversity? How did they foster the process of building consensus? In the next section, several elements of the research methodology that served to deal with the challenges are elaborated.

STIMULATING CONSENSUS

In the CSP, several elements stimulated building consensus on what constitutes good chaplaincy care. The very existence of the research community is a possible stimulus for developing consensus. In other contributions to case studies research, individual chaplains have written a case study and received feedback from a chaplain and another professional.[24] Although the case studies are commented upon, there is not yet a dialogical process for coming to consensus. The duration of four years, in which the research communities collaboratively analyzed and discussed the case studies, contributed to consensus. In other words, the basic community of researchers made the research a collaborative and communal effort from the beginning. Yet, there were several methodological strategies applied to stimulate consensus building, of which I will highlight five: using an appreciative approach, a

---

23. Schweitzer, et al., *Remembering Yesterday, Caring Today*.

24. Fitchett and Nolan, *Spiritual Care in Practice*; Fitchett and Nolan, *Case Studies in Spiritual Care*.

focus on the particular, describing the effectiveness of the care provided, the use of an analytical framework, and the addition of critical issues.

First, the CSP adopted an appreciative approach.[25] The appreciative approach lies not only in the collaborative nature of the project as such, in which the chaplains were appreciated for their contribution to the project. The appreciative approach played a visible role in the acquisition of case studies and their review in the RCs. The project presumed that when an experienced chaplain selected and described a case study as "good practice," it would offer elements of good practice. That is, again, not the same as a perfect practice. Second, the evaluative format which guided the analysis in the research communities focused on the identification of active and efficacious elements in the accompaniment of clients. The review was thus not oriented at identifying problems, raising critical questions, or at determining what other chaplains would or might have done—in other words at what did *not* happen—but it focused on what happened, why it happened, and with what result.

Appreciatively discussing a case study, though, does not guarantee that the chaplain-researchers experienced appreciation in the discussion of their work. In fact, they experienced "it as a challenge to put aside their values and convictions with regard to fellow-chaplains' cases."[26] Even though chaplains are trained to suspend their judgement in listening to clients, and even though they participated in the project as co-researchers instead of as colleague chaplains, their personal judgment could not easily be set aside. Elsewhere, I have described how this led to feelings of being criticized and unprotected.[27] In the research community of hospital chaplains, a first round of positive feedback was introduced, before the analysis started. Other chaplains mentioned the use of the third-person perspective in the discussion of the case studies as helpful to embody the role of a researcher and to "detach your mind and feelings for a while."[28] Those experiences indicate that the process of building consensus also includes the relational foundation of feeling appreciated and safe.

A second feature of the CSP that might have helped in building consensus is the focus on the particular and the observable.[29] The submitted case studies described a particular situation, with a particular client and the particular actions of the chaplain. The case studies did not pretend to offer

25. Walton and Körver, "Dutch Case Studies Project."
26. Den Toom, *The Chaplain-Researcher*, 125.
27. Den Toom, "Oneself as Another."
28. Den Toom, "Oneself as Another," 204.
29. Körver, "The Science of the Particular."

an encompassing picture of what chaplaincy is, nor an ideal image of what chaplaincy should be like. In the beginning of the project, four types of case studies were aimed for:[30] *representative* with regard to the client population, *paradigmatic* as an example of a certain approach or method of chaplaincy, *outsider case* which aims to portray a unique case, and a *critical* case to test general assumptions of common perspectives on chaplaincy. It could be expected that the first two types of cases are more likely to lead to discussions on what good chaplaincy is, as they might contrast with other views on what is representative and paradigmatic. But even then, the case studies described a particular situation. Furthermore, the focus on the particular and observable might have helped to avoid ideological discussions, as reality is often more complex and nuanced than ideological convictions.

The third methodological strategy is that the interventions, goals, and outcomes of a case are described. These three constitute a sort of interwoven unity to the case. If the three are aligned, that is, if the interventions that are employed by chaplains result in the outcomes that were aimed for, one can consider it to be a good practice. While, as indicated above, there could still be questions on the adequacy of the chaplains' actions and the validity of the goals, the case may at least be considered good in the sense that the case attains the pursued goals. In other words, the case studies could be considered good in a functional sense of being efficacious. Or in a teleological sense of being good [*tov*] in relation to an end.[31]

A fourth feature of the CSP was the use of meaning and worldview as an analytical framework for the description of chaplaincy's domain.[32] The notions of meaning and worldview, entailing the existential, spiritual, ethical, and aesthetic dimensions, were used to analyze the substantive aspects of the cases. The cases were written in the vocabulary of the submitting chaplain, expressing that chaplain's particular convictions, values, and behavior in offering care. The description allowed for the particularity of a chaplain's care in comparison with that of others. In the analysis, however, a shared vocabulary was used. The choice for the domain definition of the professional association was strategic, as most participating chaplains were members of the professional association and could therefore relate to the professional standard.[33] Although the definition is not neutral—as no

---

30. Later, these categories were not used as a selection criterion for the case studies, but as analytical categories afterwards. (See Chapter 3.) That did not mean that the distinction was not applied anymore, but the case studies did not have to be categorized a priori by the submitting chaplain-researchers.

31. See Walton, *Blest Practices*.

32. See Den Toom et al., "Rearranging the Domain."

33. That is not necessarily the case for chaplains from the RCs of Prison and Military

definition is—the definition is functional, thus capable of including various perspectives of chaplains on their profession and practices. While the formal analytical framework helped to accommodate the diversity of the profession, the variety in the case studies helped to elucidate and substantiate the categories from the analytical framework and helped the participants to see what their common ground was.[34]

A final feature of the CSP is that it also included a question on critical issues. In the format, chaplains were asked to mention critical issues that arose from the case studies. In that part of the analysis, questions like "Is this an example of good chaplaincy" can be asked. Several RCs made notes of the "critical issues" that emerged during the research process. The opportunity to address those critical issues later in the process also provided space to develop consensus on the rest of the cases. Unfortunately, however, the critical issues question in the format received less attention than intended, due to time constraints and online meetings as a consequence of the pandemic.

In conclusion, in the CSP several strategies aided the RCs in developing consensus. The question remains whether they arrived at consensus? And if so, what did consensus look like? We will look at these issues in the next section.

FORMS OF CONSENSUS

In discussing the case studies, consensus was arrived at on various levels, on the level of the research project, on the level of the case study, on the level of the research community, and on the level of reflection on the profession as a whole. In the present section, the various forms and processes of consensus are described.

First, I discuss the process of building consensus on the level of the research project. Consensus on this level does not mean consensus on a certain view or idea, but a feeling (Latin: *sentire*) together (Latin: *cum/com*). That feeling together in a collaborative research project entails both relational aspects and convictions. On a relational level, the chaplain-researchers, academic researchers, and project leaders worked on a general perspective and *modus operandi*. Considering and treating all participants in the project as fellow researchers whose perspectives are important, may have fostered that. In an international conference, for instance, not only the

---

Chaplains. While both groups of chaplains have been permitted as members since 2015, in practice the professional association primarily represents contexts of care.

34. Körver and Walton, "Door de bomen het bos." See also Chapter 2, "Observing, Interpreting, and Participating."

chairs of the research communities, but also the chaplain-researchers were explicitly asked to contribute from their research community. That helped build a collective identity as chaplaincy and academic researchers. Part of the process was to find a common direction in the research process. That relates to discussions in the Dutch context on what kind of research is suited to chaplaincy. For instance, asking chaplains about their goals and the outcomes of their care was for some participants not self-evident, as some were critical of the underlying goal rationality.[35] Building consensus on the level of research thus also meant that the chaplain-researchers needed to agree on the way in which the research was conducted, and what could be considered a good case from a methodological perspective. For instance, is the behavior described in a concrete and observable way? The process of agreeing on the project's format, and subsequently the various adaptations of the format, was a step towards consensus. In other words, consensus on what a good case was from a methodological perspective did arise.

Second, consensus was attained on the analysis of the case. At many times the research community concluded that the case was an example of "good chaplaincy." Even if the research community was not able to approve of the whole, it reached consensus on the interventions described or other specific aspects of the case studies. At least, it was acknowledged that the case was well described and that there was agreement on its analysis. The analysis by means of the four aspects of meaning and worldview helped in this respect as it was "capable of uniting the various worldview orientations."[36] The integration of the hitherto fairly novel notion of the "aesthetic" dimension of meaning and worldview also indicates that consensus was arrived at.

Third, consensus was found on the level of the research community. Within various research communities a shared language developed over time. Sometimes that was pursued explicitly in order to find a common perspective among various worldviews. In the RC Prison the chaplains agreed on a common name for the recipient of chaplaincy care. In other RCs the consensus was not actively sought, but some expressions went "viral" within the research communities. In the RC Hospital, chaplains spoke of "professional intuition," in the RC Mental Health of a "body of knowledge," and in the RC Mixed Fields of "aesthetic counseling." The fact that these research communities were arranged by field of work might have helped, but was not the only reason, as such shared expressions also emerged in the RC Mixed Fields. The substantive consensus on what chaplaincy is about did not, however, extend to the project as a whole. For that, the project was too

---

35. Den Toom, *The Chaplain-Researcher*.
36. Den Toom, *The Chaplain Researcher*, 170.

decentralized and the case studies were too much focused on the particularity of the concrete chaplaincy practice, instead of on commonalities within the profession. Seeking consensus on the project as a whole, one could say, occurred in the Academic Advisory Board and in publications on the project by the academic researchers, such as the international volume on case studies research,[37] a special issue on the CSP in German,[38] the Dutch Final Report,[39] and the present volume.

Finally, on the level of the profession as a whole, consensus was found despite whatever differences the chaplains experienced and observed, in language, worldview, and ways of working, *et cetera*. The notion of building a professional identity can help to understand that process. Professional identity consists of the dual dynamic of identification with and distinction from colleagues. On the one hand, chaplains noticed differences between them and their colleagues and distinguished themselves from them. On the other hand, despite the diversity and the distinctions, discovering and acknowledging the differences among the chaplains led to an increase in solidarity and identification with the profession as a whole. Thus, the reverse side of building consensus on chaplaincy is the process of building a professional identity. In other words, while consensus was not always reached on the level of an individual case, consensus was built on the level of the profession as a whole for which the dimensions of existential, spiritual, ethical, and aesthetic were both fundamental and unifying. In a profession where plurality seems to be the standard, and standards are often avoided, it is valuable to conclude that participation in collaborative case studies research helped to build consensus among the professional group of chaplains.

METHODICAL PROPOSALS FOR FUTURE RESEARCH

Given the fact that the CSP contributed to consensus both within the research process and among the professionals, what can be learned from the CSP for future research? We conclude with four vital elements. First, it is helpful to determine the main characteristics of a good case. Case studies can be produced for various ends. Critical cases can be described for learning purposes. When a case study seeks to understand what "good" chaplaincy is about, the pluriformity of the profession may present a challenge. To negotiate the pluriformity, it is helpful to determine some basic conditions for composing a "good" case study. In the CSP, we used the following criteria:

37. Kruizinga et al., *Learning from Case Studies*.
38. Körver et al., "Fallgeschichten, Forschung, Seelsorge."
39. Körver, et al., *Richting, Repertoire en Resultaat*.

whether a case is *good* depends on its being *representative, effective, theoretical grounded*, on *confirmation* by clients and other professionals, and on the *evaluation* and *recognition* by experienced colleagues and researchers.[40]

A second constructive element in building consensus is the use of research communities. Within the RCs, the chaplains enter into dialogue with each other and search for commonalities in the case studies. Within the communities, common vocabularies and frames emerge that aid a common understanding and appreciation of each other's work.

Third, the use of a shared analytical framework also contributes to building consensus. The analytical frame provides a shared language, despite the differences among the chaplains. When such an analytical framework is lacking, chaplains' own favorite theories and perhaps ideological notions will likely lead to conflicting views on the case studies.

Finally, focusing on concrete, observable outcomes helps in arriving at consensus on the effectiveness or the good that lies within a particular case. That focus can help to avoid ideological discussions on the profession as a whole, and turn the attention to what was good in a particular (set of) encounter(s) for a particular client. From all those particular accounts, a shared understanding of the profession can arise.

REFERENCES

Baart, Andries J. *The Presence Approach: An Introductory Sketch of a Practice*. Utrecht: Actioma, 2002.
Bernts, Ton, and Joantine Berghuijs. *God in Nederland 1966–2015*. Utrecht: Ten Have, 2016.
Cobb, Mark., et al., eds. *Oxford Textbook of Spirituality in Healthcare*. Oxford: Oxford University Press, 2012.
Den Toom, Niels. *The Chaplain-Researcher: The Perceived Impact of Participation in a Dutch Research Project on Chaplains' Professionalism*. Utrecht: Eburon, 2022.
———. "'Oneself as Another'. Combining the Roles of Chaplain and Researcher in the Dutch Case Studies Project." In *Learning from Case Studies in Chaplaincy. Towards Practice Based Evidence & Professionalism*, edited by Renske Kruizinga, et al., 198–207. Utrecht: Eburon, 2020.
Den Toom, Niels, et al. "The Professionalization of Chaplaincy. A Comparison of 1997 and 2017 Surveys in the Netherlands." *Journal of Health Care Chaplaincy* 29.1 (2023) 14–29. https://doi.org/10.1080/08854726.2021.1996810.
Den Toom, Niels, et al. "Rearranging the Domain: Spiritual Care in Multiple Dimensions."
Health and Social Care Chaplaincy 9.1 (2021) 42–59. https://doi.org/10.1558/hscc.40482.

40. See Chapter 3 "What Makes a Good Case."

Eco, Umberto. "The Roots of Conflict." *The Guardian*, October 13, 2001. https://www.theguardian.com/education/2001/oct/13/socialsciences.highereducation.

Fitchett, George, and Steve Nolan. *Case Studies in Spiritual Care. Healthcare Chaplaincy: Assessments, Interventions and Outcomes*. London: Kingsley, 2018.

———. *Spiritual Care in Practice: Case Studies in Healthcare Chaplaincy*. London: Kingsley, 2015.

Fitchett, George, et al. *Evidence-Based Healthcare Chaplaincy: A Research Reader*. London: Kingsley, 2018.

Körver, Jacques. "The Science of the Particular." In *Learning from Case Studies in Chaplaincy. Towards Practice Based Evidence & Professionalism*, edited by Renske Kruizinga et al., 71–81. Utrecht: Eburon, 2020.

Körver, Jacques, et al. *Richting, Repertoire en Resultaat. Uitkomsten van het Nederlandse Case Studies Project Geestelijke Verzorging (2016-2021)*. Utrecht: PThU-UCGV, 2023.

Körver, Jacques, et al. "Fallgeschichten, Forschung, Seelsorge: Ein inspirierendes Trio." *Wege Zum Menschen* 74.4 (2022) 300–313. https://doi.org/10.13109/weme.2022.74.4.300.

Körver, Jacques and Martin Walton. "Door de bomen het bos leren zien . . . en door het bos de bomen: Het Nederlandse Case Studies Project Geestelijke Verzorging." *KWALON* 28.1 (2023) 46–55. https://doi.org/10.5117/KWA2023.1.008.KORV.

Kruizinga, Renske, et al., eds. *Learning from Case Studies in Chaplaincy: Towards Practice Based Evidence & Professionalism*. Utrecht: Eburon, 2020.

Schuhmann, Carmen and Annelieke Damen. "Representing the Good: Pastoral Care in a Secular Age." *Pastoral Psychology* 67.4 (2018) 405–417. https://doi.org/10.1007/s11089018-0826-0.

Schweitzer, Pam, et al. *Remembering Yesterday, Caring Today: Reminiscence in Dementia Care. A Guide to Good Practice*. London: Kingsley, 2008.

Swift, Christopher, et al, eds. *A Handbook of Chaplaincy Studies: Understanding Spiritual Care in Public Places*. Farnham: Ashgate, 2015.

Visser, Anja, et al. "Goals of Chaplaincy Care: A Scoping Review of Dutch Literature." *Journal of Health Care Chaplaincy* 29.2 (2023) 176–195. https://doi.org/10.1080/08854726.2022.2080964.

Vlasblom, Jan P., et al. "Developments in Healthcare Chaplaincy in the Netherlands and Scotland: A Content Analysis of Professional Journals." *Health and Social Care Chaplaincy* 2.2 (2014) 235–254. https://doi.org/10.1558/hscc.v2i2.20409.

Walton, Martin. *Blest practices*. Valedictory Address. Groningen: PThU, 2019.

———. *Bron, rivier, delta. Teksten uit de feestrede bij het 50-jarig jubileum van de VGVZ*. Amsterdam: VGVZ, December 9, 2022.

Walton, Martin and Jacques Körver. "Dutch Case Studies Project in Chaplaincy Care: A Description and Theoretical Explanation of the Format and Procedures." *Health and Social Care Chaplaincy* 5.2 (2017) 257–280. https://doi.org/10.1558/hscc.34302.

Weber, Max. *Wirtschaft und Gesellschaft: Grundriss der verstehenden Soziologie*. Köln: Kiepenheuer & Witsch, 1964.

20

Chaplain Researchers

—Niels den Toom

"Without observer
Observation lapses
And the observed."

Hans Andreus[1]

THE CHAPLAIN AS RESEARCHER

IN THE PREVIOUS CHAPTERS, the design of the Case Studies Project (CSP) was described and nine case studies were presented and reflected upon.[2] The descriptions reveal the richness of the chaplaincy profession and help articulate it academically, building on practice-based evidence. Expanding the knowledge of chaplaincy by case studies can help chaplains to understand themselves and to elucidate for others what the importance of chaplaincy is. An interesting feature of the CSP was that it was not only research on chaplaincy but also conducted by chaplains. Chaplains received a new role of co-researcher, or chaplain-researcher. Although there were chaplain-researchers before, chaplain participation in research did not previously occur on this scale. In the current chapter, I will focus on that new role. What does being a chaplain-researcher entail, and how does being a researcher

---

1. Excerpt from "Observaties." Andreus, *Verzamelde werken*, 957, my translation. Used with permission.

2. Parts I, II, and III. The main research questions will be answered in Chapter 22.

affect chaplains' practices? The question will not be answered in an idealistic manner, describing how research ideally can be combined with practice, but grounded in empirical research. The chapter is based on the dissertation of this chapter's author in which a mixed-methods study was conducted on the perceived impact of participation in the CSP on chaplains' professionalism.[3]

The study employed a mixed-methods approach in the form of a sequential exploratory design.[4] First, the experiences of chaplains were exploratively mapped out through participant observation and qualitative interviews (N=9). Then the findings were validated with a questionnaire to determine the extent to which the experiences were representative of all participants (N=48). Subsequently, reflections on the main findings were discussed in focus groups (N=6) among the participants, leading to some philosophical and theological reflections with which we will conclude the chapter.

CONCEPTUALIZING THE CHAPLAIN-RESEARCHER

In the past decades combining the practices of chaplaincy and research has become more common. It is true that many scholars in chaplaincy studies were chaplains before their academic careers. However, the chaplain-researcher is a more recent phenomenon. The double name does not indicate how chaplaincy and research are combined. Is one of both roles dominant? Does the chaplain role help the researcher role, or is it the other way around? And what is meant by "research"? In this chapter, I will delve into understanding the dual role of the chaplain-researcher, how research relates to the practice of professionalization, and what chaplain-researchers themselves have to say about it.

In past decades, research on chaplaincy and spiritual care was primarily carried out by academics. Today, there is an expectation that spiritual care providers themselves participate in research. This is reflected in the professional standard of the American Association of Professional Chaplains.[5] The expected research literacy of chaplains is described as threefold: (1) a basic level, which mainly involves chaplains being able to read, evaluate, and apply existing research; (2) an intermediate level, where the chaplain contributes to research by performing, coordinating, analyzing, or other tasks; and finally, (3) an advanced level, where the chaplain independently

---

3. See Den Toom, *The Chaplain Researcher*.
4. Creswell and Plano Clark, *Mixed Methods Research*.
5. Association of Professional Chaplains, *Standards of Practice*.

conducts research. Initiatives such as Transforming Chaplaincy[6] work on all three levels. Although the levels logically presuppose each other, it is possible to have an intermediate level without the necessary basic literacy.[7] In this sense, one can speak of more passive research literacy, collaborative research activity, and independent research competency.

The term research literacy indicates the importance of "speaking the language of research." The notion emerged from the broader call to work towards a research-informed profession, as something important for the professional group. But how can the value of research for the profession of chaplaincy be understood? Roughly two arguments are put forward.[8] Firstly, it is often argued that conducting research contributes to the quality of spiritual care. Secondly, research contributes to the substantiation and accountability of the profession. In both cases, the effectiveness of chaplaincy and its contribution to the spiritual well-being of people are important issues.

An example of how research can contribute to practice is the conceptualization by the Dutch psychologist Giel Hutschemaekers.[9] He describes a model of the scientist-practitioner, in which practical knowledge and science go hand in hand.[10] The scientific approach helps practitioners to systematically combine the most current knowledge with their own clinical experience. The image of the "scientist" here is admittedly quite technical, as the "clinical scientist" in his model primarily conducts experimental studies and "bases his practices exclusively on results of scientific research."[11] Chaplain-researchers often use methods that are less technical, such as case studies, autoethnography, action research, *et cetera*, in which the particularity or subjectivity of both researcher and "research objects" is acknowledged.[12] Nevertheless, this model can be used to understand the relationship between the chaplain and the researcher.

In an analysis of four publications of chaplain-researchers,[13] of which two were Dutch publications, I concluded that:

6. www.transformchaplaincy.org.

7. Den Toom, *The Chaplain-Researcher*, 127–29.

8. Fitchett, "Health Care Chaplaincy as a Research-Informed Profession"; Handzo et al., "Outcomes for Chaplaincy."

9. Hutschemaekers, "De psycholoog als scientist-practitioner."

10. For an elaboration on this model, see Den Toom, "'Oneself as Another,'" 199–200.

11. Hutschemaekers, "De psycholoog als scientist-practitioner," 26–27.

12. Den Toom, *The Chaplain-Researcher*.

13. Nolan, "Autoethnography in Chaplain Case Study Research"; Kestenbaum et al., "'Taking Your Place at the Table'"; Sluijsmans, *Spanningsvol verbinden in een ziekenhuis*; Van der Leer, *Zinvolle zorg in het verpleeghuis*.

in most studies the role of chaplain-researchers is related to action research, as distinct from the quantitative approach in psychology ... in most studies the role of the researcher is emphasized primarily in the analysis and less in producing data. The research approaches of autoethnography and (participative) action research indeed allow for a close connection between being a chaplain and a researcher. However, the boundaries of research and chaplaincy easily become blurred.[14]

Thus, we observe a gap between how chaplain-researchers see their double role and how the role of scientist-researcher is described in the literature. Chaplain-researchers primarily draw upon autoethnographic methods, which is a research method in which the personal experiences of the researcher as a chaplain are described, reflected upon in relation to theory formation. On the other hand, as we already observed, most conceptualizations of the scientist-practitioner presuppose more clinical research methods. Interestingly, the CSP cannot be identified as either of them. Therefore, it is worthwhile to describe the role of the chaplain-researcher in the CSP, not only from the perspective of how their role was intended in the project, as was done in Chapters 1 and 2 of this volume, but also based on the experiences of the participating chaplain-researchers.

Chaplain-Researchers in the CSP

A previous publication, based on interview material, described how the chaplain-researchers in the CSP experienced both roles with regard to resemblance, difference, tension, and potential.[15] Towards the end of the project, I conducted a survey among the participants in the CSP (N=48), in which I asked them to indicate what they experienced as the hardest parts of conducting research. Table 20.1 below presents an overview of the results. As can be seen, working with a format (35 percent) and connecting theory to a case (35 percent) were considered most difficult, followed by asking for informed consent (21 percent). In the following, I elaborate on these three items.

---

14. Den Toom, *The Chaplain-Researcher*, 117–18.
15. Den Toom, "'Oneself as Another.'"

Table 20.1: Overview of elements considered the hardest in conducting research (N=48)

	N	%
Working with a format	17	35%
Connecting theory to a case	17	35%
Asking informed consent	10	21%
Time investment	9	19%
Applying the four dimensions of meaning (existential, spiritual, ethical, and aesthetic)	9	19%
Describing one's practice precisely and concretely	8	17%
Speaking from the third-person	6	13%
Interaction in the group	4	8%
Staying aware of my own implicit premises about the profession	2	4%
Analyzing my own case	1	2%
Bracketing my own premises about good chaplaincy care	1	2%
Asking for feedback from colleagues	1	2%

Chaplains found it hard to work with a set format. Where chaplain-researchers following more autoethnographic methods experienced great similarity between both roles of chaplain-researcher, here the chaplains experienced a difference. In the various research communities (RCs), the format functioned differently. One of the reasons for not using the format strictly, was that it was difficult to combine with a narrative approach to chaplaincy. Others, however, experienced the format as helpful, as it helped to systematically describe their work and to pay attention to various aspects of meaning and worldview.

Another issue chaplains encountered was relating theory to their practices. This is in line with another finding, that chaplains do not often work explicitly with theories.[16] This is not the same as stating that chaplains are atheoretical, as I will show below. The difficulty of connecting theory and practice has also been acknowledged in other studies.[17] One of the possible explanations for this is that chaplains' post-initial training was primarily shaped by Clinical Pastoral Education (CPE). In that approach, the focus

---

16. Den Toom et al., "The Professionalization of Chaplaincy."

17. Ragsdale and Desjardins, "Proposing Chaplaincy Theory"; White, et al., "Board Certification."

is more on the chaplain as a person ("getting in touch with feelings," as a respondent reports in the study of George Fitchett et al.)[18] than on theories and methods that underlay chaplaincy, for instance about how clients provide meaning, how spirituality relates to health, how rituals function, *et cetera*.

Finally, chaplains found it challenging to ask the client for informed consent or to do the member check.[19] One of the chaplains felt that letting the client read the case study might not benefit her, or would be another intervention in the care process. In other words, her research activities interfered with her chaplaincy care. Another chaplain indicated that he felt like he had a double agenda, instead of having the client's agenda as sole interest. In both cases, the chaplain-researchers gave their role of chaplain primacy over that of researcher.

What became clear in the CSP is that each RC had its own dynamics, even though the project showed coherence in the object of study, its collaborative dimension, and guiding format. Based on that, I define the chaplain-researchers in the CSP as "practitioners of chaplaincy who, together with academic researchers, describe and analyze their practices and that of others in a hermeneutical-methodical way, informed by their professional and theoretical knowledge and grounded as much as possible in empirical observations."[20]

HOW DOES RESEARCH AFFECT CHAPLAINCY CARE?

Now that the dual role of chaplain-researcher in the CSP has been defined, we can turn to the question of what the benefit of such a dual role is. Although the importance of research for chaplaincy has been broadly emphasized, it is important to note that the two ways in which research might contribute to chaplaincy care are assumptions that have not been previously empirically investigated. Nevertheless, various indications of the value of research for practice can be found in the literature.[21] In addition, it is interesting to look at three reflections of chaplains who worked specifically with a case study approach. In an article by Fitchett,[22] three chaplains reflect on how working with case studies was valuable for their practice.

18. Fitchett et al., "Educating Chaplains for Research Literacy," 9.
19. See Chapters 2 and 21 for more about the member check.
20. Den Toom, *The Chaplain-Researcher*, 134.
21. Kelly, "Invitation and Rationale"; Grossoehme, "Research as Chaplaincy Intervention."
22. Fitchett, "Making Our Case(s)."

One of them, Rhonda, reported that she found herself now "being more aware of the needs-interventions-outcome relationship so that I am more intentional in my approach."[23] Stephen also experienced that writing a case study enhanced his "focus upon desired negotiated outcomes with the patient/family."[24] In other words, writing in a structured way about the goals, interventions, and outcomes, made them more reflexive and attentive to an outcome-oriented approach. A second fruit of their research endeavor was that the discussion of the case studies with other colleagues was experienced as valuable. Stephen started presenting a case study in his department annually, "receiving feedback from other chaplains, and learning about the chaplaincy care provided by others."[25] Rhonda also acknowledged the value of "peer review and consultation."[26] A third fruit was reported by Dick, who was now "much more attentive to the construct and implementation of spiritual care assessments, and more disciplined about considering and characterizing spiritual care interventions before applying them."[27] Rather than the outcome or the peer review, he was more aware of his assessments and the process of choosing a certain intervention. As will be seen later, those reflections bear resemblances to the findings from the CSP. But before discussing the particular findings from the CSP, I introduce the concept of professionalism as a way of conceptualizing how research may contribute to chaplaincy as a practice.

Professionalism

That research contributes to professionalism seems obvious. Professionalism, or professionalization, is often intuitively and broadly used to denote the improvement of a practice. A closer definition of the concept helps to speak more precisely and critically about the value of research for the practice. It was Elliot Freidson who developed a value approach to professionalism.[28] That was a shift in the understanding of professionalism, which was first more naïve in following the professions' self-descriptions and less critical regarding power structures and exclusion mechanisms. In response, a power-critical approach regarded professionalism as a form of misuse of

---

23. Fitchett, "Making Our Case(s)," 11.
24. Fitchett, "Making Our Case(s)," 11.
25. Fitchett, "Making Our Case(s)," 11.
26. Fitchett, "Making Our Case(s)," 11.
27. Fitchett, "Making Our Case(s)," 11.
28. Freidson, *Professionalism, the Third Logic*.

power at the cost of clients.[29] Freidson's approach acknowledges that professionals do have power and can misuse it, but that the essence of professionalism is not found in power and status, but in the values that professions strive for and the freedom to do so. Based on Freidson's value-approach and a Dutch elaboration of his theory,[30] I developed a threefold model of professionalism. In the following, I describe each of the three dimensions of professionalism (see Figure 20.1).

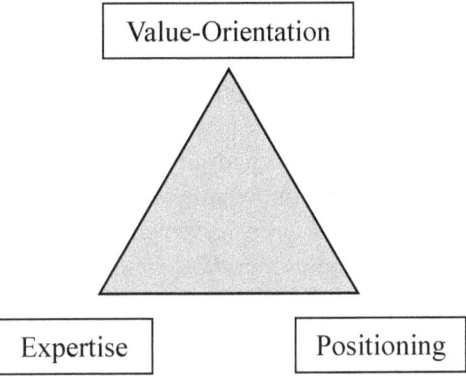

Figure 20.1: Triangle of Professionalism

Freidson argues that every profession has one or more central *values* that it pursues. Those values are the "soul" of the profession, determine both the profession's goal-orientation and the societal value of a profession. For example, doctors focus on health, lawyers on justice, *et cetera*. Although others in society also pursue those values, professionals do so on the basis of extensive *expertise*. Generally the expertise is built up through years of training and grounded in academic knowledge. However, expertise lies not only in knowledge but also in what Freidson calls discretion as the ability and freedom to choose the best option in a particular situation. Professionals often face complex situations where the best course of action cannot be determined by protocols or guidelines. Therefore, it is necessary for professionals to exercise their discretion. Of course, they must also be given the opportunity to do so. And that brings us to the third dimension of professionalism, in addition to values and expertise: *positioning*. Positioning is the extent to which a professional and a profession are embedded—both in an

---

29. For more on the shift in paradigms in the study of professions, see Chapter 2 in Den Toom, *The Chaplain-Researcher*.
30. De Jonge, *Beelden van de professional*.

organization and in society at large—and are thus facilitated in the employment of their expertise. Positioning is therefore not about the professionals and their positions themselves, but about the extent in which they are able to exercise their expertise, which in turn is aimed at the central values of their profession. Even more, certain values of the profession are not only pursued in chaplaincy, but chaplaincy is itself an expression of those values (e.g. that the vulnerable and desperate should be visited and attended to). Thus, professionalization is the continuous process of enhancing the profession's positioning and developing its expertise so that the values of the profession can be increasingly realized.

If we return to the two arguments for how research can contribute to professionalism, we can say that the first argument of quality improvement focuses on expertise and the second on accountability and substantiating the profession in relation to the profession's positioning. Ideally, both contribute in the end to a better achievement of values. In addition, the dimension of values also poses a critical question to research, namely to what extent research contributes to the central values of the profession. That provides a perspective from which the relevance and adequacy of types or focusses of research might be evaluated with regard to their contribution to professionalization.

The Impact of Participation in Research on Chaplains' Professionalism

In describing the impact of participation in the CSP on the professionalism of chaplain-researchers, I use the threefold understanding of professionalism explicated above. First, the chaplains indicated that they had become more aware of their goals and values, pertaining primarily to the value-orientation of the profession. Until then, their goals had been mostly implicit in their work, and some even said that they did not have any goal in caring for clients.[31] One of the participants concluded that "in conversations in the case study group it became fairly quickly clear that the chaplain's apparently "aimless" presence actually is not aimless at all."[32] Another reflected: "Due to my participation I am more aware of the ultimate question about my presence and my work: What is it all about in the end?"[33] In the survey, those accounts were confirmed, as 50 percent of the participants indicated that they attached more importance to setting goals in their care

31. See also Chapter 14, "Apprehending Goals."
32. Berkhout, "Interdisciplinary Work in Chaplaincy Care," 176.
33. Weeda and Muthert, "Participation in the Case Studies Project," 172.

and a considerable group actually set goals more often in their care (43 percent).[34] Their awareness of their goals included several aspects. Partially, it pertained to concrete goals they pursued for their clients, but also to focus on the outcomes of their care. In addition, the chaplains also became more reflective about their values and normative ideals that play a role in their accompaniment. For 52 percent of the chaplains, "insight in how their norms and values affect their practice" increased after participation.[35] That might seem an unexpected result for a profession, whose domain is about meaning and worldview. However, chaplains seem to have underestimated the role of their own normativity. That can partially be explained by the influence of pluralization and secularization in society. As one of the chaplains reported:

> It is tough for us, chaplains, in a secularized society. Or, we do not easily ask about someone's worldview. It is a kind of a taboo, which we have internalized. Well, those are my words. You don't discuss that (Simone2).[36]

Another explanation may be that the nondirective approach of Carl Rogers,[37] also led to a hesitant attitude of chaplains towards expressing their own values and worldview. Nevertheless, in the case studies they observed that their worldviews often play a role in their chaplaincy care. One of the participants concluded:

> Even more than that, it is what I get paid for. So, sometimes one could say "I draw the line. This shouldn't happen." Or, "This goes against everything that is important to me" . . . One becomes aware of that, that we are also normative.[38]

A second way in which participation in the CSP affected chaplains' professionalism was that their knowledge became more explicit, strengthening their expertise. Chaplains are usually academically trained and have a thorough knowledge base. Over time, their knowledge has become self-evident to them and implicitly guided their actions. As a consequence, chaplains were inclined to see their work as based on intuition or without specific theoretical knowledge. Participation in the CSP made them more aware of their knowledge. Their knowledge became explicit in the process of concretely describing their practices and motivations. Their embodied

---

34. Den Toom, *The Chaplain-Researcher*, 155. For more on chaplains and their goals, see section 6.3 of the dissertation.
35. Den Toom, *The Chaplain-Researcher*, 169.
36. Den Toom, *The Chaplain-Researcher*, 169.
37. Rogers, *The Therapeutic Relationship*.
38. Den Toom, *The Chaplain-Researcher*, 169.

knowledge became a "body of knowledge," enabling them to use it more consciously in their care for clients. One chaplain described it as a shift from "intuitive acting, that can be very wise and an art, and very good" to "more well-considered and intentional, due to which new choices emerge and various options and more conscious, professional acting."[39] After participation in the CSP, half of the chaplains indicated that they used theoretical knowledge (50 percent) and methods (48 percent) more often than before the CSP, while it remained equally often for 50 percent and 52 percent respectively.[40]

Also, chaplains were inspired to (re)read theoretical literature on chaplaincy. In addition to explicating knowledge, chaplains learned a different manner of reflecting, making them more aware of their own actions during the accompaniment of clients, but also more aware of what might be going on with the client. In particular, they became more attentive to the aesthetic aspects of meaning-making and worldview.[41]

Third, participation in the CSP also affected the chaplains' positioning. One of the issues in this respect is the articulation of the profession. The majority of chaplains (63 percent) reported having more vocabulary at their disposal to describe their profession. This was especially evident in their ability to formulate the domain and contribution of the profession in care processes and policies, and the ability to convince their managers about the value of their profession. Another aspect of positioning is the collaboration with other professionals, in particular in their charting behavior. The chaplains did not report charting more often, but rather that they were charting in a different way, focusing on "on how other disciplines might benefit more from my charting for the purpose of good care" (response from the survey).[42] Another chaplain reported an increase in describing "the effect: for instance, that someone [i.e., the client] relaxed or discovered a particular insight."[43] The latter aligns with the experience of an increased focus on outcomes from Stephen in Fitchett's article mentioned above.

The chaplains had more words at their disposal to describe and articulate their profession. Though the words varied from one chaplain to another, they nevertheless indicated that they could better describe their profession and delineate their domain. The conceptual pair "meaning-making and worldview" as a description of the domain taken from the professional

---

39. Den Toom, *The Chaplain-Researcher*, 149.
40. Den Toom, *The Chaplain-Researcher*, 140.
41. With regard to the latter see also Chapter 15, "Aesthetic Counseling and Method."
42. Den Toom, *The Chaplain-Researcher*, 174.
43. Den Toom, *The Chaplain-Researcher*, 174.

standard of the Dutch Professional Association of Spiritual Caregivers (VGVZ), had a unifying role in the plural profession. It is interesting to notice that despite the differences between chaplains in their worldview backgrounds, theoretical approaches, and styles of practice, they experienced mutual recognition in participating in the RCs. Even when the CSP led to a process of distinguishing themselves from other chaplains, they also felt increasingly connected to the profession and their professional peers. Confrontation with differentiation in the profession did not lead to the disintegration of the professional bond but to increased professional solidarity. In general, it was found that the recognition and affirmation experienced by the participants in the CSP led to increased confidence in their professional actions and to stronger professional ownership.

Professional Identity

Not only chaplains' professionalism was impacted, but participation in research also affected their professional identity. The concept of professional identity refers to the self-understanding of chaplains, in which they integrate and negotiate their professional goals, expertise, and positioning. Professional identity can be understood as the ongoing, relational, and agency oriented process of identification and differentiation with others in the professional landscape.[44] The chaplain-researchers in the CSP negotiated their professional identity in dialogue with five relationships: the relationships to the client, to chaplain-colleagues, to other professionals, to society and culture at large, and to one's personal self. Within all those relationships, the negotiation led to a clearer identity of "what kind of chaplain"[45] they are. Interestingly, the chaplains related the clarification of their professional identity to an increase in freedom and confidence. Studying one's own practices and those of their colleagues stimulated reflection on their "real" and "ideal" identities,[46] providing them "with the agency to adapt their identity when desired, and to be confident about what they consider good in their profession."[47] In addition, the reinforcement of professional identity also added focus and audacity to their professional conduct.[48] In other words,

---

44. For more on the concept of professional identity, see den Toom, *The Chaplain-Researcher*, 187–90. One of the important models I draw on is that of Ruijters and Simons, *Connecting Professionalism, Learning and Identity*.
45. Den Toom, *The Chaplain-Researcher*, 187.
46. Eteläpelto et al., "Identity and Agency."
47. Den Toom, *The Chaplain-Researcher*, 204.
48. Cf. Kestenbaum et al., "'Taking Your Place at the Table.'"

knowing who one is as a professional chaplain, helps in performing one's professionalism with confidence and in integrating professionalism in oneself. The chaplains reported that in that process they found "joy, inspiration, and nourishment."[49]

PHILOSOPHICAL AND THEOLOGICAL REFLECTIONS ON CHAPLAINCY

Now that we have seen what the impact of being a chaplain-researcher is on chaplaincy, what does that mean for chaplaincy? What insights about chaplaincy as a profession can be drawn from these findings? We reflect here on three particular and important findings: the increased goal-orientation of chaplains, the explication of their theoretical knowledge, and the increased awareness of the role of worldview in their work. Chaplaincy is not only about worldview, but is also conducted in a worldview related, spiritual manner. Therefore, in reflecting on what these findings imply for chaplaincy, we will draw on philosophical and theological resources, in order to understand professionalization in a way that corresponds to the spiritual nature of the profession of chaplaincy.

First, we reflect on the desirability of increasing goal-orientation in chaplaincy. In chaplaincy literature, particularly in the Dutch context, arguments are put forward against having a goal-orientation. The assertion is that goal-orientation instrumentalizes religion, imposes one's own agenda as a chaplain on the client, and emphasizes the results of chaplaincy over the process-character of meaning.[50] Chaplains should instead use notions of presence and sanctuary to indicate the open space they wish to provide. However, the opposition of goals on the one hand, and relations or process on the other hand, seems to be a false dichotomy. Goals can be determined in dialogue with the client. Nor is religion free from goals such as peace, reconciliation, enlightenment, *et cetera* (see also Chapter 14).[51]

In the CSP it became clear that chaplains, even if they object to a strong goal-orientation, always pursue some greater good. To indicate how those goals function in chaplaincy, the notion of "labyrinthic purposiveness" was

---

49. Den Toom, *The Chaplain-Researcher*, 207. In addition to the more individual meaning of professional identity, I have also reflected on the collective side of professional identity. See, e.g., Chapter 19.

50. In the international literature, similar arguments can be found, leading to a cautious attitude towards outcomes. See Kelly and Swinton, *Chaplaincy and the Soul*; Nolan, "Healthcare Chaplains Responding to Change." For another perspective, see Damen et al., "Outcome Research."

51. Braakhuis et al., "Professional Proximity."

put forward, referring both to the concrete goals of chaplaincy and to its purpose. Chaplains envision a certain good, or a good life, for their clients.[52] What they regard as "the good" is often intertwined with their view on life and the worldview tradition they are affiliated with. The adjective "labyrinthic" refers to the indirect way in which the accompaniment process flows. Meaning is seldom achieved immediately, but rather experienced at unsuspected moments and in surprising places. The labyrinth, as the religious pathway that diverts from the center in order to arrive at it, is a symbol of the indirect but effective manner in which chaplains accompany their clients.[53]

Second, we reflect on the fact that chaplains experience difficulties in connecting their practices to theory.[54] Instead of referring to knowledge, they often prefer notions such as empathy and intuition. The fact that they are not accustomed to speaking in terms of theories can be explained by a lack of theoretical knowledge in their education or by more principal objections against theoretical knowledge. Chaplains may for example be wary of understanding their knowledge as a sort of clinical expertise, as if they have answers to provide to their clients' questions. Also, they want to avoid reducing their clients to theories at all costs. However, neither explanation suffices. In the CSP chaplains made their "embodied knowledge" explicit, turning it into a "body of knowledge." At the same time, their body of knowledge also contains other kinds of knowledge, such as poetry, arts, and worldview-related wisdom from scriptures, theology, and philosophy, among other things. As the term theory does not sufficiently account for these other forms of knowledge, I use the phrase "professional loving wisdom." The notion of wisdom entails both practical wisdom as "the art of living" and a more contemplative wisdom that deals with the larger questions of life ("What does it mean to be human?" "Who is God?" "How can I understand suffering?").[55] The notion of "loving" wisdom, indicates that the wisdom is used in a relational way, rather than provided as information, in response to clients' questions, needs, and desires. On a more fundamental level, loving refers to the Hebrew word *yādāʾ*, including both meanings of "knowing" and "loving." Professional loving wisdom as the concept of chaplains' knowledge does not exclude theories and theoretical knowledge, but

---

52. Schuhmann and Damen, "Representing the Good."

53. Den Toom, *The Chaplain-Researcher*, see Section 9.2.

54. Ragsdale and Desjardins, "Proposing Chaplaincy Theory"; White et al., "Board Certification"; den Toom, *The Chaplain-Researcher*.

55. See Curnow, "Sophia and Phronesis"; De Lange, *Eindelijk volwassen*.

embeds them in a broader concept of knowing that aims to avoid objectifying the client.[56]

Finally, we reflect on the role of the chaplains' worldview. As Western societies increasingly become pluriform with respect to religion, including secular worldviews, chaplains' worldview backgrounds do not self-evidently match those of their clients. As was the case with the notion of goals and knowledge, chaplains also prioritize the clients' needs and worldview over that of themselves. Chaplains do not want to impose their worldview on clients, or proselytize them. Thus, they feel that their own identity should not limit their availability to clients. The result is a dichotomy between being available to every client and having a clear worldview identity. In the Netherlands, that dichotomy became concrete in a discussion in the profession on whether chaplains should be officially endorsed by a worldview organization or community or not. Endorsement was associated with being "confessional" and non-endorsement with "professional." The notion emerged that "professional" chaplains are more neutral and available to all clients. As a consequence, their worldview knowledge, inspiration and position came to play an unconscious role, limiting the professional freedom of chaplains.[57]

However, this dichotomy can also be considered spurious. In the CSP, several chaplains discovered that contrary to their self-conception, their worldview played a greater role in their practices than expected. It led to the discovery that their worldview is more intrinsically connected to the care they provide, not only as their worldview plays a role in the chaplain's care, but precisely because chaplaincy care is also an expression and embodiment of the chaplain's worldview. We proposed the idea of the post-secular to reflect on the role of worldview in a pluriform society.[58] The notion of the post-secular expresses both the reality of secularization in society and at the same the resurgence of religion. It shifts a temporal conception of religion ("religion is of the past") into a spatial concept ("religion is one of the options").[59] Rather than regarding one's religious identity as something that is no longer the "standard," the post-secular assumes that nobody can consider one's own position to be the "standard." Consequently, to understand each other in a post-secular society, it is important for all to show their colors. Chaplains can share their identity and sources in the care they provide, not from a presupposed authority, but from a fundamental understanding

---

56. Den Toom, *The Chaplain-Researcher*, see section 9.3.
57. Den Toom, *The Chaplain-Researcher*, see section 9.4.
58. Braidotti, *Transformations of Religion*.
59. Cf. Taylor, *A Secular Age*; Molendijk, "In Pursuit of the Postsecular."

of chaplaincy care as a form of dialogue. For the professionalization of chaplaincy, it is important that professionals reflect on worldview as part of their profession in a substantial and systematic manner.[60]

CONCLUSIONS

In the current chapter, I have described how the dual role of chaplain-researcher becomes increasingly important within chaplaincy care. By elaborating on how both roles are related in theory and in the practice of the CSP, I have tried to elucidate how research can benefit chaplains' practice. As every form and method of research has its own characteristics, the general term of chaplain-researcher has different nuances in different situations.

Subsequently, it became clear that while the possible fruition of combining roles is clearly stated in the literature, there is little empirical evidence to support that claim. The chaplains whom Fitchett quotes on their work with case studies indicated that they had become more aware of the relationship between needs, interventions, and outcomes, and more intentional in their approach. Another fruit was the value they attached to discussing their case studies with colleagues. Finally, they had learned to apply interventions and assessments more attentively and thoughtfully. All three changes in their practice were supported by the empirical, mixed-method study I conducted for my dissertation. Participation in the research project reinforced chaplains' professionalism on the level of their value orientation, expertise, and positioning. Chaplains became aware of their profession, were able to articulate it, and worked more goal-oriented. It led to reflections on what the profession is, how chaplains work with a labyrinthic purposiveness, are equipped with professional loving wisdom, and can let their worldview colors be seen in a post-secular society. It is this artisanship to which this volume testifies.

REFERENCES

Association of Professional Chaplains. "Standards of Practice for Professional Chaplains." APC, 2015.
Andreus, Hans. "Observations." In *Verzamelde gedichten*, 957. Amsterdam: Bert Bakker–Daamen, 1984.
Berkhout, Loes. "Interdisciplinary Work in Chaplaincy Care." In *Learning from Case Studies in Chaplaincy. Towards Practice Based Evidence & Professionalism*, edited by Renske Kruizinga, et al., 174–81. Utrecht: Eburon, 2020.

60. See for instance the research project of ERICH, "Big Stories in Chaplaincy," https://www.pastoralezorg.be/page/big-stories/.

Braakhuis, Myriam. "Professional Proximity. Seeking a Balance between Relation and Content in Spiritual Counseling." In *Learning from Case Studies in Chaplaincy. Towards Practice Based Evidence & Professionalism*, edited by Renske Kruizinga et al., 112-117. Utrecht: Eburon, 2020.

Braidotti, Rosi. *Transformations of Religion and the Public Sphere: Postsecular Publics*. Palgrave Politics of Identity and Citizenship Series. New York: Palgrave Macmillan, 2014. https://doi.org/10.1057/9781137401144.

Creswell, John W., and Vicki L. Plano Clark. *Designing and Conducting Mixed Methods Research*. Thousand Oaks: Sage, 2007.

Curnow, Trevor. "Sophia and Phronesis: Past, Present, and Future." *Research in Human Development* 8.2 (2011) 95–108.

Damen, Annelieke, et al.. "Can Outcome Research Respect the Integrity of Chaplaincy? A Review of Outcome Studies." *Journal of Health Care Chaplaincy* 26.4 (2020) 131–158. https://doi.org/10.1080/08854726.2019.1599258.

De Jonge, Ed. *Beelden van de professional: inspiratiebronnen voor professionalisering*. Delft: Eburon, 2015.

De Lange, Frits. *Eindelijk volwassen: de wijsheid van de tweede levenshelft*. Utrecht: Ten Have, 2021.

Den Toom, Niels. *The Chaplain-Researcher: The Perceived Impact of Participation in a Dutch Research Project on Chaplains' Professionalism*. Utrecht: Eburon, 2022.

———. "'Oneself as Another'. Combining the Roles of Chaplain and Researcher in the Dutch Case Studies Project." In *Learning from Case Studies in Chaplaincy. Towards Practice Based Evidence & Professionalism*, edited by Renske Kruizinga, et al., 198–207. Utrecht: Eburon, 2020.

Den Toom, Niels, et al. "The Professionalization of Chaplaincy. A Comparison of 1997 and 2017 Surveys in the Netherlands." *Journal of Health Care Chaplaincy* 29.1 (2023) 14–29. https://doi.org/10.1080/08854726.2021.1996810.

Eteläpelto, Anneli, et al. "Identity and Agency in Professional Learning." In *International Handbook of Research in Professional and Practice-Based Learning*, 645–72. Dordrecht: Springer, 2014. https://doi.org/10.1007/978-94-017-8902-8_24.

Fitchett, George. "Health Care Chaplaincy as a Research-Informed Profession: How We Get There." *Journal of Health Care Chaplaincy* 12.1–2 (2002) 67–72. https://doi.org/10.1300/J080v12n01_07.

———. "Making Our Case(s)." *Journal of Health Care Chaplaincy* 17.1–2 (2011) 3–18. https://doi.org/10.1080/08854726.2011.559829.

Fitchett, George, et al. "Educating Chaplains for Research Literacy: Results of a National Survey of Clinical Pastoral Education Residency Programs." *Journal of Pastoral Care & Counseling* 66.1 (2012) 1–12.

Freidson, Eliot. *Professionalism, the Third Logic: On the Practice of Knowledge*. Chicago: University of Chicago Press, 2001.

Grossoehme, Daniel H. "Research as Chaplaincy Intervention." *Journal of Health Care Chaplaincy* 17.3–4 (2011) 97–99.

Handzo, George F., et al. "Outcomes for Professional Health Care Chaplaincy: An International Call to Action." *Journal of Health Care Chaplaincy* 20.2 (2014) 43–53. https://doi.org/10.1080/08854726.2014.902713.

Hutschemaekers, Giel. "De psycholoog als scientist-practitioner." In *Psychologie en praktijk*, edited by Roy Kessels, et al., 15–42. Amsterdam: Boom, 2010.

Kelly, Ewan. "Introduction—Invitation and Rationale: Why Is It Necessary to Research Chaplaincy Care Practices?" In *An Invitation to Chaplaincy Research: Entering the Process*, edited by Gary E. Myers and Stephen Roberts, i–xi. HealthCare Chaplaincy Network, 2014.

Kelly, Ewan, and John Swinton, eds. *Chaplaincy and the Soul of Health and Social Care: Fostering Spiritual Wellbeing in Emerging Paradigms of Care*. London: Kingsley, 2020.

Kestenbaum, Allison, et al. "'Taking Your Place at the Table': An Autoethnographic Study of Chaplains' Participation on an Interdisciplinary Research Team." *BMC Palliative Care* 14.1 (2015) 1–10.

Molendijk, Arie L. "In Pursuit of the Postsecular." *International Journal of Philosophy and Theology* 76.2 (2015) 100–15.

Nolan, Steve. "Healthcare Chaplains Responding to Change: Embracing Outcomes or Reaffirming Relationships?" *Health and Social Care Chaplaincy* 3.2 (2015) 93–109. https://doi.org/10.1558/hscc.v3i2.27068.

———. "Introduction: Autoethnography in Chaplain Case Study Research." In *Case Studies in Spiritual Care. Healthcare Chaplaincy Assessments, Interventions and Outcomes*, edited by George Fitchett and Steve Nolan, 11–30. London: Kingsley, 2018.

Ragsdale, Judith R., and Cate M. Desjardins. "Proposing Religiously Informed, Relationally Skillful Chaplaincy Theory." *Journal of Health Care Chaplaincy* 28.2 (2022) 239–54. https://doi.org/10.1080/08854726.2020.1861533.

Rogers, Carl R. *The Therapeutic Relationship and Its Impact. A Study of Psychotherapy with Schizophrenics*. Madison: University of Wisconsin Press, 1967.

Ruijters, Manon C. P., and P. Robert-Jan Simons. "Connecting Professionalism, Learning and Identity." *Estonian Journal of Education/ Eesti Haridusteaduste Ajakiri* 8.2 (2020) 7–31.

Schuhmann, Carmen, and Annelieke Damen. "Representing the Good: Pastoral Care in a Secular Age." *Pastoral Psychology* 67.4 (2018) 405–17. https://doi.org/10.1007/s11089-018-0826-0.

Sluijsmans, Chantal. *Spanningsvol verbinden in een ziekenhuis: menslievende zorg stimuleren door normatieve professionalisering*. Delft: Eburon, 2018.

Taylor, Charles. *A Secular Age*. Cambridge: The Belknap Press of Harvard University Press, 2007.

Van der Leer, Nico. *Zinvolle zorg in het verpleeghuis: een onderzoek naar de samenhang tussen zorg en zin en de rol van de geestelijke verzorger*. Utrecht: KokBoekencentrum Academic, 2020.

Weeda, Jacqueline, and Hanneke Muthert. "What Does Participation in the Case Studies Project Mean for One's Professionalism? Preliminary Findings and Topics." In *Learning from Case Studies in Chaplaincy. Towards Practice Based Evidence & Professionalism.*, edited by Renske Kruizinga, et al., 167–73. Utrecht: Eburon, 2020.

White, Kelsey B., et al. "Board Certification of Professional Chaplains: A Qualitative Study of Stakeholder Perspectives." *Journal of Health Care Chaplaincy* 28.4 (2022) 443–466. https://doi.org/10.1080/08854726.2021.1916334.

21

On Method and Evidence
—Jacques Körver

"The modern gaze sees only one of the nutmeg's two hemispheres: that part of which is *Myristica fragrans*, a subject of science and commerce. The other half eludes it because it will only manifest itself in songs and stories."

Amitav Ghosh[1]

INTRODUCTION—CHOICES AND SELECTIONS

In this chapter we evaluate the methodological choices of the CSP: the emphasis on care for clients individually or in small groups, the use of a format for description and analysis of a case study, the use of the third person in description and discussion, the member check, working in research communities (RCs), and the Research Collaboration Group (RCG) as an advisory group. We then look at the study as participatory and practice-driven research, including the participation and recruitment of chaplains and the relationship between practice and theory, and between practice, teaching, and research. We conclude this chapter with some thoughts on the importance of qualitative research from a phenomenological and hermeneutic perspective.

---

1. Ghosh, *The Nutmeg's Curse*, 35.

CONCENTRATION ON INDIVIDUAL CHAPLAINCY CARE

The focus on dyadic forms of chaplaincy care or in small groups is artificial. The chaplain's field of work in any organization is broader and intertwined with other activities. Chaplains play a significant role in organizations, facilitate religious services, contribute to moral deliberation, organize group conversations, et cetera.[2] However, that breadth can never be addressed in one study nor in one format. Broadening the focus would be at the expense of deepening it. Our starting point was that individual and group accompaniment is the heart of chaplaincy. Chaplains themselves consider that guidance the most essential part of their work and spend the most time on it.[3] Therefore, to explore and describe the practice of chaplaincy with an eye for interventions, goals, and outcomes, it is not only worthwhile but also necessary to start with that core activity.

Although the format for describing a case includes some questions on the context of chaplaincy care (context and background of the question, referral, and communication with and feedback from other professionals),[4] the broader context of chaplaincy care received less attention. In the RC Hospital, it quickly became apparent that the specific context of a department or target group can to a great extent determine the opportunities for and limitations to chaplaincy. The size of the staff and the integration of chaplaincy in a protocol, for example, immediately affect what a chaplain can or cannot accomplish. In the RC Military "base line work," which is characterized by informal connections in a rather hierarchical and formal organization, was understood as an element of the context rather than as an organizational aspect. In the RC Prison, participants emphasized the significant overlap between their various tasks (individual contact, group discussion, celebration), which regularly led to connections being made with other tasks.

Another aspect of the format of the CSP was the focus on the behavior of chaplains, their interactions and interventions, in order to portray the practices as concretely as possible.[5] In the next step we also focused on the goals, outcomes, and theoretical underpinnings. For some participants it proved difficult, especially in the initial phase, to describe their actions concretely. Descriptions remained vague at times, and RC members did not

2. See Chapters 13 and 18.
3. Desjardins and Redl, "In Their Own Words"; Kruizinga, et al., "Enhancing the Integration."
4. See Appendix B, questions 2, 4, and 5c.
5. Walton and Körver, "Dutch Case Studies Project."

always question that. Sometimes the practice was formulated in idealistic terms in order to emphasize the particularity of a specific field of work. And sometimes participants felt that the practice included mystical dimensions that could not be expressed in words.[6] It did not always prove easy for the chairing researchers to maintain the practical focus and not resort to a theoretical position or a specific professional viewpoint. An example of the difficulty with the focus on concrete action became apparent in an initial secondary analysis of a subset of case studies on the occurrence of blessings in the chaplain's work. It appeared that blessings were frequently part of the interventions, but were often described only in a short phrase, such as "at the end of the conversation I laid hands on the client." Usually that act was not further detailed or explained, even though a whole world can lie behind that simple sentence.[7]

In part, that can only be observed in retrospect through comparison and analysis of multiple case studies. That is also the case with the collaboration of chaplains with other professionals. A quick scan of all case studies revealed that about two-thirds of the case studies involve some form of collaboration, from a casual conversation in the hallways to jointly discussing and implementing policy for a client. That issue also requires further analysis and elaboration. What can be considered collaboration, in what forms does it take place, for what purpose and with what results does it occur, what is the relationship between formal and informal consultation and collaboration, and what is the difference between the actual behavior of chaplains in this regard and how they present themselves?[8]

The final reports from the RCs reveal the fruits of the focus on direct guidance and concrete interventions.[9] At the same time, the case studies also provide a wealth of starting points for further exploration of the chaplain's behavior, particularly on the basis of a research question or hypothesis that arises from the comparison and analysis of the collected case studies, such as working with rituals in chaplaincy.[10]

---

6. Den Toom, *The Chaplain-Researcher*, 124–25. Cf. "Consensus in the Research Communities" (Chapter 19).

7. See "Rituals in Chaplaincy" (Chapter 16).

8. See "Chaplaincy in Context" (Chapter 13).

9. Körver, et al., *Richting, Repertoire en Resultaat*.

10. Veerman, "Researching Practices." See also "Rituals in Chaplaincy" (Chapter 16).

FORMAT FOR DESCRIPTION AND ANALYSIS

Along with the advantage of comparability, a major argument for a case study format was that it would encourage chaplains to reflect on their actions in a concrete, detailed, and structured way. Their capacities of observation would be stimulated precisely because the format calls attention to behavior (of the client and of the chaplain), to sensory perceptions, and, in addition, to the chaplain's inner process of reflection and decision-making. As mentioned before, some chaplains found it difficult to describe their own practice accurately and concretely. Working with the format did not come naturally to many participants, and for some it was even the most challenging element of the project.[11] Participants felt they had to press the living story into a mold, making the format feel like something instrumental that did not correspond to reality or that contradicted the principles of chaplaincy. For most, however, the format (gradually) came to function as a welcome and useful guide for putting their practice into words and providing sufficient space and structure to describe their practices.[12]

During the course of the project, a number of changes were made based on the questions, ambiguities, and discussions that arose in the RCs in response to the format. Some of those changes related to the instructions (including justification for the selection of cases, encouragement to provide descriptions that are as specific as possible, ethical guidelines, a timeline for submission, discussion and completion, and scope in words). Gradually the structure became clearer. Questions about background variables of the clients were added, as well as a question about important aspects or experiences there might be that had not yet been addressed. More explicit questions were asked about the role of worldview (of the client and the chaplain), and the role of theories and methods that were used explicitly or implicitly. Also, the format called attention to critical issues, evaluation of the review process, and a brief summary of the case study.

A very important addition was the introduction of the domain of chaplaincy as defined in the *Dutch Professional Standard Spiritual Caregiver*[13] and the four dimensions of meaning and worldview (existential, spiritual, ethical, and aesthetic) as sensitizing concepts.[14] That proved important in a twofold sense. First, it focused the attention of the chaplains on the various dimensions of chaplaincy. Through its repeated use, the four-dimensional

---

11. Den Toom, *The Chaplain-Researcher*, 120–21.
12. Den Toom, *The Chaplain-Researcher*.
13. VGVZ, *Professional Standard*.
14. Bowen, "Sensitizing Concepts."

description of meaning and worldview provided a framework for the experiences and interventions of chaplains. It helped to develop a common language for naming and clarifying aspects of the work. It helped to ensure that aspects of the work that are often left unnamed or taken for granted were nevertheless seen as conscious and powerful parts of the work, such as the aesthetic aspects[15] and the ritual interventions.[16] Second, the use of the four-dimensional description of chaplaincy helped to constantly move between the very concrete practice and the more abstract description of the professional domain.[17]

When justifying the selection of a specific care situation for a case study, chaplains had to indicate the reason for their choice: representative because of a target group, paradigmatic for the work, unusual, or critical.[18] In a later version of the format, at the end of the discussion they were asked if the motivation might have changed. More often, the discussion of this question showed that the original motivation had been deepened and that the contributor but also the other members of the RC had become more aware of what chaplaincy entails.

Reflection on the relationship between practice and theory can be seen in the same vein. That reflection was not an easy task for the participating chaplains. Many experienced a large gap between their practice and the theory they had learned in their education and training.[19] Often theory had become implicit, a "delta-like reservoir" as one participant from the RC Hospital put it, in which it is no longer possible to say exactly where or when a particular side branch or tributary fed in to the stream. The very act of explicating theory helped participants to better articulate and justify their practice, as well as correct distortions in the way they understood the theory.[20] It also served to deepen awareness of one's own professionalism and professional identity as a chaplain.

A few comments need to be made in this regard. Despite the fact that the case study was presented to clients via a member check (see below), the perspectives of those clients found only limited expression. How did they perceive the interventions and intentions of the chaplain, and how did they value the results of the accompaniment or support? In fact, there were

---

15. See "Aesthetic Counseling and Method" (Chapter 15).
16. See "Rituals in Chaplaincy" (Chapter 16).
17. Körver and Walton, "Door de bomen het bos leren zien."
18. See "What Makes a Good Case?" (Chapter 3).
19. Den Toom, *The Chaplain-Researcher*.
20. Den Toom, *The Chaplain-Researcher*, 142–46. See also "Consensus in the Research Communities" (Chapter 19).

a variety of practical issues that inhibited the member check, such as the sudden death of a client, ethical considerations, or cognitive impairments. In addition, fellow professionals were not always interested, or responded in a superficial manner. When the clients or others involved did provide feedback, there was generally a high degree of correspondence with the reporting by the chaplain. The correspondence is supported by other research. Most clients greatly appreciate a conversation with a chaplain and attach great value to that contact.[21] Appreciation increases when clients can actually express what is on their minds and when there are multiple contacts.[22] A second observation is that the case study is a form of self-reporting by the chaplain. All sorts of filters or bias may present themselves in that process, as well as socially acceptable answers or more idealistic descriptions, thereby distorting reality. There is no observation by a third party with no role in the contact. Those are caveats that could be taken into account in follow-up research.

THIRD-PERSON PERSPECTIVE

Using the third-person perspective when describing and discussing a case study did not come naturally, felt artificial, and evoked hilarity. Nevertheless, it was a tool to enable some distance from one's own practice and description. In justifying the choice of a specific case study as input into the project, the participants' own views and standards of what good chaplaincy is or should be played a role. That was also the case with the other members of an RC. The clash of views and norms did not make it easy to submit a case study of which the contributor assumed that it was an example of good chaplaincy care. Questions, even if they were informative, could be understood as critique and cause the contributor to become defensive. The "third person" functioned as a buffer or distance between one's own views and those of others. Besides an initial appreciative round of discussion of the case study, as became common in some RCs, the use of the third person had a neutralizing function for participants and helped to allow critical questions to be asked.[23]

Although other research disciplines and international case study research on chaplaincy promote the use of the first-person perspective (as a form of autoethnography) to encourage personal engagement with the

---

21. Tan, et al., "Understanding the Outcomes."
22. Snowden, et al., "'What's on Your Mind?'"
23. Den Toom, *The Chaplain-Researcher*, 127.

research object,[24] in our opinion the choice of a third-person perspective proved to be a fortunate one. That is mainly due to the review process in the RCs. In other research designs, researchers explore a topic or situation through their own involvement in it. Or a chaplain submits a case study from one's own work to a researcher, possibly structured by questions or concerns provided by the researcher. All of those studies or projects differ from the CSP in terms of the RCs. The RC presupposes a group dynamic process in which the case study is collaboratively analyzed. The benefit of the third-person perspective was not only discernible in the description of the case study, but also in the collaborative review process. Precisely in the RCs, the "third person" functioned as a neutralizing factor that stimulated the inquisitive attitude of the participants and kept the perspective of describing the professional practice of chaplains open.

MEMBER CHECK

The member check constitutes a third element for limiting subjective distortions in the case studies. The instruction for the description of the case study explicitly requested that the case study be presented to the client or the client's legal representative for feedback. The goal was to improve precision, plausibility, and applicability.

In practice, it appeared that chaplains often had reservations about presenting a first version of the case description (without the reflections) to their clients. That coincided with the reluctance to ask clients to participate in the research and then also present them with an informed consent form by which they agreed that the case study would be part of a research project, could be reviewed by others, and could be published in anonymized form. It felt like a breach of confidentiality, which is a central concern and value of chaplaincy, as if the chaplain's interest might be more important than that of the client. Of course, asking for participation in a study, submitting informed consent, and then also having clients read the description for validation is not easy. At the same time, it is a way to play the game with open cards, ethical and legal diligence, concern for client privacy, and genuine curiosity about the experience of the care process on the client's part.[25] Moreover, research shows that clients like to participate in research. They get the opportunity to clarify and organize their own experiences and contribute to improving care for future clients. That is also true even for

---

24. Abma and Stake, "Science of the Particular"; Nolan, "Introduction"; Poulos, *Essentials of Autoethnography*.

25. McCurdy and Fitchett, "Ethical Issues."

research on major life events.[26] Nevertheless, some participating chaplains were inclined, despite using a specific care process as material for a case study, not to mention anything about it to the client in question.

That in some situations it is not easy, even complicated, or utterly impossible to comply with concerns of transparency is also clear, such as in research in criminology, inaccessible working situations, or dangerous political contexts.[27] When clients have a cognitive impairment or are in circumstances that require a very high degree of privacy (as may be the case in detention or in the armed forces), the handling of the arrangements discussed above is problematic. In such situations, appropriate arrangements were sought, such as an oral informed consent, stated as such on paper by the chaplain.

In addition, inviting the client to read the description of the care process can be seen as a new intervention, where it remains to be seen what that might evoke in the client. It may be that the report reflects an interpretation on the part of the chaplain with which the client disagrees. Rejection could be the result, but also the realization that the chaplain was not on the right track or did not express underlying assumptions clearly enough. Moreover, some clients may see the report as a mirror that they expect must be particularly accurate, leaving aside whether they appreciate what they see. Others see the report rather as a portrait, in which objective representation and interpretation on the part of the chaplain intermingle.[28] Moreover, it is clear that member checks should not be applied rigidly. There may be practical as well as more theoretical or ethical concerns as in the CSP. Psychologist Sue Motulsky suggests another term: "reflexive participant collaboration."[29] In participatory research, it is important to account for the inequalities between those involved.[30] Motulsky's term is consistent with developments as they emerge in healthcare, for example, in the form of shared decision making in which the client is explicitly involved in decision-making on one's treatment or care.[31]

---

26. Boeije, *Analysis in Qualitative Research*, 43–56; Hutchinson, et al., "Benefits of Participating in Research."

27. Calvey, "Covert Ethnography in Criminology"; Kluczewska and Lottholz, "Recognizing the Never Quite Absent."

28. Madill and Sullivan, "Mirrors, Portraits."

29. Motulsky, "Is Member Checking," 402.

30. Bos and Kal, "The Value of Inequality."

31. Wirpsa and Pugliese, *Chaplains as Partners*.

RESEARCH COMMUNITIES

At the heart of the CSP were the research communities (RCs). In that context, participants presented, discussed, and analyzed their case studies. In that context they gave shape to their status as co-researchers, clarified and substantiated their actions as chaplains, and gave expression to those actions, while searching and groping for a language that connected them with and could also be meaningful for clients, colleagues, and administrators. Beforehand, there were considerations as to what case study would be suitable to reflect something of the professional inspiration and contribute to the edifice of the chaplaincy profession. Is a particular case too private? Does it represent anything? Will others recognize what and why and to what end one acted as one did? Those kinds of questions played a role in participants' minds. Sometimes there were critical questions. Occasionally, there was a lack of understanding, or even the feeling of wanting to stop. Gradually there was recognition, appreciation, sincere curiosity about what motivated everyone, what knowledge and experience everyone had in their backpacks. And especially the surprise that despite all the differences in approach, training, models, and temperament, something became visible of the commonality of the profession, of the common professional identity.

The previous sections have already mentioned a number of points that refer to the learning process that participants went through. We can outline how RCs developed over the course of the project as follows:

1. Placing their own norms and beliefs about chaplaincy in parentheses.
2. Adopting an inquisitive attitude toward each case study.
3. Describing one's own actions and their motives as concretely and in as much detail as possible.
4. Focusing on developing the profession.
5. Switching between the differentiated and concrete practice on the one hand and the more abstract four-dimensional definition of chaplaincy on the other hand.
6. Developing a common language that is also suitable for communication with other professionals.
7. Connecting action to theories and models.
8. Recognizing the dimensions of meaning and worldview in each case study.
9. Observing and describing reality methodically and carefully as a researcher.

It was a layered learning process that contributed greatly to many forms of awareness, as revealed in Niels Den Toom's research.[32] This learning process could only take place in the context of RCs functioning as laboratories of the chaplains' profession. It was notable that consensus building occurred, even though group dynamic struggles occurred from time to time as is to be expected in any task-oriented group.[33] Some factors can be identified that contributed to this consensus:

- The case studies were always discussed at length, with plenty of room for each person to contribute their questions and comments, allowing each case to be discussed from numerous perspectives. In doing so, multiple perspectives could be "true" and "valuable" at the same time.

- After the discussion, it was up to the contributor to process the questions and comments, which led to additions, corrections, new reflections, and insights. The discussion and analysis formed an ongoing process, which also allowed for critical issues often related to core themes in the recent development of chaplaincy. Not that all those themes were discussed, but they were mentioned and acknowledged, including the varying views on them.

- This method of discussion and processing revealed the differences in approach, method, theoretical background, denomination, and style. These were appreciated and tested side by side in relation to the overarching concept of chaplaincy. These differentiations that manifested themselves with increasing clarity simultaneously made visible the commonality of the profession. Differentiation led to integration, that is, learning to discern differences entailed a new integrative concept at a higher level.[34] Those differences, even in worldview background, did not diminish the sense of belonging to a common professional identity.[35]

In the RC Mixed, there were, in addition to differences in approach, method, theory, denomination, and style, also differences in the field of work. Those differences constituted an additional inspirational factor. At the same time, it turned out that the differences within the same field of work could also be extensive. However, the confrontation with the differences was stimulating in the search for the common aspects of the profession,

32. Den Toom, *The Chaplain-Researcher*.
33. See "Consensus in the Research Communities" (Chapter 19).
34. Breeuwsma, *Alles over ontwikkeling.*, 139–201; Werner, "The Concept of Development."
35. Den Toom, *The Chaplain-Researcher*, 187–211.

in which the four-dimensional definition from the Dutch professional standard formed a particularly powerful anchor as point of reference and crystallization.

In this context, it is important to reflect on the recruitment of participants for the CSP. There were four criteria that participants were required to meet: (a) extensive experience in chaplaincy,[36] (b) an interest in research, (c) willingness to commit to the project for four years and to provide at least two case studies during that time, and (d) an agreement to participate between the chaplain, the employer or supervisor, and the project leadership. We started right away, with all the lack of experience in conducting research, including lack of training or instruction in working with the format and basic research skills. Experience with and training in the basic skills of research took place in the process. That could have been done better. Some ambiguities and resentment in the early stages might have then been avoided. At the same time, it was clear that the hiccups and ambiguities in the beginning phase brought with them a special dynamic that stimulated the joint search and ensured that the project leaders and researchers did not have the recipe for all the difficulties ready in advance. In that sense, it was a search process, a search process without a detailed protocol, a journey in which the map gradually unfolded.

RESEARCH COLLABORATION GROUP

The consultation and advisory group for the benefit of the researchers and project leaders met on average twice a year during the project. The emphasis of the meetings was on exchanging experiences from the various RCs, formulating initial insights and discussing a variety of practical and theoretical issues that arose as a result of the project. Given the low frequency of the meetings, they regularly got stuck in incidental discussions. It was difficult to discern and hold on to the common thread and to join in the search for directions on the unfolding map.

That, too, could have been done better. Some possibilities could have been: (a) seeking more alignment between the working methods in the different RCs (e.g., in terms of providing theory, using the format, encouraging report making, and following the timeline); (b) thinking about and encouraging the overarching analysis of case studies both within and between RCs; (c) identifying (criteria for) good practices in the case studies;

---

36. 'Extensive' we did not specify as a set number of years. That gave us the opportunity to admit engaged participants who, although they had only been working in chaplaincy for a few years, demonstrated a reflexive and critical view of the profession.

and (d) identifying possible research themes and hypotheses for follow-up research. The fact that those opportunities did not materialize is related to the circumstance that participation in the RCG (as well as in the CSP) by the researchers was purely voluntary and for which none of the participants involved formally received time and space from their respective employers. That is an essential point to sort out for any follow-up process. Staff will have to be available. And staff means the availability of sufficient financial support.

PARTICIPATORY, PHENOMENOLOGICAL, AND HERMENEUTIC RESEARCH

In calling for a greater visibility and understanding of chaplaincy practice through case studies, George Fitchett emphasized that so little is known of that practice. Case studies serve to foster awareness among chaplains of what they actually do, why (with what goals), and to what ends (outcomes). Moreover, case studies provide accessible material for the training of chaplains, as well as for clarifying for fellow professionals, managers, and administrators what chaplaincy can provide. Fitchett, however, saw qualitative research in this form primarily as a preliminary phase for larger-scale quantitative research.[37] Later he placed more emphasis on the possibility of using case studies to explore specific themes in chaplaincy, for example, the diversity of worldview and religion and its implications for chaplaincy, or the role and contribution of chaplaincy in the context of decision-making in complex medical situations.[38] The role of rituals in chaplaincy can also be further studied and analyzed through case studies.[39]

Fitchett's main motive, however, lies with larger-scale quantitative research, for which qualitative research should provide both possible variables and hypotheses. That pursuit can be understood from a context wherein chaplaincy has to present and justify itself primarily through a quantitative, evidence-based way. Especially in the world of health care where quantitative research, and in particular the randomized controlled trial (RCT), is valued as the most important type of research. In that context, qualitative research is underappreciated and little evidential value is attributed to it. In our thinking, the latter is often based on unfamiliarity with and

---

37. Fitchett, "Making Our Case(s)."
38. Fitchett, "The State of the Art." See also Wirpsa and Pugliese, *Chaplains as Partners*.
39. Nolan, "Lifting the Lid on Chaplaincy," 13–14.

misunderstandings about the possibilities of qualitative research, as well as on the overestimation of the possibilities of quantitative research.[40]

Nationally and internationally, the CSP has contributed to the (re)valuation of qualitative research in chaplaincy. A number of reasons plays a role. (1) Through case study research, it is possible to involve chaplains as co-researchers in (participatory) research, because they are accustomed from their training to describing cases and approaching practice from a phenomenological and hermeneutic perspective. (2) Case study research has the character of practice-driven research that is in line with the current development of the profession: research that is embedded, that can be applied to practice, and that is focused on collaboration. (3) Quantitative research is not always necessary to provide evidence for the efficacy of interventions.[41] (4) Qualitative research accesses the intricate reality of meaning and worldview in practice, something that quantitative research is hardly able to do. (5) And qualitative research makes practice-based and client-based knowledge visible.[42]

On many levels, the CSP was a participatory study. Chaplains from many fields of work collaborated with researchers from five different universities. At the same time, the participants worked together with their clients. In the true sense of the word, it was a participatory research project, in which it gradually became clear that each person involved had a role to play and a task to perform. Also, it was phenomenological research, if we understand phenomenology as elucidating the direct and intuitive experience of phenomena and the intentionality of those experiences (in this case in the chaplain's interaction with the client).[43] And it was hermeneutical research, if we understand hermeneutics as interpreting those experiences and intentionality. The research aimed at moving close to that interaction and at exploring and articulating its intentionality, without immediately placing it within a specific belief or idealistic view.[44] Martin Walton emphasizes that chaplaincy is not only about the persons (*living human document*) interwoven with their context (*living human web*), but precisely about the dynamic interaction between clients and the chaplain (*living human encounter*), in which experiences can be discussed and meanings emerge, where reflections and considerations are evoked, and where perspectives for care and for

---

40. Flyvbjerg, "Five Misunderstandings"; Raad voor Volksgezondheid en Samenleving, *No Evidence without Context*.
41. Veerman, "Researching Practices."
42. Visser and Damen, "Waar moeten we het zoeken?"
43. Churchill, *Essentials of Existential*.
44. Gerkin, *The Living Human Document*.

life choices are stimulated.[45] The project presents a solid case for qualitative research in chaplaincy.

It is clear from the foregoing that practice, research, and education are aligned with each other in the case study approach. By conducting research in proximity to practice and at the service of practice, it is possible to arrive at results that can be immediately applied in teaching, training, and practice. As such, published case studies, as good practices, have already served in numerous chaplaincy training programs. And working with the format for describing and analyzing case studies developed in the CSP, stimulates in students and in experienced chaplains their research competencies: an open mind and an open perspective on reality, on the interaction of phenomena, and on differentiated and complex practices.

REFERENCES

Abma, Tineke A., and Robert E. Stake. "Science of the Particular. An Advocacy of Naturalistic Case Study in Health Research." *Qualitative Health Research* 24.8 (2014) 1150–61. https://doi.org/10.1177/1049732314543196.

Boeije, Hennie R. *Analysis in Qualitative Research*. Los Angeles [etc.]: Sage, 2010.

Bos, Gustaaf, and Doortje Kal. "The Value of Inequality." *Social Inclusion* 4.4 (2016) 129–39. https://doi.org/10.17645/si.v4i4.689.

Bowen, Glenn A. "Sensitizing Concepts." In *Sage Research Methods*, edited by Paul Atkinson, et al. Language and Qualitative Research. London: Sage, 2020. doi/10.4135/9781526421036.

Breeuwsma, Gerrit. *Alles over ontwikkeling: Over de grondslagen van de ontwikkelingspsychologie*. Amsterdam: Boom, 1993.

Calvey, David. "Covert Ethnography in Criminology: A Submerged yet Creative Tradition." *Current Issues in Criminal Justice* 25.1 (2013/07/01 2013) 541–50. https://doi.org/10.1080/10345329.2013.12035980.

Churchill, Scott D. *Essentials of Existential Phenomenological Research*. Essentials of Qualitative Methods Series. Washington, DC: American Psychological Association, 2022. doi:10.1037/0000257-000.

Den Toom, Niels. *The Chaplain-Researcher. The Perceived Impact of Participation in a Dutch Research Project on Chaplains' Professionalism*. Utrecht: Eburon, 2022.

Desjardins, Cate Michelle, and Nina Redl, eds. *In Their Own Words. Stories of Chaplains' Courage, Creativity, and Compassion During the Early Pandemic*. Chicago: Transforming Chaplaincy, 2022.

Fitchett, George. "Making Our Case(s)." *Journal of Health Care Chaplaincy* 17.1–2 (2011) 3–18. https://doi.org/10.1080/08854726.2011.559829.

———. "The State of the Art in Chaplaincy Research. Needs, Resources and Hopes." In *Learning from Case Studies in Chaplaincy. Towards Practice Based Evidence & Professionalism*, edited by Renske Kruizinga, et al., 21–35. Utrecht: Eburon, 2020.

---

45. Walton, "Introduction."

Flyvbjerg, Bent. "Five Misunderstandings About Case-Study Research." *Qualitative Inquiry* 12.2 (2006) 219–45. https://doi.org/10.1177/1077800405284363.

Gerkin, Charles V. *The Living Human Document. Re-Visioning Pastoral Counseling in a Hermeneutical Mode*. Nashville: Abingdon Press, 1984.

Ghosh, Amitav. *The Nutmeg's Curse. Parables for a Planet in Crisis*. London: John Murray, 2022.

Hutchinson, Sally A., et al. "Benefits of Participating in Research Interviews." *Journal of Nursing Scholarship* 26.2 (1994) 161–66. https://doi.org/10.1111/j.1547-5069.1994.tb00937.x.

Kluczewska, Karolina, and Philipp Lottholz. "Recognizing the Never Quite Absent: De Facto Usage, Ethical Issues, and Applications of Covert Research in Difficult Research Contexts." *Qualitative Research* 23.2 (2023) 417–33. https://doi.org/10.1177/14687941211033084.

Körver, Jacques, and Martin Walton. "Door de bomen het bos leren zien, en . . . door het bos de bomen. Het Nederlandse Case Studies Project Geestelijke Verzorging." *Kwalon* 28.1 (2023) 46–55. https://doi.org/10.5117/KWA2023.1.008.KORV.

Körver, Jacques, et al., eds. *Richting, Repertoire en Resultaat. Uitkomsten van het Nederlandse Case Studies Project Geestelijke Verzorging (2016-2021)*. Utrecht: PThU-UCGV, 2023.

Kruizinga, Renske, et al. "Enhancing the Integration of Chaplains within the Healthcare Team. A Qualitative Analysis of a Survey Study among Healthcare Chaplains." *Integrated Healthcare Journal* 4.1 (2023) e000138. https://doi.org/10.1136/ihj-2022-000138.

Madill, Anna, and Paul Sullivan. "Mirrors, Portraits, and Member Checking: Managing Difficult Moments of Knowledge Exchange in the Social Sciences." *Qualitative Psychology* 5.3 (2018) 321–39. https://doi.org/10.1037/qup0000089.

McCurdy, David B., and George Fitchett. "Ethical Issues in Case Study Publication. 'Making Our Case(s)' Ethically." *Journal of Health Care Chaplaincy* 17.1-2 (2011) 55–74. https://doi.org/10.1080/08854726.2011.559855.

Motulsky, Sue L. "Is Member Checking the Gold Standard of Quality in Qualitative Research?" *Qualitative Psychology* 8.3 (2021) 389–406. https://doi.org/10.1037/qup0000215.

Nolan, Steve. "Introduction. Autoethnography in Chaplain Case Study Research." In *Case Studies in Spiritual Care. Healthcare Chaplaincy Assessments, Interventions & Outcomes*, edited by George Fitchett and Steve Nolan, 11–32. London: Kingsley, 2018.

———. "Lifting the Lid on Chaplaincy: A First Look at Findings from Chaplains' Case Study Research." *Journal of Health Care Chaplaincy* 27.1 (2021) 1–23. https://doi.org/10.1080/08854726.2019.1603916.

Poulos, Christopher N. *Essentials of Autoethnography*. Washington, DC: American Psychological Association, 2021.

Raad voor Volksgezondheid en Samenleving. *No Evidence without Context. About the Illusion of Evidence-Based Practice in Healthcare*. Den Haag: RVS, 2017.

Snowden, Austyn, et al. "'What's on Your Mind?' The Only Necessary Question in Spiritual Care." *Journal for the Study of Spirituality* 8.1 (2018) 19–33. https://doi.org/10.1080/20440243.2018.1431031.

Tan, Heather, et al. "Understanding the Outcomes of Spiritual Care as Experienced by Patients." *Journal of Health Care Chaplaincy* 28.2 (2022) 147–61. https://doi.org/1 0.1080/08854726.2020.1793095.

Veerman, Jan Willem. "Researching Practices. Lessons from Dutch Youth Care." In *Learning from Case Studies in Chaplaincy. Towards Practice Based Evidence & Professionalism*, edited by Renske Kruizinga, et al., 46–59. Utrecht: Eburon, 2020.

VGVZ. *Professional Standard Spiritual Caregiver 2015*. VGVZ (Amsterdam: 2015). https://vgvz.nl/wp-content/uploads/2023/02/VGVZ_Professional_ Standard_2015_Main_Text_EN_v03_WITH_APPENDICES.pdf.

Visser, Anja, and Annelieke Damen. "Waar moeten we het zoeken? Op weg naar de onderzoeksagenda voor GV in de zorg." *Tijdschrift Geestelijke Verzorging* 23.97 (2020) 48–57.

Walton, Martin N. "Introduction. Researching Living Human Encounter." In *Learning from Case Studies in Chaplaincy. Towards Practice Based Evidence & Professionalism*, edited by Renske Kruizinga, et al., 9–17. Utrecht: Eburon, 2020.

Walton, Martin N., and Jacques Körver. "Dutch Case Studies Project in Chaplaincy Care. A Description and Theoretical Explanation of the Format and Procedures." *Health and Social Care Chaplaincy* 5.2 (2017) 257–80. https://doi.org/10.1558/ hscc.34302.

Werner, Heinz. "The Concept of Development from a Comparative and Organismic Point of View." In *The Concept of Development. An Issue in the Study of Human Behavior*, edited by Dale B. Harris, 125–48. Minneapolis: University of Minnesota Press, 1957.

Wirpsa, M. Jeanne, and Karen Pugliese, eds. *Chaplains as Partners in Medical Decision- Making: Case Studies in Healthcare Chaplaincy*. London: Kingsley, 2020.

22

Answering the Research Question
— Martin Walton

"Inward Stretch Outward Reach."
Rex Nettleford[1]

RESEARCH QUESTION OF THE CASE STUDIES PROJECT

THE RESEARCH QUESTION OF the Dutch Case Studies Project was threefold: (1) What do chaplains do, (2) why, and (3) to what ends, in the direct care of others (clients, patients, residents, prisoners, military personnel, *et cetera*)?[2] The formulation of the second question "why" and the third "to what ends" was too similar, as in the beginning both questions were understood in terms of the intentions and goals of the chaplain. With the third question "to what ends" we had hoped for accounts of concrete effects and outcomes of chaplaincy care that could be observed and/or reported by others and subsequently described in case studies of chaplaincy.

The second question "why" appeared to be the easiest to answer, because the question seemed to mirror prevalent discourses in chaplaincy. The question what chaplaincy "is," is often answered in terms of intention or an idealistic approach. The question "why," in the sense of intentions or purpose, includes "to what ends," whether or not those intentions are realized

---

1. Nettleford, *Inward Stretch Outward Reach*. The title is a metaphor for the formation of cultural identity in the Caribbean as a crossroad of the Americas.
2. This chapter is based on Walton, "Beantwoording vraagstelling van het CSP."

or not. The concrete description of what one has actually done (question 1) and the account of observable or reported effects proved to be a greater challenge. As the project progressed, however, the answers became more precise and detailed. A more precise formulation of the research question, or questions, is then: (1) What do chaplains do? (2) Why and to what ends do they do what they do? And (3) what is the effect or outcome of what they do?

In order to find answers to the research questions we employed a stepped analysis of the case study material. One by one the case studies were reviewed in the research communities. Each case description and each review report concluded with an answer to the research questions in the single case under consideration. In the process of multiple reviews certain perspectives arose and analyses were developed. Some of those perspectives and analyses were already being published prior to the project being completed. Others were developed in the final evaluations of the six research communities. On the basis of those perspectives, analyses, and evaluations the chairperson(s) of each research community composed a final research report, including an answer to the research question. Those reports were marked (coded) thematically and the key terms were ordered in categories (code groups). The inventory of the key terms and categories demonstrates the nuance and variation of the various reports.

On the basis of the inventory and further interpretation answers to the research questions were formulated. The answers provide a synthesis of the perspectives that were shared in various research communities, but also give an indication of accents peculiar to specific research communities. In addition, a few examples from individual case studies are provided for clarity.

The answers to the research question are thus layered, with more nuance and variation than a simple answer can provide. The answer to each question has multiple facets. And in the answers certain perspectives recur. The various dimensions of meaning and worldview, for example, illustrate both what chaplains do and why they do it, as well as being reflected in the outcomes. The aspect of value orientation is of major importance both for the chaplains and for the persons receiving care. We discovered that chaplains exercise "inward stretch" as they seek to better understand and accommodate the persons they encounter in their struggles and searches for meaning. Chaplains exercise "outward reach" in their personal, practical, and professional care responses. Our findings indicate that it is precisely the interconnection and integration of the various perspectives that make chaplaincy what it is. The answers to the research questions that follow are therefore not only multifaceted but also interrelated.

WHAT DO CHAPLAINS DO IN DIRECT CARE OF OTHERS?

To indicate what chaplains do, we speak of a repertoire of care acts (or activities) with three key aspects: *dialogue, ritual performance,* and *working with worldview (re)sources.* The threefold repertoire is acted out in a *triangle of interaction* of person, surroundings, and meaning and worldview. We then indicate the *occasions* and *topics* that play a role in contacts with chaplains, followed by various *approaches*, that is, the methods, strategies, analyses, and intervention models, that inform and underlie the care of chaplains.

Repertoire: Dialogue, Ritual & Worldview (Re)Sources

In caring for persons chaplains employ a repertoire of activities that as an interrelated whole characterizes their work. The three basic elements are (a) dialogical interaction by means of intentional conversation, counseling and non-verbal communication, (b) the performance of rituals, and (c) working with religious and other worldview and cultural (re)sources.

Dialogical Interaction

The term "interaction" is used to refer to various kinds of communication that are employed in the case studies. Conversational exchanges and the use of a variety of forms of counseling are quite common to chaplaincy, and reflect perhaps the dominant image of what chaplains do: talk with people.[3] The conversational mode is also well founded in chaplaincy training with the use of verbatims and in narrative approaches. And in the case studies, conversation, counseling, and dialogue play a major role. At the same time, it became evident in the case studies that chaplaincy does not live from words alone. A great variety of non-verbal communication is employed in the use of gestures, images, imagination, symbols, music, silence, and the physical surroundings. The non-verbal interactions can be considered dialogical in that they elicit responses and fulfill functions and techniques similar to those of verbal communication, such as offering recognition, mirroring, and reframing. For the dialogical usage of non-verbal communication, the RC Mixed Fields coined the term "aesthetic counseling,"[4] whereby aesthetic refers not just to the dynamics of beauty and art, but in an etymological

---

3. See the paragraph "Counseling and more" in Chapter 15, "Aesthetic Counseling and Method."

4. See Chapter 15.

sense to sensory perception. Tied to all these manners of communication are the skills and abilities (such as counseling techniques, "close listening,"[5] and working with sensory perception) that chaplains employ in the application of the care approaches discussed below.

Dialogical interaction also indicates the nature or style of the care, that is, the sum of attitudes that characterize the care. The nature of the care lies in the careful, sensitive, explorative, and non-judgmental[6] human interaction with others with attention for dignity, reciprocity, openness, encounter,[7] and uniqueness.

In the third place dialogical indicates the content of chaplaincy care in its intrinsic relation to meaning and worldview (see below). The term dialogue (more than, for example, conversation, counseling, or discussion) refers in this sense to an exchange on what is of fundamental value and meaning for human life. The language of chaplaincy is on the one hand everyday and experience oriented, and on the other hand metaphorical and symbolic, existential and religious. If the use of counseling techniques can be associated with "close listening," then the attention to meaning, value, and worldview can be called "focused listening."

It is important to note that the dialogue is often informal and at times structured. Structured forms can involve the implicit or explicit application of analytical models and stepped methods: narrative analysis, moral counseling, systemic approaches, an assessment tool, or coping scale. We will look more closely at methods below. One might ask if the use of structured tools and interventions, like the use of worldview (re)sources is not a distinct element of chaplaincy care, along with dialogue and ritual. The main reason for not understanding them in that way here is that however structured the tools, methods, and models might be, they function within,

---

5. This is also a term employed in the RC Mixed Fields (Walton, "Multifocale geestelijke verzorging"), as was the term "hearing to speech" from Morton, *The Journey Is Home*. In the RC Eldercare the term "listening to (enable) appearance" was employed (De Groot et al, "Van ambacht en kunst"). A style of listening by chaplains that is directed towards the person and towards depth of meaning and experience was reported in research among clients in psychiatric care. Cf. Walton, *Hoe waait de wind?*, 115–18; 127–34. See also the comments on listening and presence in Chapter 3.

6. In the RC Mental Health one spoke of an inviting, receptive, unhurried, non-judgmental, and attentive disposition. See Muthert, "Daar aansluiten."

7. This sense of encounter is drawn from dialogical philosophy, especially from Buber, *I and Thou*, and Lévinas et al., *Humanism of the Other*. Piet Verhagen states that talking about spirituality, worldview, and meaning can only proceed on the basis of relationality, in Verhagen, "The Soul Is on Air." In the case study of Potts on healing dialogue in marital therapy, Potts states that for Buber therapy is a special derivative of the I–Thou relationship. In Potts, "Martin Buber's 'Healing Dialogue.'"

that is, they are integrated into the larger dialogical context of chaplaincy.[8] That is well illustrated in the case study "I Do It My Way" (Chapter 7), in which a model with existential themes is applied to enable the client to express herself and enter into dialogue with the chaplain. Respecting and facilitating the dialogical context provide, therefore, conditions for the use of methods and models and their integration in the interaction in concrete instances of care.

Another reason not to treat methods and models separately is that many are derived from worldview perspectives and resources, such as the items of assessment tools or underlying assumptions of narrative approaches and moral counseling. Some of the methods and models are closely related to the worldview resources, While the form may become more formal with specific steps, topics, checklists, or written exercises, the function is to further the dialogical interaction on narrative, meaning, and value. One might also say that the methods and models serve to differentiate the dialogue, by opening various perspectives and structuring the dialogue.

> *The care that chaplains provide is dialogical in the sense of skilled, respectful, and meaningful communication on what is important to people.*

Ritual Performance

The term ritual performance includes a palette of symbolic, religious, and other worldview acts, from lighting a candle to reciting a holy text, from offering a blessing to the burning of letters in the framework of a ritual with music and silence, from a religious act of breaking bread and sharing Communion in the private room of a resident to a secular Memorial Day gathering of residents in the commons. Rituals structure gestures, symbolical representations, and (holy) text in an aesthetic enactment that appeals to bodily and sense experience. Chaplains generally fine tune the rituals or design new ones to respond to specific existential situations (e.g., loss, sorrow, trauma, or transiency) and to spiritual and ethical needs (e.g. comfort, forgiveness, and healing), often in situations in which other means prove insufficient. The rituals create a space in which the client can dwell and relate oneself to a situation. They offer openness for one's own interpretation and response. The space can serve as a welcome interruption of prevailing experience, as a holy place and as an occasion for holding and/or healing.

---

8. The dialogical context provides at the same time criteria for the use of methods and models and their integration in the interaction in concrete instances of care.

> Ritual performance structures aesthetic, symbolic enactment and offers another, physical, and holy space from which one can relate to a situation.

Working with Religious, Worldview, and Cultural (Re)Sources

The content of dialogical and ritual interaction lies in the intrinsic relation of chaplaincy care to meaning and worldviews, to the identity of human beings and their perspectives on their world, to what is of significance and value for them in their specific situation. That became evident in the case studies through the analysis on the basis of the four dimensions of meaning and worldview. In the existential dimension issues were framed with the help of philosophical and theological understandings.[9] In the spiritual dimension use was made of (holy) texts, meditation, rituals, and other religious and worldview practices, as well as a relation to a (religious) community.[10] In the ethical dimension community also played a role, as well as values and ethical norms derived from worldview perspectives and cultural traditions.[11] In the aesthetic dimension use was made of artistic, musical, and poetic means, of sensory elements, and of objects from the surroundings.[12]

> Working with worldview and cultural (re)sources lends chaplaincy care its characteristic color as a form of helping care.

The ground on which the threefold repertoire is acted out is the proactive, gratuitous availability (presence)[13] of the chaplain, which enables a safe

---

9. See, e.g., the use of insights of Kierkegaard in "I Do It My Way" (Chapter 7); the term "enigma" in "The Enigma of a Day" (Chapter 5); and a fable in "From Slumped to Upright" (Chapter 12).

10. See, e.g., the use of Psalms and ritual in "Wounded Warrior" (Chapter 10); of mindfulness in "From Slumped to Upright" (Chapter 12); the breaking of Communion hosts in "A Church for Charly" (Chapter 9); and the didactics on the notion of trust in "Exposure?" (Chapter 6).

11. See, e.g., the use of moral counseling in Muthert et al., "Re-Evaluating a Suicide Pact" and the term "moral injury" in "Wounded Warrior" (Chapter 10). Reflections on issues of dignity and social norms are also evident in the cases "I Do It My Way" (Chapter 7); "Wounded Warrior" (Chapter 10); and "From Slumped to Upright" (Chapter 12).

12. See, e.g., the use of objects and visual materials in "Energy *and* Inspiration" (Chapter 4) and "I Do It My Way" (Chapter 7). See also the use of ritual materials and basic elements in "A Church for Charly" (Chapter 9); and "Wounded Warrior" (Chapter 10). See the physical positioning of the chaplain in "To Honor and Confirm" (Chapter 11).

13. See the discussion in Chapter 3.

and free (hermeneutic and moral[14]) space. At times the chaplain provides a haven of confidentiality in relation to the pressures of treatment or the totalitarian character of an institution. The whole of availability and repertoire expresses itself in a broad variety of accompaniment and care practices, working with groups, and reflective and meditative practices. There are also advisory activities in the context of interdisciplinary teams. The threefold repertoire, therefore, rests upon a foundation of presence and confidentiality and is located within the context of a range of activities, but it is the house of the repertoire itself that provides chaplaincy its distinctive character in the accompaniment of individuals and groups. It is the threefold repertoire that most clearly represents the artisanship of chaplaincy.

> *Example: case study "Wounded Warrior"*
>
> In the case study "Wounded Warrior" (Chapter 10) we see how the chaplain takes time to explore the military past and present situation of the client (dialogical interaction). In response to the term "moral injury" and at the client's request, the chaplain suggests reading two Psalms (working with religious resources). Further dialogue on the texts opens for the client a path leading to human responsibility and healing (opens a moral and hermeneutic space). The Psalms also frame the ritual performance.

Triangle of Interaction: Person, Surroundings, and Meaning and Worldview

The chaplain performs the repertoire in, that is, attunes the repertoire to, a triangle of the person, the surroundings, and the realm of meaning and worldview. See figure 22.1.

Person

Initially the repertoire is employed in order to tune into the other as a unique person, a human being, and a subject. The attunement takes place, to a degree that is fitting, within a broad exploration of the (existential) situation, the sources of meaning, the cultural, worldview, and social background of the other and their needs. The chaplain seeks to understand the other person

---

14. The RC Military spoke of "opening a moral space." See Schuhmann and Pleizier, "Onder militairen." Cf. Heitink, "De geestelijk verzorger als hermeneut," and the description by Anthony Verheule of a "terror-free space" in chaplaincy in Verheule, *Angst en bevrijding*.

("living human document")[15] as far as possible in the context of their social and physical network ("living human web")[16]. Relational aspects of the care accompaniment are recognized and employed. Intercultural, interreligious, intersectional, and gender-related competences are drawn upon.

Surroundings

In the second place the surroundings and the organizational context[17] of the care are ascertained. That includes the influence of the physical and organizational surroundings (health care institution, prison, military organization, home care network, *et cetera*) on the person and their situation. Issues common to that context are signaled and analyzed.

Meaning and Worldview

In the triangle of interaction, the chaplain explores how meaning and worldview (in all four dimensions) play or can play a role in relation to the other, their needs, and (re)sources and to the surroundings.

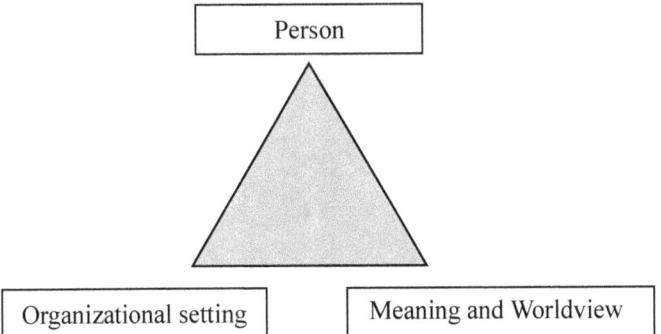

Figure 22.1: Triangle of Interaction

> *Example: RC Hospital*
>
> In oncological rehab a woman struggles with persistent fatigue and a lack of energy ("Energy *and* Inspiration," Chapter 4). On the line person—meaning the chaplain suggests after some time

---

15. Boisen, *Out of the depths*; Boisen, *The Exploration of the Inner World*.
16. Miller-McLemore, "The Living Human Web."
17. McClure, "Pastoral Theology as the Art."

to work on "inspiration." The woman responds positively, as she feels "dried up." On the line meaning—organizational (i.e., care) surroundings the chaplain introduces the term "inspiration" in the interdisciplinary team and suggests a relation between the lack of energy and the lack of inspiration. The (worldview) term "inspiration" initially encounters resistance in the team, but after some discussions working on inspiration is added to the rehab plan, in the line organizational (care) surroundings—person.

Less prevalent but not absent in the case studies is the given that the interactions in the triangle are situated within larger cultural and social contexts that in various ways influence the interactions. See figure 22.2. Some of them affect the way persons think about the nature and relevance of religion and worldview or about the identity (task) of the chaplain, as in the initial resistance to the term inspiration.[18] Other aspects are more specific as in the way Tjeerd Van de Meer analyzes how cultural and social representations of freedom conflict with the perceptions and actual options of young people in juvenile care.[19] Still others reflect contemporary views or values with regard to autonomy and self-control ("The Enigma of a Day," Chapter 5).

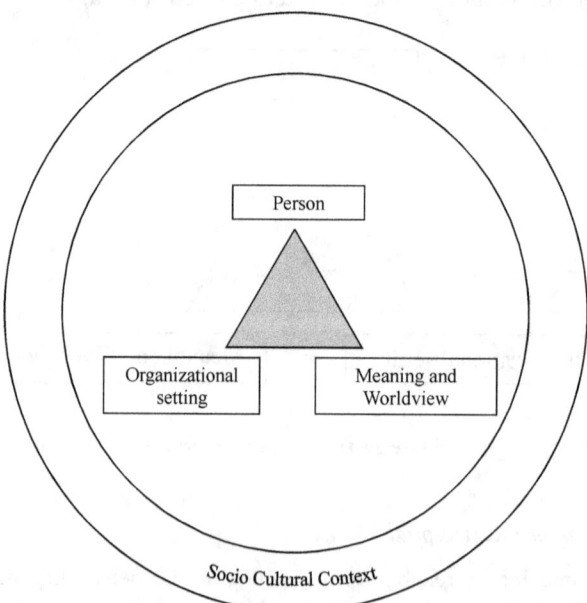

Figure 22.2: Triangle of Interaction in Context

18. See also Nolan, "He Needs to Talk!" and Pesut, "Recovering Religious Voice and Imagination" on addressing the needs of the non-religious, as discussed in Chapter 3.

19. Van der Meer, "Is MacDonald's Freedom?"

Reasons for Contact

We divide the reasons for contact into two types, occasions and issues. Often the two are closely related, but they can also differ, as in the case study "Reiteration of Ritual" (Chapter 8). The chaplain is referred to a resident following the death of the resident's daughter, but the resident only talks about childhood traumas.

Occasions

The question what chaplains do, also involves the occasions and issues they encounter. That the occasion for contact may differ from the issue that receives the most attention during the contact, is partly due to the various manners in which the contact with a chaplain come about, whether on the initiative of the other, of the chaplain, or by referral.[20] The occasion can be specific, such as the request of a ritual or confrontation with an ethical dilemma. But it can also come forth from the observation of disorientation, experience of loss, emotional stress, social isolation, moral injury, fear of death, or a desire to die, behind which another issue (of meaning) might lie. The occasion for contact or referral is sometimes the complexity, or a stacking of problems, out of which a more specific personal issue emerges. On occasion chaplains become involved when other care providers feel perplexed or powerless in the face of problematic patient conduct or lack of progress in the treatment. Or clients may turn to chaplains to talk about how they feel treated by care providers.

Issues

The issues that are present in the case studies are manifold but are generally related to the self and one's place in the world: identity and integrity, relations and connectedness, lust for life and life orientation, guilt and shame, loss and injury, anger and indignation, pain and suffering, sickness and death, desire and grief, vulnerability and vitality, weakness and strength, belief and doubt, perspective and hope.[21] In the evaluations of case studies it often

---

20. The variation in ways that contact arose and the subsequent forms that care took on was explicated in the report of the RC Hospital Care in Körver, "Wie neemt het initiatief." See also Chapter 13.

21. In the RC Hospital Care, the existential themes or dilemmas that Irvin Yalom identified proved fruitful in the analysis: isolation and relatedness, freedom and responsibility, meaning and meaninglessness, death and mortality. Like the four dimensions of meaning and worldview such categories serve as aids in the analysis ("sensitizing

became clear that in a single case study different dimensions of meaning played a role, for example, social isolation and exclusion in the existential dimension, the relation to a religious community in the spiritual dimension, stigmatization and/or inappropriate behavior in the ethical dimension, and the alienating experience of residing in a prison or care institution in the aesthetic dimension.

> *Example: Mixed Research Community*
>
> Charly is a young man with an intellectual disability and autism ("A Church for Charly," Chapter 9). To assure his rest, he generally stays in his own room and has limited contact with others (existential dimension). Because the bustle of a worship service is too much for him, his mother asks if he can receive the eucharist in his room (spiritual dimension). Once a month the chaplain celebrates a ritual of breaking and sharing the Communion host with Charly in his room. The ritual follows a rigid set pattern (aesthetic dimension). Variation causes Charly to become restless. During the ritual the conduct of Charly moves from a high level of tension to almost relaxed. The ritual has a positive influence on the conduct and well-being of Charly, and presumably affects his sense of assurance (existential and spiritual dimensions). Although the ritual was initiated for existential and spiritual reasons, and meets his (legal and ethical) right to freedom and practice of his religion, it in the meantime meets the criteria of being an indicated provision of care (from a care ethics point of view).

Method: Models and Strategies

In the performance of their repertoire chaplains employ a broad palette of methods and models with regard to (re)construction of life narratives, accompaniment of grief and dying, recovery, systemic issues, moral counseling, *et cetera*. Behind those methods and models lie practical-theoretical approaches of narrative, diaconal, and contextual nature.[22] In addition, more fundamental theoretical concerns derived from phenomenology, hermeneutics, aesthetics, and symbolic interaction play a role. Along with the models a number of "strategies" are employed, partly derived from counseling techniques, such as empathy, creating space, offering recognition, confronting ambivalences, provocation, and reframing, and partly derived

---

concepts"). Cf. Yalom, *Existential Psychotherapy*, and Körver, "Wie neemt het initiatief."

22. See Goosen, "Geestelijke verzorging."

from broader pastoral-psychological or worldview approaches, such as validation, containment, mindfulness, education, advice, multi-sided partiality, imagination, voice dialogue, reminiscence, life review, moral counseling, and engendering hope. Related to some strategies are certain roles that chaplains fulfill, such as guide, container, or intermediate, that sometimes only become evident during or after the care process. (More will be said on roles below.) Together the methods, models, strategies, and approaches constitute a professional body of knowledge, both practical and theoretical, that is an integration of formal professional knowledge, work, and life experience, and specific practices in a relational context.[23]

We summarize the methods, models, strategies, and approaches drawn from the body of knowledge under the term "method," in the etymological sense of the pursuit of a way or path. The use of method is in the case studies at times formal, systematic, and explicit, at other times informal, partial, and implicit. The application of method is twofold. Initially, method is employed to map, that is, to analyze the situation. Examples are narrative analysis or a model for end of life care to address certain issues.[24] In the second place, method is employed to guide a care process or intervention for helping the other. Examples are use of narrative models to help someone to gain insight into one's life story and clarify issues and the use of moral counseling to problematize and reframe a suicide pact.[25]

Here we remark again, as in Chapter 3, that in the case studies of the CSP little explicit use was made of formal assessment tools, as are often advanced in English language literature on chaplaincy. The analysis of the situation is simultaneously a process of mapping the situation and offering care accompaniment along the way.[26] Using various search schemas, the process often proceeds in a labyrinthic manner.[27] In a process of exchange and dialogue, of attentiveness and attunement, between the person and the chaplain, the analysis becomes a shared assessment of the situation in

---

23. This identification of a threefold source of a *body of knowledge* was made by the RC Mental Health Care. See Muthert, "Daar aansluiten."

24. Leget, *Art of Living*.

25. Muthert et al., "Re-Evaluating a Suicide Pact."

26. We understand the use of the term analysis here to parallel the use in psychotherapy in which analyzing the situation, working through the situation, and obtaining results go hand in hand. The RC Hospital spoke of "inventory, ordering, and analysis." Körver, "Wie neemt het initiatief," 155.

27. For the term "search schema" see Chapter 14, "Apprehending Goals." For the term "labyrinthic" see Chapter 20, "Chaplain Researchers." See also below under "Goals: General and Specific."

question. In that process observation (phenomenology) and interpretation (hermeneutics) play a crucial role.

Made in Holland

Five particular methods with Dutch origins were often used in the case studies. We highlight them here: two models of narrative analysis, the diamond model for end-of-life care, contextual pastoral care, and moral counseling.

Existential narrative analysis. Tjeu Van Knippenberg developed an existential, narrative approach to spiritual guidance and religious identity that he understood as "existential care for the soul."[28] The question of identity, "Who am I?," is contextualized in the conditions of time, space, and transcendence. The question of temporality, "When am I?" seeks to understand the direction of one's life in a dialectic of change and continuity. The question of space, "Where am I?", addresses the theme of connectedness in a dialectic of individuation and participation. The question of transcendence, "From where and for what am I?", is a question about the ground of one's existence in a dialectic of autonomy and heteronomy. Van Knippenberg assigns to each condition, or question, a theological theme: to time the relation of hope and despair, to space the relation of love and fear, and to transcendence the relation of faith and disbelief (or doubt). Van Knippenberg understands the soul as a capacity in humans to mediate between immanence and transcendence in the search for meaning, and he seeks to provide parameters for that search with his existential categories. The method is hermeneutic in its intention to contribute to the self-understanding of persons.

Literary narrative analysis. A more literary narrative approach is taken by Ruard Ganzevoort and Jan Visser.[29] Ganzevoort and Visser use categories of literary analysis, such as structure and plot, perspective, tone, roles, relational positioning, and intended audience. The literary categories offer an open hermeneutic space in which one can observe and analyze narrative processes. The personal stories may be or may become related to "canonical" narratives in order to render them more plausible or allow for reframing. Narrativity thus serves to underscore the parallels between written texts and living humans and thus enliven the notion of "living human documents."[30] The

---

28. Van Knippenberg, *Towards Religious Identity.*

29. Ganzevoort and Visser, *Zorg voor het verhaal*; Ganzevoort, "Narrative Approaches."

30. Boisen, *Out of the Depths*; Boisen, *The Exploration of the Inner World.*

basic goal of the method is to relate the stories of persons to the story of God.

Contextual Pastoral Care. The method of contextual pastoral care developed by Hanneke Meulink-Korff and Aad Van Rhijn[31] builds further on the systemic approach of Ivan Böszörményi-Nagy,[32] using philosophical and anthropological understandings drawn from Martin Buber[33] and Emmanuel Lévinas.[34] Notions of loyalty, indebtedness, entitlement, exoneration, responsibility, and (in)justice are rooted in an ethical understanding of others as both gift and disturbance. Practical techniques such as a dialogical attitude and multi-directed partiality allow the pastor to assist others in assessing and dealing with their (intergenerational) relations and the ethical dimensions of them.

Art of Dying. In the diamond model of end-of-life care, Carlo Leget[35] reinterprets categories from medieval approaches to the art of dying into contemporary tensions and arranges them around an understanding of inner space. Leget understands inner space as a state of mind in which persons can relate freely to what is going on in and around them. The tensions are formulated in word pairs: I—the other; doing—undergoing; holding on—letting go; remembering—forgetting, and believing—knowing, all in relation to the issues one faces when confronted with death: relations to significant others, undergoing treatment, beliefs concerning death and beyond, *et cetera*. The model can be used analytically to assist the chaplain in recognizing and locating issues that may need to be addressed, or as a scheme for exploration with the patient of challenges to be faced. The aim to enlarge the inner space of the patient is aided by the inner space (or non-anxious presence[36]) of the chaplain.

Moral Counseling. In a model for moral counseling Jack De Groot and others[37] combine a contemplative approach to counseling[38] with an ethical framework based on the work of Paul

---

31. Meulink-Korf and Van Rhijn, *The Unexpected Third.*

32. Böszörményi-Nagy et al., *Between Give and Take*; Böszörményi-Nagy, *Foundations of Contextual Therapy.*

33. Buber, *I and Thou.*

34. Lévinas et al., *Humanism of the Other.*

35. Leget, *Art of Living.*

36. Friedman, *Generation to Generation*; Friedman, *The Art of Jewish Pastoral Counseling.*

37. De Groot and Leget, "Moral Counselling"; De Groot and Van Hoek, "Contemplative Listening in Moral Issues."

38. Evers, "Contemplative Listening."

Ricœur.[39] In counseling the chaplain provides a space for the client to express a moral dilemma and the different perspectives that the client has on the dilemma. The chaplain then analyzes what the client has said from the viewpoint of what has been said about "a good life for oneself, with and for others, in just institutions." By differentiating between values, norms and convictions in relation to self, others and institutions, a grid in the form of a moral house with nine rooms can be constructed. With the client the chaplain reflects on that moral house, what moral space is most significant, and what can help the client to come to a decision regarding the moral dilemma.

Summary: What do chaplains do in direct care for others?

Chaplains work with a broad repertoire of dialogical, ritual, and worldview interactions, in order to tune in to the other person and their situation, discern the surroundings and their influence, and address issues of existential, spiritual, ethical, and aesthetic nature. They make use of a varied body of knowledge that includes practical and theoretical methods, models, strategies, and approaches. The foundation of their care lies in proactive, non-judgmental availability (presence) and the offer of a (confidential) care relation. The process of presence, observation, interpretation, analysis, and intervention is part of a continual but differentiated process.

WHY, AND TO WHAT ENDS, DO CHAPLAINS DO WHAT THEY DO?

We ascertain three perspectives on the objectives of chaplains: the values and intentions that guide their activities under the sign of a shared humanity; the goals that are pursued, of both a general and specific nature; and the roles that chaplains fulfill and seek to fulfill, expressed in both functional and metaphorical terms.

Values and Intentions: "Shared Humanity"

Chaplains are guided by a cluster of values such as human dignity and equality (justice), freedom (of religion and conscience), responsibility and

---

39. Ricœur, *Oneself as Another*.

compassion, personal and physical integrity, and resistance to social exclusion and stigmatization. Those values lead to compassionate human interactions that are expressed in availability, faithfulness, reciprocity, solidarity, and advocacy. They also express a sense of shared humanity,[40] in which both commonality and diversity are recognized. The values also shape what chaplains hope to foster in the focus on another person and their situation: sense of security, (inner) space, rest, perseverance, clarification, reflection, trust, connection, empowerment, or resilience. The orientation towards such values functions as both a (pre)condition and a general goal of chaplaincy care.

Goals: General and Specific

Although many chaplains are hesitant to (explicitly) formulate goals ahead of time, the reviews of the case studies show that goals were in fact pursued. Implicit questions and goals arise in the process of accompaniment, based in part on search schemas derived from training and practice.[41] One can speak of *labyrinthic purposiveness*.[42] Even if the path seems to diverge, one finds a way to the center of things. The goals appear in two forms. In the first place there is the guiding character of general goals derived from the value orientations discussed above and from meaning systems and worldviews. In relation to the latter, chaplains address issues of worldview and spiritual need, access religious (re)sources and support spiritual coping and a sense of coherence.[43]

At the same time and in the process of care and attunement other, more specific and concrete goals arise in relation to identity, recovery, grief, personal growth, relations, worldview or ethical issues, *et cetera*. In certain contexts, such as psychiatric care and detention a concept like recovery can also serve as a general goal, albeit from the particular perspective of chaplaincy.[44] The nature of the goals is at times existential (e.g. a greater sense of

---

40. For this emphasis see: Firet, *Het agogisch moment*; Ganzevoort and Visser, *Zorg voor het verhaal*. The Dutch term is "evenmenselijkheid," literally "like humanity." In the RC Eldercare the "employment" of reciprocity and equality were described in terms of method in De Groot et al, "Van ambacht en kunst," 186.

41. See Chapter 14.

42. Den Toom, *The Chaplain-Researcher*, 225; also 158–60. For more on the research by Den Toom, see Chapters 17, 19, and 20 in this volume.

43. The RC Hospital referred to this term of Antonovsky, that includes comprehensibility, manageability, and meaningfulness. See Antonovsky, *Unraveling the Mystery of Health*.

44. Rosie and Den Toom conducted a secondary analysis of a number of case studies on the basis of the CHIME-model of recovery (Leamy et al., "Conceptual Framework

freedom, feeling of worthiness), spiritual (basic trust, learning to pray again), ethical (appropriating other values, decision on treatment), or aesthetic (acceptance of changes in one's body, creating a place for remembrance).

Another distinction can be made between goals directed towards feelings and dispositions (restfulness, sense of spaciousness), behavior (expressing emotions, working on a relationship), and concerns of meaning and worldview (sense of dignity, a new relation to one's life story). The same distinctions will return below in discussing the effects of chaplaincy. As indicated, some participants in the CSP were not accustomed to formulating care goals explicitly. In the accompaniment process goals were often pursued implicitly and only explicitly formulated in the writing process, sometimes even retrospectively as a reflection on the effects.

Roles

Chaplains are aware that they fulfill certain roles in their care. In that sense the roles are part of what chaplains do (research question 1). In the final reports from the RCs, naming the roles is more often a part of the answer to the second research question, why chaplains do what they do. In some case studies the role or roles that the chaplain fulfilled only became clear in the review of the case study in the RC. The roles also express certain intentions of the chaplains. One chooses to fulfill a specific role in a specific situation.

Some roles are expressed in functional terms. At the foreground is often the role of a representative, either of a particular religious or other worldview denomination, or of the realm of meaning and worldview in general. Other functional roles that were named are: confidant, leader, spiritual mentor, intermediary, container, care provider, and advocate. Other roles are put in metaphorical terms: pastor, guide, signpost, sounding board, bridge, liaison, *et cetera*, of which some are implicitly or explicitly connected to worldview and cultural sources. The distinction is fluid. In secondary analysis of a number of case studies using thematic analysis, Niels Den Toom identified four roles: person of trust, representant of God/the Good, intertextual interpreter, and symbolizer of healing.[45] These roles serve to integrate values and goals, expertise and positioning of chaplains, as the basic elements of their professionalism.

---

for Personal Recovery") and contributions of chaplaincy to recovery, in: Rosie and Den Toom, "Spiritual Care and Recovery."

45. See Chapter 17.

Summary: Why do chaplains do what they do?

Chaplains are guided by a number of fundamental human values, such as dignity and freedom, that color their care provision (availability, solidarity, reciprocity) and their orientation towards the other (sense of security, space, empowerment). They pursue general goals with regard to values and meaning in order to support worldview clarification and spiritual coping. In addition, they focus on specific goals of the other with regard to feelings, behavior, and worldview orientation. In doing so they fulfill roles as religious representative, confidant, intermediary, and accompanier.

WHAT ARE THE EFFECTS AND OUTCOMES OF WHAT CHAPLAINS DO?

In the CSP we were primarily interested in effects and outcomes that had been reported or confirmed by the client, a significant other, or an involved professional, or that had been otherwise observed. The reported and observed effects were of three sorts: subjective experiences in feelings and dispositions, physical and concrete behavior, and more reflective outcomes regarding insight, self-understanding, wisdom, meaning and worldview. Often the outcomes could be distinguished but not separated as they were interrelated in a "chain of effects."

Feelings and Dispositions

For many clients a significant outcome was the experience of being "really" seen and heard, of being listened to, of "really making contact," of being able to express themselves and tell someone what was going on. In such encounters they experienced recognition, affirmation, and encouragement, with as a result "inner space,"[46] a sense of freedom, the ability to let go. That led variably to a reduction of sorrow and despondency, alleviation of feelings of guilt and of the desire to die (or in palliative settings to the acceptance of death), or to an increase of rest, relaxation, positive perspective, and hope.

---

46. Leget, *Art of Living*.

Behavior

Outcomes with regard to behavior took on three forms. A number of changes of behavior had to do with abilities or new patterns that were enabled as a result of chaplaincy care: accepting and expressing emotions, fewer claims on others, endurance, and a freer relation to loss, illness or treatment. Some behavioral changes had a process character: ability to (actively) grieve, personal growth, working on maturity, or working on a relationship. Other changes involved a specific resolution or decision: seek help, begin a recovery trajectory, seek contact with someone again, or make an (ethical) decision with regard to treatment or abstention.

Wisdom, Meaning, and Worldview

In many instances the gain as a result of contact with a chaplain was insight, self-understanding, and the ability to reflect. Insight into one's own life story, autobiographical competence,[47] was a significant part of that. A new sense of identity and dignity often played a role, but also an altered appraisal of vulnerability, relationships, life goals, and of what makes life worthwhile. Clients became aware (again) of their relation to a worldview background. Here again the dimensions of meaning and worldview provide a differentiated picture. In the existential dimension, for example, there was a freer relation to previous life events or to the enigmas of life, and acceptance of fragility. In the spiritual dimension clients (re)discovered sources of inspiration and strength, renewed faith, or found hope and trust. In the ethical dimension ethical decisions were made, value orientations realigned, and indignation over treatment became a motor for change. In the aesthetical dimension physical changes were accepted or nature was (re)discovered as a source of renewal. Many of these effects can be understood as forms of religious and worldview wisdom.

Chains of Effects

In many case studies the three sorts of outcomes were closely related to each other and influenced each other in a "chain of effects."[48] By attaining inner space, a sense of trust increased. Through an experience of trust and acceptance in a group session, memories were called forth so that it became

---

47. Van Knippenberg, *Towards Religious Identity*.

48. The term comes from the RC Eldercare, in De Groot et al., "Van ambacht en kunst," 184.

possible to reevaluate difficult experiences in the past, with as a result a more positive view of self. Finding a modus to continue living improved relations with family members. As it is not always clear what precedes what in the chain of effects, the discernment of a simple causality is hardly possible. The relation of effects to each other is often reciprocal in reinforcing each other, and the path taken is often labyrinthic in nature.[49] That makes it difficult to attribute specific outcomes to specific care processes or interventions. That seems to reflect the way in which the repertoire of chaplains is described as an interrelated whole in a triangle of interaction. The whole of the care has an effect that cannot easily be traced back to a single part of the whole. Not only are the variables virtually unlimited, but in human (dialogical) interaction all sorts of subjective aspects and perspectives play a role, so that effects are often gradually shaped rather than directly induced.

Summary: What are the effects and outcomes of what chaplains do?

Chaplaincy care leads to a broad palette of outcomes in feelings, behavior, and meaning in life, dependent upon the situation and need of the other. With regard to affect (feelings and dispositions), the basic experience of being seen and listened to is highly valued. As a result, recognition, rest, perspective, freedom, and inner space arise. With regard to behavior, people develop new patterns of dealing with emotions, grief, expectations of others, and endurance in difficult situations. They also set concrete steps in relation to recovery, relations, and ethical decisions. With regard to meaning and worldview, the gain is often insight into one's own behavior or motives, wisdom, clarification of life story, and a new sense of identity. Clients experience an increase in freedom (existential dimension), hope and trust (spiritual dimension), responsibility (ethical dimension), and acceptance in body perception (aesthetic dimension), dependent upon the situation. The gain expresses itself in new convictions and new behavior (decisions) with regard to life choices, values, and social functioning.

GOOD PRACTICES

In reflecting on case studies and identifying what they understood to be good practices, the RCs often spoke in intentional terms like faithfulness,

---

49. Den Toom, "The Chaplain-Researcher." See also Chapter 20.

allowing space, staying in the here and now, and unconditional presence.[50] That hardly sounds very specific or concrete. On the other hand, those formulations indicate that certain dispositions and intentions have a "performative effect"[51] or stand in a chain of influence and effect. Even where the descriptions are more concrete, the situation remains, as indicated above, that the three basic elements of the repertoire of chaplains, dialogical interaction, ritual performance, and working with worldview sources, form an interrelated whole and that they are performed on a relational foundation of availability (presence) and value orientation. That interrelated practice, that artisanship as a whole, needs to be recognized when specific forms of care, such as ritual renewal, use of art forms, group work, interdisciplinary interventions, *et cetera*, are labeled separately as good practices.

The label "good practices" functions, therefore, in two manners. Within a case study good practice can refer to a specific, exemplary intervention, such as the introduction of worldview language in an interdisciplinary team ("Energy *and* Inspiration," Chapter 4) or the use of an art image as means of communication in counseling ("The Enigma of a Day," Chapter 5). Good practice can also refer to a case study as a whole in which dialogical interaction, ritual performance, and working with worldview resources are integrated in the whole of care in order to induce an outcome ("Wounded Warrior," Chapter 10). In this study we have provided examples of both, specific interventions that prove effective and case studies that exemplify to a greater or lesser degree the aspect of integration to attain a goal. What our answer to the research question in the three preceding paragraphs provides is a framework, and in some respects criteria for good practices, that have been drawn from an analysis of multiple examples of (more or less) good practices.

The question is then on what basis the predicate "good" is assigned to a practice, whether as an integrated whole or a specific intervention. That is partially a normative evaluation. The interventions and case studies represent good practices to the extent that they allow the values that are fundamental to chaplaincy to be realized. An example is the use of validation as an affirmative counseling intervention to strengthen the sense of dignity of a resident, or the offer of contact that reduces the social isolation of a client. Or to put it differently, the intentions and interventions are good when they address and contribute to the good of the other, their aspirations and needs, their values and wellbeing.

---

50. See, e.g., De Groot et al., "Van ambacht en kunst."
51. Walton, *Wederwaardigheden & methoden*, 134.

In the second place, "good" has a more pragmatic meaning, where it becomes evident that in a particular situation a chaplain in an appropriate and adequate, that is, competent manner does what can be expected of a chaplain, such as tuning in to the situation of the other, pointing to aspects of meaning, or carefully performing a ritual. In a religious and worldview profession as chaplaincy, the two meanings of good, as a reflection of values and as reference to competent care, are closely intertwined, even if they do not fully coincide. The distinction was not explicated in the format and was seldom articulated in the RCs. Both meanings of good occur in the identification of good practices.[52] Together they provide criteria for good care by a chaplain.

The ascription of the term good practices rests, finally, upon three aspects of the case studies. The first is the persuasiveness of the description itself, the case that is made with the help of the format in recounting a coherent whole of presence, observation, attunement, exploration, interpretation, analysis, intervention, and (chain of) effects in which the values and competency of chaplaincy are evident. The description itself must possess a convincing character. The second aspect lies in the confirmation, where available, of the description in the feedback of those involved. The third moment is provided in the peer review by professional colleagues by means of analysis and consensus in the RCs. The good of good practices, therefore, has two layers, normative and pragmatic, that are confirmed in two, preferably three steps of coherent description, feedback, and peer review.

In describing what chaplains do, we stated that the distinctive character of chaplaincy lies in the interconnectedness of different aspects (repertoire, method, values, worldview, *et cetera*). A logical consequence is that in order to speak of good practices we must likewise observe the interconnectedness. On the basis of the findings of the CSP we arrive at a proposal for speaking of good practices in chaplaincy. A described accompaniment process in direct care for clients stands as a *good practice* when the following are applicable:

a. The chaplain employs the characteristic repertoire within the interaction triangle (what?), pursues goals that are related to the values and theoretical basis of the profession (why?), and contributes to concrete and appropriate effects in the dispositions, behavior, and life orientation of the other (with what results?).

---

52. Walton and Körver, "Dutch Case Studies Project."

b. The acts and activities of the chaplain mirror the competency of chaplaincy according to professional standards and the values of chaplaincy as a profession with regard to meaning and worldview.

c. The care provision of the chaplain forms a coherent whole that is reliably and convincingly described and that is confirmed and consented to by concerned parties and professional colleagues.

As a research endeavor the CSP was built upon a combination of research questions, the format, and the procedures of the research communities and the academic advisory board. A compliment was offered in the research on professionalization of chaplains as a result of participation. It was through that combination of approaches that the various aspects of what chaplaincy is and what good practices are, became visible as an interconnected whole, both differentiated and integrated.

REFERENCES

Antonovsky, Aaron. *Unraveling the Mystery of Health: How People Manage Stress and Stay Well.* San Francisco: Jossey-Bass, 1988.

Boisen, Anton T. *Out of the depths: An Autobiographical Study of Mental Disorder and Religious Experience.* New York: Harper, 1960.

———. *The Exploration of the Inner World: A Study of Mental Disorder and Religious Experience.* Philadelphia: University of Pennsylvania Press, 1971.

Böszörményi-Nagy, Ivan. *Foundations of Contextual Therapy.* New York: Brunner-Mazel, 1987.

Böszörményi-Nagy, Ivan, et al. *Between Give and Take: A Clinical Guide to Contextual Therapy.* New York: Brunner-Mazel, 1986.

Buber, Martin. *I and Thou.* Edinburgh: T. & T. Clark, 1958.

De Groot, Jack, et al. "OG Ouderenzorg: Van ambacht en kunst tot specialisme." In *Richting, Repertoire en Resultaat. Uitkomsten van het Nederlandse Case Studies Project Geestelijke Verzorging (2016–2021)*, edited by Jacques Körver, et al., 180–89. PThU–UCGV, 2023.

De Groot, Jack, and Carlo Leget. "Moral Counselling: A Method in Development." *Journal of Pastoral Care & Counseling* 65.1 (2011) 1–14.

De Groot, Jack, and Maria E. C. Van Hoek. "Contemplative Listening in Moral Issues: Moral Counseling Redefined in Principles and Method." *Journal of Pastoral Care & Counseling* 71.2 (2017) 106–13.

Den Toom, Niels. *The Chaplain-Researcher: The Perceived Impact of Participation in a Dutch Research Project on Chaplains' Professionalism.* Utrecht: Eburon, 2022.

Evers, Hans. "Contemplative Listening: A Rhetorical-Critical Approach to Facilitate Internal Dialog." *Journal of Pastoral Care & Counseling* 71.2 (2017) 114–21.

Firet, Jacob. *Het agogisch moment in het pastoraal optreden.* Kampen: Kok, 1988.

Friedman, Edwin H. *Generation to Generation: Family Process in Church and Synagogue.* New York: Guilford, 1985.

Friedman, Michelle S. *The Art of Jewish Pastoral Counseling: A Guide for All Faiths.* Psyche and Soul, vol. 1. London: Routledge, 2017.
Ganzevoort, Ruard. "Narrative Approaches." In *The Wiley-Blackwell Companion to Practical Theology,* edited by Bonnie J. Miller-McLemore, The Wiley Blackwell Companions to Religion. Chichester, UK: Wiley Blackwell, 2014.
Ganzevoort, Ruard, and Jan Visser. *Zorg voor het verhaal: achtergrond, methode en inhoud van pastorale begeleiding.* Utrecht: Meinema, 2018.
Goosen, Ramon. "Geestelijke verzorging volgens plan. De verhouding tussen de relationele grondhouding en de concrete doelgerichtheid in de beroepspraktijk van geestelijk verzorgers in een ziekenhuiscontext." Masters thesis, Tilburg University, 2020.
Heitink, Gerben. "De geestelijk verzorger als hermeneut." *Tijdschrift Geestelijke Verzorging* 4.14 (2000) 21–29.
Körver, Jacques. "OG Ziekenhuis: Wie neemt het initiatief, hoe, waarom en waartoe?" In *Richting, Repertoire en Resultaat. Uitkomsten van het Nederlandse Case Studies Project Geestelijke Verzorging (2016-2021),* edited by Jacques Körver, et al., 145–68. Utrecht: PThU–UCGV, 2023.
Leamy, Mary, et al. "Conceptual Framework for Personal Recovery in Mental Health: Systematic Review and Narrative Synthesis." *British Journal of Psychiatry* 199.6 (2011) 445–52.
Leget, Carlo. *Art of Living, Art of Dying: Spiritual Care for a Good Death.* London: Kingsley, 2017.
Lévinas, Emmanuel, et al. *Humanism of the Other.* Urbana: University of Illinois Press, 2006.
McClure, Barbara J. "Pastoral Theology as the Art of Paying Attention: Widening the Horizons." *International Journal of Practical Theology* 12.2 (2009) 189–210.
Meulink-Korf, Hanneke, and Aat Van Rhijn. *The Unexpected Third: Contextual Pastoral Care, Counselling and Ministry: An Introduction and Reflection.* Wellington: Christian Literature Fund, 2016.
Miller-McLemore, Bonnie J. "The Living Human Web: A Twenty-five Year Retrospective." *Pastoral Psychology* 67.3 (2018) 305–21.
Morton, Nelle. *The Journey Is Home.* Boston: Beacon, 1985.
Muthert, Hanneke. "OG GGZ: Daar aansluiten waar mensen niet willen zijn." In *Richting, Repertoire en Resultaat. Uitkomsten van het Nederlandse Case Studies Project Geestelijke Verzorging (2016-2021),* edited by Jacques Körver, et al., 190–201. Utrecht: PThU–UCGV, 2023.
Muthert, Hanneke, et al. "Re-Evaluating a Suicide Pact. Embodied Moral Counselling in a Dutch Case Study of Mental Healthcare Chaplaincy." *Tidsskrift for Praktisk Teologi* 15 (2019) 81–89
Nettleford, Rex. *Inward Stretch Outward Reach: A Voice from the Caribbean.* London: Macmillan Caribbean, 1993.
Nolan, Steve. "'He Needs to Talk!' A Chaplain's Case Study of Nonreligious Spiritual Care." *Journal of Health Care Chaplaincy* 22.1 (2016) 1–16.
Pesut, Barbara. "Recovering Religious Voice and Imagination: A Response to Nolan's Case Study "He Needs to Talk!"" *Journal of Health Care Chaplaincy* 22.1 (2016) 28–39.
Potts, Kenneth. "Martin Buber's 'Healing Dialogue' in Marital Therapy: A Case Study." *Journal of Pastoral Care* 48.4 (1994) 325–38.

Ricœur, Paul. *Oneself as Another*. Chicago: University of Chicago Press, 2008.
Rosie, Sujin., and Niels Den Toom. "Spiritual Care and Recovery in Mental Health Care. An Analysis of Spiritual Care According to CHIME." In *Recovery: The Interface between Psychiatry and Spiritual Care*, edited by Erik Olsman et al., 38-50. Utrecht: Eburon, 2023.
Schuhmann, Carmen, and Theo Pleizier. "OG Defensie: Onder militairen en tussen mensen." In *Richting, Repertoire en Resultaat. Uitkomsten van het Nederlandse Case Studies Project Geestelijke Verzorging (2016-2021)*, edited by Jacques Körver et al., 169-79. Utrecht: PThU-UCGV, 2023.
Van der Meer, Tjeerd. "Is MacDonald's Freedom?" In *Learning from Case Studies in Chaplaincy: Towards Practice Based Evidence & Professionalism*, edited by Renske Kruizinga et al., 147-52. Utrecht: Eburon, 2020.
Van Knippenberg, Tjeu. *Towards Religious Identity: An Exercise in Spiritual Guidance*. Leiden: Brill, 2002.
Verhagen, Peter J. "The Soul Is on Air; Love Is Her Weight." In *The Long and Winding Road: Religion and Mental Health through the Years*, edited by Marinus H. F. Van Uden, and Peter J. Verhagen, 181-202. International Series in Mental Health and Religion 5. Düren: Shaker, 2022.
Verheule, Anthonie F. *Angst en bevrijding: theologisch en psychologisch handboek voor pastorale werkers*. Baarn: Callenbach, 1997.
Walton, Martin. "OG Gemengd: Multifocale geestelijke verzorging." In *Richting, Repertoire en Resultaat. Uitkomsten van het Nederlandse Case Studies Project Geestelijke Verzorging (2016-2021)*, edited by Jacques Körver, et al., 135-44. Utrecht: PThU-UCGV, 2023.
———. "Beantwoording vraagstelling van het CSP." In *Richting, Repertoire en Resultaat. Uitkomsten van het Nederlandse Case Studies Project Geestelijke Verzorging (2016-2021)*, edited by Jacques Körver, et al., 58-72. Utrecht: PThU-UCGV, 2023.
———. *Hoe waait de wind? : interpretatie van geestelijke verzorging door cliënten in de ggz*. Tilburg: KSGV, 2014.
———. *Wederwaardigheden & methoden: zaligsprekingen als zoekrichtingen in seizoenen van ziekte, zinvragen & zorg*. Inaugural Address. Groningen: Protestant Theological University, 2014.
Walton, Martin., and Jacques Körver. "Dutch Case Studies Project in Chaplaincy Care: A Description and Theoretical Explanation of the Format And Procedures." *Health and Social Care Chaplaincy* 5.2 (2017) 257-80.
Yalom, Irvin D. *Existential Psychotherapy*. New York: Basic Books, 1980.

23

Looking Back and Forward

—Martin Walton, Jacques Körver, Niels den Toom

"Loves mysteries in soules doe grow,
But yet the body is his booke."

John Donne[1]

ARTISANSHIP

Chaplaincy combines attention to mysteries and meaning with personal, pertinent, practical, and professional responses to existential and embodied needs. Chaplains read the book and support the soul.[2] In the case studies we have seen how chaplains skillfully combine the repertoire of chaplaincy in dialogue, ritual, and worldview with methodical approaches and interdisciplinary communication. We have seen how they combine roles and values with goals and outcomes. We have proposed that it is precisely the combination of these basic elements, their interaction and integration that makes chaplaincy a distinctive and efficacious profession.

In the introduction to this volume we introduced the word "artisanship" as a way of portraying the professional practice and performance of chaplaincy care. Since then we have used the term sparingly. It was rather late in the process of analyzing and writing, when we looked back and tried

---

1. Donne, "The Extasie." *The Complete Poetry*, 132, in the original seventeenth century spelling.

2. See Chapter 1 on living human document, living human web, and living human encounter.

to find a general descriptive term for what we had found. And once we arrived at the term artisanship, we also realized that the term could not easily be inserted back into what we had written in relation to some particular aspect of chaplaincy. With the term artisanship we understand the practice of chaplaincy care as an intentional, coherent, and integrated whole. As an artisan, a wood carver is skilled not only in the use of instruments, but also in recognizing the type of wood, in working with the grain of the wood, and in discerning a particular form, or beauty, that can emerge from the wood. *Mutatis mutandis*, the same holds for a photographer or a poet.

The artisanship of chaplaincy expresses itself in specific practices of care *and* in the interrelatedness of those practices as a repertoire *and* in the embeddedness of those practices in the values, meaning systems, and worldview orientations that constitute its *raison d'être, and* in professional loving wisdom, *and*, most important of all, in the familiarity with human beings, their life situations, and their inspirations and aspirations. Or to put it a bit differently, artisanship is directed towards an art and combines vision with technique, precision with creativity, knowledge with intuition. As the art of care for persons in relation to meaning and worldview, chaplaincy combines art and expertise, a vision of the good with dialogical and ritual interactions, research-informed and theory-guided interventions with reciprocity and responsiveness, the breadth of human meaning with the depth of worldview traditions. Together those elements constitute a differentiated but also integrated professional practice as an artisanship.

CONTEXTS

Our depiction of chaplaincy from the case studies reflects the Dutch context. That is evident, for example, in the prominence of the domain description as meaning and worldview with four dimensions, drawn from the Dutch professional standard. Some will miss in the Dutch case studies, on the other hand, an upfront employment of a standardized assessment instrument. We hope, however, that an acquaintance with the context of our work provides a stimulus to engage in similar work in other social and cultural contexts. Our hope is that an encounter with different cultures and different fields of chaplaincy will engender curiosity and lead to comparisons with one's own practice and theoretical background. With the help of layered and multicolored differentiations in method and interventions, a common ground and perspective for chaplaincy may become visible, and a higher level of integration established.

The Dutch Case Studies Project (CSP) brought together results from different contexts in the sense of a variety of fields of work. Although five of the six Research Communities (RCs) focused upon one particular field, our answer to the research question is drawn from case studies in different fields of chaplaincy.[3] That answer also provides first of all a framework for understanding and communicating what chaplains do, not an extensive taxonomy of activities and interventions, as Massey et al. have undertaken.[4] Tailoring that framework to different fields of work, accentuating and detailing certain parts of that work in different fields, is a task that still needs to be undertaken. For that we have indicated some directions,[5] but there is still work to be done to zoom in on particular aspects of chaplaincy, for example, to see how in multiple case studies well-defined interventions in specific contexts can lead to desired results or how rituals are constructed and performed. The "subject," to use Gary Thomas's terms, of further research remains that of detailed case studies on chaplaincy, but the "object," that is, the analytical frame, form, and focus, will need further development.[6]

Undoubtedly, connecting the diverse practice of chaplaincy with an overarching description will remain a major challenge. The risk for research is to get bogged down in concrete descriptions. For practice the risk is using too abstract descriptions of the domain of chaplaincy. Transfer is needed in both directions. A sense of mystery, meaning, and value needs to be maintained, while reading the book of empirical, embodied encounters.

The focus of the CSP was on the direct accompaniment of individuals (or small groups). That means that we can say little on the basis of our research about how all sorts of other things that chaplains do and how individual care fits into that broader context. However, the things we noticed about the contributions to community,[7] suggest that the characteristic elements we have described are applicable in other areas of chaplaincy as well. The ritual character of chapel gatherings and memorial services is evident. Supporting other professionals entails dialogue with them on motivation and inspiration, and perhaps small rituals when the going gets rough. The dialogical character of moral deliberation includes not only bioethical principles, but also perspectives and priorities drawn from personal meaning systems and world views. The values chaplains stand for guide them not only in their contacts with individuals entrusted to their care, but also in

3. Chapter 22
4. Massey et al., "What do I do?"
5. Chapter 13.
6. Thomas, "A Typology for the Case Study."
7. Chapter 18.

their contacts with other staff members and managers. In other words, the elements of dialogue, ritual, and orientation to worldview, the methodical approaches, and the values and roles of chaplaincy, are things that chaplains bring to many other contexts and complexities in their work.

METHOD

We learned a lot about research methods, especially in two respects. Chaplaincy in the Netherlands has in recent decades taken a strong hermeneutical approach, interpreting persons and their narratives, both what they say and what their situation is, in relation to religious and worldview sources and narratives. While the hermeneutical approach is very much present in the case studies, the powers of observation in a phenomenological sense became increasingly important in the search for detail and for gaining a perspective on the relation between analysis, intervention, and outcome. As it turned out, the chaplains were already very observant in the act of providing care. Three things aided in getting their observations into the description of the case study. The first was the format both in its general method and in its specific questions on sensory observations and on behavior. The second was the third person perspective that helped the chaplains to "observe" their own actions and considerations. The third was the prodding by colleagues in the RCs to be more precise and more detailed in their descriptions.

That leads to the second methodological approach that had surprising results for us, the work in RCs of chaplains under the supervision of an academic researcher. In the RCs the real work of the CSP was done. There the third person perspective could be laughed at, but also employed to help shift the focus from the personal strengths and weaknesses of the chaplain in providing care to an appreciative perception of what a case study might contribute to a better understanding of professional chaplaincy care. In the RCs professional and worldview identity was differentiated and sharpened. In the RCs the role of researcher was assumed and practiced. Through the RCs chaplains became better researchers and also better chaplains. In the RCs the heart of the CSP beat, and the soul of chaplaincy was discerned.

HARVEST

What fruits has the CSP produced? From secondary research we know that participation in the CSP led to chaplains becoming more aware of their professional identity and solidarity, working more conscientiously with theory, methods, and goals, and possessing more vocabulary to tell others what they do.[8] The surge of interest among chaplains that arose at the launch of the project was mirrored in the interest of some at the end of the project to continue in some form.

A second fruit is the adaptation of the RCs model in learning communities of chaplains in exploratory research in the Netherlands in new fields of chaplaincy care (palliative home care; care for homeless persons; disaster care; *et cetera*).[9] The university center that was created as an organizational structure for the CSP, inviting researchers from other universities to participate, later expanded to include more structured collaboration with other universities, many of whom also work together in a national, government supported center of expertise on meaning and spiritual care.[10]

There were visible fruits in the form of academic, professional, and popular publications, both in primary form as case studies as in secondary form with information or analyses.[11] There was an international conference in Amsterdam in 2019 at which case studies researchers from the US and several European countries came together. Reading and evaluating case studies has become standard in chaplaincy education programs in the Netherlands. For the Dutch setting we offer several recommendations for education, training, and research:

1. Pay detailed attention in education to dialogical and ritual interactions and their effects.
2. Devote attention in education to the reciprocity of theory and practice, moving back and forth between them, in the provision of care.
3. Offer research-oriented training in (sensory) observation, description, and collaboration.
4. Use concrete descriptions of care (case studies) in supervision, peer review, and chaplaincy departments to increase the awareness of chaplains of what they do, why, and with what effects.
5. Use concrete descriptions of care (case studies) in supervision, peer review, and chaplaincy departments to increase understanding and appreciation for worldview and professional differences between chaplains.

8. Chapter 20.

9. https://www.zonmw.nl/nl/programma/zingeving-en-geestelijke-verzorging, viewed April 8, 2024.

10. https://www.ucgv.nl/background/?lang=en, viewed April 8, 2024.

11. https://www.ucgv.nl/case-studies-project/publicaties-csp/, viewed April 8, 2024. For the international publications (in English and German) of the Dutch Case Studies Project, see Appendix E.

6. Develop the CSP format or new formats for specific contexts of chaplaincy (e.g., palliative care or rehab), for other types of chaplaincy work (e.g., working with groups, consultation, ethical deliberation, rituals, worship, or memorial services), and for other settings (e.g., diaconal work and ecclesial pastoral care).

7. Pursue further analysis of multiple case studies with regard to the relations between interventions and effects.

There were also some unexpected fruits that ripened during the project. One was the realization that ritual played a greater role in practice than in prevalent descriptions and professional standards of chaplaincy. The same can be said for how chaplains work not only extensively, but also competently with aesthetic means in ways parallel to verbal interactions. We saw that community often provides a horizon for the care for individuals. We learned that despite any differences appreciation for each other's work could grow and consensus be attained.

The Dutch Case Studies Project was a journey and as a journey both an adventure and a continual challenge. Due to the nature and the size of the project we were constantly trying to catch up with ourselves and with the practical and theoretical issues that arose. However, the momentum was kept up, despite a pandemic, by the commitment of the participants and by the opportunity that was welcomed to dialogue on engaging examples of conscientious care. At the opening plenary session of the CSP, participating chaplains were invited to introduce themselves to each other as researchers. That caused some hilarity and uneasiness, but it set in motion the collaborative effort to contribute to research on chaplaincy. Key to that was the way in which chaplains learned to investigate their own practice. Together we learned that attention to detail can develop an eye for detail, that collaboration can engender collaboration, that uniformity is not essential for a sense of unity, that complexity can spark cohesion, and that the practice of chaplaincy care is an artisanship.

REFERENCES

Donne, John. *The Complete Poetry of John Donne.* Edited by John T. Shawcross. New York: New York University Press, 1968.

Massey, Kevin, et al. "What Do I Do? Developing a Taxonomy of Chaplaincy Activities and Interventions for Spiritual Care in Intensive Care Unit Palliative Care." *BMC Palliative Care* 14.1 (2015) 10.

Thomas, Gary. "A Typology for the Case Study in Social Science Following a Review of Definition, Discourse, and Structure." *Qualitative Inquiry* 17.6 (2011) 511–21.

APPENDICES

APPENDIX A

Organogram Dutch Case Studies Project

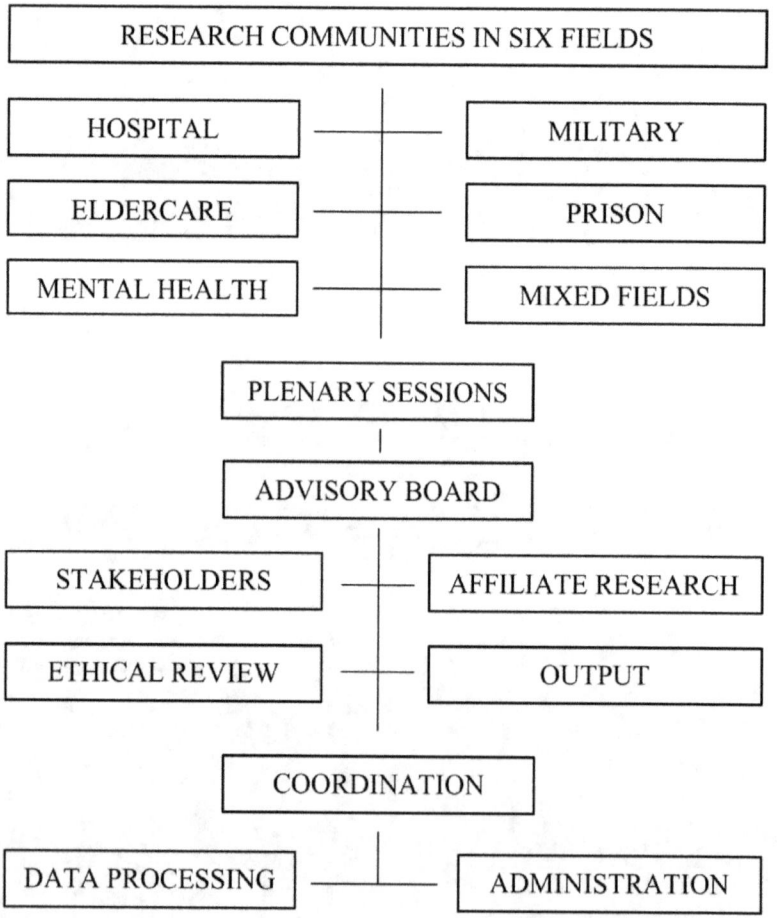

RESEARCH COMMUNITIES
8–12 chaplain-researchers chaired by one or two academic researcher(s).
6 Research Communities (RCs), 62 chaplains, and 7 chairpersons.

PLENARY SESSIONS
Convocation (2016).
Biannual meetings with all research communities.
International Conference on Case Studies Research (2019).
Concluding reports Research Communities (2021).
Presentation Final Research Report CSP (2023).

ACADEMIC ADVISORY BOARD
Research Collaboration Group (RCG):
7 chairpersons of RCs and 6 research associates from 5 universities.

STAKEHOLDERS
Employers in care organizations.
Chaplaincy services in military and prison system.
Client, branch, and professional organizations.

AFFILIATE RESEARCH
The Chaplain Researcher, PhD dissertation Niels den Toom.
Master and Bachelor theses.
Secondary analyses.
Adaptation of format for other settings.

ETHICAL REVIEW
Review by national Medical Research Ethics Committee United.
Review by local care institution ethical boards where required.
Consent forms from clients, chaplains, and chairpersons.
Data management according to Tilburg University guidelines.

OUTPUT
Valorization (enhancing the practical value of the results) by interaction between researchers and practitioners.
Data base of 101 case studies, 20+ in published form.
80+ secondary articles: reviewed, professional, and popular.

COORDINATION
Authorship format. Project development. Chairing plenary and RCG.
Cooperative agreements with chaplains, employers, and researchers.
Data processing and administration with institutional support.

APPENDIX B

Format Case Study Dutch Case Studies Project

—Martin Walton & Jacques Körver

INTRODUCTION TO THE FORMAT

Framework

Case Study

A CASE STUDY (in the framework of the Dutch Case Studies Project) is an informative and methodical description in which the accompaniment process and the contribution of (professional) chaplaincy care are demonstrated and argued with the intent of identifying (criteria or characteristics of) good practices.

Focus

The focus of the project and the format is that of direct contacts, individual or in group settings, between a professional chaplain and a client (or client system), including the context of the contacts. Other forms of contact, or chaplaincy care directed at organizational aspects, is equally worthy of research, but would require a different focus and format.

Format

For the sake of comparison and maximal gain a set format is employed. In light of the varying conditions of chaplaincy care in different contexts some flexibility is also required, for example in the use of terminology. The format is based upon examples in the literature and expanded upon with a view to the theoretical demands of the project. What follows here is a framework consisting of two phases. Not all elements will be available or relevant for all cases, but it is desirable to provide as broad a variety of description and evaluation as possible and feasible. That requires careful documentation, both with regard to protection of the involved parties and with regard to the scientific quality of the research project.

Phasing

The choice of a case and the description of it are primarily the work of the involved chaplain, though the author could be an observer (researcher or intern). The reflection and evaluation (phase 2) are situated in a case studies research community, consisting of chaplains, academic researchers, and other interested parties. In the documentation, the primary author includes the results of the discussions in the research community and submits a completed case study for approval by the research community.

The Chaplain as Researcher

The case study is to be written and discussed in the third person. That means that the chaplain submitting a case study will write and speak about him- or herself in the third person. In the discussions of the case study in the research community all, including the author, will speak of the chaplain in the third person. In that way participation in the research community is distinct from supervision (or peer review) in which personal goals and development are the focus. The primary goal of the research project is the development of the profession. *The question, for example, would not be, "Why was I (or why were you) embarrassed by this situation?" but "What is the effect of the chaplain's embarrassment on the interaction with others in the case study?"* The role of the chaplain in the case study is initially that of a practitioner who on the basis of her practice and with his practical experience submits a case study. However, in the description of the case study and in the discussions in the research community, the submitting chaplain takes on the role of co-researcher.

Accountability

Materials

The case study should be written out within a month of the last contact with the client, if not earlier. At that point additional information can have been gathered from other involved parties. In a separate document a brief list of personal data of the client is to be provided in anonymous and coded form.

The material that is provided consists of

- Reporting, partly in the form of verbatims, by the chaplain.
- Audio and video material of the contacts (optional).
- Feedback by others (clients, persons from the client system, other professional caregivers).

It is important that the case study report describes the specific and concrete activities of the chaplain and the concrete and observable responses to those activities, including detailed descriptions at key moments. The outcomes also need to be described in concrete language.

The desired length of the description in phase 1 is about 6000 words. If verbatim material is included a selection of the most relevant passages is sufficient. Material in the form of audio or video recordings, transcriptions, verbatims, that cannot be included within the case description, should be preserved in a safe manner. The length of the report on the evaluation in phase 2 should be 1000 to 1500 words.

Ethical Aspects

Although an individual case study is not a form of research for which approval by a medical-ethical review board is required, for the project as a whole, including the collection and storage of case studies material, approval has been applied for and received. In the *description* of the cases and in the *sharing* of information, close attention must be paid to the ethical, scientific, and legal frameworks of the research project.

a. Is the description sufficiently anonymous to insure and protect confidentiality?
b. Does that protection include not only the (primary) client, but also other involved parties?

c. Even if *informed consent* is not formally required, is it possible to obtain the consent of the involved parties? Where such is not possible, is a written explanation demonstrating accountability provided?

d. Has the description and interpretation of the case been checked and verified at critical points with others involved or with observing parties?

e. Is there sufficient recognition for the role and contribution of any other involved parties?

Procedure

Selection

For the development of good practices examples are needed in which chaplaincy care seems to have gone well. It is helpful to focus on the reasons or motives for the choice of a particular case, and perhaps test those reasons in dialogue with another person, for example the academic researcher. Within the framework of research on a number of case studies, criteria of variety or specialization may influence the selection. For the choice of an individual case the following perspectives can play a role.

a. Representative case from the patient group.

b. Paradigmatic case of the way the chaplain works.

c. Outsider case which by virtue of its unusual character is illuminating.

d. Critical case which tests the usual way of doing things.

It is possible that the reasons or motives for the choice of a case study only really become clear at a later moment, after comparison with other case studies.

Finalizing the Case Study

a. Someone other than the submitter takes notes on the discussion of the case study in the research community.

b. With the help of those notes the submitter writes a report on the findings of the research community, using the framework of phase 2.

c. The discussions in the research community may give occasion to altering the text of the description for the sake of clarification or correction. The alterations should remain visible in the text.

d. At the next meeting of the research community, the submitter presents a complete report that includes his/her own description *and* the written report of the findings of the research community.

e. The research community establishes the definitive text of the case study.

FORMAT

Phase 1. Description (Chaplain/Submitter)

Abstract

Provide in a few sentences a brief narrative of what the case study is about, e.g.:

- Who was the client? What was the setting? What is the subject or problem?
- How did the chaplaincy care take form? Was there a significant outcome or noteworthy characteristic?
- What was the reason for selecting the case for description?

1. Background Variables of the Person(s) in Question

Sex / Age / Living situation / Children / Education / Occupation / Religious or worldview background / Present religion or worldview / Diagnosis–Needs / Department / Size of organization / Size and composition of chaplaincy team.

2. Background and Context

a. Context: setting, institutional and physical surroundings.

b. Occasion for contact: client request, professional referral, chaplain initiative, or otherwise, including prior knowledge of the chaplain.

c. Person(s) in care: client, client system, relevant biographical information.

d. Chaplain: age, sex, education and training, position, cultural and faith background, experience, profile professional position, other relevant antecedents, preferences.
   e. Other parties involved: who and in what manner?
   f. Informed consent? In what manner was it received? If not possible, why not?
   If in written form, include as appendix.
   g. Appendices: Number? Names?

3. Accompaniment Process

   a. Initial contact, introduction, reason for contact.
   b. Exploration of the question or situation: client history, assessment tools.
   c. Clarification and interpretation of the question or situation in a spiritual sense: theories and models used.
   d. Physical observations (especially non-verbal aspects): mimicry, motoric movement, intonation, appearance, posture, eye-contact, manner in which client made contact, moods, emotional expressiveness, *et cetera*.
   e. Interactions, interventions, responses, including moments of choice, intuitions and key decisions by chaplain.
   f. Chaplaincy care plan and appointments.
   g. Outcomes, results, effects:
      - sense observations of posture, attitude, and behavior;
      - reports of effects by client, client system, or other professionals (caregivers);
      - degree to which intended goals (e.g. bereavement processes, new perspective, improvement of relations, *et cetera*) were realized.
   h. Important experiences of the client and/or chaplain, or other important aspects, not yet mentioned.

4. Communication on the Case

   f. Reporting, charting, (interdisciplinary) meetings; coordination.
   g. Evaluation with any or all parties involved.

5. Reflections and Feedback

a. Reflections by the chaplain.

b. Feedback on (the description) of the care process from the client or someone from the client system.

c. Feedback on the description from one or more other professional/caregiver(s) who had contact with the client.

6. Summary

a. What has the chaplain done, or intentionally not done (interactions, interventions, approaches)?

b. Why and for what reasons (intentions, motivations, theoretical reasons)?

c. What goal or goals did the chaplain have (purposes)?

d. What was the effect (results, outcomes)?

Phase 2. Evaluation (Research Community)

1. Observations on the Description (maximum of 20 minutes)

a. Clarification. Informative questions.

b. General comments.

2. Dimensions of Meaning, Faith, and Worldview

a. What kind of *existential* experiences or questions are central to the case study?

b. Are there *spiritual* needs, desires, or perspectives that play a role?

c. Are there *ethical* issues that play a role?

d. In what ways do *aesthetical* aspects play a role?

3. Relation of Theory and Practice

a. In what manner, i.e. with the help of what kind of approaches or methods, was care provided?

b. What role does the faith or worldview of the client, the chaplain, and/or the context play in the case?

c. What use was made, explicitly or implicitly, of theories?

d. How did the theories work in practice, and/or what reflection on theory is possible from the viewpoint of the case in question?

4. Goals and Outcomes

a. What is the result or effect? How can that be ascertained?

b. What was the intention of the chaplain?

c. Was there congruency or discrepancy between (a) and (b)? What is its significance?

5. Reflection on the Analysis in the Research Community

a. Did critical issues arise for further discussion or research?

b. Are there notable observations on the discussion in the research community?

6. Brief Summary by the Research Community

a. What has the chaplain done (interactions, interventions, approaches)?

b. Why and for what reasons (intentions, motivations, theoretical reasons)?

c. What was the effect (results, outcomes)?

d. What can be said retrospectively on the reasons for selection of the case study? What type of case study is it?

e. What would be a good title of the case study?

f. What suggestions emerge for good practices: examples, criteria, challenges?

APPENDIX C

Consent Information and Forms Dutch Case Studies Project

INFORMATION LETTER

Introduction

YOU HAVE BEEN ASKED by a chaplain to participate in the Case Studies Project, a research project that is being conducted by the Protestant Theological University and the Tilburg School of Theology. Before you decide if you want to participate in the study, it is important that you know why the research is being conducted and what it is about. Please take time to read this written information and discuss it, if you want, with family, friends, or with care providers. You can always contact us if there are questions or if anything is unclear.

What is the Goal of the Research?

The study is directed at gathering "case studies" from chaplains. A case study in this context is a description of care contacts and conversations by a chaplain. The goal of the study is to provide answers to three different questions.

1. What do chaplains do? What are their goals and what are the effects of their care?
2. Can we on the basis of what we find in the case studies develop theories that will be helpful for chaplaincy care?

3. How do chaplains learn from participating in this study and what effect does that have on their professionalization?

In total more than fifty chaplains from various institutions such as hospitals, nursing homes, and other care providers as well as prisons and the military, participate in the study. The study will last about four years until 2020. When the study has been completed, various scholarly publications will be written to present the results.

What Does the Study Involve?

If you choose to participate in the study, that means that the chaplain will write a report (case study) about the care that the chaplain provided you. If you want, the chaplain can share the report with you so that you can respond to it. The report will be anonymized. It will be discussed in a research community with other chaplains and researchers.

We also ask for your permission to gather background information, such as age, sex, religion or worldview. All of the information will remain confidential.

What Are the Advantages of Participating?

It can have an advantage for you to see the report of your contact with the chaplain on paper and have the opportunity to talk about it with the chaplain. In addition, we hope that the study will provide information for improving chaplaincy care in the future.

How Will the Data about Me Be Treated?

All of the information that is gathered during the study will be treated confidentially and used anonymously. The care report will also be anonymous. We will see to it that the publicized research information cannot be traced to you. The research data will be kept for ten years.

Do I Have to Participate?

Your participation is completely voluntary. The decision to participate or not is all yours. If you decide to participate, then we will ask you to sign the enclosed consent form. At any moment you may decide to withdraw your consent. You will not have to provide a reason for doing so. It will have no influence on your care, should you decide not to participate or later withdraw your consent.

Who is Organizing and Paying for the Study?

The study is being coordinated by Dr. J.W.G. (Jacques) Körver, Associate professor, trainer & supervisor at Tilburg University and Prof. M.N. (Martin) Walton, Extraneous Professor of Chaplaincy Studies at the Protestant Theological University. The study is being financed by the participating universities. The participation of the chaplains is being financed by their institutions.

Whom Can I Contact for Further Information?

If you have questions, then you can contact us at (. . .).

Thank you for taking the time to read this information.

CONSENT FORM FOR PARTICIPATION CASE STUDIES PROJECT

Statement

I am satisfied with the information I have received about the study. I have read the written information and have had the opportunity to ask any questions about the study. My questions have been satisfactorily answered and I understand what kind of study it is and what the goals are. I have had time to think about participating in the study.

I understand that participation is voluntary and that I can end my participation at any time and do not need to provide a reason.

I know that relevant information about me will be used for scientific research and may be published. I agree to this as long as it is done anonymously and that my privacy is guaranteed.

I know that information about me will be stored. If new research is started in the future, I can be contacted again about participating or not. I can decide that at that time.

Client

I agree to participate in the study:

Name:

Date of birth:

Signature:

Date:

Chaplain

I declare that the person named above had been informed in both writing and oral form about the study. I declare that withdrawal from participation by the person named above will have no influence on the care that is provided.

Name

Function

Signature

Date

DECLARATION OF ORAL CONSENT FOR PARTICIPATION IN THE CASE STUDIES PROJECT

Explanation

As a chaplain you have asked a patient or client to participate in the Case Studies Project: A Study of Chaplaincy Practice. As a written form of consent was not possible, you have received permission orally. You have informed the person about the goals of the study, how it is being conducted, and the possibility of withdrawing consent at any time. You have assured the person that not participating or withdrawing participation will have no influence on the care that is provided. In addition, you have explained that the information will be dealt with confidentially and that the case study will be written in an anonymous form.

Declaration

I declare that I have received oral permission for participation in the Case Studies Project from:

Client

Name

Date of birth

Chaplain

Name

Function

Signature

Date

APPENDIX D

Case Studies in Chaplaincy
Inventory of English Language Publications

INVENTORY

For our reflections in Chapter 3 on what makes a good case, we made an inventory of case studies that have been published in English since 2000. We refer in Chapter 3 to the inventory and review that Steve Nolan wrote up on 28 case studies published between 2011 and 2018 ("Lifting the Lid on Chaplaincy: A First Look at Findings from Chaplains' Case Study Research." *Journal of Health Care Chaplaincy* 27.1 (2021) 1–23). We not only used Nolan's list, but also drew upon George Fitchett's references in his 2011 call to write up case studies in chaplaincy care ("Making Our Case(s)." *Journal of Health Care Chaplaincy* 17.1–2 (2011) 3–18).

For our purposes we then focused on four journals and four volumes with case studies (adding one other journal and one other volume with one case each of which we were aware). Our inventory in the journals was carried out simply by typing "case study chaplaincy" in the search bar of the websites of the respective journals. We likely missed some articles with case material that were not formally presented as case studies. Case studies in chaplaincy printed in other journals we certainly missed. We generally excluded articles that did not have chaplaincy care as their context. Our intent was not to be exhaustive, but to have a significant sampling for the sake of understanding how case studies in chaplaincy are composed and used with respect to research.

- In the *Journal of Pastoral Care and Counseling (JPCC)*, we found three articles predating the year 2000 that we have included below, because they seek to use case material to make a point with regard to chaplaincy or counseling, by drawing salient features of a case of chaplaincy care to the foreground (1989), by demonstrating a dialogical approach to care (1994), or by illustrating how chaplaincy care can be done in an evidence informed manner (1998). They all say something about what chaplains do or can do.

- In the *Journal of Health Care Chaplaincy (JHCC)*, we found three case studies from the year 2000, all illustrating an outcome-oriented approach to chaplaincy. And then in the period 2011 to 2023, beginning with George Fitchett's call for writing up case studies in chaplaincy care in the same journal, we found an additional six case studies.

- For *Health and Social Care Chaplaincy (HSCC)*, George Fitchett and Steve Nolan edited a special number (Volume 5.2 2017) devoted to case studies research that includes six case studies.

- In the *Journal of Religion, Spirituality and Aging (JRSA)*, we found two case studies from 2016 and 2021, respectively, focused on specific care groups.

- In addition, one case study from the Case Studies Project (CSP) was published in English in 2019 in *Tidsskrift for Praktisk Teologi. Nordic Journal of Practical Theology (TPT)*. (It was reprinted a year later in slightly revised form in a volume edited by Renske Kruizinga, et al., listed below.)

The majority of the case studies that have been published have appeared in volumes dedicated to case studies research.

- Nine are to be found in the volume edited by George Fitchett and Steve Nolan, *Spiritual Care in Practice: Case Studies in Healthcare Chaplaincy*. London: Jessica Kingsley, 2015.

- Another nine are presented in their second volume: George Fitchett and Steve Nolan, eds. *Case Studies in Spiritual Care*. London: Jessica Kingsley, 2018.

- There are four chapters with case studies from the CSP in Renske Kruizinga, Jacques Körver, Niels den Toom, Martin Walton, and Martijn Stoutjesdijk, eds. *Learning from Case Studies in Chaplaincy: Towards Practice Based Evidence & Professionalism*. Utrecht: Eburon, 2020.

- Nine case studies are included in the volume edited by M. Jeanne Wirpsa and Karen Pugliese, *Chaplains as Partners in Medical Decision-Making: Case Studies in Healthcare Chaplaincy*. London: Philadelphia: Jessica Kingsley Publishers, 2020.
- In *Evidence-Based Healthcare Chaplaincy: A Research Reader*, edited by George Fitchett, Kelsey White and Kathryn Lyndes, 48–65. London: Jessica Kingsley, 2018, a reprint is included of a case study by Steve Nolan from 2016 in *Journal of Health Care Chaplaincy*. See below.

Altogether we found twenty-one case studies in journal articles and thirty-two case studies in volumes devoted to (case studies) research. Subtracting the two reprints, we arrive at fifty-one case studies, forty-eight since the year 2000, forty-five starting in 2011 with a new generation of case studies more or less in accordance with Fitchett's criteria. Of those forty-five the majority of the case studies come from chaplaincy care in the USA (26), the others from the UK (7), the Netherlands (5), Canada (3), and one each from Australia, Germany, Israel, and Iceland. If we add the nine case studies from the Netherlands in this volume, then we come to fifty-four published case studies since 2011.

Another matter of interest are the titles of the case studies. Many include the name of a client, at times followed by the medical condition. Often a quote is included in the title, from the client or from a family member. Others indicate what the case study wants to communicate: companioning, interdisciplinary communication, or the use of a particular method, approach, or theory. Some emphasize working with a particular group such as persons with a particular cultural or ethnic belonging, with the non-religious, or with "those with dementia." Still others indicate something of what happened in the care, such as dialoguing, companioning, or mediating. Some of the titles are rather extensive; others succinct. We might summarize by saying that some titles focus on who the client is, some on what the situation is, and others on what the chaplain does, with sometimes an emphasis on what chaplains need to do.

We present our inventory of case studies in chronological order, and then in the sequence in which they appear in a book or journal.

CASE STUDIES

1989 *JPC*

Gibbons, James L., and Sherry L. Miller. "An Image of Contemporary Hospital Chaplaincy." *Journal of Pastoral Care* 43.4 (1989) 355–61. (USA)

1994 JPC

Potts, Kenneth. "Martin Buber's 'Healing Dialogue' in Marital Therapy: A Case Study." *Journal of Pastoral Care* 48.4 (1994) 325–38. (USA)

1998 JPC

O'Connor, Thomas St James, and Elizabeth Meakes. "Hope in the Midst of Challenge: Evidence-Based Pastoral Care." *Journal of Pastoral Care* 52.4 (1998) 359–67. (Canada)

2000 JHCC

Berger, Julie Allen. "A Case Study: Linda." *Journal of Health Care Chaplaincy* 10.2 (2000) 35–43. (USA)

Crane, Janet R. "A Case Study Using 'The Discipline' with a Clinical Team." *Journal of Health Care Chaplaincy* 10.2 (2000) 57–68. (USA)

Rodrigues Yim, Robert J. "A Case Study of Jerry: Emphasizing Team Communication Through Use of 'The Discipline.'" *Journal of Health Care Chaplaincy* 10.2 (2000) 45–56. (USA)

2011 JHCC

Cooper, Rhonda S. "Case Study of a Chaplain's Spiritual Care for a Patient with Advanced Metastatic Breast Cancer." *Journal of Health Care Chaplaincy* 17.1–2 (2011) 19–37. (USA)

2012 JHCC

King, Stephen D. W. "Facing Fears and Counting Blessings: A Case Study of a Chaplain's Faithful Companioning a Cancer Patient." *Journal of Health Care Chaplaincy* 18.1–2 (2012) 3–22. (USA)

2013 JHCC

Risk, James L. "Building a New Life: A Chaplain's Theory Based Case Study of Chronic Illness." *Journal of Health Care Chaplaincy* 19.3 (2013) 81–98. (USA)

2015 Fitchett and Nolan (eds.), *Spiritual Care in Practice*

Grossoehme, Daniel H. "'God Tells the Doctors to Pick the Right Medicine'—LeeAnn, a 12-Year-Old Girl With Cystic Fibrosis." In *Spiritual Care in Practice: Case Studies in Healthcare Chaplaincy*, edited by George Fitchett and Steve Nolan, 31–50. London: Jessica Kingsley, 2015. (USA)

Hildebrand, Alice A. 2015 "'I Can Tell You This, but Not Everyone Understands'—Erica, a Mother of a Two-Year-Old Girl With Cancer." In *Spiritual Care in Practice: Case Studies in Healthcare Chaplaincy*, edited by George Fitchett and Steve Nolan, 51–68. London: Jessica Kingsley, 2015. (USA)

Piderman, Katherine. M. "Why Did God Do This to Me?'—Angela, a 17-Year-Old Girl With Spinal Injury." In *Spiritual Care in Practice: Case Studies in Healthcare Chaplaincy*, edited by George Fitchett and Steve Nolan, 69–89. London: Jessica Kingsley, 2015. (USA)

Ratcliffe, Rosie. "'I Am Frightened to Close My Eyes at Night in Case the Witch Comes to Me in My Sleep'—Yesuto, an African Man in His Early Thirties Troubled by His Belief in Witchcraft." In *Spiritual Care in Practice: Case Studies in Healthcare Chaplaincy*, edited by George Fitchett and Steve Nolan, 113–32. London: Jessica Kingsley, 2015. (UK)

Swift, Christopher. "'I Tried to Kill Myself. Will God Keep Me Apart From the Person I Love in the Lifeafter?'— June, a 78-Year-Old Woman Who Attempted Suicide." In *Spiritual Care in Practice: Case Studies in Healthcare Chaplaincy*, edited by George Fitchett and Steve Nolan, 133–53. London: Jessica Kingsley, 2015. (UK)

Zollfrank, Angelika A. "'My Family Wants Me to See a Priest. It Can't Hurt, Right?'—Nate, a 20-Year-Old Man and His Sexual Identity." In *Spiritual Care in Practice: Case Studies in Healthcare Chaplaincy*, edited by George Fitchett and Steve Nolan, 154–76. London: Jessica Kingsley, 2015. (USA)

Huth, Jim, and Wes Roberts. "'I Need to Do the Right Thing for Him'—Andrew, a Canadian Veteran at the End of His Life, and His Daughter Lee." In *Spiritual Care in Practice: Case Studies in Healthcare Chaplaincy*, edited by George Fitchett and Steve Nolan, 201–22. London: Jessica Kingsley, 2015. (Canada)

Redl, Nina. "'What Can You Do for Me?'—David, a Mid-60s Jewish Man With Stage IV Pancreatic Cancer." In *Spiritual Care in Practice: Case Studies in Healthcare Chaplaincy*, edited by George Fitchett and Steve Nolan, 223–41. London: Jessica Kingsley, 2015. (Israel)

Weyls, Richard C. "'Tell Her That It's OK to Release Her Spirit'—Maria, a Native American Woman, Grieving the Loss of Her Dying Mother." In *Spiritual Care in Practice: Case Studies in Healthcare Chaplaincy*, edited by George Fitchett and Steve Nolan, 242–62. London: Jessica Kingsley, 2015. (USA)

2016 *JHCC* & *JRSA*

Nolan, Steve. "'He Needs to Talk!' A Chaplain's Case Study of Nonreligious Spiritual Care." *Journal of Health Care Chaplaincy* 22.1 (2016) 1–16. (UK)

Reed, Marlette B., Annette M. Lane, and Sandra P. Hirst. "Spiritual Care for Those with Dementia: A Case Study." *Journal of Religion, Spirituality & Aging* 28.4 (2016) 338–48. (Canada)

2017 *HSCC*, special edition, Fitchett and Nolan (eds.)

Schmohl, Corinna. "'You've Done Very Well.' ('Das haben Sie sehr schön gemacht') On Courage and Presence of Mind in Spiritual Issues." *Health and Social Care Chaplaincy* 5.2 (2017) 174–93. (Germany)

Bassett, Lynn. "Space, Time and Shared Humanity: A Case Study Demonstrating a Chaplain's Role in End-of-Life Care." *Health and Social Care Chaplaincy* 5.2 (2017) 194–208. (UK)

Murphy, Karen. "'I'm Being Swallowed Up by this Illness, So Much Pain Deep Inside'— Claire, a 40-Year-Old Woman with Cancer." *Health and Social Care Chaplaincy* 5.2 (2017) 209–23. (UK)

Glenister, David. "'I Want to Make it Right'—A 46-Year-Old Woman with End Stage Renal Disease and Her Australian Aboriginal Partner Make Significant Choices." *Health and Social Care Chaplaincy* 5.2 (2017) 224–40. (Australia)

Murphy, Jeffery N. "The Chaplain as the Mediator Between the Patient and the Interdisciplinary Team in Ethical Decision Making: A Chaplaincy Case Study Involving a Quadriplegic Patient." *Health and Social Care Chaplaincy* 5.2 (2017) 241–56. (USA)

Van Loenen, Guus, Jacques Körver, Martin Walton, and Reijer de Vries, "Case Study of 'Moral Injury': Format Dutch Case Studies Project." *Health and Social Care Chaplaincy* 5.2 (2017) 281–96. (Netherlands)

2018a Fitchett (ed.) *Evidence-Based Healthcare Chaplaincy*

Nolan, Steve. "'He Needs to Talk!' A Chaplain's Case Study of Nonreligious Spiritual Care." In *Evidence-Based Healthcare Chaplaincy: A Research Reader*, edited by George Fitchett et al., 48–65. London: Jessica Kingsley, 2018. [Reprint from *Journal of Health Care Chaplaincy* 22.1 (2016) 1–16. See above.] (UK)

2018b Fitchett and Nolan (eds.). *Case Studies in Spiritual Care.*

Liz Bryson, Paul Nash, and Sally Nash. "'That's Great! You Can Tell Us How You Are Feeling'—Mark, a Recently Severely Physically Disabled 11-Year-Old Boy With a Brain Tumor." In *Case Studies in Spiritual Care: Healthcare Chaplaincy Assessments, Interventions, and Outcomes*, edited by George Fitchett and Steve Nolan, 35–51. London: Jessica Kingsley, 2018. (UK)

Jinks, Patrick. "'She's Already Done So Much'—Sarah, Diagnosed Prenatally With Trisomy 18, and Her Family." In *Case Studies in Spiritual Care: Healthcare Chaplaincy Assessments, Interventions, and Outcomes*, edited by George Fitchett and Steve Nolan, 52–70. London: Jessica Kingsley, 2018. (USA)

Hanson, Janet. "'He Is Disappointed I Am Not the Son He Wanted. I Tried and Tried to Deny I Am a Girl'—Vicki, a Male to Female Transgender Veteran." In *Case Studies in Spiritual Care: Healthcare Chaplaincy Assessments, Interventions, and Outcomes*, edited by George Fitchett and Steve Nolan, 87–101. London: Jessica Kingsley, 2018. (USA)

Sanders, Valerie C. "'I Was Able to Go to Confession'—Mrs. Helen, a Survivor Of Military Sexual Trauma Perpetrated By A Religious Leader." In *Case Studies in Spiritual Care: Healthcare Chaplaincy Assessments, Interventions, and Outcomes*, edited by George Fitchett and Steve Nolan, 102-20. London: Jessica Kingsley, 2018. (USA)

Bratt Carle, Jessica. "'God's Just Too Busy for Us Right Now'—Paul, a 10-Year-Old White Male Transitioning From Tertiary Medical Center to Pediatric Inpatient Psychiatric Hospital." In *Case Studies in Spiritual Care: Healthcare Chaplaincy Assessments, Interventions, and Outcomes*, edited by George Fitchett and Steve Nolan, 137-52. London: Jessica Kingsley, 2018. (USA)

Ásgeirsdóttir, Guðlag Helga. "Connecting Family Members Through Ritual—Jakob, Hulda and Their Family in Palliative Care." In *Case Studies in Spiritual Care: Healthcare Chaplaincy Assessments, Interventions, and Outcomes*, edited by George Fitchett and Steve Nolan, 153-69. London: Jessica Kingsley, 2018. (Iceland)

Roberts. Patricia. 2018 "'I Do Want to Get This Funeral Planned'—Daisy, a Former Colleague in Hospice Care." In *Case Studies in Spiritual Care: Healthcare Chaplaincy Assessments, Interventions, and Outcomes*, edited by George Fitchett and Steve Nolan, 170-86. London: Jessica Kingsley, 2018. (USA)

Goodman, Amy E. and Joel Baron. "'For Myself and for Your People With Whom I Pray'—Mrs. Pearlman, an 82-Year-Old Woman With a Terminal Diagnosis of Advanced Alzheimer's Disease." In *Case Studies in Spiritual Care: Healthcare Chaplaincy Assessments, Interventions, and Outcomes*, edited by George Fitchett and Steve Nolan, 187-204. London: Jessica Kingsley, 2018. (USA)

Nolan, Steve. "'I'd Like You to Get to Know About Me'—Kristof, a 50-Year-Old Atheist Academic Admitted to Hospice for Palliative Symptom Control." In *Case Studies in Spiritual Care: Healthcare Chaplaincy Assessments, Interventions, and Outcomes*, edited by George Fitchett and Steve Nolan, 223-45. London: Jessica Kingsley, 2018. (UK)

2019 *TPT*

Muthert, Hanneke, Monique Van Hoof, Martin Walton, and Jacques Körver. "Re-Evaluating a Suicide Pact. Embodied Moral Counselling in a Dutch Case Study of Mental Healthcare Chaplaincy." *Tidsskrift for Praktisk Teologi*, 36.2 (2019), 81–89. (Netherlands)

2020a Kruizinga et al. (eds.). *Learning from Case Studies*

De Vries, Reijer J., Marja Went, Martin van Hemert, Soerish Jaggan, and Geerhard Kloppenburg. "With an Open Mind for the Unexpected, Prison Chaplaincy: A Case Study." In *Learning from Case Studies in Chaplaincy. Towards Practice Based Evidence and Professionalism*, edited by Kruizinga, et al., 137–46. Utrecht: Eburon, 2020. (Netherlands)

Van der Meer, Tjeerd. "Is MacDonald's Freedom?" In *Learning from Case Studies in Chaplaincy. Towards Practice Based Evidence and Professionalism*, edited by Kruizinga, et al., 147–52. Utrecht: Eburon, 2020. (Netherlands)

Van Hoof, Monique, Hanneke Muthert, Martin Walton, and Jacques Körver. "Agreement is Agreement? Moral Counseling in a Life-Threatening Dilemma." In *Learning from Case Studies in Chaplaincy. Towards Practice Based Evidence and Professionalism*, edited by Kruizinga, et al., 153–58. Utrecht: Eburon, 2020. [Revised reprint of Muthert et al. 2019 above.] (Netherlands)

Jorissen, Gertjan, Carmen Schuhmann, Theo Pleizier, Jacques Körver, and Martin Walton. "You Can Remove a Person from the War, But Not the War from a Person." In *Learning from Case Studies in Chaplaincy. Towards Practice Based Evidence and Professionalism*, edited by Kruizinga, et al., 159–64. Utrecht: Eburon, 2020. (Netherlands)

2020b Wirpsa and Pugliese (eds.). *Chaplains as Partners*

Galchutt, Paul. "Keith's Story. 'It Was an Easy Choice. I'm Not Ready to Die'—Keith, a 59-Year-Old Living With Stage IV Bladder Cancer." In *Chaplains as Partners in Medical Decision-Making. Case Studies in Healthcare Chaplaincy*, edited by M. Jeanne Wirpsa and Karen Pugliese, 86–115. London: Jessica Kingsley, 2020. (USA)

Hogg, Jim. "Glen's Story. 'Glen's Mission'—A 72-Year-Old Man, Living Until His Sense of Purpose Was Fulfilled." In *Chaplains as Partners in Medical Decision-Making. Case Studies in Healthcare Chaplaincy*, edited by M. Jeanne Wirpsa and Karen Pugliese, 117–55. London: Jessica Kingsley, 2020. (USA)

Wirpsa, M. Jeanne. "Bob's Story. 'I Don't Want to Put Them Through Anything More. They've Already Done Enough for Me'—Bob, a Middle-Aged Husband and Father As He Faces Treatment Decisions for His Second Life-Threatening Cancer." In *Chaplains as Partners in Medical Decision-Making. Case Studies in Healthcare Chaplaincy*, edited by M. Jeanne Wirpsa and Karen Pugliese, 156–96. London: Jessica Kingsley, 2020. (USA)

Goheen, Keith W. "Rita's Story. 'Aren't We Supposed to Honor Our Mother and Father?'—Ray, Grandson of the Family Matriarch, Rita." In *Chaplains as Partners in Medical Decision-Making. Case Studies in Healthcare Chaplaincy*, edited by M. Jeanne Wirpsa and Karen Pugliese, 265–306. London: Jessica Kingsley, 2020. (USA)

Swofford, Melanie. "Mark's Story. 'Take This Trach Out; I Don't Want to Live This Way'—Mark, a Middle-Aged Man With Acute Respiratory Disease." In *Chaplains as Partners in Medical Decision-Making. Case Studies in Healthcare Chaplaincy*, edited by M. Jeanne Wirpsa and Karen Pugliese, 307–44. London: Jessica Kingsley, 2020. (USA)

Vilagos, Teresamarie T. "Aaron's Story. 'I Don't Want to Give Up on Him, but I Don't Want to Hurt Him Either'—Aaron's Family As They Struggle to Do Right by This 45-Year-Old Who Suffered a Sudden Life-Threatening Injury." In *Chaplains as Partners in Medical Decision-Making. Case Studies in Healthcare Chaplaincy*, edited by M. Jeanne Wirpsa and Karen Pugliese, 345–77. London: Jessica Kingsley, 2020. (USA)

Axelrud, Abraham. "Sarah's Story. 'If G-d Feels Sarah Should Experience a Recovery, It Will Be a Great Gift. However, if G-d Doesn't, My Belief System Will Never Change'—Leah, an Orthodox Jew, Speaking About G-d's Role in Her Daughter's Devastating Illness." In *Chaplains as Partners in Medical Decision-Making. Case*

Studies in Healthcare Chaplaincy, edited by M. Jeanne Wirpsa and Karen Pugliese, 438–66 London: Jessica Kingsley, 2020. (USA)

Kirby, Michelle. "Alma's Story. 'She's Dying From a Broken Heart'—Mary Telling the Story of Her Sister Alma's Death." In *Chaplains as Partners in Medical Decision-Making. Case Studies in Healthcare Chaplaincy,* edited by M. Jeanne Wirpsa and Karen Pugliese, 467–94. London: Jessica Kingsley, 2020. (USA)

Duncan Rosencrans, Emily. "Ayesah's Story. 'Allah Will Save Her'—Mohammed Talking About His Wife, Ayesah." In *Chaplains as Partners in Medical Decision-Making. Case Studies in Healthcare Chaplaincy,* edited by M. Jeanne Wirpsa and Karen Pugliese, 495–529. London: Jessica Kingsley, 2020. (USA)

2021 *JRSA*

Timbers, Veronica L., and Melanie Childers. "A Case Study in Group Spiritual Care for Residents of a Post-Acute Care Facility." *Journal of Religion, Spirituality & Aging* 33.1 (2021) 86–96. (USA)

2023 *JHCC*

Heikkinen, Peter J., and Benjamin Roberts. "'I See You.' A Chaplain Case Study on Existential Distress and Transdisciplinary Support." *Journal of Health Care Chaplaincy* 29.4 (2023) 406–23. (USA)

Shu, Christina. "'I Need My Granddaughter to Know Who I Am!' A Case Study of a 67-Year-Old African American Man and His Spiritual Legacy." *Journal of Health Care Chaplaincy* 29.3 (2023) 256–68. (USA)

APPENDIX E

International Publications Dutch Case Studies Project

THE FOLLOWING ARE THE international publications (in English and German) that have been produced within the CSP framework to date. The table of contents of the book edited by Renske Kruizinga et al. (*Learning from Case Studies*) is included after the list of publications. All publications (more than eighty, mostly in Dutch) published by participants (chaplains and academic researchers) can be found on the website of the *University Center for Chaplaincy Studies (UCGV)*: https://www.ucgv.nl/case-studies-project/publicaties-csp/. The CSP's final report (in Dutch) can also be downloaded from that website: https://www.ucgv.nl/case-studies-project/eindrapport-csp/. Some of De Roest's publications describe the CSP as a special example of collaborative research (in practical theology) (see the bibliography below).

Den Toom, Niels. *The Chaplain-Researcher. The Perceived Impact of Participation in a Dutch Research Project on Chaplains's Professionalism.* Utrecht: Eburon, 2022.

Den Toom, Niels, et al. "Geistesgegenwart. Über den Einfluss der Forschung auf die Professionalität von Seelsorgenden." *Wege zum Menschen* 74.4 (2022) 314–26. https://doi.org/10.13109/weme.2022.74.4.314.

Den Toom, Niels, et al. "The Professionalization of Chaplaincy. A Comparison of 1997 and 2017 Surveys in the Netherlands." *Journal of Health Care Chaplaincy* 29.1 (2023) 14–29. https://doi.org/10.1080/08854726.2021.1996810.

Den Toom, Niels, et al. "The Perceived Impact of Being a Chaplain-Researcher on Professional Practice." *Journal of Health Care Chaplaincy* 30.1 (2024) 19–32. https://doi.org/10.1080/08854726.2022.2132036.

Den Toom, Niels, et al. "Rearranging the Domain: Spiritual Care in Multiple Dimensions." *Health and Social Care Chaplaincy* 9.1 (2021) 42–59. https://doi.org/10.1558/hscc.40482.

De Roest, Henk. *Collaborative Practical Theology. Engaging Practitioners in Research on Christian Practices.* Leiden: Brill, 2020.

De Roest, Henk. "Collaborative Research." In *The Wiley Blackwell Companion to Theology and Qualitative Research*, edited by Pete Ward and Knut Tveitereid, 435–45. Hoboken: John Wiley & Sons, 2022.

Gärtner, Stefan. "Rituale in der Seelsorge nach einem Trauma. Eine Untersuchung von Fallgeschichten aus der Psychiatrie." *Zeitschrift für Pastoraltheologie* 41.2 (2021) 93–105. https://www.unimuenster.de/Ejournals/index.php/zpth/article/view/3753.

———. "Editorial. Fallstudien in der Seelsorge. Ein internationales Forschungsproject." *Wege zum Menschen* 74.4 (2022) 297–99. https://doi.org/10.13109/weme.2022.74.4.297.

———. "Muslimische Seelsorge in einem religiös geprägten Gesundheitswesens. Ein Fallbericht und seine Hintergründe." *Spiritual Care* 12.4 (2023) 333–41. https://doi.org/10.1515/spircare-2022-0067.

Gärtner, Stefan, et al. "Von Fall zu Fall. Kontext, Methode und Durchführung eines empirischen Forschungsprojekts mit Casestudies in der Seelsorge." *International Journal of Practical Theology* 23.1 (2019) 98–114. https://doi.org/10.1515/ijpt-2017-0040.

Körver, Jacques. "Das Tabu der Zielorientierung durchbrechen. Mit professioneller Intuition im Krankenhaus auf der Suche nach der Seele." *Wege zum Menschen* 74.4 (2022) 368–81. https://doi.org/10.13109/weme.2022.74.4.368.

Körver, Jacques, et al. "Fallgeschichten, Forschung, Seelsorge. Ein inspirirendes Trio." *Wege zum Menschen* 74.4 (2022) 300–13. https://doi.org/10.13109/weme.2022.74.4.300.

Kruizinga, Renske, et al., eds. *Learning from Case Studies in Chaplaincy. Towards Practice Based Evidence & Professionalism.* Utrecht: Eburon, 2020.

Muthert, Hanneke, and Irene Plaatsman. "Die Lebensgeschichte als Gefäß in der Seelsorge. Dem bisher unbekannten begegnen." *Wege zum Menschen* 74.4 (2022) 327–42. https://doi.org/10.13109/weme.2022.74.4.327.

Muthert, Hanneke, et al. "Re-Evaluating a Suicide Pact. Embodied Moral Counselling in a Dutch Case Study of Mental Healthcare Chaplaincy." *Tidsskrift for Praktisk Teologi* 36.2 (2019) 81–89. https://doi.org/https://doi.org/10.48626/tpt.v36i2.5357

Pleizier, Theo, and Carmen M. Schuhmann. "How the Military Context Shapes Spiritual Care Interventions by Military Chaplains." *Journal of Pastoral Care & Counseling* 76.1 (2022) 4–14. https://doi.org/10.1177/15423050221076462.

Rosie, Sujin, and Niels Den Toom. "Spiritual Care and Recovery in Mental Health Care. An Analysis of Spiritual Care According to CHIME." In *Recovery. The Interface between Psychiatry and Spiritual Care*, edited by Erik Olsman, et al., 38–50. Utrecht: Eburon, 2023.

Schuhmann, Carmen. "Spiritual Care, Moral Injury, and Moral Recovery." In *Recovery. The Interface between Psychiatry and Spiritual Care*, edited by Erik Olsman, et al., 85–96. Utrecht: Eburon, 2023.

Schuhmann, Carmen, and Theo Pleizier. "Wie Seelsorgende mit moralischem Stress bei Soldaten umgehen." *Wege zum Menschen* 74.4 (2022) 343–56. https://doi.org/10.13109/weme.2022.74.4.343.

Schuhmann, Carmen, et al. "How Military Chaplains Strengthen the Moral Resilience of Soldiers and Veterans: Results from a Case Studies Project in the Netherlands." *Pastoral Psychology* 72 (2023) 605–24. https://doi.org/10.1007/s11089-023-01097-5.

Van Loenen, Guus, et al. "Case Study of 'Moral Injury'. Format Dutch Case Studies Project." *Health and Social Care Chaplaincy* 5.2 (2017) 81–96. https://doi.org/10.1558/hscc.34303.

Walton, Martin N. "'Wie ein Spaziergang im Grünen'. Ästhetische Aspekte bei der Beratung durch *geestelijk verzorgers*." *Wege zum Menschen* 74.4 (2022) 357–67. https://doi.org/10.13109/weme.2022.74.4.357.

Walton, Martin N., and Jacques Körver. "Dutch Case Studies Project in Chaplaincy Care. A Description and Theoretical Explanation of the Format and Procedures." *Health and Social Care Chaplaincy* 5.2 (2017) 257–80. https://doi.org/10.1558/hscc.34302.

Kruizinga, Renske, Jacques Körver, Niels den Toom, Martin Walton, and Martijn Stoutjesdijk, eds. *Learning from Case Studies in Chaplaincy. Towards Practice Based Evidence & Professionalism*. Utrecht: Eburon, 2020.

Table of contents:

1. Introduction. Researching Living Human Encounters (*Martin Walton*)
2. The State of the Art in Chaplaincy Research. Needs, Resources and Hopes (*George Fitchett*)
3. Putting Chaplaincy Research in the Picture. The Dutch Case Studies Project (*Jacques Körver*)
4. Researching Practices. Lessons from Dutch Youth Care (*Jan Willem Veerman*)
5. Up and Down the Participation Ladder. The Use of Narratives in Collaborative Research (*Gaby Jacobs*)
6. The Science of the Particular (*Jacques Körver*)
7. Chaplains' Case Study Research. Building towards a Theory of Chaplaincy Care? (*Steve Nolan*)
8. Comparing Multiple Case Studies of (Military) Chaplaincy Care. Methodological Issues (*Theo Pleizier & Carmen Schuhmann*)
9. Professional Proximity. Seeking a Balance between Relation and Content in Spiritual Counseling (*Myriam Braakhuis*)
10. Effects of Health Care Chaplaincy. A Qualitative Study with Case Reports (*Nika Höfler & Traugott Roser*)
11. Personal Experiences in Writing a Case Study (*Paul Galchutt*)
12. With an Open Mind for the Unexpected. Prison Chaplaincy: A Case Study (*Reijer J. de Vries, Marja Went, Martin van Hemert, Soerish Jaggan, & Geerhard Kloppenburg*)
13. Is MacDonald's Freedom? (*Tjeerd van der Meer*)
14. Agreement is Agreement? Moral Counseling in a Life-Threatening Dilemma (*Monique van Hoof, Hanneke Muthert, Jacques Körver, & Martin Walton*)
15. You Can Remove a Person from the War, but not the War from a Person (*Gertjan Jorissen, Carmen Schuhmann, Theo Pleizier, Jacques Körver, & Martin Walton*)
16. What Does Participation in the Case Studies Project Mean for One's Professionalism? Preliminary Findings and Topics (*Jacqueline Weeda, & Hanneke Muthert*)
17. Interdisciplinary Work in Chaplaincy Care (*Loes Berkhout*)
18. Towards a Distinct Professional Identity. What Chaplains Have Learned in Flanders Case Study Research (*Lindsy Desmet*)

19. What Are Chaplains Learning by Producing Case Studies? (*Frieda Boeykens*)
20. 'Oneself as Another.' Combining the Roles of Chaplain and Researcher in the Dutch Case Studies Project (*Niels den Toom*)
21. Epilogue. Developing the Case (*Jacques Körver, Renske Kruizinga, Niels den Toom, & Martin Walton*)

APPENDIX F

Ritual Interventions by Chaplains in Research Community Hospital

(Chapter 16)

Case No.	Patient and context	Chaplain interventions	Nature of ritual	Purpose and result
Z1	Male, age 71, married, 2 children. Catholic. Worked as a sexton and helped dig cemetery graves. Admitted to ICU with numerous ailments, with several physicians involved. Acute deterioration leading to his death.	Upon request by wife, blessing of the sick. First explores life story and marriage. Creates space (literally) by informing and involving caregivers in ritual. Looking back and forward with wife.	A modified form of Catholic Anointing of the Sick on ICU. Focus on patient's situation and life. Involvement of family members (laying on of hands) in performance. Wife asks if there are costs involved. Next day, prayer (including Hail Mary and Lord's Prayer) and blessing, before and following death.	Embedding ritual in the care process, life story and religious background. Transition to a new situation. Trusting relationship with family, review and evaluation of life, creating space in ICU, importance of religious connection.

Z3	Female, age 71, widow, 2 children. Protestant. Prolonged ICU stay (> 1 month) due to complications after surgery. Uncertain if she will come off life support. Evasive in communication. Talking via letter board. Expecting support from "above."	Regular and faithful visits, sometimes without speaking. Prolonged contact. Holding hands. Working on trust. Probing her perception of the situation, partly based on eye contact. Prayer and blessing after each visit.	Free, spontaneous prayer with articulation of current experience, of doubt and despair and of hope and faith. Reading from Bible, e.g. Psalm 121. Laying on of hands and blessing. Usually as a conclusion (in a double sense).	Creating space for patient's story, concerns, doubt and faith, in the tension between recovery and hopelessness. Staying present, representing God's care. Space for her tears. Results of chaplain's care are recognized by son and by other caregivers.
Z4	Female, 60 years old, with partner. Formerly Protestant, no present affiliation. Wheelchair dependent, CVA, now with esophageal cancer. Admission to ICU after surgery, tracheostoma, accumulation of problems. Can barely express herself, only via writing board. Great fear (of death).	Helps her to express herself. Explores life story and loss experiences. Supplies metaphors to reach existential layer. Helps with writing letter to caregivers about experiences in ICU. Mindfulness exercise.	Mindfulness, specifically a listening exercise, to help her park thoughts if they keep going through her head. It is an exercise the woman is familiar with.	Creating space for patient's story, narrative reconstruction of life story, organizing thoughts. Woman feels less like an object of care, finds her "voice" again, room for lightness and humor.
Z5	Female, 19 years old, nurse, living with parents. Worldview unknown. Death of physician triggers recent loss experiences in private life: cousin crashed, relationship ended. Feelings of guilt. Does not allow herself a grieving process. Tension in relationship between person and profession.	Exploration of complex questions. Ordering and nuancing, relating current experiences to previous, and to life story. Referral to psychologist. Ritual on entering and leaving conversation room.	To mark the transition between work and home, the young woman always locks or unlocks the door to chaplain's study herself.	Awareness in patient of her own questions and desires. Reinterpretation of guilt. Creating her own place in the family drama and grief. More in touch with herself, feels relieved and happier.
Z6	Male, age 37, married, 3 children. Catholic. Leukemia with intensive treatment far from home (abroad), resulting in little contact with children. Apathy, mental distress.	Supporting by familiar rituals. Long-term and frequent visits. Establishing contact with church community near the hospital. Arranging airfare for children via fund raising.	Prayer service with Communion and blessing. Offering lamp with text (*God bless our home*). Bible, plant, bottle of holy water (memory of grandmother) are elements in prayer service. Wife and children bless husband, and he blesses them.	In ritual, support, affirmation, and hope emerge, as well as connection to larger faith community. Practical help alleviates some of the existential need. Children could come over.

Z7	Female, age 68, married, 2 children. Christian. Hodgkin's disease. Admission to ICU due to drug toxicity. Bipolar disorder. Overwhelming existential experiences (sister's suicide, child with autism).	Life review and inventory of (loss) experiences. Helping face and organize critical situation. Embedding in transcendence using small rituals.	Lighting candle (*light of hope and attention*) for her husband in chapel. Praying and singing together. Woman likes to sing the old songs. Chaplain's 'threshold prayer' prior to conversation.	Taking stock of and acknowledging ambivalence, regaining inner space. Enabling her to name and accept what concerns her with an eye for ambivalences in existence. She regains her strength.
Z8	Female, age 73, second partner, 1 child. Catholic. Recurrence of ovarian cancer. Extremely anxious and tense during treatments. Needs specific ritual.	Exploration of life story and social context, of Marian devotion, treatment process, death anxiety. Alignment of care with that of others. Blessing ritual.	Blessing of Rosary which she always carries with her and which gives her strength in tense moments. In chapel, sprinkling of holy water, prayer (Hail Mary) and blessing.	Learning to deal with tension, fear and uncertainty, and loneliness (in family) on the basis of trust. Recognition of her (way of) believing.
Z9	Female, 42 years old, cohabiting. Desire for children. Raised Catholic. Abortion due to severe abnormalities of child in womb. Wants stillborn child to be blessed.	Exploration and recognition of loss, grief, longing, and unmet expectations. Blessing of mother and child.	Blessing of the mother prior to the intervention. Blessing and naming of the stillborn child after the termination of pregnancy, as a lasting memory.	Unspeakable loss and grief is given a place in parents' lives. Doing justice to the integrity of child and parents. Support from an ancient religious source.
Z10	Female, 66 years old, second marriage, 1 child. Lutheran. For the third time breast cancer. Oncology rehab. Seeks energy and inspiration.	Spiritual life review, in the context of life and illness history. Working step by step toward new inspiration. Reference to small rituals.	Reference to the sanctuary where she can light a candle. Reference to Bible texts (Ex. 19:4; Deut. 32:11) that speak of God bearing her young like an eagle (referring to an image of a bird on a tapestry she wove).	Recovered inspiration and spirit by reconnecting to her religious and creative resources. Inspiration as a goal of the rehabilitation program, in addition to energy.
Z12	Woman, 77 years old, married, no children. Lutheran. Acute, brief admission due to pulmonary problems. Partner is incurably ill, causing worries, especially at night.	One-time conversation. Exploration of situation, of capacities to bear, role of faith.	Reinterpretation of knitting as ritual to find relaxation during hospital visits, and of compiling photo album as ritual to hold memories.	Assessment of issues, coping style and (faith) resources. Awareness of these and of options for dealing with tensions.

Z15	Male, 46 years old, divorced, 2 children. Refugee. Catholic. Emergency surgery due to colon cancer and stoma construction.	Easily accessible contact, exploring illness's impact through providing space for conversation. Presenting oneself as chaplain. Praying together.	Praying together and reading from the Bible, after surgery. Request to pray came when it became clear that the chaplain was a Catholic pastor.	Creating openness to acceptance of situation. Actualizing faith in praying together. Sharing common religious background.
Z16	Female, 56 years old, married, 2 children. Catholic. Bipolar disorder. Repeated admissions. Comes from family with many conflicts. She suffers from the disorder, especially in relation to her own family.	In repeated short conversations, exploring and sorting out current experiences against the background of illness and life story. Naming points of light. Offering numerous ritual options.	Visiting chapel, lighting candle (including after suicide of fellow patient), participation in liturgy. Receiving Communion in room. Prayers, texts, poems, religious magazine. After liturgy she brings rose for herself and a nurse.	Ordering and (re)constructing life story. Reframing relationship to others. Strengthening and affirming relationship to outside world and world of transcendence. Courage to live on.
Z19	Female, age 71, married, 2 children. Catholic, non-practicing. Complications after major surgery for esophageal cancer. Has been through a lot, according to nursing staff.	Close observation and tracking. Active listening. Exploring meaning of past and present experiences. Offering a candle and a card.	Lighting a candle for her several times in sanctuary. Offering a card with special text for two special life moments (euthanasia of a brother; wedding anniversary).	Providing space for and organizing profound experiences, placing them in a religious perspective. Relief, happy to express herself, new perspective.
Z21	Woman, age 70, widow, 4 children. Cancerous tumor on lower lip. Radiotherapy. Restless night, fear of what is to come, panic.	Exploring and interrogating nighttime experiences. Fear of the end is connected to previous experiences of fear and inferiority. Connecting with previous ways and sources of coping (e.g., lighting candle in church).	Referral to chapel to light a candle.	Clarifying and interpreting nocturnal restlessness. Putting experiences into religious perspective. Tapping internal spiritual resources. Woman articulates agony, gives it a place in her life story, and can better bring her life wisdom to bear.
Z23	Male, age 66, married, no children. Freemasonry. Chemo- and radiotherapy due to cancer in nasal cavities. Husband and wife search for depth and spirituality. Loss of independence. Feeling of being abandoned by environment.	Through images/metaphors connecting their story of illness, treatment, and future with meaning and spiritual perspective. Searching for new perspective after successful treatment.	Chaplain prays a 'threshold prayer' prior to the visit at the door of the sick room.	Chaplain is able to listen better, add depth, distinguish stories of husband and wife, and helps them connect with their own spiritual inner self.

www.ingramcontent.com/pod-product-compliance
Lightning Source LLC
Chambersburg PA
CBHW071148300426
44113CB00009B/1124